Simulation for Data Science with R

Harness actionable insights from your data with computational statistics and simulations using R

Matthias Templ

BIRMINGHAM - MUMBAI

Simulation for Data Science with R

First published: June 2016

Production reference: 1240616

Published by Packt Publishing Ltd.
Livery Place
35 Livery Street
Birmingham B3 2PB, UK.
ISBN 978-1-78588-116-9

www.packtpub.com

Credits

Author
Matthias Templ

Reviewer
Gerlinde Dinges

Commissioning Editor
Akram Hussain

Acquisition Editor
Vinay Argekar

Content Development Editor
Aishwarya Pandere

Technical Editor
Tanmayee Patil

Copy Editors
Safis Editing
Angad Singh

Project Coordinator
Nidhi Joshi

Proofreader
Safis Editing

Indexer
Monica Ajmera Mehta

Graphics
Jason Monteiro

Production Coordinator
Nilesh Mohite

Cover Work
Nilesh Mohite

About the Author

Matthias Templ is associated professor at the Institute of Statistics and Mathematical Methods in Economics, Vienna University of Technology (Austria). He is additionally employed as a scientist at the methods unit at Statistics Austria, and together with two colleagues, he owns the company called data-analysis OG. His main research interests are in the areas of imputation, statistical disclosure control, visualization, compositional data analysis, computational statistics, robustness teaching in statistics, and multivariate methods. In the last few years, Matthias has published more than 45 papers in well-known indexed scientific journals. He is the author and maintainer of several R packages for official statistics, such as the R package sdcMicro for statistical disclosure control, the VIM package for visualization and imputation of missing values, the simPop package for synthetic population simulation, and the robCompositions package for robust analysis of compositional data. In addition, he is the editor of the Austrian Journal of Statistics that is free of charge and open-access. The probability is high to find him at the top of a mountain in his leisure time.

I'd like to thank my wife, Barbara, for her mental support for the work on this book. In addition, my thanks goes to all the people who provide open source code to the R project.

About the Reviewer

Gerlinde Dinges works as a methodological researcher at the quality management and methods department of Statistics Austria. She studied at the University of Linz and earned a degree in statistics from the University of Vienna. Since 2002, she has been working extensively in the field of model-based estimation for business statistics and published several papers in this field. Gerlinde has broad experience in working with large (administrative) data and has participated in several European research projects. Her main research interest is in the area of explorative data analysis, business statistics, imputation, visualization, and teaching statistics. Together with her colleagues, she developed a computer-assisted teaching system to enhance and support classroom teaching in an interactive way (http://www.statistik.at/tgui).

www.PacktPub.com

eBooks, discount offers, and more

Did you know that Packt offers eBook versions of every book published, with PDF and ePub files available? You can upgrade to the eBook version at www.PacktPub.com and as a print book customer, you are entitled to a discount on the eBook copy. Get in touch with us at customercare@packtpub.com for more details.

At www.PacktPub.com, you can also read a collection of free technical articles, sign up for a range of free newsletters and receive exclusive discounts and offers on Packt books and eBooks.

https://www2.packtpub.com/books/subscription/packtlib

Do you need instant solutions to your IT questions? PacktLib is Packt's online digital book library. Here, you can search, access, and read Packt's entire library of books.

Why subscribe?

- Fully searchable across every book published by Packt
- Copy and paste, print, and bookmark content
- On demand and accessible via a web browser

Table of Contents

Preface   **vii**

Chapter 1: Introduction   **1**

What is simulation and where is it applied?   **3**

Why use simulation?   **6**

Simulation and big data   **7**

Choosing the right simulation technique   **8**

Summary   **11**

References   **11**

Chapter 2: R and High-Performance Computing   **13**

The R statistical environment   **14**

Basics in R   15

Some very basic stuff about R   15

Installation and updates   16

Help   17

The R workspace and the working directory   18

Data types   18

  Vectors in R   19

  Factors in R   21

  list   21

  data.frame   22

  array   24

Missing values   25

Generic functions, methods, and classes   **26**

Data manipulation in R   **28**

Apply and friends with basic R   28

Basic data manipulation with the dplyr package   31

  dplyr – creating a local data frame   32

  dplyr – selecting lines   33

  dplyr – order   34

dplyr – selecting columns	35
dplyr – uniqueness	37
dplyr – creating variables	37
dplyr – grouping and aggregates	38
dplyr – window functions	41
Data manipulation with the data.table package	42
data.table – variable construction	42
data.table – indexing or subsetting	43
data.table – keys	44
data.table – fast subsetting	44
data.table – calculations in groups	46
High performance computing	**47**
Profiling to detect computationally slow functions in code	47
Further benchmarking	49
Parallel computing	56
Interfaces to C++	58
Visualizing information	**60**
The graphics system in R	61
The graphics package	62
Warm-up example – a high-level plot	62
Control of graphics parameters	64
The ggplot2 package	66
References	**71**
Chapter 3: The Discrepancy between Pencil-Driven Theory and Data-Driven Computational Solutions	**73**
Machine numbers and rounding problems	**74**
Example – the 64-bit representation of numbers	77
Convergence in the deterministic case	77
Example – convergence	78
Condition of problems	**86**
Summary	**87**
References	**87**
Chapter 4: Simulation of Random Numbers	**89**
Real random numbers	**90**
Simulating pseudo random numbers	**92**
Congruential generators	93
Linear and multiplicative congruential generators	94
Lagged Fibonacci generators	98
More generators	98
Simulation of non-uniform distributed random variables	**101**
The inversion method	101

The alias method 105
Estimation of counts in tables with log-linear models 106
Rejection sampling 108
Truncated distributions 116
Metropolis - Hastings algorithm 117
   A few words on Markov chains 118
   The Metropolis sampler 126
The Gibbs sampler 129
   The two-phase Gibbs sampler 129
   The multiphase Gibbs sampler 131
   Application in linear regression 132
The diagnosis of MCMC samples 134
Tests for random numbers **141**
The evaluation of random numbers – an example of a test 142
Summary **146**
References **146**

Chapter 5: Monte Carlo Methods for Optimization Problems   **149**

Numerical optimization **153**
Gradient ascent/descent 154
Newton-Raphson methods 154
Further general-purpose optimization methods 157
Dealing with stochastic optimization **159**
Simplified procedures (Star Trek, Spaceballs, and Spaceballs princess) 159
Metropolis-Hastings revisited 163
Gradient-based stochastic optimization 165
Summary **170**
References **171**

Chapter 6: Probability Theory Shown by Simulation   **173**

Some basics on probability theory **173**
Probability distributions **174**
Discrete probability distributions 174
Continuous probability distributions 175
Winning the lottery **176**
The weak law on large numbers **178**
Emperor penguins and your boss 178
   Limits and convergence of random variables 180
   Convergence of the sample mean – weak law of large numbers 181
   Showing the weak law of large numbers by simulation 182
The central limit theorem **190**
Properties of estimators **195**
Properties of estimators 196

Confidence intervals	197
A note on robust estimators	200
Summary	**201**
References	**201**
Chapter 7: Resampling Methods	**203**
The bootstrap	**204**
A motivating example with odds ratios	205
Why the bootstrap works	208
A closer look at the bootstrap	211
The plug-in principle	212
Estimation of standard errors with bootstrapping	**213**
An example of a complex estimation using the bootstrap	216
The parametric bootstrap	**218**
Estimating bias with bootstrap	**221**
Confidence intervals by bootstrap	222
The jackknife	**226**
Disadvantages of the jackknife	229
The delete-d jackknife	230
Jackknife after bootstrap	232
Cross-validation	**235**
The classical linear regression model	235
The basic concept of cross validation	236
Classical cross validation – 70/30 method	238
Leave-one-out cross validation	240
k-fold cross validation	242
Summary	**244**
References	**245**
Chapter 8: Applications of Resampling Methods and Monte Carlo Tests	**247**
The bootstrap in regression analysis	**247**
Motivation to use the bootstrap	248
The most popular but often worst method	253
Bootstrapping by draws from residuals	258
Proper variance estimation with missing values	**263**
Bootstrapping in time series	**269**
Bootstrapping in the case of complex sampling designs	**273**
Monte Carlo tests	**278**
A motivating example	278
The permutation test as a special kind of MC test	287

A Monte Carlo test for multiple groups 290
Hypothesis testing using a bootstrap 294
A test for multivariate normality 295
Size of the test 297
Power comparisons 298
Summary **298**
References 299
Chapter 9: The EM Algorithm **301**
The basic EM algorithm **301**
Some prerequisites 302
Formal definition of the EM algorithm 303
Introductory example for the EM algorithm 304
The EM algorithm by example of k-means clustering **305**
The EM algorithm for the imputation of missing values **312**
Summary **318**
References **318**
Chapter 10: Simulation with Complex Data **321**
Different kinds of simulation and software **322**
Simulating data using complex models **324**
A model-based simple example 324
A model-based example with mixtures 327
Model-based approach to simulate data 328
An example of simulating high-dimensional data 329
Simulating finite populations with cluster or hierarchical structures 330
Model-based simulation studies **333**
Latent model example continued 334
A simple example of model-based simulation 336
A model-based simulation study 341
Design-based simulation **347**
An example with complex survey data 348
Simulation of the synthetic population 349
Estimators of interest 350
Defining the sampling design 351
Using stratified sampling 353
Adding contamination 354
Performing simulations separately on different domains 356
Inserting missing values **357**
Summary **359**
References 359

Chapter 11: System Dynamics and Agent-Based Models   363

  Agent-based models   364
  Dynamics in love and hate   368
  Dynamic systems in ecological modeling   371
  Summary   374
  References   374

Index   375

Preface

"Everybody seems to think I'm lazy

I don't mind, I think they're crazy

Running everywhere at such a speed

Till they find there's no need (There's no need)"

The Beatles in their song "I'm only sleeping"

The Monte Carlo way and simulation approach are ways to stay lazy and efficient at the same time. "Lazy", since a simulation approach is generally much easier to carry out as compared to an analytical approach — there is mostly no need for analytical approaches, and one might be crazy to neglect the whole world of statistical simulation. "Efficient", since it costs minimal efforts to get reliable results, and often simulation is the only approach to get results. The simulation approach in data science and statistics is generally a more intuitive approach compared to analytical solutions. It is not hidden behind a wall of mathematics, and using a simulation approach is often the only way to solve complex problems.

Statistical simulation has thus become an essential area in data science and statistics. It can be seen as a data-driven approach to many practical problems in data science and statistics.

In this book, theory is also explained with illustrative examples using the software environment R, for which advanced data processing features are shown in the book.

This book will thus provide a computational and methodological framework for statistical simulation to users with a computational statistics and/or data science background.

More precisely, the aim of this book is to lay into the hands of the readers a book that explains methods, give advice on the usage of the methods, and provide computational tools to solve common problems in statistical simulation and computer-intense methods.

The core issues are on simulating distributions and datasets, Monte Carlo methods for inference statistics, microsimulation and dynamical systems, and presenting solutions using computer-intense approaches. You will see applications in R not only to better understand the methods but also to gain experience when working on real-world data and real-world problems.

The author of the book has tried to make humorous and amusing examples in certain chapters in order to increase interest, staying catchy and memorable. Next to serious text on methods, curious examples on individual mortality and fertility rates of the author of the book are also present as is the system dynamics from the love/hate story of Prince Henry and Chelsy Davy, the Australian guy in the Austrian mountain trying to reach the highest mountain through an optimization problem, or the weak law of winning the lottery are presented as well.

What this book covers

Chapter 1, *Introduction*, discusses the general aim of simulation experiments in data science and statistics, why and where simulation is used, and the special case of dealing with big data.

Chapter 2, *R and High-Performance Computing*, consists of comprehensive text on advanced computing, data manipulation, and visualization with R.

Chapter 3, *The Discrepancy between Pencil-Driven Theory and Data-Driven Computational Solutions*, reports problems on numerical precision, rounding, and convergence in a deterministic setting.

Chapter 4, *Simulation of Random Numbers*, starts with the simulation of uniform random numbers and transformation methods to obtain other kinds of distributions. It includes a discussion of various types of Markov chain Monte Carlo (MCMC) methods.

Chapter 5, *Monte Carlo Methods for Optimization Problems*, introduces deterministic and stochastic optimization methods.

Chapter 6, *Probability Theory Shown by Simulation*, has a strong focus on basic theorems in statistics; for example, the concept of the weak law of large numbers and the central limit theorem are shown by simulation.

Chapter 7, *Resampling Methods*, is a comprehensive view on the bootstrap, the jackknife and cross-validation.

Chapter 8, Applications of Resampling Methods and Monte Carlo Tests, shows applications in various fields such as regression, imputation, and time series analysis. In addition, Monte Carlo tests and their variants such as permutation tests and bootstrap tests are presented.

Chapter 9, The EM Algorithm, introduces the expectation maximum method to iteratively obtain an optima. Applications in clustering and imputation of missing values are given.

Chapter 10, Simulation with Complex Data, shows how to simulate synthetic data as well as population data that can be used for the comparison of methods in general or also serve as input for agent-based microsimulation models.

Chapter 11, System Dynamics and Agent-Based Models, discusses agent-based microsimulation models and shows basic models in system dynamics to study complex dynamical systems.

What you need for this book

This book heavily depends on the software environment R, version 3.2 or newer (`https://cran.r-project.org/`). In most chapters, independent and standalone code is written to show methods and execute examples, and no additional packages of R are needed. For a few chapters, additional R packages such as deSolve, cvTools, laeken, VIM, and few others must be installed within R. The packages dplyr and ggplot2 are used throughout the book.

Optionally, the use of a script editor for R, such as RStudio (`https://www.rstudio.com/`) or Architect + Eclipse (`https://www.openanalytics.eu/architect`), is recommended.

Who this book is for

This book is for users who are familiar with computational methods and R. If you want to learn about the advanced features of R, along with computer-intense Monte Carlo methods and tools for statistical simulation, and if you prefer data-driven solutions, then this book is for you.

Conventions

In this book, you will find a number of text styles that distinguish between different kinds of information. Here are some examples of these styles and an explanation of their meaning.

R code words in text, filenames, file extensions, pathnames, and dummy URLs are shown as follows:

A block of code is set as follows:

```
[default]
love <- function(t, x, parms){
  with(as.list(c(parms, x)), {
    dPrince_Harry <- a * Chelsy_Davy
    dChelsy_Davy <- -b * Prince_Harry
    res <- c(dPrince_Harry, dChelsy_Davy)
    list(res)
  })
}
```

Any command-line input or output is written as follows:

```
dat <- matrix(c(104,11037,189,11034),2,2, byrow=TRUE)
## Loading required package: grid
> confint(oddsratio(dat, log=FALSE))
##      2.5 %      97.5 %
##   0.4324132 0.6998549
```

 Warnings or important notes appear in a box like this.

 Tips and tricks appear like this.

Reader feedback

Feedback from our readers is always welcome. Let us know what you think about this book—what you liked or disliked. Reader feedback is important for us as it helps us develop titles that you will really get the most out of.

To send us general feedback, simply e-mail feedback@packtpub.com, and mention the book's title in the subject of your message.

If there is a topic that you have expertise in and you are interested in either writing or contributing to a book, see our author guide at www.packtpub.com/authors.

Customer support

Now that you are the proud owner of a Packt book, we have a number of things to help you to get the most from your purchase.

Downloading the example code

You can download the example code files for this book from your account at http://www.packtpub.com. If you purchased this book elsewhere, you can visit http://www.packtpub.com/support and register to have the files e-mailed directly to you.

You can download the code files by following these steps:

1. Log in or register to our website using your e-mail address and password.
2. Hover the mouse pointer on the **SUPPORT** tab at the top.
3. Click on **Code Downloads & Errata**.
4. Enter the name of the book in the **Search** box.
5. Select the book for which you're looking to download the code files.
6. Choose from the drop-down menu where you purchased this book from.
7. Click on **Code Download**.

You can also download the code files by clicking on the **Code Files** button on the book's webpage at the Packt Publishing website. This page can be accessed by entering the book's name in the **Search** box. Please note that you need to be logged in to your Packt account.

Once the file is downloaded, please make sure that you unzip or extract the folder using the latest version of:

- WinRAR / 7-Zip for Windows
- Zipeg / iZip / UnRarX for Mac
- 7-Zip / PeaZip for Linux

The code bundle for the book is also hosted on GitHub at https://github.com/PacktPublishing/Simulation-for-Data-Science-with-R. We also have other code bundles from our rich catalog of books and videos available at https://github.com/PacktPublishing/. Check them out!

Downloading the color images of this book

We also provide you with a PDF file that has color images of the screenshots/ diagrams used in this book. The color images will help you better understand the changes in the output. You can download this file from `https://www.packtpub.com/sites/default/files/downloads/SimulationforDataSciencewithR_ColorImages.pdf`.

Errata

Although we have taken every care to ensure the accuracy of our content, mistakes do happen. If you find a mistake in one of our books—maybe a mistake in the text or the code—we would be grateful if you could report this to us. By doing so, you can save other readers from frustration and help us improve subsequent versions of this book. If you find any errata, please report them by visiting `http://www.packtpub.com/submit-errata`, selecting your book, clicking on the **Errata Submission Form** link, and entering the details of your errata. Once your errata are verified, your submission will be accepted and the errata will be uploaded to our website or added to any list of existing errata under the Errata section of that title.

To view the previously submitted errata, go to `https://www.packtpub.com/books/content/support` and enter the name of the book in the search field. The required information will appear under the **Errata** section.

Piracy

Piracy of copyrighted material on the Internet is an ongoing problem across all media. At Packt, we take the protection of our copyright and licenses very seriously. If you come across any illegal copies of our works in any form on the Internet, please provide us with the location address or website name immediately so that we can pursue a remedy.

Please contact us at `copyright@packtpub.com` with a link to the suspected pirated material.

We appreciate your help in protecting our authors and our ability to bring you valuable content.

Questions

If you have a problem with any aspect of this book, you can contact us at `questions@packtpub.com`, and we will do our best to address the problem.

1
Introduction

In the previous century, the Vienna University of Technology in Vienna enrolled
a bachelor study called data engineering and statistics. Basically the content
was perfectly related to the nowadays commonly-used term **data science**.
Data-oriented lectures in the area of computer science, such as storing and retrieving
data, programming, and data security, were in the curriculum, together with
applied lectures on statistics, such as multivariate statistics, biostatistics, financial
statistics, statistical learning, and official statistics. We had too few students and
after a few years the course was canceled. 16 years later, the picture completely
changed. New bachelors and masters courses on data science have been developed
everywhere in the world over the last few years. Universities have found that they
must offer studies on data science, because the industry needs experts on it, but
also developments in statistics in recent years have almost exclusively come from
an area called **computational statistics**. Statistics is the original form of computing
data, and computational statistics takes this to an extreme where methods and tools
are developed in a highly data-dependent manner, using and developing modern
computational tools. Computational statistics and data science are closely related.
Computational statistics covers a broad swathe of data science, exclusive data
management, and data security issues. Computational statistics (and therefore
also data science) has become very popular since the eighties, and it is very likely
the most influential area of statistics nowadays. In the field of computational statistics,
not only is new methodology developed, but it is also implemented in software –
nowadays almost exclusively in the old but modern **software environment R**.

Data science seems like a good term when your work is driven by data with a less strong component on method and algorithm development than computational statistics, but with a lot of pure computer science topics related to storing, retrieving, and handling data sets. It also differs from computational statistics in various aspects. For example, in the area of data visualization also pure process-related visualizations (airflows in an engine, for example) are a topic in data science but not in computational statistics.

Wikipedia defines data science as a field that:

> *"incorporates varying elements and builds on techniques and theories from many fields, including math, statistics, data engineering, pattern recognition and learning, advanced computing, visualization, uncertainty modeling, data warehousing, and high performance computing with the goal of extracting meaning from data and creating data products."*

Data science is the management of the entire modeling process, from data collection, storage and managing data, data pre-processing (editing, imputation), data analysis, and modeling, to automatized reporting and presenting the results, all in a reproducible manner. It is thus also an interdisciplinary study to extract meaning from data with statistics, by using a lot of elements in computer science, as well as general subject-matter skills. In that sense, data science is an extension and continuation of statistics. Data scientists use statistics and data-oriented computer science tools to solve the problems they face.

Statistical simulation is an essential area in data science. The core issues of this book are simulating distributions and data sets, Monte Carlo methods for inference statistics, and presenting solutions on computer-intense approaches. This book discusses various areas in statistical simulation, random number simulation, resampling, Monte Carlo methods, statistical theory explained by simulation experiments, agent-based microsimulation, and system dynamics. The aim is to put a book into the hands of readers that explains methods, gives advice on the use of those methods, and provides computational tools to solve common problems in statistical simulation and computer-intense methods.

In this book, the theory is not just explained. The theory is also made understandable with illustrative examples using the R software environment. The reader will get to grips with the R software environment. After getting the background on popular methods in the field, readers will see applications in R to better understand the methods, as well as to gain experience when working on real-world data and real-world problems.

R itself is perfectly suited to carry out simulations. It should be mentioned that the basics of R are not the topic of the book, but advanced data manipulation and advanced visualization tools are shown in R. The reader should therefore not be a complete newbie in R, and if so, should first read a very basic introduction to R.

Readers will get a brief overview of the problems and possibilities of data-driven simulation and resampling methods.

What is simulation and where is it applied?

Statistical simulation is a numerical method for conducting experiments on a computer in order to solve mathematical problems in a data-driven manner.

Each *experiment* is carried out in two steps:

1. Drawing a random outcome.
2. The subsequent application of an estimation function to the drawn data.

Random draws are made by means of simulating random numbers, such as the numbers produced by a chosen random number generator.

Simulation is applied in different ways. It is applied in **sampling** to gather information about a random object by observing many realizations of it (Kroese et al., 2014).

As computational power keeps increasing, and new methods and algorithms are being developed, opportunities present themselves to not only conduct innovative research, but also to design better social and economic policies and programs through **micro-simulation** and **agent-based modeling**, where states change over time according to defined transition probabilities. Another example is the area of **system dynamics**, which describes the interaction of populations or individuals. Both topics are part of *Chapter 11, System Dynamics and Agent-Based Models*.

With simulation experiments, one can even show the concepts of probability theory and the basic theorems of statistics. The (weak and strong) *law of large numbers* can be explained. We may repeatedly do some experiments with related probability mechanisms. The outcomes of these experiments are random – random events have outcomes that are not known with certainty, but in the long run we know the properties. To toss coins is the simplest example. The most fundamental theorem in mathematical statistics, the central limit theorem, can also be shown by simulation. Using simulation experiments, readers will be able to fully understand this important theorem, while the proof with mathematics needs very detailed knowledge of mass and probability theory. More information on simulation to show the basics in statistics is provided in *Chapter 6, Probability Theory Shown by Simulation*.

Statistical simulation is also used to show the properties of an estimation method regarding different conditions. One example is the question of how an estimator behaves under different kinds of missing values pattern, or how outliers may corrupt the estimator. When samples have been drawn with complex sampling designs from finite populations, the influence of the sampling design on the estimator of interest can be shown with design-based simulations. Both model-based simulation and design-based simulation are shown in *Chapter 10, Simulation with Complex Data*. How data might be simulated for different kind of problems is also discussed. This covers the high-dimensional data and complex synthetic populations needed for design-based simulations.

Usually, when statisticians talk about simulations, they mean **Monte Carlo simulations**. The Monte Carlo simulation method uses repeated random sampling to mimic the null hypothesis or simulate data from a model where an estimation function is applied to the simulated data.

The Monte Carlo simulation approach is also essential in **Bayesian statistics**, where **Markov chain Monte Carlo** (**MCMC**) methods are used to sample parameter values from a posterior distribution (see also Kroese et al., 2014). This will be intensively discussed in *Chapter 4, Simulation of Random Numbers*. Generally, it is crucial to have an excellent random number generator at hand that allows you to simulate uniformly distributed values. Additionally, it is crucial to transform a uniform distribution into a distribution of interest. We can do this with inversion, rejection sampling, or MCMC methods; see also *Chapter 4, Simulation of Random Numbers*.

The Monte Carlo simulation approach is also central to estimating certain numerical quantities in general, but especially to estimate **statistical uncertainty**. It turns out (*Chapter 6, Probability Theory Shown by Simulation*) that almost no mathematics is used to express the statistical uncertainty for any complex estimator. The Monte Carlo simulation method is a data-driven and computational tool. It is the perfect tool for data scientists to make statistical inferences without getting lost in the world of mathematics.

Another application of Monte Carlo simulation is **multi-dimensional integrals**, which can be solved via Monte Carlo techniques, typically by drawing random numbers out of an interval at which the integral is defined. Closely related to this is numerical **optimization**. Here, the Monte Carlo approach can be used to first solve optimization problems with complicated objective functions using a stochastic approach. The aim to introduce randomness is to avoid to converge / trap into a local optima when searching for an optima in non-convex (or non-concave) optimization functions, (more on this in *Chapter 5, Monte Carlo Methods for Optimization Problems*).

The great thing about Monte Carlo simulation is that the procedure is simple, independent of the complexity of the estimator/estimation of interest. Doing even the most complicated Monte Carlo simulation can be broken down into simple steps:

1. Identify a mathematical model – the estimation you want to apply.

2. Define the parameters in your model.

3. Create random data according to those parameters. Typically, we generate independent data sets under the conditions of interest.

4. Simulate and analyze the output of your estimations. This is typically done by computing the numerical value of the estimator/test statistic. On the original data, this should be $T(X)$. For each simulated data set we get $T_1, \dots, T_R$, that is, the numerical values of the estimator for each simulated data. If is large enough, the distribution of $T_1, \dots, T_R$ gives a good approximation of the true sampling distribution of the estimator/ test. Moreover, the sample mean of the estimates is an estimate of the true mean. The 0,025 and 0,975 quantiles of this distribution is an estimator of the confidence interval of the point estimate from $T(X)$.

Generally speaking, with Monte Carlo simulation we approximate the sampling distribution of an estimator or test statistic. The particular set of related conditions are usually parameters fitted from the original data and conditions from a null hypothesis. With Monte Carlo simulations, we can successfully express the statistical uncertainty of an estimator or receive the relevant values (for example, the *p-value*) of a hypothesis test.

Why use simulation?

Simulation can save huge amounts of time and provides very accurate answers to our questions.

Statistical inference is often handled by asymptotic normal theory, which may provide formulas for the standard errors that allow us to construct confidence intervals around point estimates. For the simple case of the simple estimator of the arithmetic mean, we can immediately choose the formula $\bar{x} \mp 1.96 \cdot s/\sqrt{n}$ for an observational vector x with n values, the arithmetic $\bar{x} = \frac{1}{n}\sum_{i=1}^{n} x_i$ and s being the standard deviation of x. However, this formula to express the confidence interval for the arithmetic mean is only true for independent identical distributed samples, sampled with simple random sampling from a population. However, in many situations the (asymptotic) distribution of the parameter of interest might not be known, and often we do not have the expertise to derive even an approximation of a formula to express the standard error of an estimator of interest. For example, this might be true for the Huber mean (Huber 1981) from data sampled with a multi-stage cluster sampling design. In other words, if the quantity of interest is a very complex function of the data or if the data is of a very complex nature, we may be able to benefit substantially from the use of a Monte Carlo simulation. Even when a formula may exist in the statistical literature to express the confidence interval, we might not be aware of it.

A very prominent **resampling method** is the **bootstrap**, intensively discussed in *Chapter 7, Resampling Methods*. In this approach, the sampling distribution of the parameter estimate is simulated by repeated sampling with replacement from the current data, and re-computing parameter estimates from each sampled data set. The distribution of these estimations expresses the variability of the estimation, thus this distribution can be used to express confidence intervals.

The approach is very similar for hypothesis tests. The distribution of the test statistics is not always known for a test. With the Monte Carlo approach to testing, data is simulated in a way that it mimics the null hypothesis, and parameters for data generation are used from the empirical data. The test statistic is calculated on the data and compared to the repeatedly simulated data. It's then a straightforward topic in *Chapter 8, Applications of Resampling Methods and Monte Carlo Tests, Monte Carlo Tests*) to receive a *p-value* for the test.

Simulation and big data

Big unstructured data is often analyzed nowadays, or used as auxiliary information. Running simulations on big data is a challenge.

Big data can be too large to fit in the memory of a desktop computer. Whenever this happens, basically three options are available to choose from. The first option is to just use a more powerful server with a larger amount of memory for your computations. Second, the data can also be stored efficiently in a database and we connect to the database for analysis. Typically, only a subset of the data is of interest, so we can just grab the interesting parts of the database, import it to R, do the analysis, and export the results back to the database. Since R has excellent features and APIs for connecting to well-known databases, this is the recommended approach. Third, aggregate and subset your data first. It is likely that you don't need such detailed information for your analysis. To give an example, imagine you want to analyze road traffic data. The measurement units on a highway usually report the speed, the distance to the next car, the lane used, and the kind of vehicle. If this is so, the data will be really huge. However, for an analysis of measurement faults, it is enough to aggregate the data and analyze 1- or 5-minute interval data.

As soon as the data sets become large, resampling methods such as the Bootstrap might cause long computation times. The usual method is to repeatedly sample data, estimate the statistic of interest, and save the results. Whenever simulations can be rerun under different settings, one may change this approach. For a method such as the Bootstrap, an additional vector can be stored for each Bootstrap sample containing information about how often a sample is included in a Bootstrap sample. Thus, instead of *storing* the Bootstrap sample, we store a vector of *0,1,...* that expresses whether a unit is included (and how often) in a Bootstrap sample. With this approach, Bootstrap samples must only be selected ones. This approach is especially useful when the Bootstrap sample selection is of a more complex nature because of special sampling designs, and simulations should be re-run again.

If estimations are done repeatedly, as in the Monte Carlo approach, it is very important to have fast implementations of the estimators in the software available. It is recommended to run everything vectorized, meaning that any function call applied to a vector or any other data structure operates directly on all of its values/elements. It is then crucial that this *loop* is implemented in a compiled language such as C or C++, as is the case with more elementary functions of base R. R provides a powerful interface to foreign languages. The use of foreign languages is often much more efficient than using non-compiled, interpreted R language directly. Appropriately implemented apply-like functions over vectors, matrices, or data frames can even be very simply parallelized. The trick is then just to use, for example, instead of an `lapply`, the call `mclapply` from the R package parallel (R Core Team 2015).

Resampling methods can be easily run on parallel processes. Monte Carlo techniques were originally designed for machines with a single processor. With today's high performance computing possibilities, the calculation can often be done by the use of many processors running in parallel (Kroese et al., 2014). Monte Carlo techniques perform efficiently in the parallel processing framework. In R, for example, only very few modifications are needed to run a Monte Carlo approach in parallel. However, when data sets get large, parallel computing might only be faster than single-core computing in Linux or OS X operating systems, since both support *forking*, while Microsoft Windows does not support this to the same extent.

A related issue is the use of effective random number generation techniques for parallel computing. It must be ensured that the random numbers used by separate workers are produced independently, otherwise the workers will return the same results. To facilitate reproducible research, it is thus necessary to provide different initializations of random numbers to all workers (see also Schmidberger et al., 2009). For example, the package rlecuyer (Sevcikova and Rossini 2015) supports these issues.

Choosing the right simulation technique

The bad news is that there is no general guidance and no general method for simulation. The choice of the right simulation technique rather depends on the underlying problem, data set, and the aim of the study.

We already mentioned in which areas simulation plays a role. Depending on the area of interest, different techniques are considered. For a Bayesian analysis, the methods differ between general inference statistics using resampling techniques, and when optimization comes into the topic. The methods change completely when interaction of populations or individuals are in focus, or when predictions about the future on an individual level (micro-simulation) are required.

However, some general questions may give a little guidance for choosing the right technique. This is illustrated in *Table 1.1*. Of course, it is often the case that a clear decision cannot be made. For example, if you work with a sample, optimization techniques might be used for several reasons, but the main aim of optimization is more general. It can be applied to samples or population data. Another example includes, for example, in agent-based microsimulation of course one can compare models, but it's not the main aim. Thus this table should give only a very rough categorization of methods for basic questions. It should be clear that optimization methods, methods for system dynamics, and agent-based micro-simulation techniques may differ to the methods that are developed to express the uncertainty of estimators, such as resampling methods.

The following table describes choosing the right simulation technique, **Monte Carlo (MC)** techniques, and resampling techniques; **Markov chain Monte Carlo (MCMC)** methods; MC test Monte Carlo techniques applied to hypothesis testing, **optimization (O)**, **system dynamics (SD)**, **agent-based modeling (ABM)**, **design-based simulation (DBS)**, and **model-based simulation (MBS)**:

Question	Yes	No
Do you work with a sample?	MC, MC test, MBS, DBS	ABM, SD
Is variability/randomness important?	MC, MC test, MBS, DBS	ABM, SD
Is the number of observations large?	ABM	SD, MCMC
Do you apply a hypothesis test?	MC test	ABM, DBS, SD, Opt
Is the sample drawn from a finite population?	DBS	MBS
Do you work with a population?	ABM, Opt, SD	MC, MC test
Do you want to compare models?	MC	ABM, SD, Opt
Do you apply Bayesian statistics?	MCMC	SD, Opt
Do you need to simulate certain distributions?	RN, MCMC	SD, Opt
Is probability theory a main issue?	ABM, MCMC	MC, MBS, DBS
Has something to be optimized?	Opt	MC, MC test, MBS
Dynamic rules of behavior within individuals.	SD, ABM	All others
Do changes to the system happen over time?	SD	All others
Can the time-frame of interest be long?	ABM, SD	All others

Please enjoy all the chapters mentioned, simulate a cozy burning fire with R's package animation (Yihui 2013) in *Figure 1.1*, and start to explore all the different issues in *Simulation for Data Science with R*:

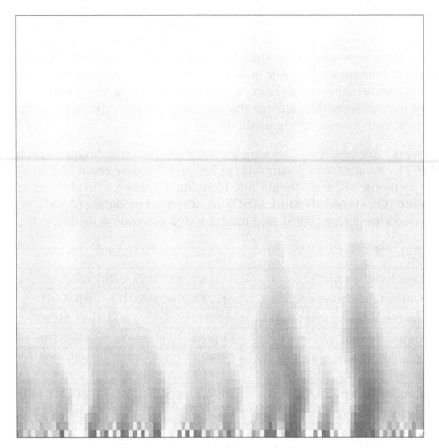

Figure 1.1: Snapshot of a simulated burning fire for your coziness

To run the burning fire simulation, have a look at the code on this website: http://yihui.name/en/2009/06/simulation-of-burning-fire-in-r/.

Summary

Simulation experiments are mostly data-dependent and thus perfectly suited for a data scientist. Different kinds of simulation techniques have been mentioned in this chapter. They are discussed in detail in the next chapters. We mentioned that simulation can be applied almost everywhere to show the properties and performance of methods, to make predictions, and to assess statistical uncertainty. We learned that no general approach exists and that quite different methods exist for different tasks, data sets, and problems. It's up to the data scientist and statistician to choose the right simulation approach.

Whenever computational power is an issue, remember that almost any simulation can be run in a parallel manner, and modern software is ready for this task.

In practice, one should not ask the question "Why did you use simulation?" to somebody who has applied simulation techniques, but rather "Why didn't you use simulation?" to somebody who did not.

References

- Eddelbuettel, D., and R. François. 2011, "Rcpp: Seamless R and C++ Integration." *Journal of Statistical Software 40 (8): 1–18.*

- Huber, P.J. 1981, *Robust Statistics*, Wiley.

- Kroese, D.P., T. Brereton, T. Taimre, and Z.I. Botev. 2014. "Why the Monte Carlo Method is so important today," *Wiley Interdisciplinary Reviews: Computational Statistics 6 (6). John Wiley & Sons*, Inc.: 386–92.

- R Core Team. 2015. *R: A Language and Environment for Statistical Computing.* Vienna, Austria: R Foundation for Statistical Computing. `https://www.R-project.org/`.

- Schmidberger, S., M. Morgan, D. Eddelbuettel, H. Yu, L. Tierney, and U. Mansmann. 2009, "State of the Art in Parallel Computing with R," *Journal of Statistical Software 31 (1).*

- Sevcikova, H., and T. Rossini. 2015. *Rlecuyer: R Interface to RNG with Multiple Streams,* `https://CRAN.R-project.org/package=rlecuyer`.

- Yihui, X. 2013. "Animation: An R Package for Creating Animations and Demonstrating Statistical Methods," *Journal of Statistical Software 53 (1): 1–27.*

2

R and High-Performance Computing

The software environment **R** (R Development Core Team, 2015) is nowadays the most commonly used software in the statistical world, and this software is heavily used in this book. The methods described in any of the following chapters are practically applied, and the application of the methods is shown using the statistical environment R. For a book on simulation and data science in R, and to efficiently apply methods, a longer R introduction is needed, especially on features that support efficient calculations.

In this chapter, you will be given a very brief introduction to the functionality of R. This introduction does not replace a general introduction to R but instead shows some useful points, such as introducing modern visualization tools and efficient data manipulation packages. These topics — among others from this chapter — are important for understanding the examples and the R code in the book.

More important than replicating a fully comprehensive R introduction would be to cover some aspects related to computer-intensive methods and expensive data simulation in data science. Thus, some packages and methods are introduced that are suitable to work efficiently with large data sets or can be efficiently applied in simulations.

Since data manipulation is always a central point in every analysis and data scientists probably spend more than 70 percent of their work in data manipulation (before applying statistical methods), we will concentrate on the packages `dplyr` (Wickham and Francois, 2015) and `data.table` (Dowle et al., 2015).

At the end of this chapter, we will discuss packages for high-performance computing (for example, package `snow`, Tierney et al., 2015) and useful profiling tools.

> Other important issues such as creating our own R packages, integrated tests, and dynamic reporting are not part of the contents of this book. However, experienced R users should make use of these important features, and it is suggested that you read specialized literature on these topics.

Experts in R may skip this chapter and immediately start with *Chapter 3*, *The Discrepancy Between Pencil-Driven Theory and Data-Driven Computational Solutions*. Newbies in R should also read an introduction to R next to or before reading this chapter.

The R statistical environment

R was founded by Ross Ihaka and Robert Gentlemen in 1994/1995. It is based on **S**, a programming language developed by John Chambers (Bell Laboratories), and Scheme. Since 1997, it has been internationally developed and distributed from Vienna over the **Comprehensive R Archive Network** (**CRAN**). R is nowadays the most popular and most used software in the statistical world. In addition, R is free and open source (under the GPL2). R is not only a statistical software, it is an environment for interactive computing with data supporting facilities to produce high-quality graphics. The exchange of code with others is easy since everybody can download R. This might also be one reason why modern methods are often exclusively developed in R. R is an object-oriented programming language and has interfaces to many other software products such as C, C++, Java, and interfaces to databases.

Useful information can be found on the following links.

- Homepage: http://www.r-project.org/ and http://cran.r-project.org (CRAN)
- Frequently Asked Questions (FAQs) lists on CRAN
- Manuals and contributed manuals at CRAN
- Task views on CRAN

R is extendable by approximately 8,400 add-on packages.

For programming, it is advisable to write the code in a well-developed editor and communicate interactively with R. An editor should allow syntax-highlighting, code-completion and interactive communication with R. For beginners but also for advanced users, RStudio is one choice (`http://www.rstudio.org/`). Experts might also use the combination of Eclipse plus its add-on StatET. Both editors provide a fully developed programming environment. They not only integrate R, they also integrate many other useful tools and software.

Basics in R

R can be used as an overgrown calculator. All the operations of a calculator can be very easily used in R; for example, addition is done with +, subtraction with -, division with /, exponential with `exp()`, logarithm with `log()`, square root using `sqrt()`, sinus with `sin()`. All operations works as expected; for example, the following expression is parsed by R, inner brackets are solved first, multiplication and division operators have precedence over the addition and subtraction operators, and so on:

```
5 + 2 * log(3 * 3)
## [1] 9.394449
```

Since R starts within one second, there is no need to have any other calculator at hand anymore.

Some very basic stuff about R

R is a function and object-oriented language. Functions can be applied to objects. The syntax is as shown in the following example:

```
mean(rnorm(10))
## [1] -0.4241956
```

With the function `rnorm`, 10 numbers are drawn randomly from a standard normal distribution. If no seed is fixed (with function `seed()`), the numbers differ from one call to another call of these function. Afterwards, the `mean` is calculated for these 10 numbers. Functions typically have function arguments that can be set. The syntax for calling a function is generally:

```
res1 <- name_of_function(v1) # an input argument
res2 <- name_of_function(v1, v2) # two input arguments
res3 <- name_of_function(v1, v2, v3) # three input arguments
```

Functions often have additional function arguments with default values. You get access to all function arguments with `args()`.

Allocation to objects are made by `<-` or `=` and the generated object can be print via object name followed by typing ENTER, such as:

```
x <- rnorm(5)
x
##  [1] -1.3672828 -2.0871666  0.4747871  0.4861836  0.8022188
```

The function `options()` allows you to modify the default setting such as to change the font, the encoding, or as shown here, we reduce the number of printed digits (internally R will not round to these digits, it's just the print):

```
options(digits = 4)
x
##  [1] -1.3673 -2.0872  0.4748  0.4862  0.8022
```

Please note that R is case sensitive.

Installation and updates

The recommended procedure to install the software consists of the following steps.

Install R: if R is already installed on the computer, ensure that it is the latest version. If the software is not installed, go to `http://cran.r-project.org/bin/` and choose your platform. Just download the executable file depended on your operating system and follow the on-screen instructions.

To install an add-on package, say package `dplyr`, type:

```
install.packages("dplyr")
```

Installation is needed only once. The content of an installed package can be used after loading the package via:

```
library("dplyr")
```

When typing `update.packages()`, R searches for possible updates and installs new versions of packages, if any are available.

The previous information was about installing the stable CRAN version of the packages. However, the latest changes are often only available in the development version of the package. Sometimes these development versions are hosted on GitHub or similar Git repository systems.

To install the latest development version, the installation of the package `devtools` (Wickham and Chang, 2015) is needed. After calling the `devtools` package, the development version can be installed via `install_github()`. We show this for package `dplyr`:

```
if(!require(devtools)) install.packages("devtools")
```

```
library("devtools")
install_github("hadley/dplyr")
```

Help

It is crucial to have basic knowledge of how to get `help` using the following command:

```
help.start()
```

By this command your browser opens and help (and more) is available.

The browsable help index of the package can be accessed by typing the following command into R:

```
help(package="dplyr")
```

To find help for a specific function, one can use `help(name)` or `?name`. As an example, we can look at the help file of function `group_by`, which is included in the package `dplyr`:

```
?group_by
```

Data in the package can be loaded via the `data()` function, for example, the `Cars93` dataset from package MASS (Venables and Ripley 2002):

```
data(Cars93, package = "MASS")
```

`help.search()` can be used to find functions for which you don't know an exact name, for example:

```
help.search("histogram")
```

This command will search your local R installation for functions approximately matching the character string `"histogram"` in the (file) name, alias, title, concept, or keyword entries. With function `apropos`, one can find and list objects by (partial) name. For example, to list all objects with partial name match of `hist`, type:

```
apropos("hist")
```

To search help pages, vignettes or task views, use the search engine at the website of R and view the results of your request (for example, `summarize`) in your web browser:

```
RSiteSearch("group by factor")
```

This reports all search results for the character string `"group by factor"`.

The R workspace and the working directory

Created objects are available in the workspace of R and loaded in the memory of your computer. The collection of all created objects is called the *workspace*. To list the objects in the workspace, type the following:

```
ls()
## [1] "x"
```

When importing or exporting data, the working directory must be defined. To show the current working directory, the function `getwd` can be used:

```
getwd()
## [1] "/Users/templ/workspace/simulation/book"
```

To change the working directory, the function `setwd` is the choice, see `?setwd`.

Data types

The objective is to know the most important data types:

- `numeric`
- `character`
- `factor`
- `logical`

The following are the important data structures:

- `vector`
- `list`
- `array`
- `data.frame`
- Special data types: missing values (NA), NULL-objects, NaN, `-inf`, `+inf`

Vectors in R

Vectors are the simplest data structure in R. A vector is a sequence of elements of the same type, such as numerical vectors, character vectors, or logical vectors. Vectors are often created with the function `c()`, for example:

```
v.num <- c(1,3,5.9,7)
v.num
## [1] 1.0 3.0 5.9 7.0
is.numeric (v.num)
## [1] TRUE
```

`is.numeric` query if the vector is of class `numeric`. Note that characters are written with parentheses.

Logical vectors are often created indirectly from numerical/character vectors:

```
v.num > 3
## [1] FALSE FALSE  TRUE  TRUE
```

Many operations on vectors are performed element-wise, for example, logical comparisons or arithmetic operations with vectors. A common error source is when the length of two or more vectors differs. Then the shorter one is repeated (*recycling*):

```
v1 <- c(1,2,3)
v2 <- c(4,5)
v1 + v2
## [1] 5 7 7
Warning message:
In v1 + v2 :
  longer object length is not a multiple of shorter object length
```

One should also be aware that R coerces internally to meaningful data types automatically. For example:

```
v2 <- c (100, TRUE, "A", FALSE)
v2
## [1] "100"   "TRUE"  "A"     "FALSE"
is.numeric (v2)
## [1] FALSE
```

Here, the lowest common data type is a string and therefore all entries of the vector are coerced to character. Note, to create vectors, the functions `seq` and `rep` are very useful.

Often it is necessary to subset vectors. The selection is made using the [] operator. A selection can be done in three ways:

- **Positive**: A vector of positive integers that specifies the position of the desired elements
- **Negative**: A vector with negative integers indicating the position of the non-required elements
- **Logical**: A logic vector in which the elements are to be the selected (TRUE), along with those that are not selected (FALSE)

Let us consider the following example:

```
data(Cars93, package = "MASS")
# extract a subset of variable Horsepower from Cars93
hp <- Cars93[1:10, "Horsepower"]
hp
##  [1] 140 200 172 172 208 110 170 180 170 200
# positive indexing:
hp[c(1,6)]
## [1] 140 110
# negative indexing:
hp[-c(2:5,7:10)]
## [1] 140 110
# logical indexing:
hp < 150
##  [1]  TRUE FALSE FALSE FALSE FALSE  TRUE FALSE FALSE FALSE FALSE
# a logical expression can be written directly in []
hp[hp < 150]
## [1] 140 110
```

Factors in R

Factors in R are of special importance. They are used to represent nominal or ordinal data. More precisely, unrecorded factors for nominally scaled data, and ordered factors for ordinal scaled data. Factors can be seen as special vectors. They are internally coded integers from *1* to *n* (# of occurrences) which are all associated with a name (label). So why should numeric or character variables be used as factors? Basically, factors have to be used for categorical information to get the correct number of degrees of freedom and correct design matrices in statistical modeling. In addition, the implementation of graphics for factors vs. numerical / character vectors differs. Moreover, factors are more efficient at storing character vectors. However, factors have a more complex data structure since factors include a numerically coded data vector and labels for each level/category. Let us consider the following example:

```
class(Cars93)
## [1] "data.frame"
class(Cars93$Cylinders)
## [1] "factor"
levels(Cars93$Cylinders)
## [1] "3"       "4"       "5"       "6"       "8"       "rotary"
summary(Cars93$Cylinders)
##      3      4      5      6      8 rotary
##      3     49      2     31      7      1
```

We note that output of `summary` is different for factors. Internally, R applies a method dispatch for generic functions such as `summary`, searching in our case if the function `summary.factor` exists. If yes, this function is applied, if not, `summary.default` is used.

list

A list in R is an *ordered* collection of objects whereas each object is part of the list and where the data types of the individual list elements can be different (vectors, matrices, data.frames, lists, and so on). The dimension of each list item can be different. Lists can be used to group and summarize various objects in an object. There are (at least) four ways of accessing elements of a list, (a) the [] operator, the operator [[]], the $ operator and the name of a list item. With `str()`, you can view the structure of a list, with `names()` you get the names of the list elements:

```
model <- lm(Price ~ Cylinders + Type + EngineSize + Origin, data =
Cars93)
## result is a list
class(model)
```

```
## [1] "lm"
## access elements from the named list with the dollar sign
model$coefficients
##     (Intercept)       Cylinders4        Cylinders5        Cylinders6
##           5.951            3.132            7.330            10.057
##       Cylinders8 Cylindersrotary        TypeLarge       TypeMidsize
##          17.835           19.828           -4.232             2.558
##       TypeSmall        TypeSporty          TypeVan        EngineSize
##          -6.086           -2.188           -5.835             2.303
##     Originnon-USA
##           5.915
```

data.frame

Data frames (in R data.frame) are the most important data type. They correspond
to the rectangle data format that is well-known from other software packages, with
rows corresponding to observation units and *columns* to variables. A data.frame is
like a *list*, where all list elements are vector/factors but with the restriction that all list
elements have the same number of elements (equal length) For example, data from
external sources to be read are often stored as data frames, data frames are usually
created by reading data but they can also be constructed with function data.frame().

A lot of opportunities exist to subset a data frame, for example with syntax: [index
row, index columns]. Again positive, negative and logical indexing is possible and
the type of indexing may be different for row index and column index. Accessing
individual columns is easiest using the $ operator (like lists):

```
## extract cars with small number of cylinders and small power
w <- Cars93$Cylinders %in% c("3", "4")  & Cars93$Horsepower < 80
str(Cars93[w, ])
## 'data.frame':    5 obs. of  27 variables:
## $ Manufacturer    : Factor w/ 32 levels "Acura","Audi",..: 11 12 25
28 29
## $ Model           : Factor w/ 93 levels "100","190E","240",..: 44
62 53 50 88
## $ Type            : Factor w/ 6 levels "Compact","Large",..: 4 4 4
4 4
## $ Min.Price       : num  6.9 6.7 8.2 7.3 7.3
```

```
##  $ Price            : num  7.4 8.4 9 8.4 8.6
##  $ Max.Price        : num  7.9 10 9.9 9.5 10
##  $ MPG.city         : int  31 46 31 33 39
##  $ MPG.highway      : int  33 50 41 37 43
##  $ AirBags          : Factor w/ 3 levels "Driver & Passenger",..: 3 3
## 3 3 3
##  $ DriveTrain       : Factor w/ 3 levels "4WD","Front",..: 2 2 2 1 2
##  $ Cylinders        : Factor w/ 6 levels "3","4","5","6",..: 2 1 2 1
## 1
##  $ EngineSize       : num  1.3 1 1.6 1.2 1.3
##  $ Horsepower       : int  63 55 74 73 70
##  $ RPM              : int  5000 5700 5600 5600 6000
##  $ Rev.per.mile     : int  3150 3755 3130 2875 3360
##  $ Man.trans.avail  : Factor w/ 2 levels "No","Yes": 2 2 2 2 2
##  $ Fuel.tank.capacity: num  10 10.6 13.2 9.2 10.6
##  $ Passengers       : int  4 4 4 4 4
##  $ Length           : int  141 151 177 146 161
##  $ Wheelbase        : int  90 93 99 90 93
##  $ Width            : int  63 63 66 60 63
##  $ Turn.circle      : int  33 34 35 32 34
##  $ Rear.seat.room   : num  26 27.5 25.5 23.5 27.5
##  $ Luggage.room     : int  12 10 17 10 10
##  $ Weight           : int  1845 1695 2350 2045 1965
##  $ Origin           : Factor w/ 2 levels "USA","non-USA": 1 2 1 2 2
##  $ Make             : Factor w/ 93 levels "Acura Integra",..: 34 39
## 76 80 83
```

A few helpful functions that can be used in conjunction with data frames are: `dim()`, reporting the dimension (number of rows and columns); `head()`, the first (default 6) rows of a data frame; and `colnames()`, the columns/variable names.

array

An array in R can have multiple dimensions. A vector is already a one-dimensional array. A matrix is a two-dimensional array, having rows and columns. Let us call a data set from package vcd stored as a four-dimensional array:

```
library("vcd")
## Loading required package: grid
data(PreSex)
PreSex
## , , PremaritalSex = Yes, Gender = Women
##
##              ExtramaritalSex
## MaritalStatus Yes  No
##      Divorced  17  54
##      Married    4  25
##
## , , PremaritalSex = No, Gender = Women
##
##              ExtramaritalSex
## MaritalStatus Yes  No
##      Divorced  36 214
##      Married    4 322
##
## , , PremaritalSex = Yes, Gender = Men
##
##              ExtramaritalSex
## MaritalStatus Yes  No
##      Divorced  28  60
##      Married   11  42
##
## , , PremaritalSex = No, Gender = Men
##
##              ExtramaritalSex
## MaritalStatus Yes  No
##      Divorced  17  68
##      Married    4 130
```

We see that the first dimension is `MaritalStatus`, the second is `ExtramaritalSex`, the third dimension is `PremaritalSex`, and the fourth dimension is `Gender`.

We can now access the elements of the array by indexing using `[]`. If we want to extract the data where `PremaritalSex` is `Yes` and `Gender` is `Men`, we type:

```
PreSex[, , 1, 2]
##               ExtramaritalSex
## MaritalStatus Yes No
##       Divorced  28 60
##       Married   11 42
```

This mean that all values from the first and second dimensions are chosen, only the first one (`Yes`) from the third and the second one (`Men`) from the last dimension is specified. This can also be done by name:

```
PreSex[, , "Yes", "Men"]
##               ExtramaritalSex
## MaritalStatus Yes No
##       Divorced  28 60
##       Married   11 42
```

Missing values

Missing values are almost always present in the data. The default representation of a missing value in R is the symbol NA. A very useful function to check if data values are missing is `is.na`. It returns a logical vector or `data.frame` depending on whether the input is a vector or `data.frame` indicating "missingness". To calculate the number of missing values, we could sum the *TRUE's* (interpreted as *1* while *FALSE* is interpreted as *0*).

```
sum(is.na(Cars93))
## [1] 13
```

All in all, 13 values are missing.

To analyze the structure of any missing values, the R package VIM (Templ, Alfons, and Filzmoser, 2012) can be used. One out of many possible plots for missing values, the matrixplot (*Figure 1*) shows all the values of the whole data frame. Interestingly, the higher the weight of the cars, the more *missings* are present in variable luggage.room:

```
require("VIM")
matrixplot(Cars93, sortby = "Weight", cex.axis=0.6)
```

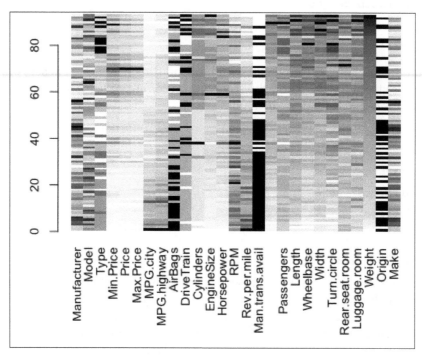

Figure 1: matrixplot from package VIM. The darker the higher the values. Missing values are in red

In package robCompositions (Templ, Hron, and Filzmoser 2011), one useful function is missPatterns, which shows the structure of missing values (we do not show the output):

```
m <- robCompositions::missPatterns(Cars93)
```

Generic functions, methods, and classes

R has different class systems, the most important ones are S3 and S4 classes. Programming with S3 classes is easy living, it's easier than S4. However, S4 is *clean* and the use of S4 can make packages very user-friendly.

In any case, in R each object is assigned to a class (the attribute `class`). Classes allow object-oriented programming and *overloading* of *generic functions*. Generic functions produce different output for objects of different classes as soon as methods are written for such classes.

This sounds complex, but with the following example it should get clearer.

As an example of a generic function, we will use the function `summary`. `summary` is a generic function used to produce result summaries. The function invokes particular methods that depend on the class of the first argument:

```
## how often summary is overloaded with methods
## on summary for certain classes
(the number depends on loaded packages)
length(methods(summary))
## [1] 137
class(Cars93$Cylinders)
## [1] "factor"
summary(Cars93$Cylinders)
##        3      4      5      6      8 rotary
##        3     49      2     31      7      1
## just to see the difference, convert to class character:
summary(as.character(Cars93$Cylinders))
##    Length     Class      Mode
##        93 character character
```

From this previous example one can see that the summary is different, depending on the class of the object. R internally looks as if a method is implemented for the given class of the object. If yes, this function is used, if not, the function `summary.default` is used. This procedure is called *method dispatch*.

In the last line of the previous example, R looked as if a function `summary.factor` was available, which was true.

 You can easily write your own generic functions, and define print, summary, and plot functions for objects of certain classes.

Data manipulation in R

For students working with perfectly prepared data from various R packages on relatively small scale problems, data manipulation is not the big issue. However, in the daily practice of a data scientist, most of the time working on data analysis does not involve applying a suitable function to an already perfectly prepared piece of data. The majority of work is done on data manipulation, in order to collect data from several sources, shape the data into a suitable format, and extract the relevant information. Thus, data manipulation is the core work, and data scientists and statisticians should possess strong data manipulation skills.

Whenever you work with data frames, the package `dplyr` provides user-friendly and computationally efficient code. One package that supports even more efficient data manipulation is the `data.table` package (Dowle et al., 2015). However, since both packages have their advantages, we report both. Also, `data.table` works with two dimensional data objects.

In any case, when working, for example, with arrays of dimensions larger than 2, `apply` is still the only choice. One example is phonological data, where for each phonological station, measurements for different species are given over time. Such data sets are typically stored as an array, in this case in a four-dimensional array.

Apply and friends with basic R

Using the `apply` family one can manipulate slices of data from matrices, arrays, lists, and data frames in a repetitive manner. These functions allow you to cross the data over certain dimensions and avoid the explicit use of `for` loops. Repetitively, functions are applied over all elements of a dimension.

Let's consider again the `Cars93` data set. The data set consists of rows (first dimension) and columns (second dimension). To apply a function over the second dimension of this data set, for example, to calculate the number of missing values over the columns, the call looks like the following:

```
## function to be applied afterwards
func <- function(x){
  return(sum(is.na(x)))
}
## apply func on all columns (second dimension (2))
## and store it to na
na <- apply(X = Cars93, MARGIN = 2, FUN = func)
## show those with missings
```

```
na[ na > 0 ]
## Rear.seat.room    Luggage.room
##                2              11
```

Here, x must be an array (note that a matrix is a 2-dimensional array), MARGIN is the dimension where FUN is applied.

 This apply call is basically the same as the for loop.

```
p <- ncol(Cars93)
na_for <- numeric(p)
for(i in 1:p){
  na_for[i] <- func(Cars93[, i])
}
```

```
identical(as.numeric(na), na_for)
## [1] TRUE
```

While one can always use for loops, the code from apply is much shorter.

When a given function should be applied on a list (note that a data.frame is also internally treated as a list), lapply might be your friend. The output returned is also a list that has the same number of elements as the object passed to it.

In a previous code call, we assigned a list output to an object called m:

```
m <- robCompositions::missPatterns(Cars93)
class(m)
## [1] "list"
```

We apply a function, for example, length(), to all elements of a list by using lapply to access the length of each list element:

```
lapply(m, length)
## $groups
## [1] 3
##
## $cn
## [1] 3
##
```

```
## $tabcomb

## [1] 81

##

## $tabcombPlus

## [1] 28

##

## $rsum

## [1] 93
```

`sapply` works basically as `lapply`, but simplifies the output if possible. For example:

```
s <- sapply(m, length)
```

is no longer a list (as for lapply) but a vector of integers.

```
s
##       groups       cn    tabcomb tabcombPlus      rsum
##            3        3         81          28        93
class(s)
## [1] "integer"
```

The function `aggregate` is similar to `apply`. Its difference lies in the function argument, which allows it to subset the data set and apply a function on these subsets. Let us have a look at the function arguments:

```
args(aggregate)
## function (x, ...)
## NULL
```

Since we see only the arguments from the generic, but we want to apply the functions to the `Cars93` data frame, we may look to see if there is a method for data frames implemented:

```
methods(aggregate)
## [1] aggregate.cv*         aggregate.cvSelect*  aggregate.cvTuning*
## [4] aggregate.data.frame aggregate.default*   aggregate.formula*
## [7] aggregate.Spatial*    aggregate.ts         aggregate.zoo*
## see '?methods' for accessing help and source code
args(aggregate.data.frame)
## function (x, by, FUN, ..., simplify = TRUE)
## NULL
```

To make group-wise statistics, this function can now be applied on our example data, for example, to calculate the median `Horsepower` and `Weight` of cars for each cylinder class (`Cylinders`):

```
aggregate(Cars93[, c("Horsepower", "Weight")], by =
list(Cars93$Cylinders), median)
##   Group.1 Horsepower Weight
## 1       3       70.0   1965
## 2       4      110.0   2705
## 3       5      138.5   3602
## 4       6      170.0   3515
## 5       8      210.0   3935
## 6  rotary      255.0   2895
```

Similar functions to aggregate are `by` (another print output), `summarize` from package `Hmisc` (Harrell Jr, 2016), and `summarize` and `group_by` from package `dplyr`, discussed as follows.

Basic data manipulation with the dplyr package

The base R's functionality on data manipulation is nice, but in some situations the `dplyr` package is more intuitive and, more importantly, much faster than the base R data manipulation functions. Since this book is about data simulation, and it also discusses computer-intense methods, computational speed is very important, especially for larger simulations.

The package `dplyr` offers functions for:

- Filtering of observations
- Variable selection
- Recoding
- Grouping
- Aggregation (in groups)

 Other useful packages such as `reshape2`, `stringr`, or `lubridate` are not covered in this book.

- `data.table` is discussed later

Additional packages, such as the `dplyr` package, sometimes make life easier, and as previously mentioned, the calculation time can be considerable faster.

Some of the steps in data management can be *abstracted*. Such tasks include: *selection* of rows or columns — *ordering* of data — *recoding*, *grouping*, and *aggregation*.

Here are some further reasons for an additional package such as `dplyr`:

- Only a few important keywords to remember
- Consistency
- Works with different inputs
- `data.frame`, `data.tables`, `sqlite`
- Simple (but new) syntax
- Less code, less error
- From now on in this section the following applies (since this is the `dplyr` language): a column corresponds to a variable and a line corresponds to a observation

First, the package must be loaded (and once to be installed):

```
library("dplyr")
```

 Some vignettes (short instructions) are available, see `help(pa = "dplyr")`.

dplyr – creating a local data frame

A *local* data frame can be created using `tbl_df()`.

Why do we need this? Because it offers more efficient print outputs and no chance of accidentally printing huge data sets, which can lead to memory problems or long waiting time.

Remember, `Cars93` is a *data.frame*:

```
class (Cars93)
## [1] "data.frame"
```

We then convert to a *local* data frame for dplyr and look at the new print output that is done by dplyr:

```
Cars93 <- tbl_df(Cars93)
class(Cars93)
## [1] "tbl_df"      "tbl"          "data.frame"


## print(Cars93) # output suppressed
```

dplyr – selecting lines

Using the function slice(), one can select rows according to their line number:

```
slice(Cars93, 1) # first line, output suppressed
```

You can also select multiple rows at once.

Note that c() creates a vector from the input numbers, and function n() returns the number of observations (lines). We will select the 1, 4, 10, 15 and the last line of the data:

```
slice (Cars93, c(1,4,10,15, n ()))
## Source: local data frame [5 x 27]
##
```

	Manufacturer	Model	Type	Min.Price	Price	Max.Price	MPG.city
##	(fctr)	(fctr)	(fctr)	(dbl)	(dbl)	(dbl)	(int)
## 1	Acura	Integra	Small	12.9	15.9	18.8	25
## 2	Audi	100	Midsize	30.8	37.7	44.6	19
## 3	Cadillac	DeVille	Large	33.0	34.7	36.3	16
## 4	Chevrolet	Lumina	Midsize	13.4	15.9	18.4	21
## 5	Volvo	850	Midsize	24.8	26.7	28.5	20

```
## Variables not shown: MPG.highway (int), AirBags (fctr), DriveTrain
(fctr),
##    Cylinders (fctr), EngineSize (dbl), Horsepower (int), RPM (int),
##    Rev.per.mile (int), Man.trans.avail (fctr), Fuel.tank.capacity
(dbl),
##    Passengers (int), Length (int), Wheelbase (int), Width (int),
##    Turn.circle (int), Rear.seat.room (dbl), Luggage.room (int), Weight
##    (int), Origin (fctr), Make (fctr)
```

The function `filter()` can select rows that satisfy a condition.

Example, all observations where variable `Manufacturer ==` is Audi when at the same time the value of variable `Min.Price` is > 25:

```
filter(Cars93, Manufacturer == "Audi" & Min.Price > 25)
## Source: local data frame [2 x 27]
##
##    Manufacturer  Model    Type Min.Price Price Max.Price MPG.city
##          (fctr) (fctr)  (fctr)     (dbl) (dbl)     (dbl)    (int)
## 1          Audi     90 Compact      25.9  29.1      32.3       20
## 2          Audi    100 Midsize      30.8  37.7      44.6       19
## Variables not shown: MPG.highway (int), AirBags (fctr), DriveTrain
(fctr),
##    Cylinders (fctr), EngineSize (dbl), Horsepower (int), RPM (int),
##    Rev.per.mile (int), Man.trans.avail (fctr), Fuel.tank.capacity
(dbl),
##    Passengers (int), Length (int), Wheelbase (int), Width (int),
##    Turn.circle (int), Rear.seat.room (dbl), Luggage.room (int), Weight
##    (int), Origin (fctr), Make (fctr)
```

dplyr – order

With `arrange()` you can sort the data by one or more variables. By default it is sorted in ascending order, with `desc()` descending:

```
Cars93 <- arrange (Cars93, Price)
Cars93 ## output suppressed
```

You can also sort by multiple variables:

```
head(arrange(Cars93, desc (MPG.city), Max.Price), 7)
## Source: local data frame [7 x 27]
##
##    Manufacturer  Model   Type Min.Price Price Max.Price MPG.city
##          (fctr) (fctr) (fctr)     (dbl) (dbl)     (dbl)    (int)
## 1           Geo  Metro  Small       6.7   8.4      10.0       46
## 2         Honda  Civic  Small       8.4  12.1      15.8       42
## 3        Suzuki  Swift  Small       7.3   8.6      10.0       39
## 4        Subaru  Justy  Small       7.3   8.4       9.5       33
```

```
## 5        Toyota  Tercel  Small      7.8   9.8      11.8        32
## 6         Ford Festiva  Small      6.9   7.4       7.9        31
## 7      Pontiac  LeMans  Small      8.2   9.0       9.9        31
## Variables not shown: MPG.highway (int), AirBags (fctr), DriveTrain
(fctr),
##    Cylinders (fctr), EngineSize (dbl), Horsepower (int), RPM (int),
##    Rev.per.mile (int), Man.trans.avail (fctr), Fuel.tank.capacity
(dbl),
##    Passengers (int), Length (int), Wheelbase (int), Width (int),
##    Turn.circle (int), Rear.seat.room (dbl), Luggage.room (int), Weight
##    (int), Origin (fctr), Make (fctr)
```

dplyr – selecting columns

Function `select()` allows you to select variables from the data set:

```
head (select (Cars93, Manufacturer, Price), 3)
## Source: local data frame [3 x 2]
##
## Manufacturer Price
##        (fctr) (dbl)
## 1        Ford   7.4
## 2     Hyundai   8.0
## 3       Mazda   8.3
```

For a sequence of variables, the operator `:` can be used:

```
head (select (Cars93, Manufacturer:Price), 3)
## Source: local data frame [3 x 5]
##
## Manufacturer  Model  Type Min.Price Price
##        (fctr) (fctr) (fctr)    (dbl) (dbl)
## 1        Ford Festiva  Small      6.9   7.4
## 2     Hyundai  Excel  Small      6.8   8.0
## 3       Mazda    323  Small      7.4   8.3
```

Negative indexing is possible, while all variables with the letter prefix minus (-) are excluded:

```
select (Cars93, -Min.Price, -Max.Price) # output suppressed
```

Some functions are useful within `select ()`:

- `starts_with()`
- `ends_with()`
- `contains()`
- `matches()`
- `num_range()**`

For example:

```
head (select (Cars93, starts_with ("Man")), 3)
## Source: local data frame [3 x 2]
##
##    Manufacturer Man.trans.avail
##          (fctr)          (fctr)
## 1          Ford             Yes
## 2       Hyundai             Yes
## 3         Mazda             Yes
head (select (Cars93, contains ("Price")), 3)
## Source: local data frame [3 x 3]
##
##    Min.Price Price Max.Price
##        (dbl) (dbl)     (dbl)
## 1      6.9   7.4       7.9
## 2      6.8   8.0       9.2
## 3      7.4   8.3       9.1
```

Both `select ()` and `rename ()` can be used to rename variables by simply using a `new = old` syntax. `select ()` returns only the specified variables:

```
head (select (Cars93, myPrize = Price, Min.Price))
## Source: local data frame [6 x 2]
##
##    myPrize Min.Price
##      (dbl)     (dbl)
## 1     7.4       6.9
## 2     8.0       6.8
## 3     8.3       7.4
## 4     8.4       6.7
## 5     8.4       7.3
## 6     8.6       7.3
```

dplyr – uniqueness

Functionality `distinct()` can be used to keep only unique rows:

```
Cars93_1 <- select(Cars93, Manufacturer, EngineSize)
dim (Cars93_1)
## [1] 93   2
Cars93_1 <- distinct(Cars93_1)
dim (Cars93_1)
## [1] 79   2
```

By default, all variables are used to assess whether a row multiple occurs in the data set:

```
dim(Cars93)
## [1] 93 27
dim( distinct (Cars93, Manufacturer) )
## [1] 32 27
# based on two variables:
dim(distinct(Cars93, Manufacturer, EngineSize))
## [1] 79 27
# based on two variables, second is rounded:
dim(distinct(Cars93, Manufacturer, rr=round(EngineSize)))
## [1] 57 28
```

dplyr – creating variables

With function `mutate()` one can add new variables and retains the old variables:

```
m <- mutate(Cars93, is_ford = Manufacturer == "Ford")
m[1:3, c(1,28)]
## Source: local data frame [3 x 2]
##
## Manufacturer is_ford
##        (fctr)   (lgl)
## 1         Ford    TRUE
## 2      Hyundai   FALSE
## 3        Mazda   FALSE
```

Function `transmute()` retains only the listed variables, in this case it looks almost the same as the previous example. We do not show an output here:

```
transmute(Cars93, is_ford = Manufacturer == "Ford", Manufacturer)
```

Newly created variables can be used again in the same statement:

```
head (transmute(Cars93, Manufacturer, is_ford = Manufacturer == "Ford",
num_ford = ifelse (is_ford, -1, 1)), 3)
## Source: local data frame [3 x 3]
##
##    Manufacturer is_ford num_ford
##          (fctr)   (lgl)    (dbl)
## 1          Ford    TRUE       -1
## 2       Hyundai   FALSE        1
## 3         Mazda   FALSE        1
```

dplyr – grouping and aggregates

One often wants to perform calculations in *groups*. Previously, we saw examples using the `apply` family of the base R package. For data frames, the `dplyr` package supports grouping. The syntax of the package `dplyr` is much more elegant than using the base R packages for grouping and aggregation. `dplyr` supports grouping with the function `group_by()`, which creates the subsets, and `summarize()`, which is used to calculate statistics that must provide exactly one number. Package `dplyr` provides additional, useful aggregation statistics such as the `first_value(x)`, `last_value(x)`, `nth_value(x)` of a variable.

Let us show grouping by using the variable `Manufacturer` and by calculating the group size, the minimum of the variable `Prize` and the maximum of the variable `Prize`:

```
by_type <- group_by (Cars93, Type)
summarize (by_type,
 count = n(),min_es = min(EngineSize),
 max_es = max(EngineSize)
)
## Source: local data frame [6 x 4]
##
##        Type count min_es max_es
##      (fctr) (int)  (dbl)  (dbl)
## 1 Compact      16    2.0    3.0
```

```
## 2    Large    11    3.3    5.7
## 3  Midsize    22    2.0    4.6
## 4    Small    21    1.0    2.2
## 5   Sporty    14    1.3    5.7
## 6      Van     9    2.4    4.3
```

Via `group_by ()` functions are applied on defined groups. Note that `dplyr` supports the *pipeline* syntax from R package `magrittr` (Bache and Wickham, 2015). For the preceding call, one can also write:

```
Cars93 %>%
  group_by(Type) %>%
  summarize(count = n(), min_es = min(EngineSize), max_es =
max(EngineSize) )
## output suppressed since equally to previous output
```

The *pipeline* operator can be interpreted for the preceding example: first the `Cars93` data set is chosen and then `group_by` is applied to this data set. `summarize` is then applied to the result of `group_by`. So in general, it makes it possible to provide commands like in a *pipe* together. The output of the previous is first input into the following command. The commands are performed from left to right (in the direction of the *arrow*).

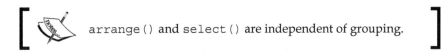 arrange () and select () are independent of grouping.

Let's take another example, in order to report the first two observations per group:

```
by_type <- group_by(Cars93, Type)
slice (by_type, 1: 2)
## Source: local data frame [12 x 27]
## Groups: Type [6]
##
```

```
##      Manufacturer     Model      Type Min.Price Price Max.Price MPG.city
##            (fctr)    (fctr)    (fctr)     (dbl) (dbl)     (dbl)    (int)
## 1        Pontiac   Sunbird   Compact       9.4  11.1      12.8       23
## 2           Ford     Tempo   Compact      10.4  11.3      12.2       22
## 3       Chrylser  Concorde     Large      18.4  18.4      18.4       20
## 4      Chevrolet   Caprice     Large      18.0  18.8      19.6       17
```

```
## 5       Hyundai   Sonata Midsize   12.4  13.9     15.3      20
## 6       Mercury   Cougar Midsize   14.9  14.9     14.9      19
## 7          Ford   Festiva   Small    6.9   7.4      7.9      31
## 8       Hyundai    Excel   Small    6.8   8.0      9.2      29
## 9       Hyundai   Scoupe  Sporty    9.1  10.0     11.0      26
## 10          Geo    Storm  Sporty   11.5  12.5     13.5      30
## 11    Chevrolet Lumina_APV    Van   14.7  16.3     18.0      18
## 12    Chevrolet    Astro     Van   14.7  16.6     18.6      15
## Variables not shown: MPG.highway (int), AirBags (fctr), DriveTrain
(fctr),
##    Cylinders (fctr), EngineSize (dbl), Horsepower (int), RPM (int),
##    Rev.per.mile (int), Man.trans.avail (fctr), Fuel.tank.capacity
(dbl),
##    Passengers (int), Length (int), Wheelbase (int), Width (int),
##    Turn.circle (int), Rear.seat.room (dbl), Luggage.room (int), Weight
##    (int), Origin (fctr), Make (fctr)
```

We have shown by example that `dplyr` provides a simple syntax. Again, the operator `%>%` syntax makes it even more easily readable:

```
## output suppressed since the same as above
Cars93 %>% group_by(Type) %>% slice(1:2)
```

Let's take another example. We want to compute a new variable `EngineSize` as the square of `EngineSize`, and for each group we want to compute the minimum of the new variable. In addition, the results should be sorted in descending order:

```
Cars93 %>% mutate(ES2 = EngineSize^2) %>% group_by(Type) %>%
summarize(min.ES2 = min(ES2)) %>% arrange(desc(min.ES2))
## Source: local data frame [6 x 2]
##
##        Type min.ES2
##      (fctr)    (dbl)
## 1    Large   10.89
## 2      Van    5.76
## 3  Compact    4.00
## 4  Midsize    4.00
## 5   Sporty    1.69
## 6    Small    1.00
```

dplyr – window functions

`summarize()` works for functions that return one single value. To make more complex aggregations, *window functions* can be used.

There are different types of *window functions*:

- **Ranking/ordering**: `row_number()`, `min_rank()`, `percent_rank()`, and so on
- **Offsets**: `lag()`, `lead()`
- **Cumulative functions**: `cumsum()`, `cummin()`, `cummax()`, `cummean()`, and so on

Let's perform a simple example. Calculate the cumulative sum and average value within each group of `Type`:

```
Cars93 %>%
  group_by(Type) %>%
  arrange(Type) %>%
  select(Manufacturer:Price) %>%
  mutate(cmean = cummean(Price), csum = cumsum(Price))
## Source: local data frame [93 x 7]
## Groups: Type [6]
##
##       Manufacturer      Model     Type Min.Price Price cmean   csum
##             (fctr)     (fctr)   (fctr)     (dbl) (dbl) (dbl)  (dbl)
## 1          Pontiac    Sunbird  Compact       9.4  11.1 11.10   11.1
## 2             Ford      Tempo  Compact      10.4  11.3 11.20   22.4
## 3        Chevrolet    Corsica  Compact      11.4  11.4 11.27   33.8
## 4            Dodge     Spirit  Compact      11.9  13.3 11.77   47.1
## 5        Chevrolet   Cavalier  Compact       8.5  13.4 12.10   60.5
## 6       Oldsmobile    Achieva  Compact      13.0  13.5 12.33   74.0
## 7           Nissan     Altima  Compact      13.0  15.7 12.81   89.7
## 8         Chrysler    LeBaron  Compact      14.5  15.8 13.19  105.5
## 9            Mazda        626  Compact      14.3  16.5 13.56  122.0
## 10           Honda     Accord  Compact      13.8  17.5 13.95  139.5
## ..             ...        ...      ...       ...   ...   ...    ...
```

Data manipulation with the data.table package

The package `data.table` is not included in the base R installation and must be installed once. It allows very efficient aggregation of large data sets (for example, data with several gigabytes of memory), efficient merging (`join`) of several objects, adding and deletion of variables, and efficient importing of data sets (`fread()`). The syntax is easy to learn but it is different to the syntax of base R.

Let us first convert a `data.frame` to a `data.table` using function `data.table`. We again use the `Cars93` data, and print the data table — the print output differs from base R and also from `dyplyr`. Note that each `data.table` is also a `data.frame` and both can be accessed as a list:

```
require(data.table)

Cars93 <- data.table(Cars93)

Cars93 ## print output suppressed
```

The utility function `tables()` lists all `data.table` objects in the memory and gives information on the dimension and needed memory for each data table:

```
tables()
##          NAME    NROW NCOL MB
## [1,] Cars93     93    27   1
##          COLS
## [1,] Manufacturer,Model,Type,Min.Price,Price,Max.Price,MPG.city,MPG.
highway,AirBags,D
##          KEY
## [1,]
## Total: 1MB
```

data.table – variable construction

Using the `$` operator, new variables can be constructed. As an example, we will create a new variable where the values are TRUE if the manufacturer is `Ford`:

```
Cars93$tmp1 <- Cars93[, j = Manufacturer == "Ford"]
```

We can modify a variable by the `:=`-syntax directly (a very nice feature!)

```
Cars93[, tmp2 := rnorm(nrow(Cars93))]
```

Note that these modifications are done *by-reference* — no copy of the data is needed internally.

To delete variables, one of the two following possibilities can be used:

```
Cars93[, tmp1:=NULL]
Cars93$tmp2 <- NULL
```

data.table – indexing or subsetting

The indexing is done differently than in base R. Two parameters are used, i: for the rows of the data.table and j: for the columns of the data.table.

We use [] as an indexing operator, but it works slightly differently. j is an *expression* in the scope of the actual object. Using with=FALSE: j is evaluated as a vector of names or numbers.

Let us extract rows. We suppress the output in the following code listing to avoid filling the book with output from the Cars93 data:

```
Cars93[i = 2] # second row, all columns
Cars93[i = c(1,5)] # first and fifth row, all columns
Cars93[i = -c(1:5)] # exclude the first five rows
```

Now let us extract columns. See the details on the following code listing:

```
Cars93[j = 3] # this does not work since 3 evaluates to 3
## [1] 3
Cars93[j = "Price"] # extract "Price" does not work since "Price"
evaluates to "Price"
## [1] "Price"
Cars93[j = Price] # this works, since variable Price exists in the scope
of Cars93
##  [1]  7.4  8.0  8.3  8.4  8.4  8.6  9.0  9.1  9.2  9.8 10.0 10.0 10.1
10.3
## [15] 10.9 11.1 11.1 11.3 11.3 11.4 11.6 11.8 12.1 12.2 12.5 13.3 13.4
13.5
## [29] 13.9 14.0 14.1 14.4 14.9 15.1 15.6 15.7 15.7 15.8 15.9 15.9 15.9
16.3
## [43] 16.3 16.5 16.6 17.5 17.7 18.2 18.4 18.4 18.5 18.8 19.0 19.1 19.1
19.3
## [57] 19.5 19.5 19.7 19.8 19.9 20.0 20.2 20.7 20.8 20.9 21.5 22.7 22.7
23.3
## [71] 23.7 24.4 25.8 26.1 26.3 26.7 28.0 28.7 29.1 29.5 30.0 31.9 32.5
33.9
## [85] 34.3 34.7 35.2 36.1 37.7 38.0 40.1 47.9 61.9
```

```
Cars93[i=1:3, j = "Price", with = FALSE] # also works
##    Price
## 1:  7.4
## 2:  8.0
## 3:  8.3
```

Indexing can also be done more sophisticatedly. For example, if we wanted to extract the first three rows, extract all variables, calculate a new variable that is the price range, or calculate the mean price, we could do the following:

```
Cars93[1:3, .(Price, Horsepower, Diff.Price = Max.Price - Min.Price,
Mean.Price = mean(Price))]
##    Price Horsepower Diff.Price Mean.Price
## 1:  7.4          63        1.0        7.9
## 2:  8.0          81        2.4        7.9
## 3:  8.3          82        1.7        7.9
```

.() is short for list().

data.table – keys

data.table objects can be grouped according to a key. Based on such a key, calculations are very efficient. By using setkey(), a key can be set for a data.table:

```
setkey(Cars93, Type) # equally: setkeyv(dt, "x")
```

More than one key can be defined for a data.table. Now sorting is done automatically regarding this key. Actual key variables can be displayed with key():

```
key(Cars93)
## [1] "Type"
```

data.table – fast subsetting

By using keys, we can increase the performance of subsetting:

```
setkey(Cars93, Type)
Cars93["Van"] # all rows with Type == "Van" (output suppressed)
```

For more than two keys — for example, to extract all observations with Type equal to Van, DriveTrain equals 4WD and Origin equals non-USA — we can apply the following:

```
setkey(Cars93, Type, DriveTrain, Origin)
Cars93[.("Van", "4WD", "non-USA")]
##      Manufacturer  Model Type Min.Price Price Max.Price MPG.city MPG.
highway
## 1:       Mazda      MPV  Van      16.6  19.1     21.7       18      24
## 2:       Toyota  Previa  Van      18.9  22.7     26.6       18      22
##          AirBags DriveTrain Cylinders EngineSize Horsepower  RPM
## 1:         None        4WD         6        3.0        155 5000
## 2: Driver only        4WD         4        2.4        138 5000
##      Rev.per.mile Man.trans.avail Fuel.tank.capacity Passengers Length
## 1:          2240              No               19.6          7    190
## 2:          2515             Yes               19.8          7    187
##      Wheelbase Width Turn.circle Rear.seat.room Luggage.room Weight
Origin
## 1:        110    72          39           27.5           NA   3735 non-
USA
## 2:        113    71          41           35.0           NA   3785 non-
USA
##                Make
## 1:      Mazda MPV
## 2: Toyota Previa
```

Let's compare efficiency on a data set with characters. We use the microbenchmark package (Mersmann 2015) for this purpose. We see that data.table is more than 60 times faster than base R, and in this case dplyr is the slowest:

```
require(microbenchmark)
N <- 1000000
dat<- data.table(
  x=sample(LETTERS[1:20], N, replace=TRUE),
  y=sample(letters[1:5], N, replace=TRUE))
head(dat, 3)
##    x y
## 1: M a
```

```
## 2: B a
## 3: I e
setkey(dat, x,y)

microbenchmark(
    data.table = dat[list(c("B", "D"), c("b", "d"))],
    dplyr = dat %>% slice(x %in% c("B", "D") & y %in% c("b", "d")),
    baseR = dat[x %in% c("B", "D") & y %in% c("b", "d")]
)
## Unit: milliseconds
```

##	expr	min	lq	mean	median	uq	max	neval
##	data.table	1.13	1.276	1.571	1.351	1.487	7.382	100
##	dplyr	70.27	80.049	96.965	83.216	88.785	267.583	100
##	baseR	69.65	76.685	95.777	82.128	87.722	281.426	100

data.table – calculations in groups

We can do calculations in groups by using by. In the following example, we will calculate the arithmetic mean price, the interquartile price range, and the median price:

```
Cars93[, .(mean = mean(Price), IQR = IQR(Price), median = median(Price)),
by = Type]
```

##	Type	mean	IQR	median
## 1:	Compact	18.21	7.30	16.15
## 2:	Large	24.30	6.95	20.90
## 3:	Midsize	27.22	17.42	26.20
## 4:	Small	10.17	2.70	10.00
## 5:	Sporty	19.39	8.25	16.80
## 6:	Van	19.10	0.70	19.10

There is further functionality in the data.table package. See .SD to apply functions to more than one variable, .N for the number of elements in each group, and merge to efficiently join data sets.

High performance computing

Initially, it is important to measure which lines of code take the most computation time. Here, you should try to solve problems with the processing time of individual calculations by improving the computation time. This can often be done in R by *vectorization*, or often better by writing individual pieces of code in a compilable language, such as **C, C++***, or **Fortran****.

In addition, some calculations can be parallelized and accelerated through parallel computing.

Profiling to detect computationally slow functions in code

Take an example where you have written code for your data analysis but it runs (too) slow. However, it is most likely that not all your lines of code are slow and only a few lines need improvement in terms of computational time. In this instance it is very important to know exactly what step in the code takes the most computation time.

The easiest way is to find this out is to work with the R function `system.time`. We will compare two models:

```
data(Cars93, package = "MASS")
set.seed(123)
system.time(lm(Price ~ Horsepower + Weight + Type + Origin, data=Cars93))
##    user  system elapsed
##   0.003   0.000   0.002
library("robustbase")
system.time(lmrob(Price ~ Horsepower + Weight + Type + Origin,
data=Cars93))
##    user  system elapsed
##   0.022   0.000   0.023
```

The user time is the CPU time for the call and evaluation of the code. The elapsed time is the sum of the user time and the system time. This is the most interesting number. `proc.time` is another simple function, often used inside functions:

```
ptm <- proc.time()
lmrob(Price ~ Horsepower + Weight + Type + Origin, data=Cars93)
##
## Call:
```

```
## robustbase::lmrob(formula = Price ~ Horsepower + Weight + Type +
Origin,     data = Cars93)
##  \--> method = "MM"
## Coefficients:
##   (Intercept)      Horsepower         Weight        TypeLarge
TypeMidsize
##     -2.72414         0.10660        0.00141          0.18398    3.05846
##       TypeSmall      TypeSporty        TypeVan   Originnon-USA
##     -1.29751         0.68596       -0.36019          1.88560
proc.time() - ptm
##    user  system elapsed
##   0.025   0.000   0.027
```

To get a more precise answer about the computational speed of the methods, we should replicate the experiment. We can see that `lm` is about 10 times faster than `lmrob`:

```
s1 <- system.time(replicate(100, lm(Price ~ Horsepower + Weight + Type +
Origin, data=Cars93)))[3]
s2 <- system.time(replicate(100, lmrob(Price ~ Horsepower + Weight + Type
+ Origin, data=Cars93)))[3]
(s2 - s1)/s1
## elapsed
##   10.27
```

However, we don't know which part of the code makes a function slow:

```
Rprof("Prestige.lm.out")
invisible(replicate(100,
              lm(Price ~ Horsepower + Weight + Type + Origin,
data=Cars93)))
Rprof(NULL)
summaryRprof("Prestige.lm.out")$by.self
##                    self.time self.pct total.time total.pct
## ".External2"            0.04    22.22       0.04     22.22
## ".External"             0.02    11.11       0.02     11.11
## "[[.data.frame"         0.02    11.11       0.02     11.11
## "[[<-.data.frame"       0.02    11.11       0.02     11.11
## "as.list"               0.02    11.11       0.02     11.11
## "lm.fit"                0.02    11.11       0.02     11.11
## "match"                 0.02    11.11       0.02     11.11
## "vapply"                0.02    11.11       0.02     11.11
```

We can see which function calls relate to the slowest part of the code.

A more detailed output is reported by using the following. However, since the output is quite long, we have redacted it for the book version (but it is available when running the code bundle that accompanies this book):

```
require(profr)
## Loading required package: profr
parse_rprof("Prestige.lm.out")
```

 Plots are implemented to show the profiling results.

Further benchmarking

Finally, we will show a data manipulation example using several different packages. This should show the efficiency of data.table and dplyr.

To run the following code snippets, it is mandatory to load the following since the functionality used is included in those packages:

```
library(microbenchmark); library(plyr); library(dplyr);
library(data.table); library(Hmisc)
```

The task is to calculate the groupwise (Type, Origin) means of Horsepower, for example:

```
data(Cars93, package = "MASS")
Cars93 %>% group_by(Type, Origin) %>% summarise(mean = mean(Horsepower))
## Source: local data frame [11 x 3]
## Groups: Type [?]
##
##        Type  Origin       mean
##      (fctr)  (fctr)      (dbl)
## 1  Compact      USA  117.42857
## 2  Compact  non-USA  141.55556
## 3    Large      USA  179.45455
## 4  Midsize      USA  153.50000
## 5  Midsize  non-USA  189.41667
```

```
## 6      Small     USA  89.42857
## 7      Small non-USA  91.78571
## 8     Sporty     USA 166.50000
## 9     Sporty non-USA 151.66667
## 10       Van     USA 158.40000
## 11       Van non-USA 138.25000
```

First, we calculate the same with base R, where we also write a `for` loop for calculating the mean. We do this extra dirty for benchmarking purposes:

```
meanFor <- function(x){
  sum <- 0
  for(i in 1:length(x)) sum <- sum + x[i]
  sum / length(x)
}


## groupwise statistics
myfun1 <- function(x, gr1, gr2, num){
  x[,gr1] <- as.factor(x[,gr1])
  x[,gr2] <- as.factor(x[,gr2])
  l1 <- length(levels(x[,gr1]))
  l2 <- length(levels(x[,gr1]))
  gr <-  numeric(l1*l2)
  c1 <- c2 <- character(l1*l2)
  ii <- jj <- 0
  for(i in levels(x[,gr1])){
    for(j in levels(x[,gr2])){
      ii <- ii + 1
      c1[ii] <- i
      c2[ii] <- j
      vec <- x[x[,gr2] == j & x[,gr1] == i, num]
      if(length(vec) > 0) gr[ii] <- meanFor(vec)
    }
  }
```

```
  df <- data.frame(cbind(c1, c2))
  df <- cbind(df, gr)
  colnames(df) <- c(gr1,gr2,paste("mean(", num, ")"))
  df
}


## groupwise using mean()
## attention mean.default is faster
myfun2 <- function(x, gr1, gr2, num){
  x[,gr1] <- as.factor(x[,gr1])
  x[,gr2] <- as.factor(x[,gr2])
  l1 <- length(levels(x[,gr1]))
  l2 <- length(levels(x[,gr1]))
  gr <-  numeric(l1*l2)
  c1 <- c2 <- character(l1*l2)
  ii <- jj <- 0
  for(i in levels(x[,gr1])){
    for(j in levels(x[,gr2])){
      ii <- ii + 1
      c1[ii] <- i
      c2[ii] <- j
      gr[ii] <- mean(x[x[,gr2] == j & x[,gr1] == i, num])
    }
  }

  df <- data.frame(cbind(c1, c2))
  df <- cbind(df, gr)
  colnames(df) <- c(gr1,gr2,paste("mean(", num, ")"))
  df
}
```

For data.table, we will create a data table:

```
Cars93dt <- data.table(Cars93)
```

We now run the benchmark using `microbenchmark` and plot the results. For the plot syntax, refer to the section on visualization:

```
op <- microbenchmark(
  ## pure for loops
  MYFUN1 = myfun1(x=Cars93, gr1="Type", gr2="Origin",
                  num="Horsepower"),
  ## pure for loops but using mean
  MYFUN2 = myfun2(x=Cars93, gr1="Type", gr2="Origin",
                  num="Horsepower"),
  ## plyr
  PLYR = ddply(Cars93, .(Type, Origin), summarise,
               output = mean(Horsepower)),
  ## base R's aggregate and by
  AGGR = aggregate(Horsepower ~ Type + Origin, Cars93, mean),
  BY = by(Cars93$Horsepower,
          list(Cars93$Type,Cars93$Origin), mean),
  ## Hmisc's summarize
  SUMMARIZE = summarize(Cars93$Horsepower,
                  llist(Cars93$Type,Cars93$Origin), mean),
  ## base R's tapply
  TAPPLY = tapply(Cars93$Horsepower,
             interaction(Cars93$Type, Cars93$Origin), mean),
  ## dplyr
  DPLYR = summarise(group_by(Cars93, Type, Origin),
                  mean(Horsepower)),
  ## data.table
  DATATABLE = Cars93dt[, aggGroup1.2 := mean(Horsepower),
                   by = list(Type, Origin)],
  times=1000L)
```

The output can now be visualized, see the following screenshot:

```
m <- reshape2::melt(op, id="expr")
ggplot(m, aes(x=expr, y=value)) +
  geom_boxplot() +
  coord_trans(y = "log10") +
  xlab(NULL) + ylab("computation time") +
  theme(axis.text.x = element_text(angle=45))
```

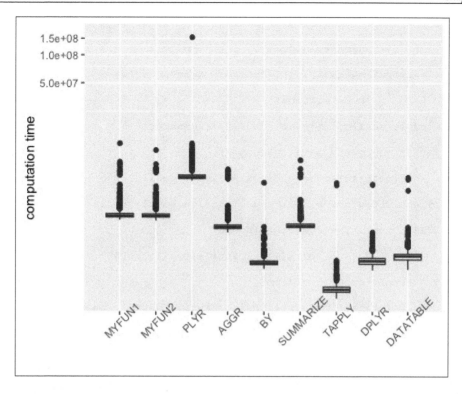

We can see that both `dplyr` and `data.table` are no faster than the others. Even the dirty `for` loops are almost as fast.

But we get a very different picture with large data sets:

```
library(laeken); data(eusilc)
eusilc <- do.call(rbind,
    list(eusilc,eusilc,eusilc,eusilc,eusilc,eusilc,eusilc))
eusilc <- do.call(rbind,
    list(eusilc,eusilc,eusilc,eusilc,eusilc,eusilc,eusilc))
dim(eusilc)
## [1] 726523       28
eusilcdt <- data.table(eusilc)

setkeyv(eusilcdt, c('hsize','db040'))


op <- microbenchmark(
```

```
  MYFUN1 = myfun1(x=eusilc, gr1="hsize", gr2="db040",
                 num="eqIncome"),

  MYFUN2 = myfun2(x=eusilc, gr1="hsize", gr2="db040",
                 num="eqIncome"),

  PLYR = ddply(eusilc, .(hsize, db040), summarise,
               output = mean(eqIncome)),

  AGGR = aggregate(eqIncome ~ hsize + db040, eusilc, mean),

  BY = by(eusilc$eqIncome, list(eusilc$hsize,eusilc$db040), mean),

  SUMMARIZE = summarize(eusilc$eqIncome,
                        llist(eusilc$hsize,eusilc$db040), mean),

  TAPPLY = tapply(eusilc$eqIncome,
               interaction(eusilc$hsize, eusilc$db040), mean),

  DPLYR = summarise(group_by(eusilc, hsize, db040),
                 mean(eqIncome)),

  DATATABLE = eusilcdt[, mean(eqIncome), by = .(hsize, db040)],

  times=10)
```

Again, we plot the results, as shown in the following screenshot:

```
m <- reshape2::melt(op, id="expr")

ggplot(m, aes(x=expr, y=value)) +

  geom_boxplot() +

  coord_trans(y = "log10") +

  xlab(NULL) + ylab("computation time") +

  theme(axis.text.x = element_text(angle=45, vjust=1))
```

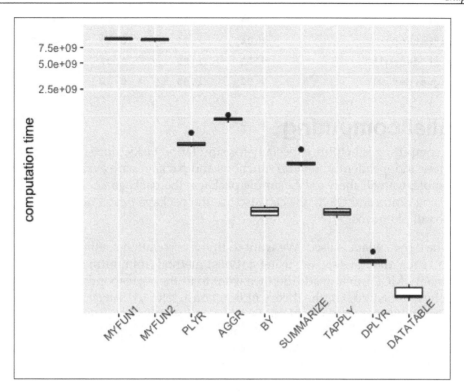

We can now observe that data.table and dylr are much faster than the other methods (the graphics shows log-scale!).

We can further profile the functions, for example, for *aggregate* we see that calling gsub and prettyNum needs the most computation time in function aggregate:

```
Rprof("aggr.out")
a <- aggregate(eqIncome ~ hsize + db040, eusilc, mean)
Rprof(NULL)
summaryRprof("aggr.out")$by.self
##                         self.time self.pct total.time total.pct
## "gsub"                       0.52    48.15       0.68     62.96
## "prettyNum"                  0.16    14.81       0.16     14.81
## "<Anonymous>"                0.10     9.26       1.08    100.00
## "na.omit.data.frame"         0.06     5.56       0.12     11.11
## "match"                      0.06     5.56       0.08      7.41
## "anyDuplicated.default"      0.06     5.56       0.06      5.56
```

## "[.data.frame"	0.04	3.70	0.18	16.67
## "NextMethod"	0.04	3.70	0.04	3.70
## "split.default"	0.02	1.85	0.04	3.70
## "unique.default"	0.02	1.85	0.02	1.85

Parallel computing

Parallel computing is helpful, especially for simulation tasks, since most simulations can be done independently. Several functions and packages are available in R. For this example, we will show only a simple package, the package snow (Tierney et al., 2015). Using Linux and OS X, one can also use the package parallel, while foreach works for all platforms.

Again, the Cars93 data is used. We want to fit the correlation coefficient between Price and Horsepower using a robust method (minimum covariance determinant - MCD), and in addition we want to fit the corresponding confidence interval by a Bootstrap. For the theory of Bootstrap, refer to *Chapter 3, The Discrepancy Between Pencil-Driven Theory and Data-Driven Computational Solutions.* Basically, we take Bootstrap samples (using sample()) and for each Bootstrap sample we calculate the robust covariance. From the results (R values), we take certain quantiles which can then be used for determining the confidence interval:

```
R <- 10000
library(robustbase)
covMcd(Cars93[, c("Price", "Horsepower")], cor = TRUE)$cor[1,2]
## [1] 0.8447
## confidence interval:
n <- nrow(Cars93)
f <- function(R, ...){
  replicate(R, covMcd(Cars93[sample(1:n, replace=TRUE),
      c("Price", "Horsepower")], cor = TRUE)$cor[1,2])
}
system.time(ci <- f(R))
##    user  system elapsed
##  79.056   0.265  79.597
quantile(ci, c(0.025, 0.975))
##    2.5%  97.5%
## 0.7690 0.9504
```

The aim is now to parallelize this calculation. We will call the package snow and make three clusters. Note that you can make more clusters if you have more CPUs on your machine. You should use the number of CPUs you have minus one as the maximum:

```
library("snow")
cl <- makeCluster(3, type="SOCK")
```

We now need to make the package robustbase available for all nodes as well as the data and the function:

```
clusterEvalQ(cl, library("robustbase"))
clusterEvalQ(cl, data(Cars93, package = "MASS"))
clusterExport(cl, "f")
clusterExport(cl, "n")
```

We can also set a random seed for each cluster:

```
clusterSetupRNG(cl, seed=123)
## Loading required namespace: rlecuyer
## [1] "RNGstream"
```

With clusterCall we can perform parallel computing:

```
system.time(ci_boot <-
                 clusterCall(cl, f, R = round(R / 3)))
##    user  system elapsed
##   0.001   0.000  38.655
quantile(unlist(ci_boot), c(0.025, 0.975))
##    2.5%  97.5%
## 0.7715 0.9512
```

We see that we are approximately twice as fast, and we could be even faster if we had more CPUs available.

Finally, we want to stop the cluster:

```
stopCluster(cl)
```

Interfaces to C++

Interfaces to C++ are recommended in order to make certain loops faster. We will show a very simple example to calculate the weighted mean. It should highlight the possibilities and let readers first get into touch with the package Rcpp (Eddelbuettel and Francois, 2011; Eddelbuettel, 2013), which simplifies the use of C++ code dramatically compared with R's .Call function.

Two great communicators of R, Hadley Wickham and Romain, used this example in their tutorials.

We want to compare the runtime of an example using R as an interpreted language, and also using Rcpp. We want to calculate the weighted mean of a vector.

A naive R function could look like that. We will use only interpreted R code:

```
wmeanR <- function(x, w) {
  total <- 0
  total_w <- 0
  for (i in seq_along(x)) {
    total <- total + x[i] * w[i]
    total_w <- total_w + w[i]
  }
  total / total_w
}
```

There is also a function called weighted.mean available in the base installation of R, and weightedMean in package laeken (Alfons and Templ, 2013).

Let us also define the Rcpp function. The function cppFunction compiles and links a shared library, then internally defines an R function that uses .Call:

```
library("Rcpp")
## from
## http://blog.revolutionanalytics.com/2013/07/deepen-your-r-experience-
with-rcpp.html
cppFunction('
  double wmean(NumericVector x, NumericVector w) {
  int n = x.size();
  double total = 0, total_w = 0;
  for(int i = 0; i < n; ++i) {
```

```
    total += x[i] * w[i];
    total_w += w[i];
  }
  return total / total_w;
  }
')
```

Now, let's compare the methods:

```
x <- rnorm(100000000)
w <- rnorm(100000000)
library("laeken")
op <- microbenchmark(
  naiveR = wmeanR(x, w),
  weighted.mean = weighted.mean(x, w),
  weighedMean = weightedMean(x, w),
  Rcpp.wmean = wmean(x, w),
  times = 1
)
## Warning in weightedMean(x, w): negative weights
op
## Unit: milliseconds
##           expr   min    lq  mean median    uq   max neval
##         naiveR 92561 92561 92561  92561 92561 92561     1
##  weighted.mean  5628  5628  5628   5628  5628  5628     1
##    weighedMean  4007  4007  4007   4007  4007  4007     1
##     Rcpp.wmean   125   125   125    125   125   125     1
```

Again, we draw a plot to visualize the results, as in the following screenshot globally:

```
m <- reshape2::melt(op, id="expr")

ggplot(m, aes(x=expr, y=value)) + geom_boxplot() + coord_trans(y =
"log10") + xlab(NULL) + ylab("computation time") + theme(
        axis.text.x = element_text(angle=45, vjust=1))
```

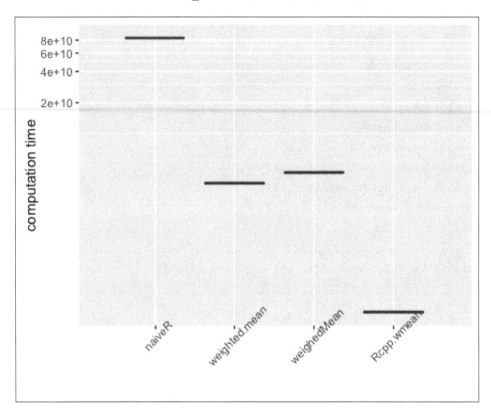

Visualizing information

In many chapters, results are visualized using the graphics capabilities of R. Thus, we will give a very short introduction to the base graphics package, plus a short introduction to the package ggplot2 (Wickham, 2009).

The reader will learn briefly about the graphical system in R, different output formats for traditional graphics system, customization and fine tuning of standard graphics, and the ggplot2 package.

Other packages such as ggmap, ggvis, lattice, or grid are not touched on here. **Interactive** graphics are also beyond the scope of this book (Google Charts, rgl, iplots, JavaScript, and R).

The graphics system in R

Many packages include methods to produce plots. Generally, they either use the functionality of the base R package called graphics or the functionality of the package grid.

For example, the package maptools (Bivand and Lewin-Koh, 2015) includes methods for mapping; with this package one can produce maps. It uses the capabilities of the graphics package. Package ggplot2 is based on the grid package and uses the functionality of the grid package for constructing advanced graphics.

Both packages, graphics and grid, include basic plot methods, and both packages use the graphical system of the operating system for plotting, which is hidden from the user. These graphical features from the operating system are attached by the graphical devices (?grDevices) of R, which also include support for colors and fonts.

The graphical output is either on screen or saved as a file. The screen devices pop-up as soon as a function such as plot() * is called. Typical screen devices are X11()** (X Windows window), windows() (Microsoft Windows window), and quartz (OS X). File devices include postscript() (PostScript format), pdf() (PDF format), jpeg() (JPEG), bmp (bitmap format), svg() (scalable vector graphics), and cairo() — the cairo-based graphics device that comes with its own graphic library to generate PDF, PostScript, SVG, or bitmap output (PNG, JPEG, TIFF), and X11.

In practice, there is almost no difference between plotting on the screen or in a PDF. Note that the current state of a device can be stored and copied to other devices.

The most common graphic devices are X11(), pdf(), postscript(), png(), and jpg().

For example, to save in pdf:

```
pdf(file = "myplot.pdf")
plot(Horsepower ~ Weight, data = Cars93)
dev.off ()
```

The available graphics devices are machine dependent. You can check the available ones using `?Devices`.

Note that various function arguments such as `width`, `height`, and `quality`, ..., can be used to modify the output.

The main question is which output format should be used?

The answer is rather simple: `X11` for displaying the image (automatically with, for example, RStudio); and `pdf` (or PostScript) for line graphics. These graphics are scalable without losing quality. `png` (or `jpg`) should be used for pixel graphics or graphics with many data points. Pixel graphics are not scalable without losing quality. `svg` has advantages in the browser (scalable, responsive — important in web design), but it does not include all fonts.

The graphics package

The package `graphics` is the traditional graphics system. Even though there are other packages for visualization available that produce publication quality plots perfectly, the graphics package is mainly used for producing figures quickly in order to explore content on-the-fly. Within this package, different types of function exist:

- **High-level graphics functions**: Opens a device and create a plot (for example, `plot()`)

- **Low-level graphics functions**: Add output to existing graphics (for example, `points()`)

- **Interactive functions**: Allow interaction with graphical output (for example, `identify()`)

Typically, a combination of multiple graphics functions is used to create a plot.

Each **graphics device** can be seen as a (abstract) **sheet of paper**. Thus with the graphics package we can draw using **many** pens in many colors, but **no eraser** is available. Multiple devices can be simultaneously opened and one can draw in one (the "active") graphics device.

Warm-up example – a high-level plot

We want to plot filled circles where the size depends on the absolute value of y and the color depends on the value of x:

```
x <- 1:20 / 2 # x ... 0.5, 1.0, 1.5, ..., 10.0
y <- sin(x)
plot(x, y, pch = 16, cex = 10 * abs(y), col = grey(x / 14))
```

We have already learned that `plot()` is a high-level plot function, and that we can add something to an existing plot with a low-level plot function. Let's add some text, a curve and a line, as seen in the following figure:

```
plot(x, y, pch = 16, cex = 10 * abs(y), col = grey(x / 14))
text(x, y, 1:20, col="yellow")
curve(sin, -2 * pi, 4 * pi, add = TRUE, col = "red")
abline(h = 0, lty = 2, col = "grey")
```

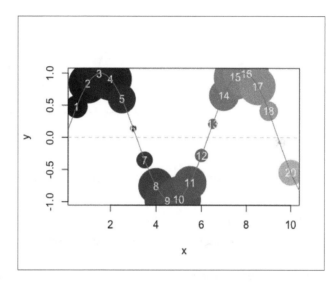

The function `plot()` is a **generic function**. It is overloaded with methods, and R selects the method depending on the class of the object to be plotted (**method dispatch** of **R**). It also shows different outputs depending on the **class** of the object to be plotted.

This can be seen in the following, where a numeric vector is first plotted, and then a factor, and then a data frame with one variable as a factor, and finally an object of class `ts`, as shown in the following figure:

```
par(mfrow=c(2,2))
mpg <- mtcars$mpg
cyl <- factor(mtcars$cyl)
df <- data.frame(x1=cyl, x2=mpg)
tmpg <- ts(mpg)
plot(mpg); plot(cyl); plot(df); plot(tmpg)
```

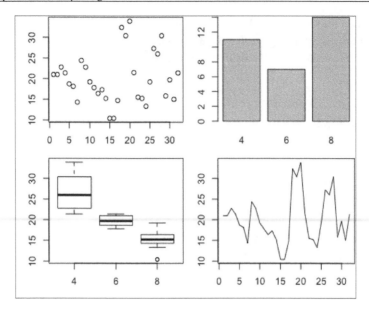

To know which plot methods are currently available, one can type `methods(plot)` into R:

```
tail(methods(plot)) ## last 6
## [1] "plot.TukeyHSD"  "plot.tune"      "plot.varclus"    "plot.
Variogram"
## [5] "plot.xyVector"  "plot.zoo"
## number of methods for plot
length(methods(plot))
## [1] 145
```

Subsequent calls produce (almost) equivalent results. Note that the last call uses the formula interface of R, see `?formula`:

```
plot(x=mtcars$mpg, y=mtcars$hp)
plot(mtcars$mpg, mtcars$hp)
plot(hp ~ mpg, data=mtcars)
```

Control of graphics parameters

Customizing graphics and changing the default output is almost always necessary, because: **high-level** plot functions do not always produce the desired final result, functionality for the fine tuning of graphics is necessary (colors, icons, fonts, line widths, etc); you need information about the plot regions and coordinate system to place the output of **low-level** functions, multiple graphs on a page.

Graphical parameters are the key to changing the appearance of graphics, including, for example, colors, fonts, linetypes, and axis definitions.

Each open device has its own independent list of graphics parameters and most parameters can be directly specified in high- or low-level plotting functions.

Important: all graphic parameters can be set via function par, see ?par. The most important function arguments of par are: mfrow for multiple graphics, col for colors, lwd for line widths, cex for the size of symbols, pch for selecting symbols, and lty for different kinds of lines.

In the following examples we will only discuss the control of colors.

Here are some possibilities: in R you can default address colors by name via colors(). rgb() to mix red-green-blue. Using hsv() is even better as it offers a pre-defined set of pallets with rainbow colors and many others, for example, ?rainbow, predefined set of palettes with palette().

Predefined palettes using the RColorBrewer package (Neuwirth, 2014).

Multiple plots with package graphics can be done via par(mfrow = c (2,2)). However, a more flexible is to use the function layout, see ?layout for examples.

We will show one example for layout by constructing a plot that doesn't exist in R. Note that a slightly modified version of this example was used in the lectures of Friedrich Leisch.

We will first calculate some numbers that are used afterwards to place the graphics:

```
## min und max in both axis
xmin <- min(mtcars$mpg); xmax <- max(mtcars$mpg)
ymin <- min(mtcars$hp); ymax <- max(mtcars$hp)


## calculate histograms
xhist <- hist(mtcars$mpg, breaks=15, plot=FALSE)
yhist <- hist(mtcars$hp, breaks=15, plot=FALSE)


## maximum count
top <- max(c(xhist$counts, yhist$counts))
xrange <-  c(xmin,xmax)
yrange <- c(ymin, ymax)
```

We now produce the following figure:

```
m <- matrix(c(2, 0, 1, 3), 2, 2, byrow = TRUE)
## define plot order and size
layout(m, c(3,1), c(1, 3), TRUE)
## first plot
par(mar=c(0,0,1,1))
plot(mtcars[,c("mpg","hp")], xlim=xrange, ylim=yrange, xlab="", ylab="")
## second plot -- barchart of margin
par(mar=c(0,0,1,1))
barplot(xhist$counts, axes=FALSE, ylim=c(0, top), space=0)
## third plot -- barchart of other margin
par(mar=c(3,0,1,1))
barplot(yhist$counts, axes=FALSE, xlim=c(0, top), space=0, horiz=TRUE)
```

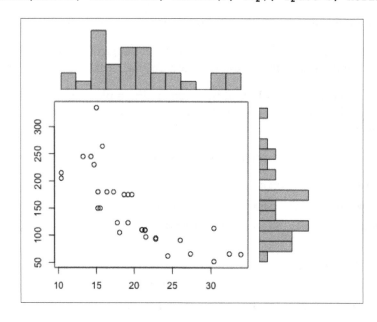

The ggplot2 package

Why use `ggplot2`?

- Gives a consistent and systematic approach to generating graphics
- Based on the book *Grammar of Graphics* by Wilkinson (1999)
- Very flexible

- Customizable, allows you to define your own themes (for example, for cooperative designs in companies)
- But slow and not as easy to learn

In `ggplot2`, the parts of a plot are defined independently. The anatomy of a plot consists of: data, must be a data frame (object of class `data.frame`); and **aesthetic mapping**, which describes how **variables** in the data are mapped to visual properties (aesthetics) of geometric objects. This must be done within the function `aes()`. **assignment**, where values are mapped to visual properties. It must also be done outside the function `aes()`. geometric objects (geom's, aesthetic will be mapped to geometric objects), for example, `geom_point()` - statistical transformations, for example, function `stat_boxplot()`, scales, coordinate system, position adjustments, and faceting, for example, function `facet_wrap`.

Aesthetic means "something you can see", for example, colors, fill (color), shape (of points), linetypes, size, and so on. Aesthetic mapping to geometric objects is done using function `aes()`.

To make a scatterplot with `Horsepower` and `MPG.city` for the `Cars93` data set, you use the following command:

```
library("ggplot2")
ggplot(Cars93, aes(x = Horsepower, y = MPG.city)) + geom_point(aes(colour
= Cylinders))
```

This command generates the following output:

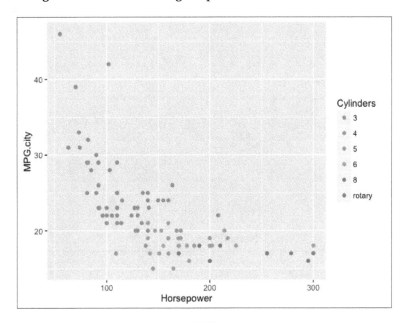

Here, we mapped Horsepower to the x variable, `MPG.city` to the y variable, `Cylinders` to color (within `aes()`!). We used `geom_point` to tell `ggplot2` to produce a scatterplot. Note that a statistical transformation is always defined, mostly this, as in our example, is the identity (leave the points as they are).

Note that each type of geom accepts only a subset of aesthetics (for example, setting `shape` in `aes()` and makes no sense when mapped to `geom_bar`) We add a geom by using `+`.

We can simple use more than one geom, here we also add a scatterplot smoothing, and we perform an aesthetic mapping of weights to color (within `aes()`). Automatically, a legend is produced, as seen in the following screenshot:

```
g1 <- ggplot(Cars93, aes(x=Horsepower, y=MPG.city))

g2 <- g1 + geom_point(aes(color=Weight))

g2 + geom_smooth()

## geom_smooth: method="auto" and size of largest group is <1000, so
using loess. Use 'method = x' to change the smoothing method.
```

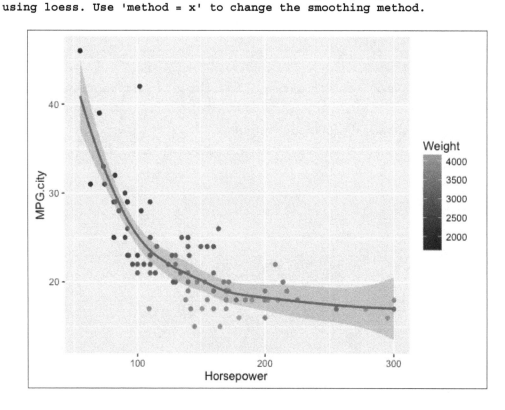

We still have g1 available in our workspace, so we can add something else, for example, text, resulting in following screenshot:

```
g1 <- g1 + geom_text(aes(label=substr(Manufacturer,1,3)), size=3.5)
g1 + geom_smooth()
## geom_smooth: method="auto" and size of largest group is <1000, so
using loess. Use 'method = x' to change the smoothing method.
```

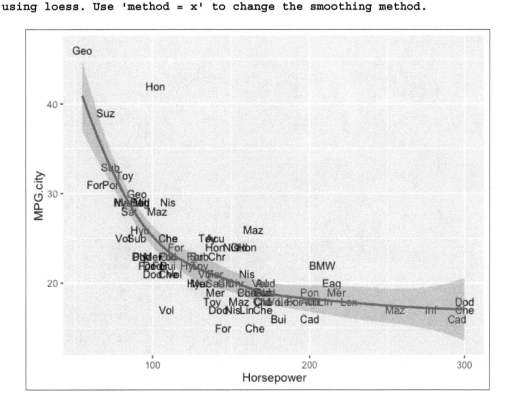

Each block of a ggplot2 is defined by a list of parameters. To make life easy, sensible standard default parameter values are set.

All (geoms) are associated with statistical transformations. For some geoms, the data is modified, for example, geom_boxplot. Note that geom_boxplot must not be called whenever the statistical transformation stat_boxplot is called — automatically ggplot2 knows that it should use geom_boxplot.

With scales, aesthetics for variables can be defined, such as color and fill (color), size, shape, linetype, and so on, by using the function **scale_**.

A "standardized" graphic for each group in the data can be done — for one grouping variable use facet_wrap(), for two grouping variables use facet_grid().

We will show one example of how to set the syntax for `facet_wrap`, and we use another theme for the following output:

```
gg <- ggplot(Cars93, aes(x=Horsepower, y=MPG.city))
gg <- gg + geom_point(aes(shape = Origin, colour = Price))
gg <- gg + facet_wrap(~ Cylinders)  + theme_bw()
gg
```

The output is as follows:

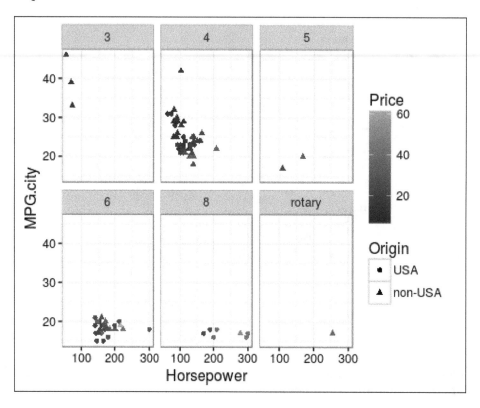

Note that themes can be used for cooperative design. Two themes comes with ggplot2: `theme_gray()` (the default one), and `theme_bw()`.

Take a look at more information on themes by typing `?theme_gray` into R references:

References

- Alfons, A., and M. Templ. 2013. "Estimation of Social Exclusion Indicators from Complex Surveys: The R Package laeken." *Journal of Statistical Software* 54 (15): 1–25. http://www.jstatsoft.org/v54/i15/.

- Bache, S.M., and W. Wickham. 2014. magrittr: A Forward-Pipe Operator for R. https://CRAN.R-project.org/package=magrittr.

- Bivand, R., and N. Lewin-Koh. 2015. Maptools: Tools for Reading and Handling Spatial Objects. https://CRAN.R-project.org/package=maptools.

- Dowle, M., A. Srinivasan, T. Short, S. Lianoglou, R. Saporta, and E. Antonyan. 2015. Data.table: Extension of Data.frame. https://CRAN.R-project.org/package=data.table.

- Eddelbuettel, D., and R. Francois. 2011. "Rcpp: Seamless R and C++ Integration." *Journal of Statistical Software* 40 (8): 1–18.

- Harrell Jr, F.E. 2016. Hmisc: Harrell Miscellaneous. https://CRAN.R-project.org/package=Hmisc.

- Mersmann, O. 2015. Microbenchmark: Accurate Timing Functions. https://CRAN.R-project.org/package=microbenchmark.

- Neuwirth, E. 2014. RColorBrewer: ColorBrewer Palettes. https://CRAN.R-project.org/package=RColorBrewer.

- R Core Team. 2015. R: A Language and Environment for Statistical Computing. Vienna, Austria: R Foundation for Statistical Computing. https://www.R-project.org/.

- Revolution Analytics, and S. Weston. 2015. Foreach: Provides Foreach Looping Construct for R. https://CRAN.R-project.org/package=foreach.

- Templ, M., K. Hron, and P. Filzmoser. 2011. RobCompositions: An R-Package for Robust Statistical Analysis of Compositional Data. John Wiley; Sons.

- Tierney, L., A.J. Rossini, N. Li, and H. Sevcikova. 2015. Snow: Simple Network of Workstations. https://CRAN.R-project.org/package=snow.

- Venables, W.N., and B.D. Ripley. 2002. Modern Applied Statistics with S. Fourth. New York: Springer. http://www.stats.ox.ac.uk/pub/MASS4.

- Wickham, H. 2009. Ggplot2: Elegant Graphics for Data Analysis. Springer-Verlag New York. http://ggplot2.org/book/.

- Wickham, H., and W. Chang. 2016. Devtools: Tools to Make Developing R Packages Easier. `https://CRAN.R-project.org/package=devtools`.

- Wickham, H., and R. Francois. 2015. dplyr: A Grammar of Data Manipulation. `https://CRAN.R-project.org/package=dplyr`.

- Wilkinson, L. 2005. The Grammar of Graphics (Statistics and Computing). Secaucus, NJ, USA: Springer-Verlag New York, Inc.

3

The Discrepancy between Pencil-Driven Theory and Data-Driven Computational Solutions

Questions on numerical precision and rounding errors with a wide range of applications are especially considered within the area of *numerical mathematics*. But statistics and data science are also tangled with problems on rounding and numerical precision, and data scientists should be aware of this. Of course, such problems also depend on the architecture of the computer. Even numbers that are measured with the highest degree of precision cannot be represented exactly on a computer. Some of the problems are of a general nature. It becomes critical if, for example, analytical properties of estimators differ in theory (on paper) and practice (with computers).

The goal of this chapter is to raise awareness of the mentioned topics. The reader should be sensitized to the concepts of machine numbers and rounding, as well as issues in convergence and the condition of problems. These concepts do not directly support other chapters, but they should be basic knowledge for any data scientist and statistician. In addition, the chapter content can be seen as a warm-up for computer-oriented and data-driven analysis that is the content of the next chapters.

Machine numbers and rounding problems

A computer cannot store any value of a continuous distribution exactly, and continuous values get discretized (rounded) on a fine scale. The rounding of values and storage of values as machine numbers should always be kept in mind; for most applications, this doesn't lead to any problems.

"Most" means "not always". Some examples are shown in the following topics that will leave most users without background knowledge in machine numbers perplexed and irritated.

As a motivating example, the following "bug" report (software R) serves as an example:

From: focus17@libero.it

To: R-bugs@biostat.ku.dk

Subject: error in function trunc

Date: Fri, Jul 2007 15:03:58 +0200 6 (CEST)

The following command will get a wrong result:

*trunc (2.3 * 100)*
[1] 229

Answer Duncan Murdoch: That is the correct answer. 2.3 is not representable Exactly; The actual value used is slightly less.

Remark: `trunc()` is the largest integer in cutting a value off after the decimal point. It is generally the case that a random number cannot be accurately stored in a floating point arithmetic.

Thus, you should not wonder anymore about the following:

```
round(1.49999999999999)
## [1] 1
round(1.4999999999999999)
## [1] 2
```

`1.499999999999999` can't be represented internally, thus it gets rounded to `1.5`. When `round()` is applied, the result is `2`. It is the case that `1.499999999999999` actually gets stored as `1.50000000000000` because of limitations on floating point precision.

This also shows in the next example:

From: wchen@stat.tamu.edu

To: R-bugs@biostat.ku.dk

Subject: [Rd] match () (PR # 13135)

Date: Tue, 7 Oct 2008 00:05:06

The match function does not return values properly. Take a look at the following example:

a <- seq(0.6, 1, by = 0.01)
match(0.88, a)
[1] 29
match(0.89, a)
[1] NA
match(0.94, a)
[1] 35

Answer Brian Ripley:

FAQ Q7.31 strikes again!

0.89 is not a member of seq(0.6, 1, by = 0.01)*, since 0.01 cannot be represented exactly in a binary computer.

Many users wonder about rounding. According to the help page on `round()`, `round(1.5)` could be either `1` or `2`. This may be in contradiction with what you learned in primary school and what you experience in software such as Microsoft Excel (that `1.5` is always rounded up to `2`), and so it is in R for `round(1.5)`, but it does not apply to rounding off a 5 in general. From the R help for `round()`, we get further clarity: *For rounding off a 5, the IEC 60559 standard is expected to be used, 'go to the even digit'.*

In case you did not recognize it, IEC 60559 is an international standard, whereas Excel is not.

Usually, it is rare for round() to be called explicitly in R code since rounding is usually going on inside print routines.

In case you want to force rounding such as 0.5 to 1, you may add a very small number to your value so that it is round:

```
excel_round <- function (x, digits) round (x * (1 + 1e-15), digits)
round(0.5, digits = 0)
## [1] 0
excel_round(0.5, digits = 0)
## [1] 1
```

We can summarize the rounding issue with the wonderful sentence of Kernighan and Plauger, 1982:

> *"10.0 times 0.1 is hardly ever 1.0."*

Floating point representations are characterized by the following four parameters:

- Base, *b > 1* for example, 2
- Smallest and largest exponent *emin < 0*, and *emax > 0* integer
- Mantissa length *m*

A number is thus represented as follows:

$$x = (-1)^{u_0} b^e \sum_{i=1}^{m} u_i \, b^{-i}$$

Here, *e* is an exponent and $u_i \in \{0,1\}$

If the decimal representation of a value is indicated with *m* digits, a maximum error equals $\epsilon_m = b^{-m}$, which is often referred to as machine precision or machine epsilon. The machine epsilon can be used to estimate the maximum distance between two neighboring numbers.

Example – the 64-bit representation of numbers

For the 64-bit binary representation of numbers, $m = 53$, $e_{min} = -1022$ and $e_{max} = 1024$, with the maximum absolute distance between two machine numbers expressed as follows:

$$|\tilde{x} - x| \le \epsilon_m|x|$$

This distance (and more) can be displayed in R with the following:

```
.Machine$double.eps
## [1] 2.220446e-16
.Machine$double.digits
## [1] 53
.Machine$double.xmax
## [1] 1.797693e+308
```

All this has far-reaching consequences in practice – primarily with regard to the convergence of algorithms.

Convergence in the deterministic case

Under the term **convergence**, we can think about the idea that a sequence of random numbers converge to a fixed value, or of the increasing similarity of outcomes to a certain value, or that a sampled probability distribution grows increasingly similar to a certain distribution, or that the series formed by calculating the expected value of the outcome's distance from a particular value may converge to 0.

The convergence of iterative methods and procedures, as well as the convergence of simulations, are very important topics in statistical simulation and data science problems. We say that an iterative algorithm has been converged when the expected value is below a (small and problem-dependent) threshold.

Furthermore, the convergence of sequences of random variables to some limit random variable is a basic concept in probability theory, and its applications to statistics and stochastic processes, (see *Chapter 6, Probability Theory Shown by Simulation*).

In the following, the convergence of a sequence is in main focus. Convergence in this context is defined by:

$$\lim_{n\to\infty} a_n = a \quad \Leftrightarrow \quad \forall \varepsilon > 0 \; \exists N \in \mathbb{N} \; \forall n \ge N: \; |a_n - a| < \varepsilon$$

It is known that, for example, the following series converges (alternating harmonic series):

$$\lim_{n\to\infty} \sum_{k=1}^{n} \frac{(-1)^{k+1}}{k} = \ln2$$

And, as an example of a series that diverges (harmonic series), refer to the following:

$$\sum_{k=1}^{\infty} \frac{1}{k}$$

Similarly, the exponential function may be represented as a series of $e^x = \sum_{n=0}^{\infty} \frac{x^n}{n!}$.

The convergence of these series can be proved analytically. The convergence of these series, however, may not always be the case when doing calculations on a computer.

Example – convergence

Let's have a look at one of the series given, $\sum_{k=1}^{\infty} \frac{1}{k}$. In R, this will look like the following:

```
masch <- function(maxit=10000){
  summe <- 0
  summeNeu <- n <- 1
  ptm <- proc.time()
  while(summe != summeNeu & n < maxit){
    summe <- summeNeu
    summeNeu <- summe + 1/n
    n <- n + 1
  }
  time <- proc.time() - ptm
  list(summe=summeNeu, time=time[3])
}
masch(10000)$summe
## [1]  10.78751
masch(1000000)$summe
## [1]  15.39273
masch(10000000)$summe
## [1]  17.69531
```

Thus, you may not be able to decide on a computer whether this series diverges (at least not after 10 minutes of computing time). We can also see that the number calculated increases nonlinearly with the number of recursions. This is also shown in the following table. We increase the numbers of iterations by a factor of 10:

```
SEQ <- c(10,1000, seq(100000,10000000,length=10))
df <- cbind(SEQ, t(as.data.frame(sapply(SEQ, masch))))
df
```

	SEQ	sum	time
	10	3.828968	0
	1000	8.484471	0.004
	1e+05	13.09014	0.444
	1200000	15.57505	5.264
	2300000	16.22564	10.164
	3400000	16.6165	15.076
	4500000	16.8968	19.848
	5600000	17.11549	24.643
	6700000	17.29483	29.573
	7800000	17.44685	34.485
	8900000	17.57878	39.41
	1e+07	17.69531	44.204

However, the series $e^x = \sum_{n=0}^{\infty} \frac{x^n}{n!}$ results in a completely different conclusion. For $x = 1$ the result should be the irrational (Euler) number e. After 19 iterations oldsum == newsum, although e should be an irrational number:

```
x <- 1
oldsum = 0
newsum = n = term = 1
while(oldsum != newsum){
  oldsum = newsum
  term = 1/factorial(n)
  n = n + 1
  newsum = oldsum + term
  print(paste("n = ", n, ". Diff = ", term, ". Sum = ", newsum, sep=""))
}
## [1] "n = 2. Diff = 1. Sum = 2"
```

```
## [1] "n = 3. Diff = 0.5. Sum = 2.5"
## [1] "n = 4. Diff = 0.166666666666667. Sum = 2.66666666666667"
## [1] "n = 5. Diff = 0.0416666666666667. Sum = 2.70833333333333"
## [1] "n = 6. Diff = 0.00833333333333333. Sum = 2.71666666666667"
## [1] "n = 7. Diff = 0.00138888888888889. Sum = 2.71805555555556"
## [1] "n = 8. Diff = 0.000198412698412698. Sum = 2.71825396825397"
## [1] "n = 9. Diff = 2.48015873015873e-05. Sum = 2.71827876984127"
## [1] "n = 10. Diff = 2.75573192239859e-06. Sum = 2.71828152557319"
## [1] "n = 11. Diff = 2.75573192239859e-07. Sum = 2.71828180114638"
## [1] "n = 12. Diff = 2.50521083854417e-08. Sum = 2.71828182619849"
## [1] "n = 13. Diff = 2.08767569878681e-09. Sum = 2.71828182828617"
## [1] "n = 14. Diff = 1.60590438368216e-10. Sum = 2.71828182844676"
## [1] "n = 15. Diff = 1.14707455977297e-11. Sum = 2.71828182845823"
## [1] "n = 16. Diff = 7.64716373181982e-13. Sum = 2.71828182845899"
## [1] "n = 17. Diff = 4.77947733238739e-14. Sum = 2.71828182845904"
## [1] "n = 18. Diff = 2.81145725434552e-15. Sum = 2.71828182845905"
## [1] „n = 19. Diff = 1.56192069685862e-16. Sum = 2.71828182845905"
```

We will give another example of rounding errors that we face in everyday work. For the estimation of the standard deviation, two mathematically equivalent formulas exist (with the theorem of Steiner, one can bring one form to the other):

- As done in R: $s = \dfrac{1}{n-1}\sqrt{\sum_{i=1}^{n}(x_i - \bar{x})^2}$ with $\bar{x} = \dfrac{1}{n}\sum_{i=1}^{n}x_i$

- As done in previous versions of Excel: $s = \sqrt{\dfrac{1}{n-1}\left(\left(\sum_{i=1}^{n}x_i^2\right) - \bar{x}^2\right)}$

The calculation of the standard deviation with the latter formula is easier to do without the help of computers if the numbers are integers. However, it can be shown that the latter formula leads to numerical instabilities (larger rounding errors).

Let's take a look with the help of R:

```
## first formula for the standard deviation:
s1 <- function(x){
  s <- sum((x - mean(x))^2)
    return(sqrt(1/(length(x)-1) * s))
}
## second formula for the standard deviation:
```

```
s2 <- function(x){
#    s <- 1/(length(x)-1) * sum(x^2) - mean(x)^2
     s <- sum(x^2) - 1/length(x) * sum(x)^2
     return(sqrt(1/(length(x)-1) * s))
}
## wrapper function:
st <- function(x, type) {
  switch(type,
         precise = s1(x),
         oldexcel = s2(x)
         )
}
## generating 1000 random numbers from standard normal distribution:
x <- rnorm(1000)
## show more digits:
options(digits=16)
## results:
st(x, "precise")
## [1] 1.034835048604582
st(x, "oldexcel")
## [1] 1.034835048604582
```

Both give the same results. However, let's try an experiment to show the differences. The outcome should always be 0.50125, but we will see that because of numerical instabilities, this is not always true, especially for the second formula:

```
stall <- function(x){
    c(precise=st(x, "precise"), excel=st(x, "oldexcel"))
}
## generate numbers (zeros and ones)
x <- rep(0:1,100)
stall(x)
##              precise              excel
## 0.5012547071170855 0.5012547071170855
X <- matrix(nrow=length(x), ncol=10)
X[,1] <- 1
for(n in 2:ncol(X)) X[, n] <- x + 10^(2 * (n - 1))
```

```
colnames(X) <- 2 * (1:ncol(X) - 1)
dim(X)
## [1] 200  10
## first four observations:
head(X,4)
##       0   2     4       6         8           10            12
## [1,] 1 100 10000 1000000 100000000 10000000000 1000000000000
## [2,] 1 101 10001 1000001 100000001 10000000001 1000000000001
## [3,] 1 100 10000 1000000 100000000 10000000000 1000000000000
## [4,] 1 101 10001 1000001 100000001 10000000001 1000000000001
##                     14    16    18
## [1,] 100000000000000 1e+16 1e+18
## [2,] 100000000000001 1e+16 1e+18
## [3,] 100000000000000 1e+16 1e+18
## [4,] 100000000000001 1e+16 1e+18
options(digits=5)
apply(X, 2, stall)
##           0       2       4       6       8      10      12      14 16
## 18
## precise 0 0.50125 0.50125 0.50125 0.50125 0.50125 0.50125 0.50125  0
## 0
## excel   0 0.50125 0.50125 0.50125 0.00000 0.00000     NaN 0.00000  0
## 0
```

A critical general question for any iteration is how many iterations are needed until convergence. Let's take a look at the infinite geometric series $\sum_{i=0}^{\infty} q^i$ that generally converges if $|q| < 1$. It has as the following formula:

$$\sum_{i=0}^{\infty} q^i = \frac{1}{1-q} \quad \text{for} \quad |q| < 1$$

Let's concentrate on the special choices of q, q = 0.5, and $q = 2$, where these series, $\sum_{i=0}^{\infty} 2^{-i}$, should diverge in the first case and converge in the second case, where for the second case $\sum_{i=0}^{\infty} 2^{-i} = \dfrac{1}{1-\frac{1}{2}} = 2$ holds. For $q = 2$ the series converges to 2 even with relatively small *i* *(i = 55)*, as shown as follows:

```
konv <- function(q = 2){
  s <-  0
    snew <- term <- i <- 1
    while(s != snew){
      s <- snew
        snew <-  s + q^(-i)
        i <- i + 1
    }
    list(iteration = i, total = snew, lastterm = 2^(-i))
}
konv()
## $iteration
## [1] 55
##
## $total
## [1] 2
##
## $lastterm
## [1] 2.7756e-17
```

And for *q = 0.5* it diverges:

```
konv(q = 0.5)
## $iteration
## [1] 1025
##
## $total
## [1] Inf
##
## $lastterm
## [1] 2.7813e-309
```

One can see that the last terms are already smaller than the machine number.

One final example about convergence is as follows. Consider the R code for the computation of e^x from earlier, and we compare the accuracy of the calculation with the `exp ()` function. How large is the error?

```
expsum <- function(x){    oldsum <- 0
    newsum <- n <- term <- 1
    while( oldsum != newsum )
    {    oldsum <- newsum
        term <- term * x/n
        n <- n + 1
        newsum <- oldsum + term
    }
    list(iteration = n, summe = newsum)
}
x <- 1:1000
absError <- sapply (x, function (x) abs (exp (x) - expsum (x) $ sum))
relError <- absError / exp (x)
```

For double precision (and 64-bit), $\epsilon_m = 2^{-53}$ (approximate 16 decimal places) $|\tilde{x} - x| \le \epsilon_m|x|$:

```
roundingError <- sapply(x, function(x) 2^(-53)*exp(x))
```

In the following graph, (*Figure 3.1*) we can see how the rounding error explodes with the increasing values of **x**:

```
plot(x[1: 600], roundingError[1:600], log = "xy", xlab = "log (x)", ylab
= "log (rounding errors)", type = "l")
```

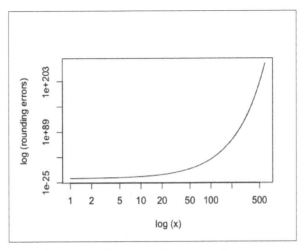

Figure 3.1: Varying numbers for x and corresponding rounding errors

Consider now for a different **x** the number of iterations until convergence. Will the number of iterations increase with increasing **x** on a linear scale? In what manner?

We vary x between 0 and 20 with increment 0.1 and produce and show the result in *Figure 3.2*:

```
x <- seq(0, 20, by=0.1)

iter <- sapply(x, function(x) expsum(x)$iteration)

plot(x, iter, xlab="x", ylab="No. of iterationen until convergence",
type="l")
```

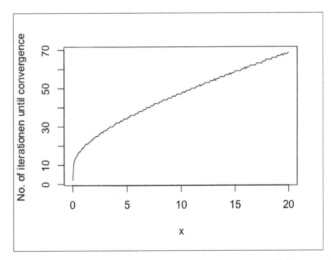

Figure 3.2: The number of iterations needed for the convergence of different values of x

The linearity between **x** and the number of iterations until convergence it seems is given if $x > 3$ up to a breakpoint at large for large **x** (overflow, in the preceding graphic not shown).

Condition of problems

Other well-known problems of rounding errors are described in the foundations of computational mathematics. In the following, we consider another rounding problem that is related to the numerical precision of matrix operations. For the condition of a problem, in most cases, the reciprocal condition number is estimated in computer programs. The smaller the reciprocal condition number (or the higher the condition number), the worse is the condition of the problem.

The 2-norm condition number (in R it is `kappa()`) represents the ratio of the largest to the smallest non-zero singular value of a matrix, while `rcond()` computes an approximation of the reciprocal condition number; take a look at the details.

A poorly conditioned problem is, for example, as follows:

```
library("Matrix")
## reciprocal approximate condition number
rcond(Hilbert(9)) ## worse
## [1] 9.0938e-13
## reciprocal condition number
x1 <- cbind(1, 1:10)
head(x1, 3)
##      [,1] [,2]
## [1,]    1    1
## [2,]    1    2
## [3,]    1    3
rcond(x1) ## much better
## [1] 0.05278
```

Such instability (ill-conditioned problems) occurs mainly in case of multi-collinearity in regression analysis. Multi-collinearity occurs if one (or more) predictor variable(s) can be well described by a linear combination of other predictor variables. This leads to serious numerical problems of classical approaches, often even to senseless estimates.

Summary

Data scientists are confronted with both the problems, rounding errors, and instabilities because of numerical precision problems.

In R, one should be aware that printing a result does not mean that you see the exact number. It's just rounded off on given digits (*default = 7*), but internally, the numbers are saved with more digits.

In any case, we saw in this chapter that the floating point arithmetic of a computer cannot represent all numbers, and almost every number is rounded to the next even digit. By reading this chapter, you learned the basic knowledge of machine numbers and rounding. This knowledge is mandatory for any data scientist and statistician although these problems play a minor role in the following chapters. We also saw in this chapter convergence issues: how to observe convergence for a given problem. This will be continued and extended in the following chapters, such as in *Chapter 4*, *Simulation of Random Numbers*, and *Chapter 5*, *Monte Carlo Methods for Optimization Problems*.

References

The Elements of Programming Style, Second Edition by Brian W. Kernighan and P.J. Plauger, 1982, New York, NY, USA: McGraw-Hill, Inc.

4
Simulation of Random Numbers

Can you imagine a statistical simulation to evaluate and compare methods without generating random numbers? Can you imagine a Bayesian approach without drawing random numbers from predictive or prior distributions? Can you imagine any game of chance without the concept of randomness? Can you imagine a world without randomness?

Generally speaking, the statistics and probability theory is based on abstract concepts of probability space and random numbers. An elegant mathematical theory has been developed, which takes its starting point from random numbers.

Specially applied research areas such as computational statistics, data science, and statistical simulation employ the concept of random numbers. Hereby, often a large number of **independent and identically distributed (i.i.d)** random numbers are generated/needed, especially for simulation purposes.

However, in computer applications, surprisingly the random numbers are mostly simulated with deterministic algorithms, which is somehow in contradiction with the basic theory. The first part of this chapter mainly deals with the problem of deterministic random number generation. But let's first take a look at real random numbers.

Real random numbers

Generated *real (true)* random numbers should be realizations of independent identically distributed random variables, and they should be unpredictable, meaning that the next generated number is unpredictable from the previously generated random numbers. The lottery and gambling industries, for example, rely on them. But are true/real random numbers also useful in statistics? Before answering this question, we will discuss real random number generation.

As a source of random numbers, the following random number generators might be used:

- Flipping a coin, rolling dice, roulette, and so on
- The decaying of a radioactive source
- Noise from the atmosphere (www.random.org)

It can be observed that a physical process is behind the generation of true random numbers.

By generating, for example, a sequence of zeroes and ones, these bits should be equally likely and independently occur from each other. To evaluate this property, statistical tests can be used.

However, true random number generators have some disadvantages in applications in data science and statistical simulation:

- They are often computationally expensive to generate
- The implementation is usually difficult and time-consuming, and thus more costly
- Reproducibility is not a given
- Whether random numbers will be generated is normally not checked

A striking example is a coin getting damaged on being tossed. Here the probability of landing on the head (side) of the coin will change. In general, unobserved and uncontrollable processes might have influence on a true random generator, and such an influence can hardly be verified. For example, random numbers obtained from hits of gamma rays on a detector might be occasionally be influenced by changes of the magnetic field.

Nevertheless, mainly because the reproducibility of any result is a very important concept, real number generators are mostly not used in statistics, statistical simulation, and data science applications. The field of applications for true random number generators are especially in cryptography and slot machines, as it is often required that the generated random numbers be absolutely unpredictable.

The R package, `random`, directly accesses `www.random.org`. With the facilities of this website, true random numbers can be collected. The random number generator is based on atmospheric noise and the measurement of gamma-rays that hit (us and) the surface of our Earth. Using the `randomNumbers` function, random numbers are streamed from this website:

```
library("random")
x <- randomNumbers(n=10000, col=2, min=0,
        max=1e+06, check=TRUE) / 1000000
```

As a first indicator of the random number generator working properly, the original values are plotted against the lagged values (see *Figure 4.1*). This means that the first value is plotted against the second, the second value against the third, and so on. If there is a certain structure visible in the following figure, the values might be auto-correlated:

```
n <- length(x)
df <- data.frame(x1 = x[1:(n-1)], x2 = x[2:n])
ggplot(df, aes(x = x1, y = x2)) + geom_point(size = 0.1) +
xlab("random numbers from random.org") + ylab("lag 1")
```

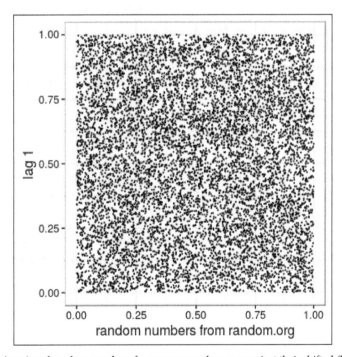

Figure 4.1: A series of random numbers from www.random.org against their shifted (lag 1) values

Not all tests, for example the Diehard test battery at `https://www.phy.duke.edu/~rgb/General/dieharder.php`, passed by this generated true random numbers.

Simulating pseudo random numbers

Pseudo random numbers are the basis for almost any statistical (Monte Carlo) simulation, and they are used in a huge variety of problems in statistics. Simulating them well is crucial for valid outputs on Monte Carlo simulations, and also resampling methods rely on the quality of pseudo random numbers.

We can distinguish between (at least) two kinds of pseudo random number generators:

- **Arithmetic random number generators**: They are based purely on, as the name suggests, arithmetic. Irrational numbers like $\sqrt{2}$ and e may be used as random number generators by making use of the fractional part of any multiples used. However, it is difficult to determine whether irrational numbers, as yet, have a periodicity. In addition, irrational numbers can only be presented as (finite) machine numbers in a computer; irrational numbers are rarely used in practice to generate random numbers.

- **Recursive arithmetic random number generators**: They are based on the calculation of a new random number from one or more previous numbers. Reproducibility is given by setting an initial value (seed) to ensure that exactly at the point of rerunning the programme, the same random numbers are generated. These algorithms for generating random numbers are deterministic because they follow a precise calculation rule. A sequence of pseudo random numbers is therefore deterministic.

A pseudo-random generator is a construct of $(S, \mu, f, \mathcal{U}, g)$ with the initial state S (finite and machine numbers), the probability distribution μ on S to produce the initial state (seed) , the transition function $f \colon S \to S$, as well as the solution space $\mathcal{U}$, and the output function $g \colon S \to \mathcal{U}$

Logically, $\mathcal{U}$ describes the machine numbers in the interval *(0,1)*. The current state is given by $s_i = f(s_{i-1})$ for $i \geq 1$, and the result (the pseudo-random numbers) by:

$$u_i = g(s_i) \in \mathcal{U}.$$

An essential characteristic of a pseudo-random number generator is the period.

$$S < \infty \;\Rightarrow\; \exists l \geq 0 \land j \geq 0 : s_{l+j} = s_l$$

$$\Rightarrow \forall i \geq l \; \exists s_{i+j} = s_i \land u_{i+j} = u_i$$

Here, the smallest j characterizes the period length of the pseudo-random generator.

For a 32-bit computer, the maximum period is limited with 2^{32}. Good pseudo-random number generators have a period close to 2^k, with k being the bit representation of the computer (nowadays usually it is 64-bit; on older computers, it may be 32-bit or less).

Congruential generators

Congruential generators are popular because of their simplicity. But, even with their simplicity, they can work well under certain conditions, and many software products still use certain types.

A congruential generator is defined by the following parameters:

- Number $n \in \mathbb{N}^+$ of the state values, order
- Mode $m \in \{2,3,4,\ldots\}$
- Coefficient $a_1,\ldots,a_n \in \{0,\ldots,m-1\} \in \mathbb{Z}_0$
- Increment $b \in \{0,\ldots,m-1\}$
- Start values $x\_1, ..., x\_n \{0, ..., m\text{-}1\}$ (seed)

For $i > n$ one sets now:

$$x_i = \left(\left(\textstyle\sum_{k=1}^{n} a_k\, x_{i-k}\right) + b\right) \text{ modulo } m$$

The state at the time, i is therefore $s_i = (x_{i-n}, \ldots, x_i)^{T}$.

By a suitable choice of m, and b, the maximum period can be obtained (see, for example, (Knuth 1998)).

Linear and multiplicative congruential generators

The simplest congruential generators are linear and multiplicative congruential generators.

Often, n (see the previous occurrence) equals 1. If this is the case, then the previous equation simplifies to the following:

$$y_i = (ay_{i-1} + b) \text{ modulo } m$$

As a toy example, let $a = 2$, $y_0 = 1$, $b = 1$, and $m = 10$. Then, the random numbers are 1, 3, 7, 5, 1, 3, 7, 5, 1, 3, 7, 5, 1, and so on. The period is 4.

Maximum period length can be achieved by the appropriate choice of b (with b and m prime to each other) m and a.

A good choice is, for example, $m = 2\text{^}32$, $a = 69069$, $b = 23606797$.

A so-called multiplicative congruential results when $b = 0$.

The literature on linear and multiplicative congruence generators state that these generators have a hyperplanes behavior. If we lag the sequence $(u_i)_{i \geq 0}$ in k tuples $(u_0, \dots, u_{k-1}), (u_1, \dots, u_k), \dots, (u_{n+1}, \dots, u_{n+k})$, then these k tuples (in $\mathbb{R}^k$) lay on a maximum of $\sqrt{km} \cdot k!$ parallel hyperplanes.

Figure 4.2 shows that result for *k = 3* using a bad choice of parameter values (m = 100000000, a = 2, b = 1, y_0 = 0, n = 120000), and *Figure 4.3* shows a good choice of parameter values (m = 2^{32}, a = 69069, b = 23606797, y_0 = 0, n = 120000):

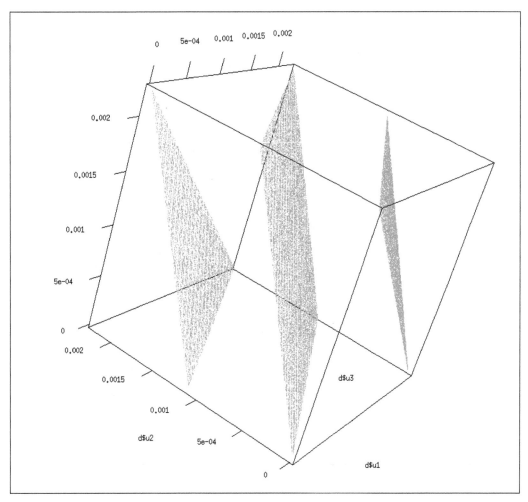

Figure 4.2: Lagged random numbers with a bad choice of parameters for the linear congruential generator. The lagged series falls into three 2-dimensional planes

Another (better) choice of parameters may lead to much better results; take a look at *Figure 4.3*:

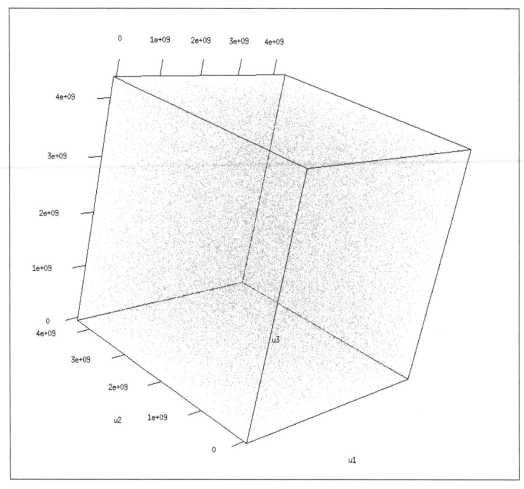

Figure 4.3: Lagged random numbers with a good choice of parameters of the linear congruential generator

With another example, we look at a very prominent linear congruential generator, **Randu**. Randu, which was constructed by IBM and used for many years, acting as a standard generator for random numbers at IBM mainframes.

This generator is determined by the parameter setting $y_{j+1} = (65539 \cdot y_j) \mod 2^{31}$. This results in integer pseudo-random numbers y_j in the interval $[1, 2^{31} - 1]$.

These random numbers may easily be transformed into rational numbers in *[0,1]* using the transformation $X_j = \dfrac{y_j}{2^{31}}$.

To best observe the differences and the bad behavior of Randu, the following code produces interactive 3D rotatable graphics (not shown in this book). The results of Randu look almost as bad as the result in *Figure 4.1*. By running the following code it can be clearly seen that the points fall in 15 two-dimensional planes:

```
seed <- 123
randu <- function(n) {
  for (i in 1:n) {
    seed <<- (65539 * seed) %% (2^31)
      result[i] <- seed / 2^31
  }
  return(result)
}
plot3S <- function(func, n=10000) {
  x <- func(n)
  require("rgl")
  x1 <- x[1:(n-2)]
  x2 <- x[2:(n-1)]
  x3 <- x[3:n]
  plot3d(x1, x2, x3, size=3)
  play3d(spin3d())
}
```

To see the results, run the following lines:

```
plot3S(randu)
## to compare it with R's standard generator
plot3S(runif) ## (Mersenne-Twister)
```

Since Randu was widely used in the early 1970s, many results from that time are seen as suspicious. The reason for using these parameter values for this linear congruential generator is that the random numbers could be drawn quickly using special features of some computer hardware. IBM corrected it and Randu is not used anymore.

Simple, linear, and multiplicative congruential often have short periods, why it may be advantageous to multiple connect linear congruential generators.

Lagged Fibonacci generators

Another kind of generators is defined by the Fibonacci type of generators. This class of random number generator is aimed at being an improvement on the linear congruential generator discussed earlier.

By choosing $n = 2$, $a_1 = a_2 = 1$ and $b = 0$, the Fibonacci generator results originally with $y_i = (y_{i-1} + y_{i-2}) \bmod m$.

Lagged Fibonacci generators are given by $y_i = (y_{i-r} \otimes y_{i-s}) \bmod m$

where $s < r$ and $\otimes$ an arithmetic operation from $+, -, *$ or the *or*-operator $\oplus$.

An example for a lagged Fibonacci generator is $y_i = (y_{i-55} - y_{i-24})$, also known as RAN3.

More generators

Of course, there exists more advanced methods than the pseudo random generators discussed earlier. The good news is that they are ready-to-use; the bad news is that they are often very complex, and it is out of scope of this book to explain them. In the following examples, we look at applications of these methods using R.

The default random number of R is the Mersenne Twister algorithm (Matsumoto and Nishimura 1998). This generator ensures uniform distribution in 624 dimensions. This can be seen by typing:

```
RNGkind()
## [1] "Mersenne-Twister" "Inversion"
```

One realizes that the Mersenne Twister algorithm is the default in R. In addition, the inversion method (see next section) uses the inversion method to transfer values from uniform to a normal distribution. In *Figure 4.4*, random numbers from this choice are shown on the left-hand side graphics, while the results with the Super-Duper algorithm (Reed, Hubert, and Abrahams, 1982) and the Box-Muller method (Box and Muller, 1958) are shown on the right:

```
ok <- RNGkind()
op <- par(mfrow=c(1,2), mar=c(3,4,2,2))
set.seed(111)
```

```
hist(rnorm(1000), main="Mersenne Twister, Inversion", freq=FALSE,
xlim=c(-4,4), ylim=c(0,0.43), cex.main=0.7)
```

```
curve(dnorm(x), col = 2, lty = 1, lwd = 2, add = TRUE)
```

```
RNGkind("Super", "Box-Muller")
```

```
RNGkind()
```

```
## [1] "Super-Duper" "Box-Muller"
```

```
hist(rnorm(1000), main="Super-Duper, Box-Muller", freq=FALSE,
xlim=c(-4,4), ylim=c(0,0.43), cex.main=0.7)
```

```
curve(dnorm(x), col = 2, lty = 1, lwd = 2, add = TRUE)
```

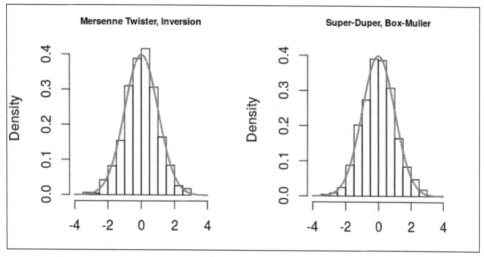

Figure 4.4: Random numbers once drawn with Mersenne Twister and the inversion method (left) and once drawn with the Super-Duper and transferred to standard normal distribution with the Box-Muller method

However, many more generators can be used even in base-level R.

When generating random numbers, we can immediately also think of random walks as an example. For this example, 200,000 random numbers are generated and stored in a matrix of a 100,000 observations and 2 columns.

On a random walk, it is assumed that a drunken man who is too drunk to even exhibit a sense of direction will come back to the pub that he left, and also that he can find the way to his apartment whenever can he still manage to walk. We also assume that he is in good physical shape so that he can walk very, very long (an infinite distance). In order to gain some assurance that the drunkard finds his way home after every pub visit, we repeat this 50 times, resulting in 50 tracks (the tracks go from black to light grey).

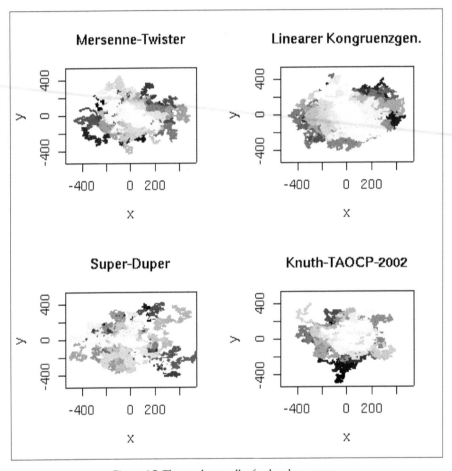

Figure 4.5: The random walk of a drunken person

Simulation of non-uniform distributed random variables

So far, the simulation of the same random variable was discussed. In fact, the generation of uniform random numbers is a very important step. The methods for generating non-uniform random numbers are different. The main aim is to transform random numbers from a uniform distribution to another distribution. Generally, a uniformly distributed random variable, can accordingly be transformed and modified to obtain other distributions.

The inversion method

The condition is that uniformly distributed random numbers are already generated in the interval [0,1]. The inversion method takes advantage of the fact that a distribution function is also defined in the interval [0,1].

Let $F_V(x)$ be the distribution function of V. Through the plug-in of a uniform random number $g \sim U(0,1)$ into the inverse distribution function $F_V^{-1}(g)$, we get a random number with the distribution V.

A prerequisite for the application of an inversion process is therefore the existence of the analytic form of the inverse function, or at least of an approximation of the inverse function. If approximated, the quality of random numbers depends heavily on how well the inverse function can be approximated.

Let X be a continuous random variable with the distribution function $F(x)$. Generally meant for a p quantile of the distribution function $F: F^{-1}(p) = \min\{x|F(x) \geq p\}$.

Let U be a uniformly distributed random variable on the interval [0,1]. Then $X := F^{-1}(U)$ has the wanted distribution with the distribution function F (x). We don't give the proof for this *theorem*, but refer to any classical book on mathematical statistics, all of which include this proof.

Let's get into practice and start with a very simple discrete distribution: the Bernoulli distribution. From random numbers following a uniform distribution, it is very simple to transfer them to a Bernoulli distribution $(X \sim \mathcal{B}(\pi))$ that is determined by one parameter π. Using R, this could look like ($\pi = 0.2$):

```
u <- runif(100, 0, 1)
ifelse(u <= 0.2, 0, 1)
##   [1] 1 0 0 0 1 1 1 1 1 1 1 1 1 1 1 1 1 1 1 1 1 1 1 1 1 1 1 1 0 1 1 1 1 1
1 1 1
```

```
##   [36] 0 1 1 1 1 1 1 0 0 1 1 1 1 1 1 0 1 1 0 1 1 1 1 1 1 0 0 0 1 0 1
1 0 0
##   [71] 1 1 1 0 1 1 0 1 1 1 1 1 1 1 1 1 1 1 0 1 1 1 0 1 1 1 1 1 1 1
```

How can we show this graphically? In the following figure, we see that a random number equal to **0.554** was drawn from U(0,1). Since it is larger than **0.2**, it is projected to be **1**:

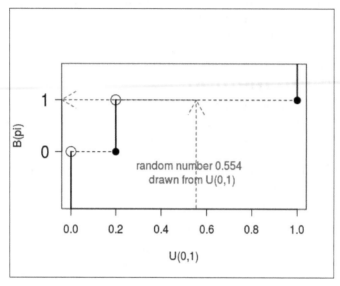

Figure 4.6: From uniform U(0,1) to Bernoulli $B(\pi = 2)$ distributions. $F^{-1}(U)$ equals 0 for uniform random numbers smaller than 0.2, otherwise they are 1

The following example shows the generation of continuous distribution — the exponential distribution.

The distribution of the exponential is given by $F(x) = 1 - e^{-\lambda x}$ with $\lambda > 0$. $F^{-1}(u)$, which is now determined as follows:

$$u = 1 - e^{-\lambda x} \Leftrightarrow e^{-\lambda x} = 1 - u \Leftrightarrow -\lambda x = \log(1 - u) \Leftrightarrow x = -\frac{1}{\lambda}\log(1 - u)$$

Because of $U \sim \mathcal{U}(0,1) \Leftrightarrow 1 - U \sim \mathcal{U}(0,1)$ the following holds $X = -\frac{1}{\lambda}\log(U)$ with distribution F(X).

Graphically this looks like the following screenshot:

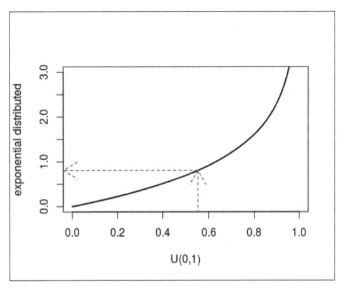

Figure 4.7: Transforming random numbers from a uniform distribution to an exponential distribution

From *Figure 4.7*, it is easily visible that the exponential distribution must be right-skewed since most values will be small in this example. For the same value (**0.554**) as the one drawn in the previous example, the resulting projected value is approx. `0.807`.

Let's switch to R. With the inversion method and the function `runif()`, we can simulate exponentially distributed random numbers using the inverse exponential function. The resulting figure (*Figure 4.8*) shows the simulated exponential distributions with a different parameter, λ:

```
library("MASS")
invExp <- function(n, lambda = 1) {
  u <- runif(n)
  x <- -(1/lambda) * log(u)
  return(x)
}
lambda <- c(0.5, 1, 2, 5)
par(mar = c(3,3,3,0), mfrow = c(2, 2))
for (l in lambda) {
  sample <- invExp(10000, l)
```

```
truehist(sample, nbins = 20, col = "limegreen",
         main = paste("lambda =", 1), xlab = "")
curve(dexp(x, 1), from = 1e-10, add = TRUE)
}
```

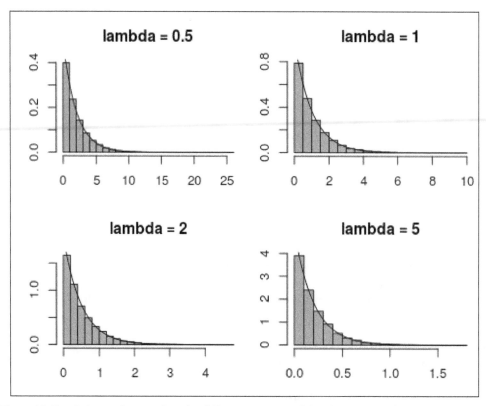

Figure 4.8: Simulating random numbers that follow an exponential distribution using the inversion method

We also see that the inversion method is very easy to apply as soon as the inverse distribution function is known. However, $F^{-1}(u)$ is often analytically difficult or impossible to compute. Even the inverse of the normal distribution is not known exactly and has to be approximated. Approximation is often done by fitting polynomials. For other distributions, such as the Beta distribution, other methods are generally used — such as the rejection methods that is explained afterwards.

The alias method

This method allows one to simulate categorical variables.

Maybe you often used the function `sample` in R to simulate discrete random numbers with given probabilities? Following is an example:

```
sample(1:3, 10, replace = TRUE, prob = c(3/7,1/7,3/7))
##  [1] 3 3 1 3 1 3 1 3 3 3
```

But how such an algorithm may work behind the very important `sample` function?

Basically, the alias method (Walker 1977) can be used to simulate discrete (univariate) random numbers with a given probability function $P(X = x_i) = p_i$, $1 \le i \le n$.

The basic rule is that the random numbers are drawn *from* a rectangle, where the height of the rectangle is $\frac{1}{n}$, and the width is given by n, with n being the number of different categories.

Let's visualize (see *Figure 4.9*, on the left-hand side) our previous example where we simulated discrete values from 1 to 3 with probabilities the being 3/7, 1/3, and 3/7. A so-called *setup* method is used to rearrange this bar chart into a rectangle. The good news is that this is always be possible:

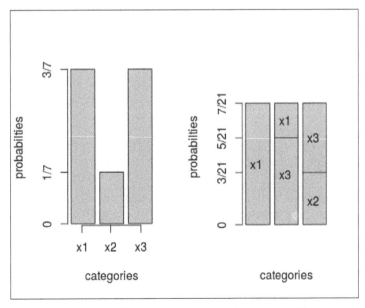

Figure 4.9: On the left are the probabilities for the three categories. On the right is the transformation to a rectangular format

So, for our example, the three probabilities must be rearranged to form a rectangular format.

For the rectangular representation in *Figure 4.9*, we see that in the *x* axis' direction, two categories are represented twice. For example, in the second bin, x_1 and x_3 are stacked together. The alternative value (here it is x_3) of a region is called the alias value.

We illustrate the corresponding alias values in the following table:

i	xi	pi	ai	ri
1	x1	3/7	x1	1
2	x3	3/7	x1	5/7
3	x2	1/7	x3	3/7

To generate the random numbers, the following algorithm will be used:

- Simulate two random numbers u_1 and u_2 independently drawn from $U \sim U(0,1)$

- Set $z = \lceil nu_1 \rceil$

- If $u_2 \leq r_z$ return x_z, otherwise return a_z

Coming back to our example, this means that we first draw a random number from $U(0,1)$. Imagine this is 0.1. We calculate $z = \lceil 3 \cdot 0.1 \rceil = 1 \rightarrow$ we are in the first bin and choose x_1. Imagine that the next number drawn from $U(0,1)$ is 0.5. Then, $z = 2$. We then have to draw another random number, u_2 from $U(0,1)$; imagine this is 0.2. Since $0.2 \leq r_i = 5/7$, we choose u_2.

The alias method was shown on a very simple example, but it is a straightforward process to apply the alias method to simulate discrete values with more categories.

Estimation of counts in tables with log-linear models

Simulating the values of a table is needed for constructing advanced independence tests (if the cell values of a table are independent to each other) or if only margins are available but the (expected) cell values are needed.

Let's focus on a practical example of independence tests. We use the following tabulated values containing counts for the 24-hour precipitation for a season at the rain-gauge:

	Spring	Summer	Autumn	Winter	Sum
30	275	302	357	198	1132
60	56	20	43	37	156
125	52	29	53	44	178
250	65	17	52	69	203
500	37	15	54	58	164
1000	23	5	50	42	120
Sum	508	388	609	448	1953

For example, for the Pearson χ^2-test of independence, expected cell counts are estimated, typically by multiplying the margins and dividing by the total counts. For the first cell value, the expected value would be $\frac{1132 \cdot 508}{1953} = 294.45$.

However, the cell values can also be estimated using log-linear models. This is not only useful in the case of independence tests, but also for other applications to estimate frequencies, for example, in the research area of statistical disclosure control, whereas small estimated frequencies violate laws on privacy.

Using log-linear models to estimate the cell values (frequencies), it is important to assume a certain distribution assumption of counts. Generally, the assumption that the underlying distribution of cell counts is a Poisson distribution is well accepted.

The focus is on the cell probabilities. These cell probabilities can be modeled with a logit link function in a regression model:

$$\text{logit} p = \log o = \log \frac{p}{1-p} = \beta_0 + \beta_1 x_1 + \beta_2 x_2 + \cdots + \beta_k x_k$$

With k as the number of cell values. o is for *odds*.

Exposing this formula leads to the following:

$$e^{\text{logit} p} = o = \frac{p}{1-p} = e^{\beta_0 + \beta_1 x_1 + \beta_2 x_2 + \cdots + \beta_k x_k} = e^{\beta_0} e^{\beta_1 x_1} e^{\beta_2 x_2} \ldots e^{\beta_k x_k}$$

The inverse of the logit function is called logistic function. If logit $(\pi) = z$, then $\pi = \frac{e^z}{1+e^z}$

Let's take hands dirty in R on an example using our two-dimensional table with precipitations:

```
x <- data.frame("spring" = c(275,56,52,65,37,23),
                       "summer" = c(302,20,29,17,15,5),
                       "autumn" = c(375,43,53,52,54,50),
                       "winter" = c(198,37,44,69,58,42))
```

The following cell values are estimated with a log-linear model:

```
xx <- expand.grid(rownames(x), colnames(x)) # all combinations
x1 <- xx[,1]
x2 <- xx[,2]
y <- as.vector(t(prop.table(x))) # cell probabilites
form <- y ~ x1:x2  # modell
mod <- glm(form, family="poisson") # estimation
pred <- (predict(mod))  # prediction
pred <- exp(pred)/(1+exp(pred))  # transf. with logistic function
round(matrix(pred, ncol=4, byrow=TRUE) * sum(x)) # table
##        [,1] [,2] [,3] [,4]
## [1,]   241  262  302  180
## [2,]    54   20   42   36
## [3,]    51   29   52   43
## [4,]    63   17   51   67
## [5,]    36   15   53   56
## [6,]    23    5   49   41
```

These expected values can now be inputted to an $(\pi) = z$ test of independence.

Rejection sampling

How to simulate random numbers from a normal distribution when we don't know the inverse of the normal distribution? How to simulate random numbers from a Beta distribution? How to generally simulate random numbers from a distribution where we know the density function?

The answer is to use rejection sampling: a very intuitive and simple (but very powerful) method to simulate random numbers from almost any distribution.

The rejection method is based on densities rather than distribution functions as used with the inversion method. The basis is drawing numbers from an easy-to-simulate distribution and accepting them based on a certain acceptance criteria (or rejecting them based on a rejection criteria).

If random numbers with the density function $f(x)$ are generated, and there is another density function (proposal density) $h(x)$ with $g(x) = ah(x) \geq f(x)$, then the following algorithm simulates random numbers with the density $f(x)$:

1. Generate the independently random variables $z_i \sim h$ and $u_i \sim U(0,1)$.

2. If $u_i \leq \dfrac{f(z_i)}{g(z_i)} = \alpha(z_i)$ accept and put $x_i = z_i$.

3. Otherwise, discard and go 1.

This general concept is now shown in action, first by simulating values from a normal distribution.

Simulating values from a normal distribution

As a first example, we simulate random numbers from a normal distribution using rejection sampling.

As proposal distribution (the easy-to-simulate values distribution), the Cauchy distribution is taken. For the Cauchy distribution, the inverse of the distribution function can be analytically expressed without any approximations.

We want to simulate random numbers from $N(0,1)$. The density of the standard normal distribution is, $f(x) = \dfrac{1}{\sqrt{2\pi}} e^{-\frac{1}{2}x^2}$ and from the Cauchy distribution $h(x) = \dfrac{1}{\pi} \cdot \dfrac{1}{1+x^2}$.

One can show the following

$$a = \sup_{x \in \mathbb{R}} \frac{f(x)}{h(x)} = \sqrt{\frac{2\pi}{e}} \approx 1.52$$

The acceptance probability is given by the following:

$$\alpha(z) = \frac{f(z)}{a \cdot h(z)} = \frac{\dfrac{1}{\sqrt{2\pi}} e^{-\frac{1}{2}z^2}}{\sqrt{\dfrac{2\pi}{e}} \dfrac{1}{\pi} \dfrac{1}{1+z^2}} = \frac{\sqrt{e}}{2}(1 + z^2) e^{-\frac{1}{2}z^2}$$

For illustration, the theoretical values of a Cauchy and a normal distribution are calculated:

```
x <- seq(-5, 5, length = 200)
dc <- dcauchy(x, location = 0, scale = 1)
dn <- dnorm(x, mean = 0, sd = 1)
```

The comparison of the two densities by plotting their estimated densities is done with the following code snippet. The output is presented in *Figure 4.10*:

```
par(mfrow=c(1,2))
plot(x, dn, type="l")
lines(x, dc, col="blue", lty=2)
legend("topright", col=c("black", "blue"), lty=c(1,2), legend =
c("normal", "Cauchy"), cex=0.5)
plot(x, dn/dc, type="l")
```

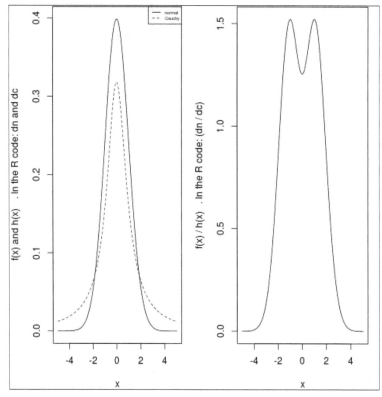

Figure 4.10: On the left are the densities of the standard normal and standard Cauchy distributions. The Cauchy distribution is broader, but it doesn't fully cover the normal distribution (since for any density f(x) = 1 holds). On the right are the ratios between the normal and Cauchy densities. The highest ratio is around 1 is to 1

The optimal choice for parameter a is determined next. The optimal choice is the minimal value where a·h(x) fully covers f(x) for any x:

```
foo <- function(x) dnorm(x)/dcauchy(x)
opt <- optimize(foo, c(0, 4), maximum=TRUE)
a <- opt$objective
a
## [1] 1.520347
ah <- a * dc
```

The densities of the Cauchy distribution as well as the normal distribution are both below a·h(x) for any x and h(x); see *Figure 4.11*:

```
plot(x, dn, type="l", ylim=c(0,0.5), lwd=2)
lines(x, dc, col="blue", lty=2)
lines(x, ah, col="blue", lty=2, lwd=2)
legend("topright", col=c("black", "blue", "blue"), lty=c(1,2,2),
lwd=c(1,1,2), legend = c("normal", "Cauchy", "a * Cauchy"), cex=0.5)
```

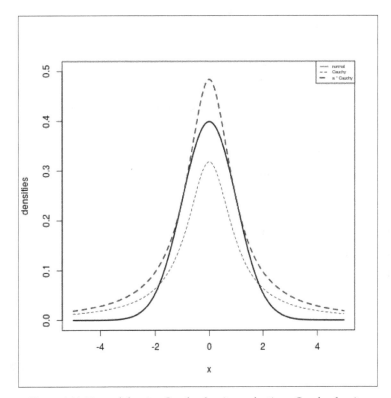

Figure 4.11: Normal density, Cauchy density, and a times Cauchy density

The difference between a·h(x) is illustrated as follows:

```
plot(x, dn, type="l", ylim=c(0,0.5), lwd=2)
polygon(x, dn, col="gray")
polygon(c(x, rev(x)), c(dn, rev(ah)), col="blue")
```

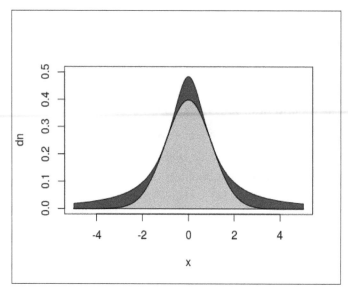

Figure 4.12: Differences between and

The acceptance probability can be written as a function, as well as the rejection sampling:

```
alpha <- function(x){
    dnorm(x)/(1.520347 * dcauchy(x))
}


rejectionNorm <- function(n) {
    x <- rcauchy(10000,0,1)
    u <- runif(10000)
    return(na.omit(ifelse(u <= alpha(x), x, NA)))
}
```

We can now simulate random numbers from a normal distribution using rejection sampling, and we show the corresponding empirical distribution by a histogram, and we also show the theoretical density curve; take a look at *Figure 4.13*:

```
set.seed(123)

x <- rejectionNorm(10000)

hist(x, prob=TRUE)

curve(dnorm(x), lty = 1, lwd = 2, add = TRUE)
```

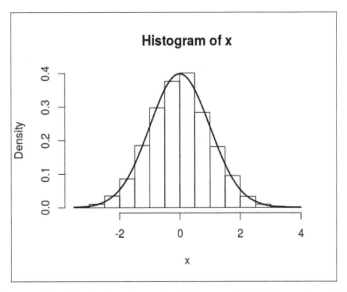

Figure 4.13: A histogram of simulated values from a standard normal distribution using rejection sampling. The curve shows the theoretical density

Simulating random numbers from a Beta distribution

We already showed how to use the rejection method for simulating normally distributed values. But, how does this work for other distributions? The answer is easy: the same as before. We use a proposal distribution where two issues should be fulfilled:

- The acceptance probability should be high. Note that this issue is not as important as it was in earlier since considerable good results can often be produced with a low acceptance rate, and simulating random numbers from a proposal distribution is often not time consuming.

- The proposal density times s should cover the whole range of f(x).

Let $Z \sim \text{Beta}(2,2)$ be a random variable with density $f(z) = 6z(1 - z)$ in $[0,1]$v.

As proposal density, we can (always) use a $U(0,1)$ distribution, as the following figure shows:

```
curve(dbeta(x, shape1 = 2, shape2 = 2), from = 0, to = 1,
  xlab = "", ylab = "", main = "")
## a * h(x):
abline(h = 1.5, lty = 2)
```

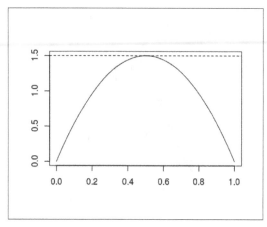

Figure 4.14: f(x) (Beta(2,2) distribution) (solid line) and a·h(x) (uniform distribution times a) (dashed line)

If Z Beta(2,2) is distributed with density $f(x)$, and U is uniformly distributed on $[0,1]$ with density $h(x)$, then $f(z) = 6z(1-z) \leq \frac{3}{2}h(z) = \frac{3}{2} =: g(z)$.

The acceptance probability is given by $\alpha(z) = \frac{f(z)}{g(z)} = 6z(1-z)\frac{2}{3} = 4z(1-z)$:

```
rsBeta <- function(n) {
  z <- runif(n)
  u <- runif(n)
  ind <- (u <= 4 * z * (1 - z))
  return(z[ind])
}
set.seed(123)
sample1 <- rsBeta(10000)
acceptS <- length(sample1) / 10000
acceptS
## [1] 0.6716
```

Let's plot this, we define a function for it:

```
library(MASS)
plot1 <- function(s, shape1=2, shape2=2){
  truehist(s, h = 0.1, xlim = c(0, 1), #ylim = c(0,2),
          col="white", main = "", xlab = "")
  curve(dbeta(x, shape1 = shape1, shape2 = shape2),
        from = 0, to = 1, add = TRUE)
  d <- density(s, from = 0, to = 1, adjust = 2,
              kernel = "gaussian")
  lines(d$x, d$y, lty = 2)
  legend("topright",
        legend = c("true density", "density of simulated values"),
        col = c(1, 1), lty = c(1, 2), cex = 0.6)
}
```

This produces the results shown in *Figure 4.15*, showing our results from simulating values of a *Beta(2,2)* using the rejection sampling approach:

```
plot1(sample1) # produces a histogram and curve, shown below:
```

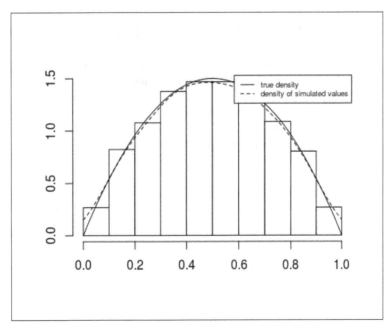

Figure 4.15: A histogram of simulated values from a Beta(2,2) distribution using rejection sampling

In the previous example, we also see that the acceptance rate is not as bad; we even took the easiest proposal distribution.

We can extend the previous example by simulating random numbers from a distribution in an arbitrary interval. For this purpose, it is necessary to calculate the upper bound a. For $\alpha = 2.5$ and $\beta = 6.5$, the following code does the job:

```
rsBeta2 <- function(n, shape1=2.5, shape2=6.5){
    a <- optimize(f=function(x){dbeta(x,shape1,shape2)},
            interval=c(0,1), maximum=TRUE)$objective
    z <- runif(n)
    u <- runif(n, max=a)
    ind <- (u <= dbeta(z,shape1,shape2))
    return(z[ind])
}
sample2 <- rsBeta2(10000)
```

Truncated distributions

We are coming back to the case where the inverse distribution function is known or can be approximated.

To generate random numbers within an interval [a,b], all numbers outside this interval are discarded using a rejection method. But this can be very inefficient when the interval is small in comparison to the whole range of values that must be accepted or rejected. So, how to avoid rejection values but simulate only values in such an interval?

Faster as rejection here is the inversion method. Let $X \sim F$ and Y the distribution of restricted to an interval [a,b]. Then, for the distribution function G of Y it is as follows:

$$
G(y) = \begin{cases} 0, & y < a \\ \dfrac{F(y) - F(a)}{F(b) - F(a)}, & a \le y < b \\ 1, & y \ge b \end{cases}
$$

$Y = F^{-1}(F(a) + U(F(b) - F(a)))$ is therefore a random number with the distribution function G(y).

As an example, we look at the Cauchy distribution. We only wanted values in an interval [4,5]. With the rejection method, we would reject this percentage of values, and to simulate 10 values in this interval, we could do this:

```
# percentage of rejection
(1- (pcauchy(5) - pcauchy(4))) * 100
## [1] 98.48538
v <- rcauchy(1000)
v <- v[v >= 4 & v <= 5]
v
##  [1] 4.598988 4.117381 4.902618 4.933402 4.453769 4.630756 4.693866
##  [8] 4.785372 4.768864 4.274614 4.471191 4.340737 4.641484 4.059680
## [15] 4.639054 4.135258
v[1:10]
##  [1] 4.598988 4.117381 4.902618 4.933402 4.453769 4.630756 4.693866
##  [8] 4.785372 4.768864 4.274614
```

Using the inversion method, this becomes what is displayed next:

```
Fa <- pcauchy(4)
Fb <- pcauchy(5)
u <- runif(10, min = 0, max = Fb - Fa)
qcauchy(Fa + u)
##  [1] 4.575576 4.607166 4.717217 4.151208 4.672747 4.582442 4.914843
##  [8] 4.774956 4.962344 4.038282
```

This saves a considerable amount of computation time, especially for large scale simulations.

Metropolis - Hastings algorithm

Almost all of the previously discussed methods worked with either inversion (if the inverse of the distribution function is known or determined by numerical integration) or rejection sampling. These methods have in common that i.i.d. random numbers are simulated.

The main goal is, as in the previously discussed methods, to simulate random numbers from a theoretical distribution. With the **Markov chain Monte Carlo (MCMC)** methods, we cannot simulate i.i.d random numbers but correlated variables of a Markov chain. The violation of the i.i.d. assumption is often taken into account to solve more difficult problems. Next, the most common method for MCMC sampling is discussed — the Metropolis-Hastings algorithm.

A few words on Markov chains

Some basic notation and theory about Markov chains are useful to understand the next sections on all kinds of Metropolis Hastings and Gibbs samplers.

A Markov chain $\{x^{(t)}\}$ is a sequence of dependent random variables $X^{(0)}, X^{(1)}, X^{(2)}, ..., X^{(t)}$, where the probability distribution of $\{x^{(t)}\}$ given $X^{(0)}, ..., X^{(t-1)}$ only depends on the previous state $X^{(t-1)}$. The conditional probability is called the transition kernel or Markov kernel K: $X^{(t+1)}|X^{(0)}, X^{(1)}, X^{(2)}, ..., X^{(t)} \sim K(X^{(t)}, X^{(t+1)})$.

For example, for a simple random walk Markov chain, the following applies:

$X^{(t+1)} = X^{(t)} + \epsilon_t$ with independently of $X^{(t)}$.

```
## Simple random walk Markov chain:
n <- 10; set.seed(123)
x <- numeric(n)
for(i in 2:n){
  x[i] <- x[i-1] + rnorm(1)
}
x
##  [1]  0.0000000 -0.1488433 -0.2237392  0.4429488  0.3460754  2.4281334
##  [7]  2.2873937  3.4153892  2.2176013  3.1395324
```

The Markov kernel $K(X^{(t)}, X^{(t+1)})$ corresponds here to a $N(X^{(t)}, 1)$ density, and thus the following code is equivalent to the previous lines:

```
set.seed(123)
x <- numeric(n)
for(i in 2:n){
  x[i] <- rnorm(1, mean = x[i-1])
}
x
##  [1]  0.0000000 -0.1488433 -0.2237392  0.4429488  0.3460754  2.4281334
##  [7]  2.2873937  3.4153892  2.2176013  3.1395324
```

A Markov kernel can always be formulated. From the previous example, we see that the representation with a Markov kernel is equivalent to an out defined Markov chain. We also can observe that the next state (value) only depends on the previous state (value).

A stationary stochastic process is given when a probability function exists with the following condition: if $X^{(t)} \sim f$, then $X^{(t+1)} \sim f$.

From the existence of a stationary process it follows that, independently from the starting value, a sample from the stationary distribution is generated as long as the period is long enough. Later this will be noted as the burn-in phase–the MCMC needs a certain amount of *time* to produce values from a stationary distribution, thus the first values belonging to the burn-in phase will be deleted. More details on this burn-in phase will follow later.

Also, each "region" can be achieved with positive probability for the defined region. And with an infinite imaginary Markov chain, one can get to any point again (recurrence). Compare our example in the first section of this chapter with the drunken person that goes home from the pub. He will come back to the pub with positive probability.

Furthermore, the limit distribution of $X^{(t)}$ is f (ergodicity). This property has far-reaching consequences. Be K a Markov chain that produces an ergodic Markov chain with stationary distribution. Then, for an integrate function h holds in *average*:

$$\frac{1}{T}\sum_{t=1}^{T} h\left(X^{(t)}\right) \rightarrow \mathbb{E}_f[h(X)]$$

What is the meaning that the law of large numbers and for MCMC methods is applicable (ergodic theorem). This also means that one chain may not converge with the expected value $\mathbb{E}_f[h(X)]$, but when repeating over and over (generating independently a series of Markov chains) the law of large numbers holds. This is equivalent to the standard theory.

From now on, we will no longer continue with the theory of convergence of MCMC methods but will take this result from the literature: as long as the recurrence of a chain is given, the MCMC converges. The question later on is just how fast the MCMC will converge. In other words, an MCMC often takes a long time to converge, so it is always necessary to evaluate the convergence speed.

As for rejection sampling, the aim of the next method is to find a way to generate samples from a target density f. However, as mentioned earlier, MCMC methods have a disadvantage: the i.i.d assumption is violated since the next simulated value always depends on the previous value. In other words, the samples are correlated. In addition, over a long time, the simulated values do not follow the wanted distribution, that is, the initial samples may follow a very different distribution. This is especially true if the algorithm's starting point is in a region of low density. Therefore, a burn-in period is necessary, where an initial number of samples are thrown away (often the first 1000 or so).

So, why do we want to use such methods as the Metropolis-Hastings method described next?

It is because most simple rejection sampling methods suffer from the "curse of dimensionality", since the probability of rejection increases exponentially with the number of dimensions. Since Metropolis–Hastings and other MCMC methods do not have this problem to such a degree, they are often the only possible working solution. As a result, MCMC methods are often the only methods that can produce samples for high-dimensional statistical models. Moreover, the Metropolis-Hastings algorithm will, for example, always work even if it is sometimes difficult to set up the algorithm.

Note that auto-correlation can be reduced by thinning the simulated sequence of random numbers. This means that after the burn-in phase, every 10th simulated value or so is kept. However, this also means that a very large number of samples will be needed.

The basic Metropolis-Hastings algorithm was published by Metropolis et al. 1953. The presented version is based on the generalized algorithm by (Hastings 1970).

The algorithm in general is described as follows:

- It must specify to a given state X_t how to generate the next state
- There is a candidate point, Y, generated from a proposal distribution
- If this candidate point is accepted, the --> chain moves to state Y at time $t + 1$ and $X_{t+1} = Y$
- Otherwise, the chain stays in state
- Required conditions are as follows:
    - Irreducibility: a non-zero probability of transitioning (even if it occurs in more than one step) from any state to any other state
    - Positive recurrence: if the expected time till we return is finite
    - Aperiodicity

Through a Markov kernel K with station stationary distribution f, a Markov chain $(X^{(t)})$, $t = 0,1,...$ is generated so that the limit distribution of $(X^{(t)})$ is equal to f. The difficulty is in finding a kernel K.

Let f be a density with associated conditional probability density $q(y|x)$, which is easy to simulate in practice. From q, we need only to substantially know that the ratio $f(Y)/q(Y|X)$ is known and $q(.|X)$ has enough variability to cover f.

It always holds: for each conditional density q, a Metropolis-Hasting kernel, with stationary distribution f, can be constructed.

The Metropolis-Hastings algorithm is broken down as follows (also take a look at Robert and Casella 2010):

1. Choose a proposal distribution $q(\cdot |X_t)$

2. Generate x_0 from q and set t = 0

3. Repeat (at least until the chain converges to a stationary distribution):

    1. Draw y from $q(\cdot |x_t)$

    2. Draw $u \sim U(0,1)$

    3. Set:

$$x^{(t+1)} = \begin{cases} y_t & \text{withprobability } \rho(x^{(t)}, y_t) \\ x^{(t)} & \text{withprobability } 1 - \rho(x^{(t)}, y_t) \end{cases}$$

4. With

$$\rho(X, Y) = \min\left\{\frac{f(Y)}{f(X)} \frac{q(X|Y)}{q(Y|X)}, 1\right\}$$

5. $t = t + 1$

Let's look at an example to simulate random numbers from a Rayleigh distribution with the Metropolis-Hastings algorithm (see also Rizzo 2007).

The Rayleigh distribution is used for modeling lifetimes. The density is given by the following:

$$f(x) = \frac{x}{\sigma^2} e^{x^2/(2\sigma^2)}, \quad x \geq 0, \sigma > 0$$

For the proposal distribution, an χ^2 distribution is selected. This distribution is just as skewed as the Rayleigh distribution. In the following list, we show the implementation in the software R, thus we index with 1 (instead of 0). This results in the following sequence:

1. Take for $g(\cdot \,|X_t)$ the density of an $\chi^2(X)$.

2. Generate X_0 from the $\chi^2(1)$, put $t = 1$, and store the result in x[1].

3. Repeat from $i = 2, \dots, N$:

    1. Simulate y from $\chi^2(df = X_t) = \chi^2(df = x[i\text{-}1])$

    2. Draw a random number, $u \sim U(0,1)$

    3. With x[i-1], compute the following:

    4. $r(x_t, y) = \frac{f(y)\ g(x_t|y)}{f(x_t)\ g(y|x_t)}$

    5. where f is the density of the Rayleigh distribution with the parameter σ, $q(Y, X_t)$ of the $\chi^2(df = X_t)$ - density at the point Y evaluated, and $q(X_t, Y)$ the x_t - density at the point x_t evaluated.

    6. If $u \leq r(x_t, y)$ then y is accepted and $X_{t+1} = y$ is set; otherwise $X_{t+1} = X_t$ applies. We save X_{t+1} in x[i]

    7. $t = t + 1$

Furthermore, it holds (Rizzo 2007):

$$r(x_t, y) = \frac{f(y)g(x_t|y)}{f(x_t)g(y|x_t)} = \frac{ye^{-y^2/2\sigma^2}}{x_t e^{-x_t^2/2\sigma^2}} \times \frac{\Gamma(x_t/2)2^{x_t/2}x_t^{y t/2-1}e^{-x_t/2}}{\Gamma(y/2)2^{y/2}y^{x_t/2-1}e^{-y/2}}$$

This formula can be further simplified. In addition, we simplify the example further by analyzing the Rayleigh and the χ^2 densities separately; see also Rizzo 2007. For the Rayleigh (-) density serves the following R code:

```
f <- function(x, sigma){
  if(any(x < 0)) return(0)
  stopifnot(sigma > 0)
  return((x / sigma^2) * exp(-x^2 / (2*sigma^2)))
}
```

In the following simulation, a Rayleigh (4) is sampled by means of the proposal distribution:

```
i <- 2
xt <- x[i-1] <- rchisq(1, 1)
y <- rchisq(1, df=xt)
```

And, for every y, $r(x_{i-1}, y)$ is calculated. We summarize all this in the following function:

```r
rrai <- function(n = 10000, burnin = 1000, thin = 10, sigma = 4, verbose
= TRUE){
  ## raileigh density
  f <- function(x, sigma){
    if(any(x < 0)) return(0)
    stopifnot(sigma > 0)
    return((x / sigma^2) * exp(-x^2 / (2*sigma^2)))
  }
  x <- numeric(n)
  x[1] <- rchisq(1, df=1)
  k <- 0; u <- runif(n)
  for(i in 2:n){
    xt <- x[i-1]
    y <- rchisq(1, df=xt)
    num <- f(y, sigma) * dchisq(xt, df=y)
    den <- f(xt, sigma) * dchisq(y, df=xt)
    if(u[i] <= num/den){
      x[i] <- y
    } else {
      x[i] <- xt
      k <- k + 1 # y is rejected
    }
  }
  if(verbose) cat("acceptance rate:", (k-burnin)/n/thin, "\n")
  ## burn-in:
  if(burnin > 1) x <- x[(burnin+1):length(x)]
  ## thining:
  return(x[seq(1, length(x), thin)])
}

r <- rrai(n = 10000, thin = 1, burnin = 1)
## acceptance rate: 0.4045
r <- rrai(n = 10000, thin = 10, burnin = 1000)
## acceptance rate: 0.02982
length(r)
## [1] 900
```

We see that the acceptance rate is only about 40 percent without thinning and skipping the first values, and about 3 percent with thinning (`thin=10`) and the burn-in phase.

To see the generated sample as a realization of a stochastic process, we can plot it against the index as a polygon line (note that `qplot` is a short for `ggplot`). *Figure 4.16* shows the simulated random numbers (*y-axis*) related to the sequence of generation (index) (*x-axis*):

```
qplot(1:length(r), r, geom="line", xlab="", ylab="random numbers from
Rayleigh(4)")
```

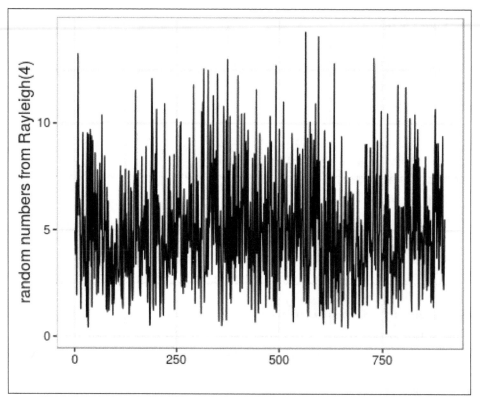

Figure 4.16: Index against simulated random numbers using the Metropolis-Hastings algorithm. The burn-in is excluded and thinning was applied to reduce auto-correlation

The simulated random numbers can be also compared with theoretical quantiles to evaluate whether they follow a Rayleigh distribution. We use the Q-Q plot for this. If the points follow a line, we can expect that our simulated sample is drawn from a Rayleigh distribution. As we see from the following plot (*Figure 4.17*), this should be the case. To generate this figure, theoretical quantiles of the Rayleigh distribution, as well as the empirical quantiles, are calculated and plotted against each other:

```
a <- ppoints(length(r))

sigma <- 4

QR <- sigma * sqrt (-2 * log (1-a)) # quantiles of Rayleigh

Q <- quantile(r, a)

qqplot(QR, Q, main = "", xlab = "Rayleigh quantile", ylab = "sample
quantile")
```

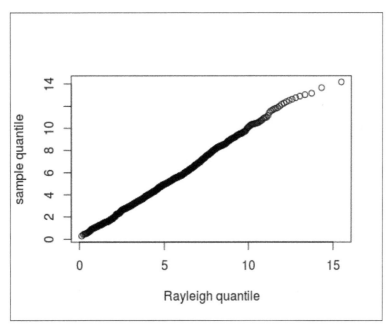

Figure 4.17: The Q-Q plot. Comparing theoretical quantiles of the Rayleigh distribution with the sample quantiles (simulated with the Metropolis-Hastings algorithm)

This example was just to see how a Metropolis-Hastings algorithm works. We choose this example as similar in (Rizzo 2007) just for didactic reasons. Note that it would be much cheaper (in terms of rejection rate) and more advantageous (in terms of i.i.d samples) to use rejection sampling for this purpose.

The Metropolis sampler

The Metropolis sampler is a simpler version of the basic algorithm since it covers the special case of the distribution to generate being symmetric.

If we consider a symmetrical distribution, $q(X|Y) = q(Y|X)$, the acceptance probability only depends on the ratio $f(Y_t)/f(X_t)$.

This gives us the opportunity to explain again the main functionality of the Metropolis-Hastings based on this simplified version.

In the following, we sample a new value, y_t, and decide on the ratio, $\frac{f(y_t)}{f(x_t)}$, if we accept this value or not:

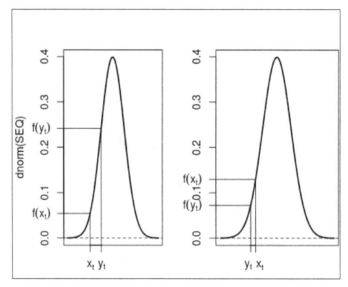

Figure 4.18: A new value, y_t, is simulated from the proposal distribution, and the acceptance probability is calculated by $q(X|Y) = q(Y|X)$. On the left, the new value y_t is accepted with probability 1, since the ratio is larger than 1. On the right, the new value is accepted with $f(yt)/f(xt) = 0.56$.

In the following two examples, we also take in each case a symmetrical distribution.

First, we want to simulate random values from a Beta distribution with the Metropolis-Hastings algorithm (we have done this already with the rejection method). The density that is considered to simulate it again is B(2,2) and B(1,2). A candidate for a proposal density q is (again) U(0,1). This algorithm is implemented in the following code using the `function` parameters n (the number of simulated values), `burnin` (the burn-in phase), `thin` (thinning), `cand` (candidate distribution), `target` (target distribution), `shape1` (shape parameter 1), and `shape2` (shape parameter 2):

```
mh <- function(n=10000, burnin=1000, thin=10, cand=runif,
        target=dbeta, shape1=2, shape2=2){
    if(burnin >= n){
        stop("burnin is larger than the number of simulations")
    }
    x <- rep(cand(1), n) # initialization
    for(i in 2:n){
        y <- cand(1)
        rho <- target(y,shape1,shape2)/
                    target(x[i-1], shape1, shape2)
        x[i] <- x[i-1] + (y - x[i-1]) * (runif(1) < rho)
    }
  # burn-in
    x <- x[(burnin+1):n]
  return(x[seq(1, length(x), thin)])
}
```

The densities of the simulated random numbers from the two Beta distributions are plotted and shown in *Figure 4.19*:

```
par(mfrow=c(1,2))
plot(density(mh()), main = "", xlab = "")
plot(density(mh(shape1=1)), main = "", xlab = "")
```

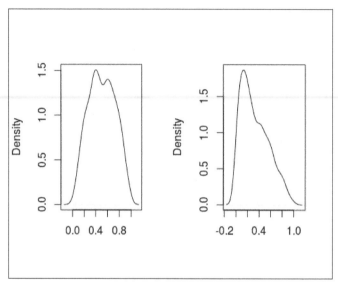

Figure 4.19: Simulated random numbers from a Beta(2,2) and Beta(1,2)

With the previous function, it is now easy to simulate random numbers from other distributions. Let's do it for the Gamma distribution, specially random numbers from G(2,4). A candidate for a density q is N(1,2):

```
rgamma <- mh(cand = rnorm, target = dgamma)
```

All the given examples according to the Metropolis-Hastings algorithm can be easily carried out with rejection sampling, and it should be made with rejection sampling since the disadvantage of non-i.i.d samples is prevented with rejection sampling. We took these two examples to show how a Metropolis-Hastings works.

To implement a Metropolis-Hastings algorithm for more complex problems is difficult, problem-specific and goes beyond this book. For basic reading, refer to (A. Gelman et al. 2013) and (Robert and Casella 2010), and do take a look at problem-specific implementations of the Metropolis-Hastings algorithm.

The Gibbs sampler

The Gibbs sampler also belongs to the class of MCMC methods. Initially, the algorithm named after Gibbs, a physician, was described by (S. Geman and D.Geman 1984). It can be seen as a one-step Metropolis-Hastings algorithm where every value is accepted. The Gibbs sampler can be perfectly used for sampling from a large set of variables/parameters by sampling each variable/parameter in turn.

For motivation, we start with the two-phase Gibbs sampler.

The two-phase Gibbs sampler

Given random variables X and Y with joint distribution $p(X,Y)$ and conditional distribution $p_{Y|X}$ and $p_{X|Y}$.

The two-phase Gibbs sampler to simulate a Markov chain (X_t, Y_t) is as follows:

- Fix X_0
- For $t = 1, 2, ...,$ draw:
    - $y_t \sim p_{Y|X}(\cdot | x_{t-1})$
    - $x_t \sim p_{X|Y}(\cdot | y_{t-1})$

This is assuming that from the conditional distributions, samples can be drawn.

For a bivariate normal distribution, it is as follows: $(X, Y) \sim N_2\left((0,0)^t, \begin{pmatrix} 1 & \rho \\ \rho & 1 \end{pmatrix}\right)$

This is the Gibbs sampler determined for x_t: $\begin{array}{l} y_{t+1}|x_t \sim N(\rho x_t, 1 - \rho^2) \\ x_{t+1}|y_t \sim N(\rho y_{t+1}, 1 - \rho^2) \end{array}$

The following holds (without proof): $X_{t+1}|X_t \sim N(\rho^2 x_t, 1 - \rho^4)$

After recursion $X_{t+1}|X_0 \sim N(\rho^{2t} x_0, 1 - \rho^{4t})$:

and the Markov chain at $t \to \infty$ converges to $N(0,1)$.

Let's write a program for a 2-phase Gibbs sampler to simulate a bivariate normal distribution as described earlier. We select a bad start from a low density region to see the need of the burn-in phase; take a look at the left-hand side graphics in *Figure 4.20*. Note that thinning can be applied to reduce auto-correlation. Auto-correlation is seen in the middle plot of *Figure 4.20* — the next values depends on the previous ones:

```r
gibbs_bivariate <- function(n = 1000, rho = 0.9, start = 0, burnin = 100,
thin = 1){
  x <- y <- numeric(n)
    s <- 1 - rho^2
    x[1] <- start # to show effect of burnin
    for(t in 1:(n-1)){
        y[t+1] <- rnorm(1, rho*x[t], s)
        x[t+1] <- rnorm(1, rho*y[t+1], s)
    }
    s <- seq(burnin+1, n, thin)
    return(cbind(x[s], y[s]))
}
par(mfrow=c(1,3))
set.seed(123)
## bad start:
b0 <- gibbs_bivariate(n=200, start = 30, burnin=0)
## plot the results
plot(b0, type="o", xlab="x", ylab="y", main="burnin 0",
        cex.main=1.3, cex.lab=1.3)
set.seed(123)
plot(b0[20:200,], type="o", xlab="x", ylab="y", main="burnin 20",
        cex.main=1.3, cex.lab=1.3, col=grey(20:200/200))
set.seed(123)
plot(b0[20:200,], pch=20, xlab="x", ylab="y", main="burnin 20",
        cex.main=1.3, cex.lab=1.3)
```

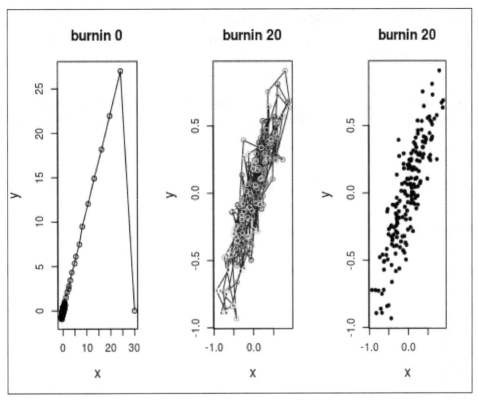

Figure 4.20: Bivariate normal distributed data simulated with a Gibbs sampler. On the left are all the simulated random numbers. In the middle is the after burn-in, showing the autocorrelation of data points. On the right are simulated random numbers after the burn-in

The multiphase Gibbs sampler

To explain the multiphase Gibbs sampler, the following notation is used: Let $\mathbf{X} = (X_1, ..., X_p)$ the X_i's single or multi-dimensional components with corresponding conditional densities $f\_1, \ldots, f_p$, with

$$X_i | x_1, x_2, ..., x_{i-1}, x_{i+1}, ..., x_p \sim f_i(x_i | x_1, x_2, ..., x_{i-1}, x_{i+1})$$

for $i = 1, ..., p$.

For the transition of $X^{(t)}$ to $X^{(t+1)}$, the multiphase Gibbs sampler can be described as follows:

For iteration $t = 1, 2, ...$ given $x^{(t)} = (x_1^{(t)}, ..., x_p^{(t)})$ simulate,

1. $X_1^{(t+1)} \sim f_1(x_1 | x_2^{(t)}, ..., x_p^{(t)})$
2. $X_2^{(t+1)} \sim f_2(x_2 | x_1^{(t)}, x_3^{(t)}, ..., x_p^{(t)})$
3. $X_p^{(t+1)} \sim f_p(x_p | x_1^{(t)}, ..., x_{p-1}^{(t)})$

Application in linear regression

The Gibbs sampler is often used in the context of regression analysis and the fit of regression parameters. A simple example that shows the basic principles of Gibbs sampling in the regression context is shown next.

Let the data pairs, $(x_1, y_1), (x_2, y_2), ..., (x_n, y_n)$ be defined with the following linear dependency $y_i = \alpha + \beta x_i + \epsilon_i$ where α and β are unknown and have to be estimated, and $\epsilon \sim N(0, \sigma^2)$. It is:

$$f(y_i | \alpha, \beta, x_i, \sigma^2) = \frac{1}{\sqrt{2\pi\sigma^2}} \exp\left(\frac{1}{2\sigma^2} (y_i - \alpha - \beta x_i)^2\right)$$

From the likelihood given by:

$$L(\alpha, \beta, \sigma^2) = \prod_{i=1}^{n} f(y_i | \alpha, \beta, x_i, \sigma^2) =$$

$$\prod_{i=1}^{n} \frac{1}{\sqrt{2\pi\sigma^2}} \exp\left(\frac{1}{2\sigma^2} (y_i - \alpha - \beta x_i)^2\right)$$

the following conditional distributions for the estimated parameters results (without proof):

$$\alpha | \beta, \sigma^2, \mathbf{x}, \mathbf{y} \sim N\left(\bar{y} - \beta\bar{x}, \frac{\sigma^2}{n}\right) \quad \beta | \alpha, \sigma^2, \mathbf{x}, \mathbf{y} \sim N\left(\left(\sum_{i=1}^{n} x_i y_i - \alpha n\bar{x}\right) / \sum_{i=1}^{n} x_i^2, \frac{\sigma^2}{\sum_{i=1}^{n} x_i^2}\right)$$

$$\sigma^2 | \alpha, \beta, \mathbf{x}, \mathbf{y} \sim Gamma\left(\frac{4}{(n-1)^2}, \frac{4}{(\sum_{i=1}^{n}(y_i - \alpha - \beta x_i)^2)^2}\right)$$

The code for this simple regression problem is as follows. The parameters `alpha`, `beta`, and `tau` define the starting values:

```
lreg <- function(y, x, time, alpha = 0, beta = -2, tau = 1, burnin = 0,
thin = 1){
    n <- length(y)
    ## alpha, beta, tau defining varibles
    res <- matrix(, ncol=3, nrow=time)
    for(i in 1:time){
        alpha <- rnorm(1, mean(y)   -beta * mean(x), 1 / (n  *tau))
        m <- (sum(x * y) - alpha * n * mean(x)) / sum(x**2)
```

```
        s <- 1 / (tau * sum(x**2))
        beta <- rnorm(1, m, s)
        w <- y - alpha - beta * x
        tau <- rgamma(1, ((n / 2) + 1), (sum(w**2) / 2))
        res[i,] <- c(alpha, beta, tau)
    }
    s <- seq(1, length((burnin + 1):nrow(res)), thin)
    res <- res[((burnin+1):nrow(res))[s], ]
    res <- data.frame(res)
    colnames(res) <- c("alpha", "beta", "tau")
    return(res)
}
```

We took a similar example as in (Robert and Casella 2010) because it is just perfect for didactic reasons. *Figure 4.21* shows the results of the Gibbs sampler for the Cars93 data set from the package MASS. In practice, we would iterate longer than 100, and we skip the burn-in. In addition, we could again apply thinning to reduce the auto-correlation of the parameter estimates. The darker the lines in *Figure 4.21*, the higher the iteration, that is, we start off bad but it soon converges to the solutions drawn in black:

```
data(Cars93, package = "MASS")
set.seed(123)
time <- 100
res <- lreg(Cars93$Price, Cars93$Horsepower, time = time)
par(mar = c(4,4,0.1,0.1))
plot(Cars93$Horsepower, Cars93$Price, pch=20, xlab = "Horsepower", ylab =
"Price", type = "n")
range <- 1 - sqrt(1:time/time)
range <- range + 0.1
#range <- range/sum(2*range)
for(i in 1:time){
    abline(a = res[i, 1], b = res[i, 2], col=gray(range[i]))#sqrt(1-i/
size)))
}
```

```
abline(a = res[i, 1], b = res[i, 2], col="red", lty=2,lwd=3)#sqrt(1-i/
size)))
```

```
points(Cars93$Horsepower, Cars93$Price, pch=20)
```

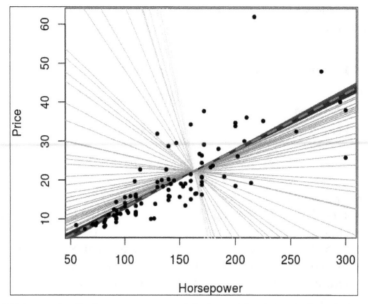

Figure 4.21: Regression fits for t = 1, ... ,100 with bad start. The darker the line, the larger the t.
The dashed line i is the solution after 100 fits

The diagnosis of MCMC samples

Monitoring convergence is important for the following situations:

- When some generated chains have not converged to the target distribution
- When the number of sufficient iterations is unknown
- When the length of the burn-in sample is unknown
- When slow convergences cannot be detected by examining a simple chain

By examining several parallel chains, slow convergence should be more evident
to observe.

In general, the following diagnostics are helpful:

- Plot simulated values against the index 1 to T, T with being the length of the simulated random numbers. This gives an indication about the burn-in time and possible convergence. If the simulated series of random numbers (chain) does not converge, increase the length of the chain, that is, simulate more random numbers.

- Repeat the previous item several times. This gives you more confidence in the burn-in time.

- Make a plot of the auto-correlation using the **autocorrelation function** (ACF). that measures the correlation of the simulated random numbers with the lagged (lag) simulated random numbers. The slow decrease of ACF indicates slow convergence, and high values indicate auto-correlation. This can be used to find independent subsamples. In other words, if auto-correlation is visible, apply thinning of the simulated chain.

- If possible, run the MCMC algorithm with very high T multiple times, independently (for example, 5-20). This gives an indication of convergence.

- For a single indicator of convergence, the Gelman-Rubin method (R. Gelman A. 1992) might be used. This method is based on comparing the behavior of several generated chains with respect to the variance of univariate summary statistics. We need the between (B) and within (W) sequence variance. The between-sequence variance is $B = \frac{1}{k-1}\sum_{i=1}^{k}\sum_{j=1}^{n}(\overline{\phi}_{i.} - \overline{\phi}_{..})^2$, where $\overline{\phi}_{i.} = \frac{1}{n}\sum_{j=1}^{n}\phi_{ij}$ and $\overline{\phi}_{..} = \frac{1}{nk}\sum_{i=1}^{k}\sum_{j=1}^{n}\phi_{ij}$. Within the ith sequence, the sample variance is $s_i^2 = \frac{1}{n}\sum_{j=1}^{n}(\phi_{ij} - \overline{\phi}_{i.})^2$.

- And, the pooled estimate of the within sample variance is as follows:

$$W = \frac{1}{nk-k}\sum_{i=1}^{k}(n-1)s_i^2 = \frac{1}{k}\sum_{i=1}^{k}s_i^2$$

- The between-sequence and within-sequence estimates of variance are combined to estimate an upper bound:

$$\hat{Var}(\phi) = \frac{n-1}{n}W + \frac{1}{n}B$$

- The GB statistic is the estimated potential scale reduction:

$$\sqrt{\hat{R}} = \sqrt{\frac{\hat{Var}(\phi)}{W}}$$

- This measures the factor by which the SD of ϕ could be extending the chain.

- This indicator decreases to 1 as the length of the chain tends to infinity, and it should be close to 1 if the chain has approximately converged to the target distribution.

Let's switch again to R. We've already done some simple diagnostics for random numbers simulated by the bivariate Gibbs sampler as well as for our example in regression. In addition, we will now plot the simulated values against the index (for our regression problem); take a look at *Figure 4.22*. We start again badly for demonstration issues. We observe that a short burn-in phase and fast convergence is indicated. To get more sureness on it, one can rerun this example (using other seeds and other starting values):

```
set.seed(123)
g <- lreg(Cars93$Price, Cars93$Horsepower, time = 500)
g1 <- cbind(g, "index" = 1:nrow(g))
g1 <- reshape2::melt(g1, id=c("index"))
ggplot(g1, aes(x = index, y = value)) + geom_line() + facet_
wrap(~variable, scales = "free_y")
```

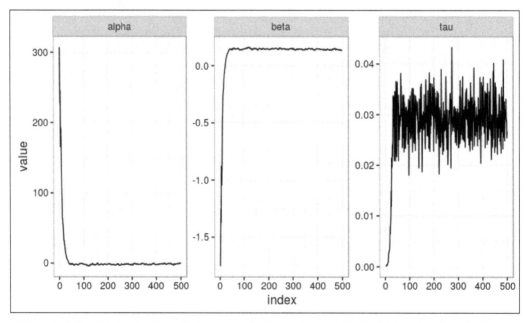

Figure 4.22: Simulated values from the Gibbs sampler (regression with Cars93 data) against the index for all three estimated parameters

We clearly see that the Gibbs sampler suffers from auto-correlation for different lags. To get closer to an i.i.d sample, thinning should be done with a thinning of approximately 15 or larger. This would result in the need to simulate more random numbers (15 times or larger). *Figure 4.23* is produced by plotting the `acf()` result. The ACF plot in the following graph should indicate autocorrelation problems:

```
plot(acf(g))
```

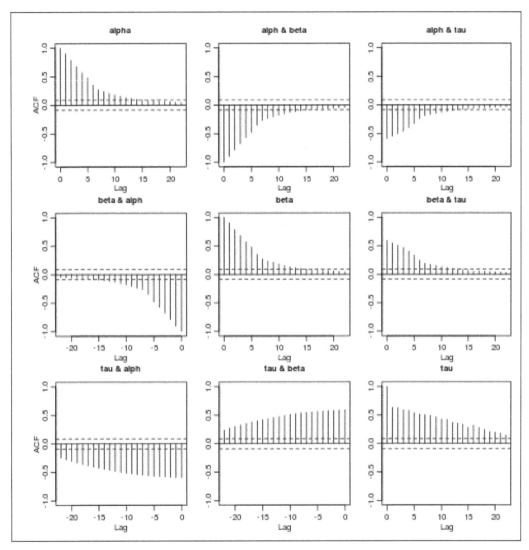

Figure 4.23: The ACF plot for alpha, beta, and tau diagonals, along with combinations of them

Next, we run M chains ($M = 5$ here) with a larger sequence at different starting values. After basic plotting, we convert them to mcmc objects (package coda), since the Gelman-Rubin method as well as the diagnostic plot from Brooks and Gelman (1998) is easy to produce with such objects. We allow relatively bad starts—this is not necessary and a start with rnorm(1, 0, 1) would be better, but we want to see more about the burn-in phase just for demonstration issues:

```
library("coda")
time <- 2000; M <- 5
set.seed(12345)
df <- lreg(Cars93$Price, Cars93$Horsepower, time = time)
for(i in 2:M){
   df <- rbind(df, lreg(Cars93$Price, Cars93$Horsepower, time = time))
}
df$M <- factor(rep(1:M, each = time))
df$index <- rep(1:time, M)
df <- reshape2::melt(df, id = c("M", "index"))
ggplot(df, aes(x = index, y = value, group = M, colour=M)) + geom_
line(alpha = 0.5) + facet_wrap(~variable, scales = "free_y")
```

Figure 4.24 shows the results for all 5 independently drawn chains. The burn-in phase seems to be short:

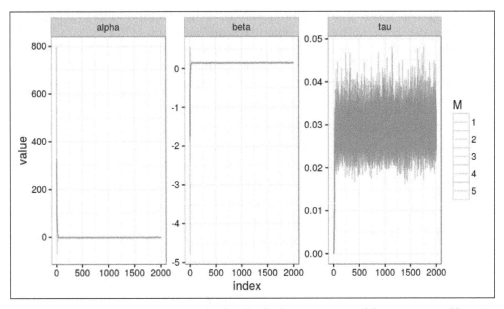

Figure 4.24: Multiple times sampled random values for the three parameters of the regression problem using the Gibbs sampler

```
## Brooke-Gelman
gl <- list()
M <- 15
set.seed(12345)
for(i in 1:M){
  gl[[i]] <- lreg(Cars93$Price, Cars93$Horsepower, time = time)
}
gl <- lapply(gl, function(x) mcmc(as.matrix(x)))
## look also at summary(g)  (not shown here)
gelman.diag(gl, autoburnin = FALSE)

## Potential scale reduction factors:
##
##       Point est. Upper C.I.
## alpha      1.07       1.07
## beta       1.07       1.07
## tau        1.00       1.00
##
## Multivariate psrf
```

The results give us the median potential scale reduction factor and its 97.5 percent quantile. We also get a multivariate potential scale reduction factor that was proposed by (Brooks and Gelman 1998). The function `gelman.plot` shows the evolution of Gelman and Rubin's shrink factor as the number of iterations increases. Note that if `autoburnin` is set to `TRUE`, then the first half of simulated random numbers are removed:

```
gelman.plot(gl, autoburnin = FALSE)
```

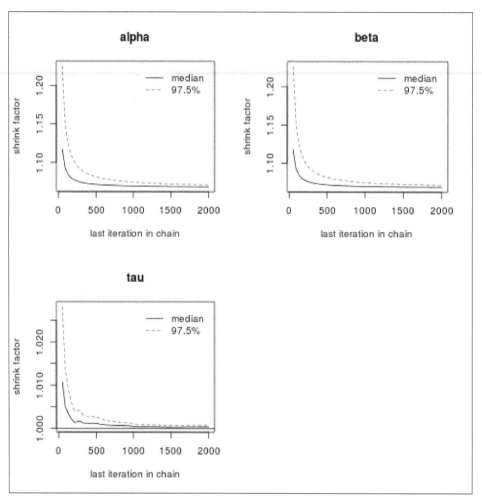

Figure 4.25: The evolution of the shrink factor for increasing the number of iterations

Figure 4.25 shows the `gelman.plot`. We see that the shrink factor converges to almost 1 for larger iterations. This might be an indication that the burn-in should be kept longer.

With all these findings, we can conclude that a good chain would be as follows:

```
burnin <- 1000
time <- burnin + time * 20
g <- lreg(Cars93$Price, Cars93$Horsepower, time = time, burnin = burnin,
thin = 20)
```

Tests for random numbers

In the previous sections of this chapter, random numbers have been simulated with different approaches. Most of the tests for random number generations tests if the basic random number generator, the random number generator that simulates uniformly distributed random numbers, is doing a good job.

We saw already in the beginning of the chapter plots, where we show a sequence of simulated random values against the sequence with lag 1 (and lag 2 for three-dimensional plots).

The random number generators are typically tested on whole test batteries defined by different tests. An original collection of tests can be found at `http://stat.fsu.edu/pub/diehard/`. These are the so-called *DieHard* tests from Marsaglia.

Since the code of Marsaglia is no longer maintained, and there are already more tests available, we refer additionally to the *dieharder* tests at `http://www.phy.duke.edu/~rgb/General/dieharder.php`. A Linux version of the R package `RDieHarder` is available at CRAN.

They include, for example, the birthday spacings test where it is tested if the spaces between points on a large interval are asymptotically, exponentially distributed. The name is based on the birthday paradox. The parking lot test places randomly unit circles in a 100 x 100 square, where a circle is successfully parked if it does not overlap with another circle. Having 12,000 circles generated, the number of successfully parked circles should follow a certain normal distribution. The minimum distance test randomly places 8,000 points in a 10,000 x 10,000 square; the minimum square distance between the pairs should be exponentially distributed with a certain mean. Now short: random spheres test randomly choose points in a cube, build certain spheres and the sphere's volume should be exponentially distributed with a certain mean. The squeeze test outcome should follow a certain distribution. Overlapping test sums should be normally distributed with characteristic mean and variance. Frequency counts on specific intervals should follow a certain distribution., and so on, and so forth.

What almost all tests have in common is that the results should follow a certain distribution, that is, the basic idea of almost all tests is the same.

The null hypothesis is generally as follows:

$$H_0: u_i \overset{i.i.d.}{\sim} U$$

This means that the simulated random numbers should be drawn from a uniform distribution and identical independent distributed.

The evaluation of random numbers – an example of a test

The presented test is a typical test for random number generators. It is based on evaluating the distribution of counts.

For the random numbers generated on a circle with radius 1 (say big_circle), a large number of circles with radius r can be defined. The following function result is a logical vector that indicates if points lay in a circle that is fully within the big_ circle:

```
circle <- function(x, r=0.05){
    repeat{
        x1 <- runif(1,-1,1)
        x2 <- runif(1,-1,1)
        if( sqrt(x1^2 + x2^2) <= (1 - r) ) break
    }
    inCircle <- ((x[,1] - x1)^2 + (x[,2] - x2)^2) <= r^2
    return(inCircle)
}
```

The number of points in the circle should have a Poisson distribution with the mean r^2. Thus, we count for each circle the number of points and create a test for the counts.

The following figure should explain the cutting of circles visually:

```
set.seed(123)
## take possible radii
x <- matrix(runif(10000, -1, 1), ncol=2)
## radii to the square
r2 <- rowSums(x^2)
## r2 smaller than 1 are kept
x1 <- x[r2 <= 1, ]
```

```
par(mar = c(2,2,0.1,0.1))
plot(data.frame(x1), pch=20)
for(k in 1:8) points(data.frame(x1[circle(x1, 0.2),]), col=k, pch=20)
```

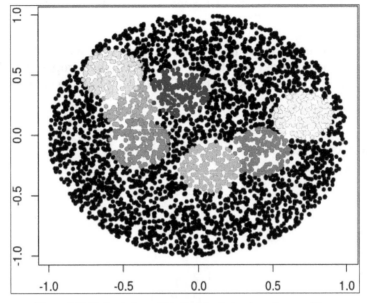

Figure 4.25: Eight circles within the big circle, at random positions

We repeat the cutting of circles 2,000 times and count for each circle the number of points included:

```
set.seed(123)
z <- replicate(2000, sum(circle(x1)))
```

Tabulated, this yields the following values:

```
TAB <- table(z)
TAB
## z
##    2    3    4    5    6    7    8    9   10   11   12   13   14   15   16   17   18
19
##    4   20   40   81  115  190  233  278  253  220  195  152   91   53   43   19   11
2
```

This means that in this simulation, once there was just one observation inside one specific circle. Most circles have around 9 or 10 values included, that is, the mode is 9 and the median count is as follows:

```
laeken::weightedMedian(as.numeric(names(TAB)), as.numeric(TAB))
## [1] 10
```

However, the variance might be high. We now want to test whether extreme events occur by chance. The observed counts may also be visually compared with the theoretical counts of a Poisson distribution. This looks good; see *Figure 4.27*:

```
lambda <- nrow(x1) * 0.05^2
PROB <- dpois(as.numeric(names(TAB)), lambda)
b <- barplot(TAB / length(z))
points(b, PROB, col="red", pch=16)
```

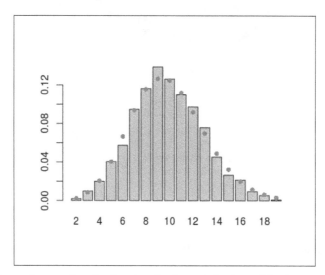

Figure 4.27: The observed counts (bar chart) against the theoretical values of the Poisson distribution (points)

We now want to reduce to 6 classes and assign our simulated values based on these classes:

```
## the five classes:
QP <- qpois(seq(0,1,by=1/6), lambda)
QP
## [1]    0    7    8   10   11   13  Inf
## frequency counts in those classes
TAB1 <- table(cut(z, QP, include.lowest=TRUE))
TAB1
```

```
##
##      [0,7]     (7,8]     (8,10]   (10,11]   (11,13]  (13,Inf]
##       450       233        531      220        347      219
```

Since we do not know the population and have only one sample (our simulation) simulated, we must take the uncertainty into account and apply a statistical test. We use the χ^2 goodness-of-fit test. Next, the theoretical quantiles and the theoretical class widths are calculated, which exactly express the probabilities to fall into the classes:

```
ppois(QP, lambda)
## [1] 5.235307e-05 2.333321e-01 3.490914e-01 6.008619e-01 7.128626e-01
## [6] 8.746304e-01 1.000000e+00
## 0 should be in the left class:
QP1 <- QP
QP1[1] <- -1
## probablities for each class:
PROB1 <- diff(ppois(QP1, lambda))
PROB1
## [1] 0.2333321 0.1157593 0.2517704 0.1120008 0.1617678 0.1253696
## goodness-of-fit test:
chisq.test(TAB1, p=PROB1)
##
##  Chi-squared test for given probabilities
##
## data:  TAB1
## X-squared = 7.8928, df = 5, p-value = 0.1622
```

We are not in the rejection region, and thus the null hypothesis — the number of points in the circles with radius r^2 is Poisson distributed — cannot be rejected. Thus, the Mersenne-Twister random number generator has passed this test.

Summary

Generally, in science, every result should be reproducible, especially in quantitative analysis. This is possible by setting the *seed* of a deterministic pseudo random number generator. Secondly, and also very crucial, is to have a well-working random number generator to simulate random numbers from a uniform distribution. R's default random number generator, the Mersenne-Twister register-based algorithm, works pretty well. Simulated random numbers should possibly not be auto-correlated, and they should have a very long period. Otherwise, results might be biased and not trustable.

Based on uniform random numbers, random numbers from other distributions can be simulated. The important methods are the inversion method and rejection sampling. Especially rejection sampling, which can be broadly used and results in independent identical distributed random numbers.

For very specific tasks, this i.i.d. assumption must be rejected, and other methods are the only way to simulate (multivariate) distributions. We presented variants of the Metropolis-Hastings algorithm: the basic, the independent, and finally, the Gibbs sampler. The rejection rates are lower than for the rejection method (for Gibbs, without thinning and burn-in, the rejection rate is zero). From a long example on regression, the quality of the simulated chain was reported. The final conclusions was that a long burn-in phase along with thinning might be necessary to reduce autocorrelation. This resulted in simulating 61,000 random numbers with the Gibbs sampler, where only 3,000 are kept.

To evaluate a random number generator, one test was presented. It was out of our scope to present further tests. However, almost all tests work on the same scheme. To count or measure something and test if this result follows a certain distribution.

Almost all follow-up chapters must rely on the quality of the random number generators. The methodology in the next chapters (such as resampling methods, Monte-Carlo optimization, or Monte-Carlo tests) use random number generators, and often, random numbers from specific distributions must be simulated.

References

- Box, G.E.P., and M.E. Muller. 1958. "A Note on the Generation of Normal Random Deviates," *Annals of Mathematical Statistics* 29: 610–11.

- Brooks, S.P., and A. Gelman. 1998. "General Methods for Monitoring Convergence of Iterative Simulations," *Journal of Computational and Graphical Statistics* 7 (4): 434–55.

- Gelman, A., J.B. Carlin, H.S. Stern, D.B. Dunson, A. Vehtari, and D.B. Rubin. 2013. *Bayesian Data Analysis, Third Edition.* Chapman & Hall/CRC Texts in Statistical Science. Taylor & Francis.

- Gelman, Rubin, A. 1992. „Inference from Iterative Simulation Using Multiple Sequences," *Statistical Science* 7 (4). *Institute of Mathematical Statistics*: 457–72.

- Geman, S., and D. and Geman. 1984. „Stochastic Relaxation, Gibbs Distributions, and the Bayesian Restoration of Images," *IEEE Trans. Pattern Anal. Mach. Intell* 6 (6): 721–41.

- Hastings, W.K. 1970. „Monte Carlo Sampling Methods Using Markov Chains and Their Applications," *Biometrika* 57 (1): 97–109.

- Knuth, D.E. 1998. *The Art of Computer Programming, Volume 2: Seminumerical Algorithms.* Addison-Weley, third edition.

- Matsumoto, M., and T. Nishimura. 1998. „Mersenne Twister: A 623-Dimensionally Equidistributed Uniform Pseudo-Random Number Generator," *ACM Transactions on Modeling and Computer Simulation* 8 (1): 3–30.

- Metropolis, N., A. W. Rosenbluth, M. N. Rosenbluth, A. H. Teller, and E. Teller. 1953. „Equation of state calculations by fast computing machines," *J. Chem. Phys* 21: 1087–92.

- Reeds, J., S. Hubert, and M. Abrahams. 1982–4AD. *C Implementation of SuperDuper.* University of California at Berkeley.

- Rizzo, M.L. 2007. *Statistical Computing with R.* Chapman & Hall/ CRC the R Series. Taylor & Francis. `http://books.google.at/ books?id=BaHhdqOugjsC`.

- Robert, C., and G. Casella. 2010, *Introducing Monte Carlo Methods with R*, New York: Springer.

- Walker, A.J. 1977. "An Efficient Method for Generating Discrete Random Variables with General Distributions," *ACM Transactions on Mathematical Software* 3 (3): 253–56.

5
Monte Carlo Methods for Optimization Problems

Function optimization was applied in *Chapter 4, Simulation of Random Numbers* to find the maximum of a normal density divided by a Cauchy density as well as to find the extreme of a Beta distribution function. In this chapter, we will concentrate on two-dimensional problems and note that the mentioned methods can be extended to multi-dimensional problems. To convey a feeling of how optimization methods work, we start with a story set in the Austrian Alps.

When I wrote these lines we suddenly had foggy weather in Austria. And I imagined the scenario of a guy from Australia visiting Austria. Note that kangaroos exist only in the zoo in Austria, and that 70 percent of Austria is covered by mountains (part of the Alps). Assume that the Australian guy has no prior information (no maps, no conversations, no guide at all) and he starts to climb the mountains. These mountains represent, in other words, a three-dimensional complex non-concave function. The Australian guy will arrive at Vienna airport but due to the foggy weather today in Austria, he doesn't see much. His aim is to climb to the top of the highest mountain in Austria (3.799 meters), see *Figure 5.1*:

Figure 5.1: Google Maps photo showing the reliefs of the Alps. The position of the highest mountain - the Grossglockner - is visualized by a red marker

What options will he have to find the highest spot?

- **The first strategy (steepest gradient to nowhere)**: The Australian guy follows the steepest direction until he burns 50 calories (measured by his calorie count watch). After this, he again follows the steepest direction at the current point as long as he burns another 50 calories. Using this strategy he will end at a mountain called *Hohe Wand* at the high of 1.132 meters, or even at the next very small hill at around 200 meters high. Surely, he was not very successful with his strategy (optimization method). He is trapped in a local maxima. Most of the simpler traditional optimization methods will end up at this level, and most of the optimization methods work in a similar way. On each point reached, the direction of the steepest path is chosen, and the length of the walk generally depends on the steepness at this point.

- **The second strategy (good first shot but dead)**: He waits until the fog disappears. Then from the airport, the mountain named *Schneeberg* is the highest spot that he is able to see. Of course he will climb the *Schneeberg* (2.076 meters) since he believes that he can reach his goal (maximum) there. When he follows the usual track, he will not detect that *Schneeberg* is far from being the highest mountain of Austria. On top he is so exhausted that he will not look around and he will believe that he was on the highest summit in Austria. He got to a higher level with strategy one, but he was trapped in a local maxima, which is still a nice place, but far from his goal to get to the highest summit of Austria. The optimization methods must somehow be sophisticated (good sight) to reach the summit of the *Schneeberg* by choosing one path/step (usually not possible in the reality of numbers and functions). Typically, by only taking one path/step it is not possible to find a local optima. However, an algorithm may jump out of a local optima, as we will see next.

- **The third strategy (the iron-men wizard)**: The Australian guy might be strong and not exhausted from climbing the *Schneeberg* or any mountains. On the summit of *Schneeberg* he will see that a mountain called *Großer Priel* (2.515 meters) is higher, but on top of this mountain he will become aware that around 70 kilometers away there is an even higher summit, called *Dachstein* (2.995 meters). On *Dachstein*, he is sure that he has reached his goal, because of the curvature of the earth he will not see a higher point, since some mountains almost as high block the sight to much higher mountains in Tirol. He is almost successful in reaching his goal in terms of language: he reached the highest mountain, not of Austria, but of the federal district of Upper Austria. He is again trapped in a local maxima. The optimization method is already incredibly sophisticated since it jumps out of a local maxima several times. Most of the optimization methods will not be able to jump out of such local maxima, nor can they reach a local maxima with one step. The more realistic option is: following the steepest decent path to a maxima, this local maxima can be rejected by looking at the minimal altitude to which one must climb down in order to go another way up (cf. topological watershed algorithm, Bertrand, 2005).

- **The fourth strategy (Star Trek)**: He takes a grid, of say 1000 points on the map and assumes that he is such an experienced climber able to reach these points by foot. It is not likely, but it is possible to reach a higher summit on *Dachstein* using this approach. Anyhow, with this strategy he will spend some months of his life climbing, although he needs almost half a year to reach all points to be able to prove which was the highest of them. This optimization method works well only if a very high number of points are chosen (fine grid) and if they can't be reached by climbing, teleportation is possible since otherwise it would take too long to find the highest point out of the 1000 mentioned.

- **The fifth strategy (spaceballs)**: A similar strategy would be to select 1000 points randomly. The probability of reaching the highest point is equal to the previous strategy. However, if he comes back for this task next year as well and if he again selects 1000 points, he will most likely reach a higher summit than only with strategy four. If the new drawn points are conditioned on the highest of spots from the first points, this is even more effective (*Spaceballs Princess*).

- **The sixth strategy (spin-the-bottle)**: Our Australian guy in Austria thinks it is best to take a bottle and play the spin-the-bottle game at each point he arrives. So he spins the bottle until it stops, and then chooses this randomly selected direction with the condition that the randomly chosen direction went upwards in altitude. Let's assume that at first he has full power, so he could take a longer path in this direction. The paths get shorter after each spin-the-bottle game, since he becomes tired. Probably with this strategy he will reach the nearby mountain *Sonnenberg* (484 meters) south of the airport, but it is also likely that he will reach the *Kahlenberg* (447 meters) or probably the *Rax* in the south-east (2.007 meters).

- **The seventh strategy (the drunken lucky sailor)**: He will look at the best directions from Vienna airport and at certain length of local walks, but he is crazy and chooses the best direction randomly by a certain degree, and also he multiplies the optimal length with twice of the contents of his half-liter sized beer served by a waiter at the airport. He will repeat this approach at every step done (place reached). The choosing of the angle may also depend on other factors, such as how much beer he has already drank and at which place the beer is served. This strategy is most probably more time consuming, but he may not be trapped in local maxima if the amount of beer is well chosen. This, of course, is challenging. He probably won't reach the highest summit of Austria, the *Grossglockner* (3.798 meters), but if the parameters are well chosen, he might have a (minimal) chance.

We might be able to continue to report on many other possible scenarios, but since this is not a book on optimization only, we will stop here and ask if the mentioned scenarios have any similarities. It should also be mentioned that the optimization problems that the Australian guy has to solve are too complex, since the Austrian mountains are far from being concave. Note that for concave or convex problems, the solutions are trivial. Please also note that the problem for the Australian guy was to find an optima on a three-dimensional surface. In statistics, problems in higher dimensions occur frequently also.

If we take a closer look at the scenarios above, we can group scenarios 1-4 to the topic of deterministic rules (traditional optimization methods). Starting at Vienna airport for each of the scenarios, the same summits are reached. Scenarios 5 to 7 differ in that aspect. Assuming that the angle and length of the paths are not fixed and this depends highly on the waiter's fate, we can group these two scenarios to the topic of stochastic random rules (a.k.a stochastic (Monte Carlo) optimization).

Before we discuss stochastic methods, we will briefly touch upon classical methods.

Numerical optimization

The aim is to find the extreme values (for example, maxima or minima) of a function *f(x)* or of an implicit equation *g(x) = 0*. In focus it is therefore the optimization problem *max h(x)*. Or in other words, we search for a value $\mathbf{x}_0 \in \mathbb{R}^n$ that holds:

- $f(\mathbf{x}_0) \leq f(\mathbf{x}) \; \forall \mathbf{x} \in \mathbb{R}^n$ (global maxima)
- $f(\mathbf{x}_0) \geq f(\mathbf{x}) \; \forall \mathbf{x} \in \mathbb{R}^n$ (global minima)

Basically, two kinds of approaches exist to solve a complex optimization problem, as already mentioned:

- The pure deterministic approach
- The stochastic approach

Deterministic means in this chapter to follow strict rules to achieve the maxima without any randomness included. While the numerical deterministic solution of the problem depends on the analytical properties of the objective function h (for example, convexity and smoothness), the stochastic approach is of more general use.

For the following examples we use the following function, where afterwards we want to find its minimum. The optima of our modified 2D Rosenbrock function (mountains) should be at (1,1):

```
mountains <- function(v) {
  (1 - v[1])^2 + 100 * (v[2] - v[1]*v[1])^2 +
  0.3*(0.2 - 2*v[2])^2 + 100 * (v[1] - v[2]*v[2])^2 -
  0.5*(v[1]^2 +5*v[2]^2)
}
```

The contour plot shows contour lines (also known as isolines or isopleths) of a function of two variables as a curve, where points on this line/curve have a constant value. The contour plot from our mountains is shown in *Figure 5.2* (the solution of the Newton-Raphson method is already visualized).

Gradient ascent/descent

The gradient descent method is a first-order derivative optimization method for unconstrained nonlinear function optimization. For function maximization we speak about ascent method, for minimization, we call it descent. We show this method for didactical reasons and continue afterwards with more powerful ones.

The steepest descent search is an extension that goes in the direction of the line of the gradient in each step, basically an optimum step is done, also referred to as a steepest step.

The aim is to locate the maximum/minimum of a function. For initialization, a starting point has to be selected. For this point as well as for any point reached later on, the derivative of the function is calculated. A next (new) point is selected in direction of the gradient of the functions derivative at a distance of (the step size parameter) from the current point.

We do not show the implementation of this method, since it fails completely when applied to the function `mountains`, but we refer to simpler examples that are implemented in the R package animations. A very simple example where this method is successful is shown here:

```
library("animation")
grad.desc()
```

And a function where already this simple method fails can be seen by executing this code:

```
ani.options(nmax = 70)
par(mar = c(4, 4, 2, 0.1))
f2 = function(x, y) sin(1/2 * x^2 - 1/4 * y^2 + 3) * cos(2 * x + 1 -
  exp(y))
grad.desc(f2, c(-2, -2, 2, 2), c(-1, 0.5), gamma = 0.3, tol = 1e-04)
```

Newton-Raphson methods

The Newton-Raphson method is the most famous deterministic optimization method. At each point, the first derivative determines the line to follow to the next point, and the second derivative is used to select the direction of the line. More precisely, Newton-Raphson methods are based on the recursion:

$$x_{i+1} = x_i - \left[\frac{\delta^2 f}{\delta x \delta x^T} (x_i) \right]^{-1} \frac{\delta f}{\delta x} (x_i)$$

Wherein the matrix of the first derivative is called the gradient, and the matrix of the second derivative is known as the Hessian matrix. This method depends strongly on the starting value.

In R a Newton-type algorithm is implemented in function `nlm`. The first function argument is the function to be minimized. In the following example we plug-in our function `mountains` and store each solution for the first 10 steps and visualize them in *Figure 5.2*. We start somewhat badly so that we can see how this algorithm falls into the local minima:

```
n <- 300
## to define a grid
x <- seq(-1, 2, length.out = n)
y <- seq(-1, 2, length.out = n)
## evaluate on each grid point
z <- mountains(expand.grid(x, y))
## contour plot
par(mar = c(4,4,0.5,0.5))
contour(x, y,  matrix(log10(z), length(x)),
        xlab = "x", ylab = "y", nlevels = 20)
## Warning in matrix(log10(z), length(x)): NaNs produced
## starting value
sta <- c(0.5,-1)
points(sta[1], sta[2], cex = 2, pch = 20)
## solutions for each of 20 steps
sol <- matrix(, ncol=2, nrow = 21)
sol[1, ] <- sta
for(i in 2:20){
    sol[i, ] <- nlm(mountains, sta, iterlim = i)$est
}
## optimal solution
sol[21, ] <- nlm(mountains, sta)$est
points(sol[21, 1], sol[21, 2], cex = 3, col = "red", pch = 20)
## path visually
lines(sol, pch=3, type="o")
## now let's start better (dashed line)
sta <- c(0,-1)
for(i in 2:20){
```

```
    sol[i, ] <- nlm(mountains, sta, iterlim = i)$est
}
sol[1, ] <- sta
sol[21, ] <- nlm(mountains, sta)$est
points(sta[1], sta[2], cex = 2, pch = 20)
points(sol[21, 1], sol[21, 2], cex = 3, col = "red", pch = 20)
lines(sol, pch=3, type="o")
```

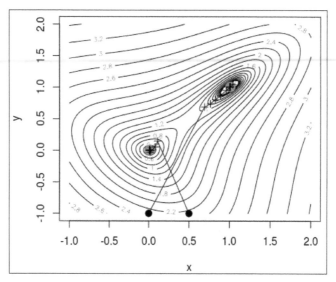

Figure 5.2: Contour plot of our two mountains (defined modified Rosenbrock function). The maxima is at (1,1). Two solutions (red filled circles) with different starting values are shown, whereas each step of the Newton-Raphson solution is indicated by a cross and path (line). The starting value is drawn with a black circle.

We can see that for this 2-dimensional example, the Newton-Raphson gradient method works well if the starting point chosen is not too bad.

As already mentioned, the Newton-Raphson method is deterministic, that is, it always reaches the same initial starting values always at the same solution.

A global optimum can be found very quickly and easily, if the function is convex/concave. However, if the function to be optimized is not convex/concave and if several local optima exist, the Newton-Raphson method will probably only find a local optimum.

Further general-purpose optimization methods

The standard function to solve general-purpose optimization problems in R is `optim`. Several methods are implemented:

- **The Nelder-Mead method (Nelder and Mead 1965)**: This is the default method that is relatively slow. It will work reasonably well for non-differentiable functions.

- **The BFGS method**: This is a quasi-Newton method, especially useful if the Hessian is unavailable or is too expensive to compute at every iteration. As the method of Nelder and Mead 1965 it is relatively robust against wrong step sizes.

- **The CG method (Fletcher and Reeves 1964)**: This is a conjugate gradients method, which is generally more fragile than the BFGS method, but computationally more efficient, thus used for larger problems.

- **The "L-BFGS-B" method (Byrd, Nocedal, and Zhu 1995)**: This allows box constraints for each variable. Of course, the initial value must satisfy these constraints.

- **The SANN method (Belisle 1995)**: It implemented using a simulated annealing approach. It uses a Metropolis function for the acceptance probability. It is not a general-purpose method and it is relatively slow, but it can be very useful in receiving a good solution on a very rough surface.

We will apply these methods to our function `mountains`. Note that we need a `for` loop to save the solution after every step to see how the algorithms work on this problem. From *Figure 5.3* we see that it highly depends on the starting value if a local or global maxima is reached. Note that for all methods, the global optima at *(1,1)* is approximately reached, not exactly, but it is a matter of computation time to come closer and closer to *(1,1)*:

```
## wrapper for all methods of optim
optims <- function(x, meth = "Nelder-Mead", start = c(0.5, -1)){
  sol <- matrix(, ncol = 2, nrow = 21)
  sol[1, ] <- start
  for(i in 2:20){
    sol[i, ] <- optim(start, mountains, method = meth,
                    control = list(maxit=i))$par
  }
  sol[21,] <- optim(start, mountains)$par
```

```
  points(start[1], start[2], pch=20, cex = 2)
  points(sol[21, ], sol[21, ], pch = 20, col = "red", cex = 3)
  lines(sol[, 1], sol[, 2], type = "o", pch = 3)
}
## plot lines for all methods
par(mar=c(4,4,0.5,0.5))
contour(x, y,  matrix(log10(z), length(x)), xlab = "x", ylab = "y",
nlevels = 20)
optims()   # Nelder-Mead
optims("BFGS")
optims("CG")
optims("L-BFGS-B")
optims("SANN")
optims("Brent")
optims(start = c(1.5,0.5))
```

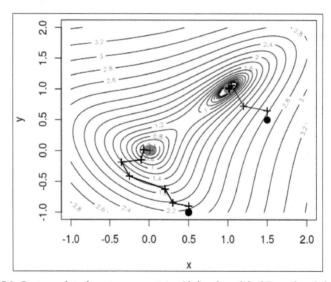

Figure 5.3: Contour plot of our two mountains (defined modified Rosenbrock function). The maxima is at (1,1). For the starting point at (0.5,-1) all methods supported by the function optim converge to the local minima, while at the starting point at (1.5,0.5) they all reach the global optima even on the same path. Each step of the solutions are indicated by a line from the starting point (black filled circle) to the final solution (red filled circle)

It should be noted that other functions and packages are also useful, such as the R packages `nloptr` (Johnson 2014) and `optimx` (Nach and Varadhan 2005). Lastly, it should be mentioned that the R package `ROI` (Hornik, Meyer, and Theussl 2013) provides an interface/wrapper to many solvers. It consists of an optimization infrastructure, a sophisticated framework for handling optimization problems in R.

Dealing with stochastic optimization

In difference to deterministic optimization, by using stochastic optimization one can find a different solution with the same starting values. This should also allow us to trap not (always) to a local optima.

Simplified procedures (Star Trek, Spaceballs, and Spaceballs princess)

As mentioned in the introduction of this chapter, in principle a (fine) grid, which should cover the whole distribution of f, can be used and evaluated for each grid point (*Star Trek*). Those grid coordinates having a maximum/minimum, provide an approximate solution of the optimization problem. Grid-based deterministic solutions to other problems are, for example, the Stahel-Donoho estimator for outlier detection (Stahel 1981a) (Stahel 1981b) or the raster-based search for principal components of a data set using grid-based projection pursuit methods (Croux, Filzmoser, and Oliveira 2007).

To move from this deterministic approach to an approach which includes randomness, one can just sample points over the whole distribution of f (*Spaceballs*). If the probability of selecting a point is equal over the whole space, the probability to a find solution, say A, is equal to the deterministic approach.

This approach can lead to good results for low-dimensional problems, but it is computationally too slow to find good solutions for higher-dimensions. Naturally, this approach can be modified by a sequential draw of points, for example, starting by drawing a set of points and drawing the next set of points depending on the values of the first set of points. For maximization in a two-dimensional problem this means that more data points are selected (for a follow-up draw of points) around higher points. We will not consider this, but only choose a set of points and mark the highest. For each of these points f is evaluated and the maximum is the approximate extreme value. If f is compact, we may, for example, draw from a uniform distribution m observations simulate:

$$f_m^* = \max(f(u_1), \ldots, f(u_m))$$

is then the approximate solution of:

$$\max_{x \in \mathbb{R}} f(\mathbf{x})$$

The maximum in red (see the following plot, *Figure 5.4*), found with an evaluation of *m = 1.500* draws between -2 and 5 from a bivariate uniform distribution:

```
## define grid
n <- 1500
set.seed(1234567)
x1 <- runif(n, min = -2, max = 5)
y1 <- runif(n, min = -2, max = 5)
z1 <- matrix(, ncol = n, nrow = n)
## evaluate on each grid point
for(i in 1:n){
  for(j in 1:n){
      z1[i,j] <- mountains(c(x1[i], y1[j]))
  }
}
## determine optima
w <- which(z1 == min(z1), arr.ind=TRUE)
## plot results
par(mar=c(4,4,0.5,0.5))
contour(x, y,  matrix(log10(z), length(x)), xlab = "x", ylab = "y",
nlevels = 20)
## Warning in matrix(log10(z), length(x)): NaNs produced
points(x1[w[1]], y1[w[2]], pch = 20, col = "red", cex = 3)
points(x1, y1, pch=3)
```

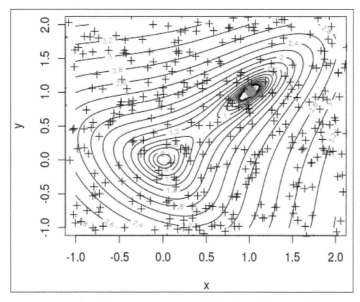

Figure 5.4: Contour plot of our two mountains (defined modified Rosenbrock function) showing the Spaceballs solution

This approach is, of course, too simplistic, but remember we already mentioned an improvement of *Spaceballs*. Let's consider the *Spaceballs princess* approach, that is, let's iterate to get better solutions. The idea is the following:

1. Sample points randomly, compute the values of the function, and select those points with highest values.

2. *Repeat*, at the fittest points located, draw values from a normal distribution, and again select the fittest points.

This is implemented in the package RCEIM (Krone-Martins 2014), which can be used for multidimensional function optimization. The method does not impose strong conditions on the function to be optimized, and we can easily apply it to our two mountains problem. Again, we save all immediate solutions and display all fittest points for each step of the algorithm. The plot in *Figure 5.5* shows those points from light gray (early stage) to black (fittest points at step 20). We also plot red crosses for the best solution in each step. All are located nearby the optimum. The final solution is marked by a large filled red circle:

```
library("RCEIM")
set.seed(123)
sol <- best <- list()
```

```
## save solution for each step
for(i in 2:20){
  a <- ceimOpt(mountains, nParam = 2, maxIter = i)
  sol[[i]] <- a$EliteMembers
  best[[i]] <- a$BestMember
}
## plot the results for each step
par(mar=c(4,4,0.5,0.5))
contour(x, y,  matrix(log10(z), length(x)), xlab = "x", ylab = "y",
nlevels = 20)
## Warning in matrix(log10(z), length(x)): NaNs produced
greys <- grey(rev(2:20 / 20 - 0.099))
for(i in 2:20){
  points(sol[[i]][,1], sol[[i]][,2], col = greys[i])
  points(best[[i]][1], best[[i]][2], col = "red", pch = 3)
}
points(best[[i]][1], best[[i]][2], col = "red", pch = 20, cex = 3)
```

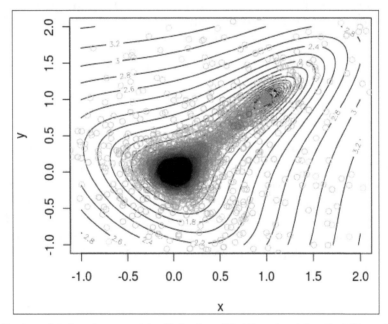

Figure 5.5: Contour plot of our two mountains (defined modified Rosenbrock function). Two solutions with equal starting values are shown, whereas each step of the random walk Metropolis-Hastings solution is indicated by a filled circle (for the first solution) or a cross (for the second solution)

It is readily apparent that this simplified procedure can be inefficient for higher dimensions. On the other hand, there are a wide range of applications, especially in case if the objective function is very complex.

Metropolis-Hastings revisited

A simple stochastic search algorithm, a random Monte Carlo Metropolis-Hastings algorithm, could then be used to generate a sequence $\theta_{j+1} = \theta_j + \epsilon_j$ and f will be evaluated given parameters θ_j and θ_{j+1}. If the value of is higher for θ_{j+1} we go in to accept, otherwise we don't move. ϵ might be chosen from a normal distribution with changing variance: the longer the sequence, the lower the variance.

For our two-dimensional example (`mountains`), a kind of random walk Metropolis-Hastings algorithm might then be defined for a sequence $x_t = (x_t, y_t)$, $t = 1, 2, \dots$ as $x^{(t+1)} = x^{(t)} + \epsilon_t$ with $\epsilon_t \sim MVN(0, \sigma_i)$, with σ_i decreasing with larger t.

The following code implements this kind of random walk Metropolis-Hastings algorithm for an optimization problem in two dimensions:

```
## Simple random walk Metropolis Hastings:
rmh <- function(n = 20, start = c(0,-0.5), stepmult = 10){
  x <- matrix(, ncol = 2, nrow = n)
  x[1, ] <- start
  sol <- mountains(start)
  for(i in 2:n){
    x[i, ] <- x[i-1, ] + rmvnorm(1, mean = c(0, 0),
                         sigma = stepmult * diag(2) / n)
    solnew <- mountains(x[i, ])
    # accept only a better solution:
    if(solnew > sol) x[i, ] <- x[i-1, ]
    if(solnew < sol) sol <- solnew
  }
  return(x)
}
```

Let's take two walks from the same starting point:

```
library("mvtnorm")
set.seed(12345)
n <- 200
x1 <- rmh(n, start = c(1.5,0))
x2 <- rmh(n, start = c(1.5,0))
```

Again, the solutions are visualized for each step of the algorithm. In *Figure 5.6* it can be seen that once the algorithm trapped into the local minima while at the same starting point, the other time the algorithm was successful to find the optimal solution:

```
par(mar=c(4,4,0.5,0.5))
contour(x, y,  matrix(log10(z), length(x)), xlab = "x", ylab = "y",
nlevels = 20)
## Warning in matrix(log10(z), length(x)): NaNs produced
points(x1[1, 1], x1[1, 2], pch = 4, cex = 3)
points(x2[n, 1], x2[n, 2], pch = 20, col = "red", cex = 3)
points(x1[n, 1], x1[n, 2], pch = 20, col = "red", cex = 3)
lines(x1[, 1], x1[, 2], type = "o", pch = 3)
lines(x2[, 1], x2[, 2], type = "o", col = "blue", lty = 2)
```

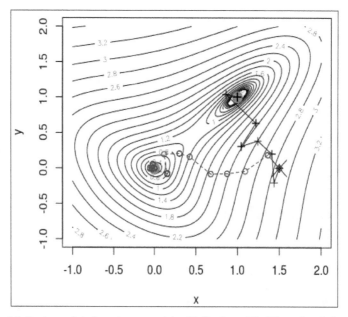

Figure 5.6: Contour plot of our two mountains (defined modified Rosenbrock function).
Two solutions with equal starting values are shown, whereas each step of the
random walk Metropolis-Hastings solution is indicated by a filled circle
(for the first solution) or a cross (for the second solution)

Gradient-based stochastic optimization

Remember the scenario of *the drunken sailor* described in the introduction to this chapter? We made a note that the direction and step size of a gradient algorithm might be modified using a kind of randomization.

Based on the Newton-Raphson method, which is basically a sequence of $\theta_{j+1} = \theta_j + \alpha_j \nabla f(\theta_j)$, $\alpha_j > 0$, for the stochastic gradient method, a random error ζ_j, ζ uniformly distributed on the unit circle is drawn.

The gradient in the previous formula is modified regarding the central difference quotient, $\nabla h(\theta_j) = \frac{f(\theta_j + \beta_j \zeta_j) - f(\theta_j - \beta_j \zeta_j)}{2\beta_j} \zeta_j$ with a (β_j) sequence of positive real numbers. The difference quotient is an approximation of the local derivative.

New values θ_{j+1}, $\theta_{j+1} = \theta_j + \frac{\alpha_j}{2\beta_j} \delta f(\theta_j, \beta_j, \zeta_j)\zeta_j$ are not exactly in the direction of steepest ascent of in θ_j, because every time some random direction dependent on the size of β_j and α_j is selected. Such directions are given preference here where $f(\theta_j + \beta_j\zeta_j) - f(\theta_j - \beta_j\zeta_j)$ is large.

To achieve convergence one must note the following (without proof):

- The deterministic sequence (α_j), $i = 1, 2, \dots$ includes positive monotonically increasing numbers
- The deterministic sequence (α_j) includes positive monotonically increasing numbers
- $\sum \alpha_j$ should diverge
- $\sum (\alpha_j/\beta_j)^2$ should converge

By the random choice of direction it can (sometimes) be avoided to trap and stay in a local optimum. Directions where is large are preferred. The performance of the algorithm depends strongly on the choice of α and β, and to choose both parameters it turns out in practice is a very difficult, almost unsolvable, task.

The following code implements the stochastic gradient approach described previously. Starting values as well as parameters for the sequences of α_i and β_i are included as function parameters:

```
stoGrad <- function(start = c(0, -0.5), j = 1500, p = 0.1){
  theta <- matrix(start, ncol=2)
  diff <- iter <- 1
  alpha <- sapply(1:100, function(x) 1 / (j+1) )
  beta  <- sapply(1:100, function(x) 1 / (j+1)^(p) )
```

```
while( diff > 10^-5 & !is.nan(diff) & !is.na(diff) ){
    zeta <- rnorm(2)
    zeta <- zeta / sqrt(t(zeta) %*% zeta)
    grad <- alpha[iter] * zeta * (mountains(theta[iter, ] + beta[iter] *
zeta) -
            mountains(theta[iter, ] - beta[iter] * zeta)) / beta[iter]
    theta <- rbind(theta, theta[iter, ] - grad)
    diff <- sqrt(t(grad) %*% grad )
    iter <- iter + 1
  }
  list(theta = theta[1:(iter-1), ], diff = diff, iter = iter-1)
}
```

The following plot (*Figure 5.7*) shows the solution to the stochastic gradient method. Even if it is a simple 2-dimensional example, it took some time to find a good choice for the sequence of β_i and α_i to achieve convergence and to find a good solution:

```
set.seed(123)

s1 <- stoGrad()

par(mar=c(4,4,0.5,0.5))

contour(x, y,  matrix(log10(z), length(x)), xlab = "x", ylab = "y",
nlevels = 20)

## Warning in matrix(log10(z), length(x)): NaNs produced

plotLine <- function(x, ...){
  lines(x$theta[,1], x$theta[,2], type = "o", ...)
  points(x$theta[x$iter, 1], x$theta[x$iter, 1], pch = 20, col = "red",
cex = 3)
}

plotLine(s1, pch = 3)

points(0, -0.5, pch = 20, cex = 1.5)

plotLine(stoGrad(), col = "blue", pch = 4)

plotLine(stoGrad(start = c(1.5, 0)), pch = 3, lty = 2)

plotLine(stoGrad(start = c(1.5, 0)), col = "blue", pch = 4, lty = 2)

points(1.5, 0, pch = 20, cex = 1.5)
```

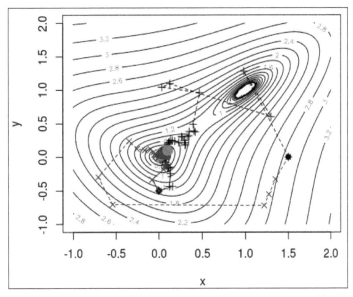

Figure 5.7.: Contour plot of our two mountains (defined modified Rosenbrock function). Four solutions, with two of them each with equal starting values, are shown, whereas each step of the solution is visualized. The starting point is indicated with a black filled circle, the final solution with a red filled circle

The implemented stochastic gradient approach is sensible to parameters j and p. We can see that modifying the parameter p to higher values leads to better results (see *Figure 5.8*):

```
set.seed(123)
s1 <- stoGrad(p = 2.5)
par(mar=c(4,4,0.5,0.5))
contour(x, y,  matrix(log10(z), length(x)), xlab = "x", ylab = "y",
nlevels = 20)
## Warning in matrix(log10(z), length(x)): NaNs produced
plotLine <- function(x, ...){
  lines(x$theta[,1], x$theta[,2], type = "o", ...)
  points(x$theta[x$iter, 1], x$theta[x$iter, 1], pch = 20, col = "red",
cex = 3)
}
plotLine(s1, pch = 3)
points(0, -0.5, pch = 20, cex = 1.5)
```

```
plotLine(stoGrad(p = 2.5), col = "blue", pch = 4)
plotLine(stoGrad(start = c(1.5, 0), j=1500, p=2.5), pch = 3, lty = 2)
plotLine(stoGrad(start = c(1.5, 0), j=1500, p=2.5), col = "blue", pch =
4, lty = 2)
points(1.5, 0, pch = 20, cex = 1.5)
```

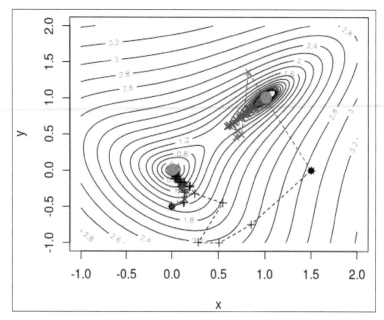

Figure 5.8: Contour plot of our two mountains (defined modified Rosenbrock function).
Four solutions, two of them each with equal starting values, are shown, whereas
each step of the solution is visualized. The starting point is indicated with a black filled
circle, the final solution with a red filled circle

The package `nloptr` (Johnson 2014) has an improved stochastic ranking evolution
strategy for nonlinearly constrained global optimization implemented (Runarsson
and Yao 2005):

```
library("nloptr")
set.seed(123)
## mountains function with modified function parameters
mountains1 <-
function(x) ((1 - x[1])^2 + 100 * (x[2] - x[1]*x[1])^2 +
    0.3*(0.2 - 2*x[2])^2 + 100 * (x[1] - x[2]*x[2])^2 -
    0.5*(x[1]^2 +5*x[2]^2))
x0 <- c(0.5, -1)
lb <- c(-3, -3)
```

```
ub <- c(3, 3)
sol <- matrix(, ncol=2,nrow=21)
## solution on each step
for(i in 1:20){
  sol[i, ] <- isres(x0 = x0, fn = mountains1, lower = lb, upper = ub,
maxeval = i)$par
}
par(mar=c(4,4,0.5,0.5))
contour(x, y,  matrix(log10(z), length(x)), xlab = "x", ylab = "y",
nlevels = 20)
## start
points(sol[1, 1], sol[1, 2], pch = 20, cex = 2)
## optima found
sol[21,] <- isres(x0 = x0, fn = mountains1, lower = lb, upper = ub)$par
points(sol[21, 1], sol[21, 2], pch = 20, col = "red", cex = 3)
## way to optima
lines(sol[,1], sol[,2], type = "o", pch = 3)
```

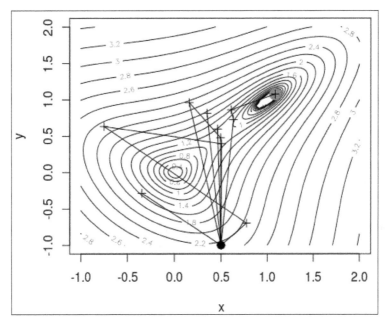

Figure 5.9: Contour plot of our two mountains (defined modified Rosenbrock function).
Each step of the solution via the ISRES implementation is visualized. The starting point is
indicated with a black filled circle, the final solution with a red filled circle

Summary

Having all methods in mind that are presented in this book, one should be able to find the best optimizer for any given problem. To choose the optimizer, the dimensionality and complexity of the problem play a role as well as the shape of the function to optimize.

Numerical optimization methods were introduced in this chapter, but special care was given to stochastic methods to solve optimization problems. The advantages of traditional numerical optimization methods are in general that they are computationally efficient and reach an optima more quickly. The optim function in R has many of these methods implemented, and also the optimx and the ROI package are wrappers to many optimizers.

However, optima found by general-purpose numerical optimization methods must not be equal to the global optima, as soon as the function to be optimized is not convex or concave. Stochastic gradient methods (our *drunken sailor*) may avoid trapping into local extrema, but in any case will find different paths when re-running them, even when starting on the same starting point. Stochastic gradient methods depend on various parameters, and a major drawback of the stochastic gradient methods is trying to find a good set of parameters. Only with a well-chosen set of parameters, the stochastic gradient methods can find good solutions, otherwise only local extrema are selected as optima.

Even very simple methods such as our *Spaceballs approach, but especially our Spaceball princess approach* often can avoid trapping into local extrema, but the costs of receiving a good solution in higher dimensional problems can be huge. Nevertheless, such approaches are often the only possibility to get a good solution if the function to be optimized has many local extrema—think of the problems that our Australian guy had to face when he wanted to find the highest mountain of Austria in foggy weather. *Spaceball princess* and its implementation in package RCEIM will most likely find the summit of the *Grossglockner*, while other solvers will most likely trap into local extrema.

We also discovered that the Metropolis-Hastings approach is easy to implement, and for our two mountains problem we got good results in a short time.

References

- Belisle, C.J.P. 1995. "Convergence Theorems for a Class of Simulated Annealing Algorithms on Rd," *J. Applied Probability* 29: 885–95

- Bertrand, G. 2005. "On Topological Watersheds," *Journal of Mathematical Imaging and Vision* 22 (2-3): 217–30

- Byrd, R.H., J. Nocedal, and C. Zhu. 1995. "A Limited Memory Algorithm for Bound Constrained Optimization," *SIAM J. Scientific Computing* 16: 1190–1208

- Croux, C., P. Filzmoser, and M. Oliveira. 2007. "Algorithms for Projection-Pursuit Robust Principal Component Analysis," *Chemometrics and Intelligent Laboratory Systems* 87: 218–25

- Fletscher, R., and C.M. Reeves. 1964. "Function Minimization by Conjugate Gradients," *Computer Journal* 7: 148–54

- Hornik, K., D. Meyer, and S. Theussl. 2013. *ROI: R Optimization Infrastructure,* https://CRAN.R-project.org/package=ROI

- Johnson, S.G. 2014. *Improved Stochastic Ranking Evolution Strategy,* https://CRAN.R-project.org/package=nloptr

- Krone-Martins, A. 2014. *RCEIM: RCEIM - R Cross Entropy Inspired Method for Optimization,* https://CRAN.R-project.org/package=RCEIM

- Nach, J.C., and R. Varadhan. 2005. "Unifying Optimization Algorithms to Aid Software System Users: Optimx," *Journal of Statistical Software* 43 (9). IEEE: 1–14

- Nelder, J.A., and R. Mead. 1965. "A Simplex Method for Function Minimization," *The Computer Journal* 7 (4). *Oxford University Press*: 308–13

- Runarsson, T.P., and X. Yao. 2005. "Search Biases in Constrained Evolutionary Optimization," *Systems, Man, and Cybernetics, Part C: Applications and Reviews, IEEE Transactions* on 35 (2). IEEE: 233–43

- Stahel, W.A. 1981a. *Breakdown of Covariance Estimators. Research Report* 31. *Research Report* 31

- 1981b. "Robuste Schätzungen. Infinitesimale Optimalität Und Schätzungen von Kovarianzmatrizen," *PhD thesis, Swiss Federal Institute of Technology* (ETH)

6

Probability Theory Shown by Simulation

"I cannot believe that God plays dice with the cosmos."

– Albert Einstein

This section includes simulation experiments to show some aspects of probability theory and mathematical statistics. It will turn out that simulations make it easy to understand basic theorems. The weak law of large numbers, but especially the central limit theorem, are discussed in detail. The latter is probably the most important theorem in statistics and worth discussing in detail. First, some very well-known basics are introduced.

Some basics on probability theory

Probability theory is a branch of mathematics, and it forms the basics to infer from a sample to a population. Together with the field of analytical statistics, probability theory is used in the field of stochastic to describe random events. Stochastic modeling in turn uses probabilistic concepts—randomness and laws regarding randomness—for the modeling and analysis of real random processes (for example, in economic forecasting). Let's introduce some notation and basic concepts.

A random process or random experiment is any procedure that can be infinitely repeated and has a well-defined set of possible outcomes. For example, rolling a die is a random experiment.

The set of outcomes is denoted by $\Omega = \{..., \omega, ... \}$. These are all possible outcomes of the random experiment. Example: for rolling a die, $\Omega = \{1, ..., 6\}$.

A random variable, $x = \{X_1, ..., X_k\}$, can take on a set of possible different values (by chance), each with an associated probability.

The output of the random experiment is a random variable. Example, even numbers on a die.

An event A: the experimental output, x, has a specific property, A. Events are therefore subsets of Ω. In our dice example, event A, *throw an even number*, means the quantity $\{2,4,6\}$.

The probability, P(A), is the probability that a particular event A occurs. Example: For the event A, "toss the head of a coin", the probability is $P(A) = \frac{1}{2}$.

Probability distributions

We take a small excursus to probability distributions, since they are used frequently in the book. The theoretical distributions are, both in descriptive and in mathematical statistics, of central importance:

- To approximate functions, such as a description of empirically observed frequency distributions in descriptive statistics

- The determination of probabilities for results of certain random experiments in mathematical statistics

Some important theoretical distributions are, for example, the Binomial distribution, the Poisson distribution, the hyper-geometrical distribution, the uniform distribution, the exponential distribution, the normal distribution, the χ^2 distribution, and the t distribution.

Discrete probability distributions

Married or not married, in the Austrian population, defines already a discrete probability distribution. Discrete distributions are in general very important and we should take a closer look at them, since they are needed in the following chapters.

One calls the function that assigns each elementary event, j, its probability, p_j the probability function of the observed distribution. It is as follows:

- $\Omega_X = \mathbb{Z}$ defined area for x (integers!)
- $P(\{j\}) = P(X = j) = p_j$

- $p_j \geq 0$ for all $j \in \Omega_x$
- $\sum_{j \in \Omega_x} p_j = 1 \Rightarrow P(\Omega_x) = 1$

The distribution function defines the probability of an experiment, $x \leq j$, and it holds:

- $F_j = P(x \leq j)$ for all $j \in \Omega_x$
- $F_j = \sum_{i \leq j} p_i$

As an example of a discrete probability distribution, we name the Binomial distribution.

A Bernoulli-model consists of a sequence of Bernoulli-experiments (Binomial distribution where $n = 1$), with the following conditions:

- For each trial, only two outcomes (events) are possible, say A and $\overline{A}$ (= *not A*, the complementary)
- Probabilities for A and $\overline{A}$ are a constant of all experiments, $P(A) = p$ and $P(\overline{A}) = 1 - p$. In summary, n replications will be done and the individual experiments are independent. The frequency $h_n(A)$ is in $h_n(A) \in \{0, 1, \ldots, n\}$

The Binomial distribution B(n, p) we can derive as follows, that is the probability that the event A occurs exactly x times in n replicates is derived as follows:

The event A occurs only with the first x experiments: $\underbrace{A, A, \ldots, A}_{x-\text{times}}, \underbrace{\overline{A}, \overline{A}, \ldots, \overline{A}}_{(n-x)\text{times}}$.

The probability of this sequence of independent experiments is $p^x(1 - p)^{n-x}$.

Considering all possible arrangements $\binom{n}{x}$ the following applies:

$P(h_n(A) = x) = \binom{n}{x} p^x (1 - p)^{n-x}$, where $\binom{n}{x} = \dfrac{n!}{(n-x)! x!}$ is the Binomial coefficient.

Continuous probability distributions

One calls the function $a \mapsto F(a) = P(x \leq a)$ the distribution function of the probability distribution of x. F(a) is the probability to observe $X \leq a$. Also, for F(x) it holds:

- $\Omega_x^{\square} = R$
- $0 \leq F(x) \leq 1$
- F(x) is a monotone increasing: given $x_1 \leq x_2$ it follows that $F(x_1) \leq F(x_2)$

The derivative of the distribution function $f(x) = F'(x)$ is called the density of the distribution of x. It holds that $f(x) \geq 0$ and $\int_{-\infty}^{\infty} f(x)dx = 1$.

As a representative of a continuous probability distribution, we mention the normal distribution. Normal distribution is the most important distribution in mathematical statistics. Not many technical and biological data follow an approximately normal distribution, but estimated parameters do. Normal distribution is the basis of many estimation and testing methods.

Winning the lottery

Let us look at the lottery numbers from Britain from the last seven months. With some tricks we can grep them from the Internet:

```
library("RCurl")

URL <- "https://www.national-lottery.co.uk/results/euromillions/draw-
history/csv"

lotto <- read.csv(textConnection(getURL(URL)))
```

The structure of these data sets is as follows:

```
str(lotto)
## 'data.frame':    52 obs. of  10 variables:
##  $ DrawDate           : Factor w/ 52 levels "01-Apr-2016",..: 24 18
12 6 49 45 37 33 25 21 ...
##  $ Ball.1             : int  7 2 32 8 4 10 17 11 13 1 ...
##  $ Ball.2             : int  15 26 34 23 5 17 26 14 14 5 ...
##  $ Ball.3             : int  28 27 40 24 25 31 32 15 32 9 ...
##  $ Ball.4             : int  31 40 45 34 28 32 34 27 37 22 ...
##  $ Ball.5             : int  42 49 48 38 43 42 43 44 48 38 ...
##  $ Lucky.Star.1       : int  10 5 1 3 6 2 2 2 1 2 ...
##  $ Lucky.Star.2       : int  11 10 10 7 11 5 10 7 7 10 ...
##  $ UK.Millionaire.Maker: Factor w/ 52 levels
"BDM196361","BDN010072",..: 50 47 45 43 32 38 35 31 26 22 ...
##  $ DrawNumber         : int  902 901 900 899 898 897 896 895 894 893
...
```

Let us see if some numbers are drawn more frequently. *Figure 6.1* shows a bar chart of these frequencies:

```
numbers <- unlist(c(lotto[,2:5]))

library("ggplot2")
```

```
qplot(factor(numbers), xlab = "Gewinnzahlen")   +
  theme_bw() +
  theme(axis.text.x=element_text(angle=90)) +
  scale_y_continuous(breaks=0:10)
```

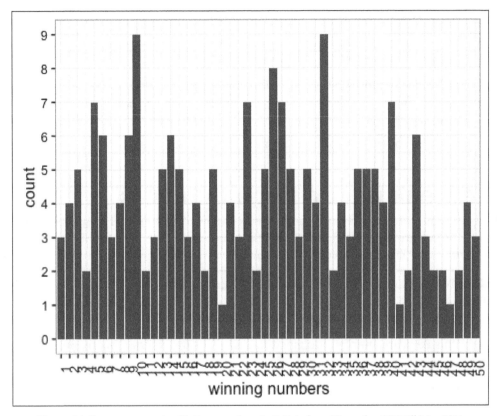

Figure 6.1: Frequency counts of lottery numbers in Britain from November 2015 till May 2016

Yeah! Anyone uneducated in statistics probably would now choose the numbers 5, 6, 10, 32, and 43 for the next lottery, believing that those numbers have a higher probability of being chosen for the next lottery game. Along the lines of: they were drawn more frequently in the past, so they will also be drawn more frequently in the future. Or some people will do the opposite by choosing those numbers that have almost never been drawn, reasoning that they now must appear.

People who know some of the basics of probability theory would rather think of a uniform distribution regarding the frequencies of drawn lottery numbers. But when looking at *Figure 6.1*, can we really believe this is true? Can we believe that the probability of a number being drawn in the British lottery is 1/50?

By no means! The number of draws is just too small. But can we believe in this when the number of draws will be increased?

We may now formulate some questions that we will answer shortly:

- We saw that the results differ. Do these differences depend on the sample size? (n in our case.)

- How large is the probability of drawing lottery number 1 when we would have n = 1000 draws? Will it converge to 1/50?

- What is the value of $P(A = 1)$, if $n \to \infty$?

- Will randomness follow any laws? What laws on random variables can be formulated?

- Is one set of experiments enough to draw conclusions?

The weak law on large numbers

The questions from the previous section led us to limit theorems. The most important limit theorems are the (weak) law of large numbers, the theorem of (Glivenko, 1933) and (Cantelli, 1933), and the central limit theorem.

First we will have a look at the weak law of large numbers. The strong law of weak numbers is mathematically more sophisticated, but tells (almost) the same story.

The weak law of large numbers is a very intuitive concept; Jakob Bernoulli even thought this 20 years after he published it in 1713, as the *golden theorem*. But if we take a closer look at this *law*, we jump into a whole world of mathematical statistics.

The weak law of large numbers is applied in betting offices, in financial assessments and for insurance, and so on. It builds the foundation of statistics, and data scientists should be aware of it. By understanding the weak law of large numbers and the central limit theorem, one understands the basics of mathematical statistics.

Emperor penguins and your boss

Take the population of emperor penguins at the South Pole into consideration (or replace emperor penguins with the length of workpieces...). The expected value of the height of emperor penguins is then the arithmetic mean of the height of the emperor penguins in the population.

Your boss gives you the task of naming this expected value. One possibility would be to measure the height of each emperor penguin from the South Pole. However, this would be too time consuming. The alternative is to randomly select some of the emperor penguins, for example, n emperor penguins from the population:

Figure 6.2: Emperor penguins at the South Pole

So, we measure the random variables $X_1, \ldots, X_n$ of n emperor penguins. The arithmetic mean is defined as $\overline{X}_n = \frac{X_1 + \cdots + X_n}{n}$. $X_1, \ldots, X_n$ are independent and identically-distributed random variables.

Assume that we now select the *n* emperor penguins from the population and we assume that we do not apply any complex sampling design, but draw the sample using simple random sampling. Thus each emperor penguin is equally likely to be drawn from the population. The result is an estimate of expectation: the height of emperor penguins in the population. Reminder: the expected value is the average of the entire population, while the sample mean is the average of the (smaller) randomly-drawn sample. The expected value is a number, while the sample mean is a random variable since the sample is randomly drawn. The estimation result will be different when re-drawing n emperor penguins.

With $\overline{X}_n$ we can give our boss an estimate of the expected value. If $n \to \infty$ then our estimated value will be close to the expected value.

But what does "close" mean? And in what sense? And is that really true?

Let's look at the bigger picture. A very interesting question is to ask what happens when we have more and more random variables available, when we increase the number of random variables over and over?

What happens if $n \to \infty$. The limit theorems provide evidence on this. They deal with the question of what happens when we have a large amount of random variables available.

In this book we want to illustrate the characteristics of the law of large numbers by means of simulation. We skip the mathematical proofs.

Limits and convergence of random variables

In *Chapter 3, The Discrepancy between Pencil-Driven Theory and Data-Driven Computational Solutions,* we already defined convergence of deterministic sequences. But what is the meaning of convergence of random variables? Each random variable is drawn (randomly) from a distribution, so instead of a_n, we consider random variables. We hope that eventually, the sequence of random numbers or the sequence of probability distributions converges to a number, a. *Figure 6.3* illustrates this. The greater the sample, the smaller/narrower this distribution should get:

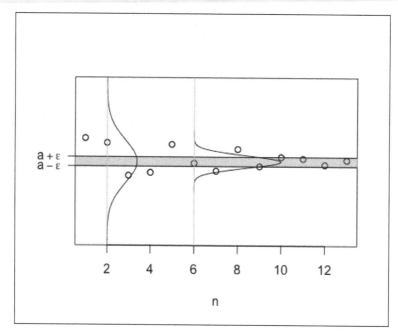

Figure 6.3: Beyond a certain sample size, the distribution should lie within the ϵ-bound around a. The probability that the white surface under the density is visible, should converge to zero for large n

The distribution should become narrower and narrower with increasing n, so that it is eventually within the interval. Stated differently, the probability that the area under the probability distribution is outside the interval defined by $[a + \epsilon; a - \epsilon]$ should converge to zero.

Mathematically, this means that a sequence of random variables, X_n, converges to a *in probability*. Almost all the probability density of X_n should be sufficiently concentrated near to a. For every $\epsilon > 0$:

$$\lim_{n \to \infty} P(|X_n - a| \geq \epsilon) = 0)$$

The probability that random numbers are outside this interval gets smaller and smaller when n tends to infinity. In other words, the limit value of this probability is zero. We say also: the sequence X_n converges in probability to a.

Convergence of the sample mean – weak law of large numbers

Let us have a closer look at the expected value and the variance of the mean. We can easily show that:

$$E(\overline{X}_n) = \frac{E(X_1) + E(X_2) + \cdots + E(X_n)}{n} = \frac{n\mu}{n} = \mu$$

Since the expected value of a random number is exactly its expectation, and:

$$Var(\overline{X}_n) = \frac{n\sigma^2}{n^2} = \frac{\sigma^2}{n}$$

The larger the sample, the smaller the variance of the estimate and the smaller the uncertainty.

The inequality of Chebyshev (see, for example, Saw, Yang, and Mo 1984) applies:

$$P(|\overline{X}_n - \mu| \geq \epsilon) \leq \frac{Var(\overline{X}_n)}{\epsilon^2} = \frac{\sigma^2}{n\epsilon^2}$$

$\overline{X}_n$ converges in probability to μ. $\epsilon > 0$: $P(|\overline{X}_n - \mu| \geq \epsilon) \leq \frac{\sigma^2}{n\epsilon^2} \to 0$.

The law of large numbers thus tells us that the sample mean converges to the true mean, but in a special way: in probability.

Showing the weak law of large numbers by simulation

Consider the simplest of all simple examples, the toss of a coin. We want to flip a coin again and again and we surely agree that the coin is *fair*, when the observed probability of tossing a *head* (or *number*) is approximately *0.5*, and if the next outcome of the next throw is not dependent on the previous result (independence). In other words, we want to evaluate whether the probability of the event *A* is equal to *1/2*, *P(A) = 0.5*. This can also be expressed with the binomial distribution:

$B (A = 'head', size = 1, p (A) = 0.5) = 0.5$

In R this can be calculated with the function `dbinom`:

```
dbinom(x = 0, size = 1, prob = 0.5)
## [1] 0.5
```

We want to perform the random experiment *throw the coin* n times and we evaluate the results. In R, we can use either the function `sample` or the function `rbinom` to simulate a coin toss. For one throw of a coin the code looks like this:

```
sample(c("head", "number"), size = 1)
## [1] "head"
# alternativ:
rbinom(n = 1, size = 1, prob = 0.5)
## [1] 0
```

We write a function which simulates the tosses of a coin and which evaluates the probabilities of *head* after n experiments, as well as calculating the absolute error to the true probability. The nice thing about this experiment is that we know the truth *(P(A) = 0.5)*. This is not the case in practice:

```
simCoin <- function(n, p = 0.5, repl = 1){
  stopifnot(n > 0 | !is.vector(n) | p < 0 | p > 0 | !is.vector(repl))
  ## function for one simulation
  r <- function(){
    res <- rbinom(n, 1, p)
    tosses <- 1:n
    pA <- cumsum(res) / 1:n
    abserror <- abs(pA - p)
    return(data.frame(res = res, tosses = tosses, pA = pA,
    abserror = abserror))
  }
}
```

```
## simulation
df <- r()
if(repl > 1){
  for(i in 2:repl){
    df <- rbind(df, r())
  }
}
## return
df$repl <- rep(1:repl, each = n)
ll <- list(res = df$res, tosses = df$tosses, pA = df$pA,
           absfehler = df$abserror, repl = as.factor(df$repl))
class(ll) <- "Coin"
return(ll)
}
## print
print.Coin <- function(x, ..., s = NULL){
  if(!is.null(s)){
  cat("After", s, "random draws: the estimated P(A) =", x$pA[s], "\nand
the absolute error", x$absfehler[s], "\n")
  } else {
    m <- max(x$tosses)
  cat("After", m, "random draws: the estimated P(A) =", x$pA[m], "\nand
the absolute error", x$absfehler[m], "\n")
  }
}
The first n = 10 tosses of the coin:
## for reproducibility
set.seed(1234)
# 10 throws
simCoin(10)
## After 10 random draws: the estimated P(A) = 0.7
## and the absolute error 0.2
```

So if we throw only 10 times, the error might be very large. We expect that the error gets smaller when we throw more often (increase the sample size n):

```
set.seed(1234)
sim <- simCoin(5000)
```

```
print(sim, s=100)
## After 100 random draws: the estimated P(A) = 0.45
## and the absolute error 0.05
print(sim, s=1000)
## After 1000 random draws: the estimated P(A) = 0.518
## and the absolute error 0.018
print(sim, s=5000)
## After 5000 random draws: the estimated P(A) = 0.5014
## and the absolute error 0.0014
```

What we already see is that the larger n, the closer the estimated value (ratio of *head* to number of throws) and the true value/expectation.

By visualizing the results we gain even more knowledge. We first define a `plot` function:

```
plot.Coin <- function(x, y, ...){
  df <- data.frame(res = x$res, tosses = x$tosses, pA = x$pA,
  repl=x$repl)
  if(length(unique(df$repl)) == 1){
    ggplot(df, aes(x=tosses, y=pA)) +
     geom_line() + geom_abline(intercept = 0.5) + ylim(c(0,1)) +
     theme(legend.position="none")
  } else if(length(unique(df$repl)) > 10){
    gg <- ggplot(df, aes(x=tosses, y=pA, group=repl)) +
     geom_line() + geom_abline(intercept = 0.5) + ylim(c(0,1))
    ## add median line and confidence interval
    dfwide <- reshape2::dcast(df, tosses ~ repl, value.var="pA")
    dfwide <- dfwide[, 2:ncol(dfwide)]
    med <- apply(dfwide, 1, median)
    q025 <- apply(dfwide, 1, quantile, 0.025)
    q975 <- apply(dfwide, 1, quantile, 0.975)
    stat <- data.frame(med=med, q025=q025, q975=q975,
                      n=1:max(x$tosses),
                      repl=max(as.numeric(df$repl)))
    gg +
      geom_line(data=stat, aes(x = n, y = med), colour = "red", size=1) +
      geom_line(data=stat, aes(x = n, y = q025), colour = "orange",
      size=0.7) +
```

```
      geom_line(data=stat, aes(x = n, y = q975), colour = "orange",
      size=0.7) +

      theme(legend.position="none")

  } else {

    ggplot(df, aes(x=tosses, y=pA, colour = repl)) +

      geom_line() + geom_abline(intercept = 0.5) + ylim(c(0,1))

  }

}
```

In *Figure 6.4*, the coin is tossed 5000 times in total and the observed probability (frequency of heads divided by the number of throws) is plotted as a line. A line is not quite correct because the number of throws is discrete. We do not want to be too critical because this representation gives a smoother image, as shown in *Figure 6.4*:

```
plot(sim)
```

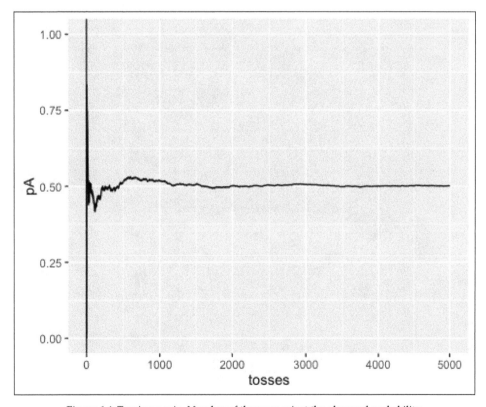

Figure 6.4: Tossing a coin. Number of throws against the observed probability.

We see that:

- Apparently, the observed probability converges to the expected value.
- Changes in the observed probability according the step n to $n = n + 1$ are getting smaller with increasing n. That is clear. If, after five times and throwing a *head* twice *(P(A)=2/5)*, then in the next throw the observed probability *(P(A)=3/6=1/2)* or *P(A)=2/6=1/3*. If the coin has already been thrown 1000 times, a new throw of the coin hardly alters the observed probability at all.

We see intuitively that the law of large numbers should work. We want to repeat the experiment, at first 10 times. We toss the coin 10×5,000 times and show the result in *Figure 6.5*:

```
set.seed(1234)

sim <- simCoin(n = 5000, repl = 10)

plot(sim)
```

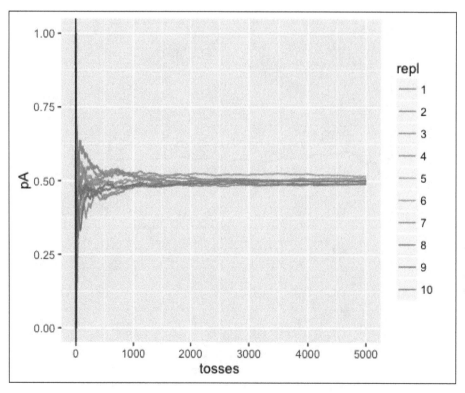

Figure 6.5: Tossing a coin. Number of throws against the observed probability.
10 replications of 5000 throws each.

However, we can observe that not every line (simulation of 5000 coin tosses) converged to 1/2 after 5000 tosses. Is there something wrong? Not at all. It's just because we took only 5000 tosses. We can also show that the law of large numbers works correctly when repeating the simulation more often and taking the median of it as well as certain quantiles on the tails. In the mean, the curves must converge to 1/2 and the quantiles must become smaller with increasing sample size.

Let us repeat the simulation 1000 times; we toss the coin repeatedly, 1000 times 5000 throws each. The result is shown in *Figure 6.6*:

```
sim <- simCoin(n = 5000, repl = 1000)
plot(sim)
```

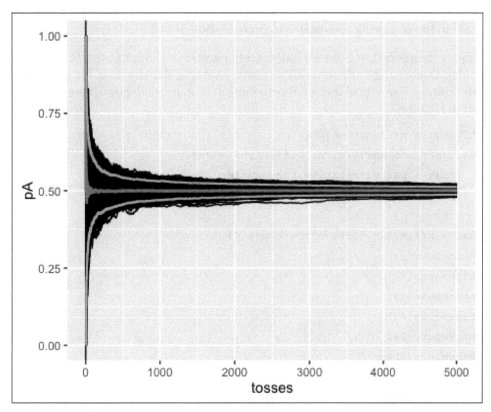

Figure 6.6: Tossing a coin. Number of throws against the observed probability.
1000 replications of 5000 throws each.

What can we know?

- We recognize that the weak law of large numbers *works,* even if we cannot perform the experiment infinitely often. The mean curve converges soon to 1/2. (We also observe that our random number generator works well.)

- The dispersion decreases with increasing sample size, but not linearly with the sample size. Doubling the sample size implies *not* a reduction of uncertainty by a factor of 1/2. The standard deviation decreases by $\sqrt{n}$ (compare the formula for the preceding variance).

In *Figure 6.6,* we have the 1000 results for each *n* and we averaged (the median, red line) them for any number of throws. Also the 2.5 and 97.5 percentile are calculated and shown in the figure (orange lines) drawn. This provides information about the decrease in the scattering around the expected value of 1/2.

As already mentioned, we cannot indefinitely perform a random experiment on the computer. Decreasing variance with increasing sample size can also, for example, be shown with the theoretical binomial distribution *B (n, p = 0.5).* For different *n* this is shown in *Figure 6.7:*

```
plotbinomcoin <- function(n){
  plot(0:n/n, dbinom(0:n, n, 0.5), type = "h",
       xlab = paste("relative frequencies (n =", n,")"),
       ylab = "p")
}
par(mar = c(4,4,0.5,0.5), mfrow = c(4,2))
plotbinomcoin(10)
plotbinomcoin(20)
plotbinomcoin(40)
plotbinomcoin(80)
plotbinomcoin(160)
plotbinomcoin(320)
plotbinomcoin(5000)
plotbinomcoin(10000)
```

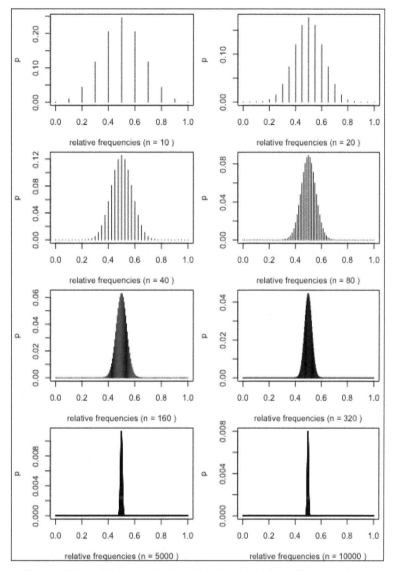

Figure 6.7: Visualization for the toss of a coin and the law of large numbers:
The larger n, the narrower the distribution around the value ½.

What does the figure show? When looking at the upper left graphics, it shows the theoretical probabilities for 10 tosses. For example, the probability is about 0.05 to toss two *heads* out of 10 tosses of a coin. The example in *Figure 6.7* also shows, in turn, that the deviations of the observed probabilities to the expected value to be greater than to an arbitrarily small number $\epsilon > 0$, with growing *n* is more and more unlikely. For the upper graphics in *Figure 6.7* we see that the distribution shrinks, largely by increasing the sample size.

To repeat: for a sequence of random variables $X_1, X_2, X_3, \ldots$ with $E(|X_i|) < \infty$ the weak law of large numbers holds if for all positive values,
$\varepsilon: \lim_{n \to \infty} P(|\bar{X}_n - \mu| > \varepsilon) = 0.$

The central limit theorem

The classical theory of sampling is based on the following fundamental theorem.

> When the distribution of *any population* has finite variance, then the distribution of the *arithmetic mean* of random samples is approximately *normal*, if the *sample size* is sufficiently large.

The proof of this theorem is usually about 3-6 pages (using advanced mathematics on measure theory). Rather than doing this mathematical exercise, the "proof" is done by simulation, which also helps to understand the central limit theorem and thus the basics of statistics.

The following setup is necessary:

- We draw samples from populations. This means that we know the populations. This is not the case in practice, but we show that the population can have any distribution as long as the variance is not infinite.
- We draw many samples from the population. Note that in practice, only one sample is drawn. For simulation purposes, we assume that we can draw many samples.

For the purpose of looking at our defined populations (pop = TRUE) and the distribution of arithmetic means from samples of these populations, we define the following function. In the first quarter of the code, the normal distribution is used, followed by the uniform and exponential distribution, and in the fourth quarter of the code, the Beta distribution is used:

```
cltSim <- function (n = 1, reps = 10000, nclass = 16, pop = TRUE,
estimator = mean) {
    old.par <- par(oma = c(0, 0, 1.5, 0), mfrow = c(2, 2),
    mar = c(4,4,2,0.5))
    on.exit(par(old.par))
    ## normal:
    norm.mat <- matrix(rnorm(n * reps), ncol = n)
    norm.mean <- apply(norm.mat, 1, estimator)
    x <- seq(min(norm.mean), max(norm.mean), length = 50)
    normmax <- max(dnorm(x, mean(norm.mean), sd(norm.mean)))
```

```
tmp.hist <- hist(norm.mean, plot = FALSE, prob = TRUE,
nclass = nclass)

normmax <- max(tmp.hist$density, normmax) * 1.05

hist(norm.mean, main = "normal", xlab = "x", col = "skyblue",
    prob = TRUE, ylim = c(0, normmax), nclass = nclass)

lines(x, dnorm(x, mean(norm.mean), sd(norm.mean)))

## exponential:

exp.mat <- matrix(rexp(n * reps, 1/3), ncol = n)

exp.mean <- apply(exp.mat, 1, estimator)

x <- seq(min(exp.mean), max(exp.mean), length = 50)

expmax <- max(dnorm(x, mean(exp.mean), sd(exp.mean)))

tmp.hist <- hist(exp.mean, plot = FALSE, prob = TRUE,
nclass = nclass)

expmax <- max(tmp.hist$density, expmax) * 1.05

hist(exp.mean, main = "exponential", xlab = "x", col = "skyblue",
    prob = TRUE, ylim = c(0, expmax), nclass = nclass)

if(pop) lines(x, dexp(x, 1/3)) else lines(x, dnorm(x, mean(exp.mean),
sd(exp.mean)))

## uniform:

unif.mat <- matrix(runif(n * reps), ncol = n)

unif.mean <- apply(unif.mat, 1, estimator)

x <- seq(min(unif.mean), max(unif.mean), length = 50)

unimax <- max(dnorm(x, mean(unif.mean), sd(unif.mean)))

tmp.hist <- hist(unif.mean, plot = FALSE, prob = TRUE,
nclass = nclass)

unimax <- max(tmp.hist$density, unimax) * 1.05

hist(unif.mean, main = "uniform", xlab = "x", col = "skyblue",
    prob = TRUE, ylim = c(0, unimax), nclass = nclass)

if(pop) lines(x, dunif(x)) else lines(x, dnorm(x, mean(unif.mean),
sd(unif.mean)))

## Beta:

beta.mat <- matrix(rbeta(n * reps, 0.35, 0.25), ncol = n)

beta.mean <- apply(beta.mat, 1, estimator)

x <- seq(min(beta.mean), max(beta.mean), length = 50)

betamax <- max(dnorm(x, mean(beta.mean), sd(beta.mean)))

tmp.hist <- hist(beta.mean, plot = FALSE, prob = TRUE,
nclass = nclass)
```

```
betamax <- max(tmp.hist$density, betamax)
hist(beta.mean, main = "Beta", xlab = "x", col = "skyblue",
    prob = TRUE, ylim = c(0, betamax), nclass = nclass)
if(pop){
  lines(x, dbeta(x, 0.35, 0.25))
  mtext(paste("Populations"), outer = TRUE, cex = 1.2)
} else {
  lines(x, dnorm(x, mean(beta.mean), sd(beta.mean)))
  mtext(paste("sample size =", n), outer = TRUE, cex = 1.2)
}
}
```

First the distribution of our chosen populations is shown (lines) and one realization of those populations each (histogram), see *Figure 6.8*:

```
cltSim()
```

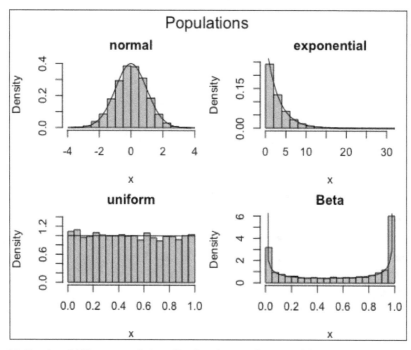

Figure 6.8: Density of different populations (lines) and one realization of those populations (histogram)

For these populations, we want to draw 10,000 samples of size *n* = 2. For each sample, we then calculate the arithmetic means. Thus 10,000 sample means are obtained. The distribution of the sample means is then visualized; see *Figure 6.9*. The lines correspond to the theoretical normal distributions, and the histogram corresponds to the distribution of sample means:

```
cltSim(2, pop = FALSE)
```

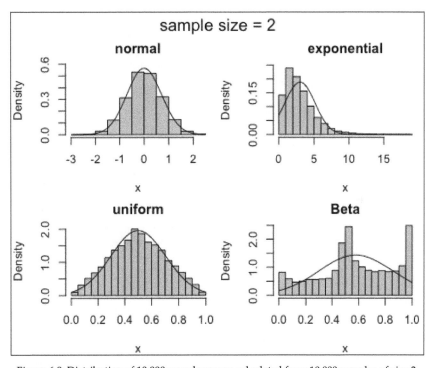

Figure 6.9: Distribution of 10,000 sample means calculated from 10,000 samples of size 2.

For sample size *n* = 2 the distribution of sample means is not normally distributed, except the samples are drawn from a standard normal distributed population. The distribution of sample means regarding the Beta distribution is tri-modal. This can be easily explained. Remember that samples of size *n* = 2 are repeatedly drawn from a Beta distribution (see *Figure 6.5*, the graphic at the right bottom). It is very likely that either two small values, two large values, or one large and one small value is drawn. The arithmetic mean of a sample of size 2 from a Beta distribution is thus likely to be at the tail or in the center of the distribution of sample means. No valid inference statistics can be made in a classical manner if the central limit theorem fails as shown here.

However, what will change if we increase the sample size from 2 to 10? The result is shown in *Figure 6.10*. Except for the exponential distributed population, the sample means are approx. normal:

```
cltSim(10, pop = FALSE)
```

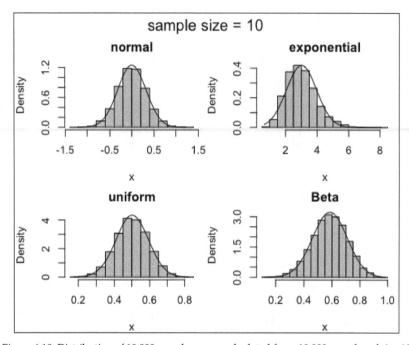

Figure 6.10: Distribution of 10,000 sample means calculated from 10,000 samples of size 10

We easily would observe if we further increase n, for example, *n = 30*, that all distributions of sample means drawn from these distributions are approximately normal. Moreover, if the sample size is large enough, the sample means are approximately normal independent of how the population looks (as soon the variance of the population is finite): the central limit theorem.

Of course, in practice one will only draw one sample (and not 10,000) from a population with unknown characteristics. However, if the sample is large enough (say *n = 50*), we know about the characteristics of an estimator such as the sample mean. The validity of the central limit theorem has far-reaching consequences in statistics. Almost every classic test is based on this knowledge. Even with the appreciation of classical confidence intervals for sample means, this confidence interval is symmetric, adopted by the estimated parameters because we know that the sample means are normally distributed.

This works for almost any estimator, even for highly non-smooth statistics such as the median; see *Figure 6.11*. Also, the sample medians are approximately normally distributed whenever the sample size is large enough:

```
cltSim(n = 100, pop = FALSE, estimator = median)
```

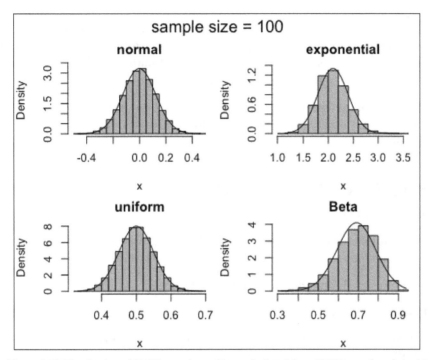

Figure 6.11: Distribution of 10,000 sample medians calculated from 10,000 samples of size 10

Properties of estimators

Especially in the following chapters, designations such as bias or asymptotic unbiasedness will be used repeatedly. These expressions are used to describe properties of an estimator. These terms are explained briefly here.

Assumption: The distribution of the sample elements X_i has an unknown parameter θ. A function t that approximately estimates from the sample values the parameter θ is given by:

$$\hat{\theta} = t(x_1, \dots, x_n).$$

Generally a function of a sample, $t = t(x_1, \ldots, x_n)$ is noted as *statistics*. In the case of estimation of parameters, we talk about a function for estimation, short *estimator t*. The realization of an estimator, $T = t(X_1, \ldots, X_n)$ such as $t = t(x_1, \ldots, x_n)$ is called *estimation*.

Depending on the sample obtained, other results for the point estimate are gained. For example, if 1,000 people are asked about their income by drawing 1,000 people from a finite population, the mean income would differ when another 1,000 people are drawn. Practically speaking, performed point estimates are therefore only useful when the accuracy of the results is considered.

In other words, a point estimate alone contains no information on accuracy. Thus an interval estimator must also be estimated that expresses the uncertainty of the point estimate.

Properties of estimators

What is a good estimator?

It is desirable, for example, that for repeated drawn samples, the sample estimates spread around *in the middle* of the true parameter (unbiasedness).

The following terms define the properties of estimators:

- **Unbiasedness**: $E(\hat{\theta}) = \theta$
- **Consistency**: $T_n \rightarrow \theta$ (when increasing the sample size, the estimator is closer to the population parameter)
- **Efficiency**: Unbiased estimator with minimal variance

There are different methods to find useful estimators for parameters of a distribution, the so-called *maximum likelihood* method being the most important.

Other important terms include:

- **Bias**: $\text{Bias}_\theta = E(\hat{\theta}) - \theta$
- **Asymptotic unbiasedness**: $\lim_{n \to \infty} E(\hat{\theta}) = \theta$
- **Mean squared error (MSE)**: $\text{MSE} = E([\hat{\theta} - \theta]^2)$ or $\text{MSE} = \text{var}(\hat{\theta}) + \text{Bias}_\theta^2$

If no bias is present, the MSE reduces to the comparison of the variances of estimated statistics. In other words, the MSE and the variance are equivalent in this case.

This all sounds nice, but how do you estimate the bias without knowing the true population parameter θ? How do you evaluate asymptotic unbiasedness when θ is unknown, as it is the case in practice? And how do you estimate the MSE if the bias is unknown?

For some estimators, all these questions have been answered by mathematical calculus, but in general we can answer those questions only by simulation studies. In other words, the properties of an estimator are typically evaluated by model-based simulations when the sample is drawn with simple random sampling, and evaluated with design-based simulation studies when the sample is drawn with complex sample designs (see *Chapter 10, Simulation with Complex Data*).

Confidence intervals

Along with point estimates, confidence intervals are commonly reported to show the reliability of the point estimates. For example, a confidence interval can be used to describe how reliable estimates from surveys are. The average hourly wages of employees taken from a simple random sample survey of 1000 respondents might be 31 Euros. A 99% confidence interval for the average income of the population might be 25 to 37 Euros. However, since there is no negative income, the confidence intervals must not be always symmetric, as is the case also for voting-intentions, for example. We will not cover these special cases, but refer to Hron, Templ, and Filzmoser (2013).

Generally, from the observed data, a lower and upper bound — an estimated interval — for the parameter θ is estimated. θ is unknown but fixed (an actual parameter in the population). The estimated interval, however, depends on the observations in the sample and is therefore random. Often, θ is contained therein, but sometimes, it is not. The calculation formula should be such that, for example, $100(1 - \alpha)$ = 95% (significance level α = 0.05) of all samples provide a θ covering interval. Increased coverage (α small) means the larger the estimated confidence intervals.

In a nutshell: We are looking for two estimates, U and O, specifying the limits of the confidence interval for a given coverage of $100(1 - \alpha)$ percent:

$P(U \le \theta \le O) = 1 - \alpha$

Formulas on confidence intervals depend on the whether the variance of θ is known or not. For smaller samples, one has to estimate the confidence intervals via a t distribution instead of the standard normal. However, if the sample size is sufficiently large, the t distribution is approximately equal to the normal distribution.

Remark: using the t-distribution instead of the normal distribution for the distribution of sample means was introduced by William Sealy Gosset's 1908 paper in Biometrika (Gosset, 1908) under the pseudonym "Student". Gosset worked in the "chemical" department at the Guinness Brewery in Dublin, Ireland. Chemical measurements, or measurements in general, were expensive, and thus he had to deal with very small sample sizes. Obviously, Guinness either did not want their competitors to know that they were using the t-test to test the quality of raw material (official version), or the bosses of Guinness might have said to him that he should brew good beer and not spend his time on an extensive paper about the later-named t-distribution. In any case, Gosset published the paper under the pseudonym "Student". It became one of the most important papers in statistics.

For an unknown standard deviation, the confidence interval for the sample mean is given by $[\overline{x} - t_{\alpha/2;n-1} * \frac{\sigma}{\sqrt{n}}, \overline{x} + t_{\alpha/2;n-1} * \frac{\sigma}{\sqrt{n}}]$, with α being the significance level, σ the standard deviation, and n the sample size. Symmetric confidence intervals (and the approximately normal distribution — here the t-distribution) can be used since of the validity of the central limit theorem.

Let's take a small exercise. We use the income variable of the *Prestige* data and estimate the arithmetic mean and confidence interval:

```
library("car")
data("Prestige")
m <- mean(Prestige$income)
m
## [1] 6797.902
p <- dim(Prestige)[1]
se <- sd(Prestige$income) / sqrt(p)
tval <- qt(0.975, df = p - 1)
cat(paste("KI: [", round(m - tval * se, 2), ",", round(m + tval * se, 2),
"]"))
## KI: [ 5963.92 , 7631.88 ]
```

Let's come back to explanations of the confidence interval. Let's draw 10 samples of size $n = 50$ each from a exp(1)-distribution. The density of the exponential distribution is given by $f(x) = \lambda e^{-\lambda x}$. Each sample leads to a different estimation of μ and to another estimated interval. How many intervals contain the true value of $\mu = 1$? This is shown in *Figure 6.12*:

```
set.seed(11112)
alpha <- 0.05
normval <- qnorm(1 - alpha/2)
```

```
numsamp <- 50; numsim <- 10
normmat <- matrix(0, nrow = numsim, ncol = 2)
y <- 1:numsim; ymat <- rbind(y, y)
for (i in 1:numsim) {
   samp <- rexp(numsamp)     # generate random exponentials
   sampmean <- mean(samp)
   sampse <- sqrt(var(samp) / numsamp)
   normmat[i, ] <- c(sampmean - normval * sampse, sampmean + normval *
sampse)
}
matplot(t(normmat), ymat , pch = " ", yaxt = "n", ylab = "",
xlab="confidence intervals") # empty plot
matlines(t(normmat), ymat, lty = rep(1, numsim), col = 1)
abline(v = 1)
```

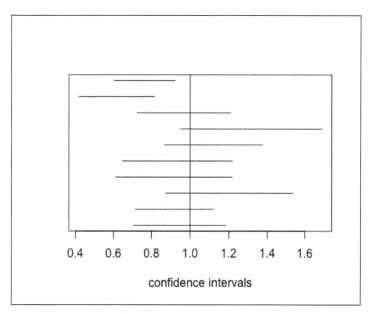

Figure 6.12: 10 draws from exp(1) and corresponding confidence intervals

We can observe that only eight of the estimated intervals cover the true population parameter indicated by a vertical line. Does that mean that the confidence interval was not properly specified? Not at all!

Were one to repeat the procedure described more often, in average 95 out of 100 unrealized intervals should contain the true value of $\mu = 1$ of (given $\alpha = 0.05$).

A note on robust estimators

We discuss here the case that all data values are correctly measured but large values may let the variance of an estimator explode.

Often in practice, there is the problem of having to either opt for a method which provides distorted estimates with smaller variance, or for a method which supplies unbiased estimates with large variance.

Figure 6.13 serves as striking example for the representation of the problem. Shooter **B** (Bias) actually shoots every time below the middle of the target. He is close to the middle, but biased, and the spread of his shots is low. The other shooter, in blue, shoots without bias (in "mean" he shoots in the middle) but the variance is large. Which strategy — unbiased with large variance or biased with low variance — would you choose?

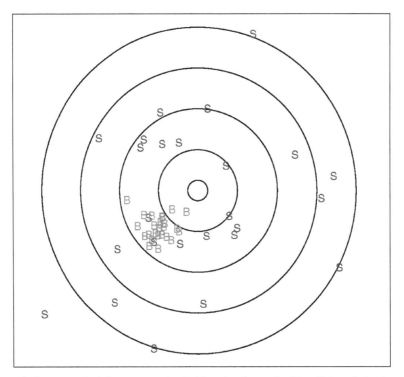

Figure 6.13: Two shooters with different strategies. In blue, the shooter "unbiased", in red, the shooter "biased"

If, for example, the unemployment rates of the regions of Austria should be compared, and the variance of the estimates is too high, then a ranking of regions may not be possible, since the confidence intervals of the unemployment rates will overlap a lot. In such a case, a possibly biased robust estimator with low variance is preferable, even though they might be biased in different directions.

In any case, to evaluate if the biased or unbiased estimator (and in general, any estimator) is preferable, the previously discussed MSE should be taken. Always, the trade-off between the variance and the bias has to be incorporated.

Summary

In this chapter, the data scientist approach to probability was shown. Probability concepts was not presented as a mathematical exercise, but some of the most important theorems when working with samples have been shown by simulation: the law of large numbers and the central limit theorem.

The concept of convergence of a mean was shown by tossing a coin. To toss a coin is something very basic in statistics. Think on selecting a person from a sampling frame or not. The Binomial but also the Poisson distribution can be motivated from this. The binomial distribution was shown in this chapter.

Both concepts — the law of large numbers as well as the central limit theorem, lead to confidence intervals, that are — in classical statistics — just a definition. This concept works as soon as the central limit theorem holds.

Also in content of this chapter were the properties of estimators. Bias, unbiasedness, asymptotic unbiasedness, and so on, have been introduced. These wordings will be consequently used in the next chapters. We mentioned the problem of determining unbiasedness or bias, since the population parameters are not known. We refer again to Chapter 10, which is dedicated to simulation experiments with the aim of evaluating estimators according to bias and variance for real data.

Estimating confidence intervals with classical methods has been introduced. The next chapter goes beyond that. There we will use resampling methods for variance estimation/estimating confidence intervals. This data-driven approach will turn out to be much more flexible and optimal to use for practitioners and data scientists.

References

- Gosset, W.S. 1908. "The Probable Error of a Mean", *Biometrika* 6 (1): 1–25

- Hron, K., M. Templ, and P. Filzmoser. 2013. "Estimation of a Proportion in Survey Sampling Using the Logratio Approach", *Metrika* 76 (6): 799–818

- Venn, J. 1880. "On the Diagrammatic and Mechanical Representation of Propositions and Reasonings", *The London, Edinburgh and Dublin Philosophical Magazine and Journal of Science* 10 (58): 1–18

7
Resampling Methods

"Dear friend, theory is all gray, and the golden tree of life is green."

– Johann Wolfgang von Goethe, Faust

For a lot of people, classical statistical inference is hard to understand, because it is packed with mathematics. Moreover, it is often very difficult and complex to demonstrate the properties of even relatively simple estimators in an analytical manner. Often it is even impossible to express the properties of estimators using mathematical formulas.

In the case of estimating confidence intervals or by carrying out a statistical test, distribution requirements must be assumed when applying classical statistics, basically the distribution of a test statistic. The mathematical formulation for estimating a classical confidence interval for a parameter θ (and point estimate $\hat{\theta}$) can often be very complex or even impossible. Imagine you want classical confidence intervals not only for the very simple arithmetic mean, but also for the median, for the 10 percent trimmed mean, for the *Huber-mean*, for regression coefficients of a robust MM-regression, the variance of the Gini from data obtained by a complex sampling design, and so on. Do you know the analytical expression or an approximation of it?

Generally, the procedure for making inference on an estimated parameter θ remains as simple as for the arithmetic mean when using resampling methods. No matter how mathematically complicated θ is, using resampling methods, statistical inference becomes simple.

It is shown that resampling methods can be used for almost all problems of statistical inference and properties of a point estimate can be relatively easily estimated from very complex estimators.

Since resampling methods are generally computationally intensive, resampling methods have been developed only since the 1980s and, of course, could only be used successfully with powerful computers.

As for the reason why resampling methods are still rarely used as classical inference methods, one can only speculate. One reason may be that many statisticians are often more mathematically oriented and also that many of them are not as well versed in programming.

This changes in that time when data science gets popular. In any case, making inferences using data-oriented resampling approaches is perfectly suited to data scientists. No powerful skills in mathematics and statistics are needed, but programming skills and computational power counts. With resampling methods, data scientists have very powerful methods on hand to solve almost any tasks related to statistical uncertainty.

The next parts of this book, of course, do not include any methods but are inspired by some books on bootstrapping (Efron and Tibshirani 1993; Shao and Tu 1995; Davison and Hinkley 1997; Chernick 1999; Hjorth 1994; Mammen 1992; Politis, Romano, and Wolf 1999; Good 1993; Westfall and Young 1993).

The bootstrap

The bootstrap is the most popular resampling method to express the uncertainty of an estimate; in other words, to estimate the variance of an estimated statistic of interest. But why is it called bootstrap? Tall boots may have a tab, loop or handle at the top known as a bootstrap; see *Figure 7.1*:

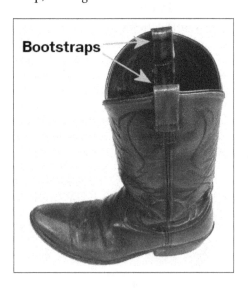

This bootstrap allows us to use our fingers to pull the boots on. But the term is used as a synonym for more. In the 19th century, the idiom "to pull oneself up by one's bootstraps was already being used as an example of an impossible task:

"It is conjectured that Mr. Murphee will now be enabled to hand himself over the Cumberland river or a barn yard fence by the straps of his boots" (Freeman 2009). This is just what the bootstrap is about in statistics. We will see that we use a bootstrap to make inference just with our boots (sample data).

In the following section, we will show with a motivating example that we get basically the same results with the bootstrap in comparison to analytical solutions. We will then explain the fundamental concept of the bootstrap and answer the question of why we can do an impossible task related to statistical inference with the bootstrap. Afterwards, we will discuss the practical application of the bootstrap in detail using R.

Before we start with the example, this famous quote – saying a lot of truth about the bootstrap approach – should be repeated:

> "*Statistics is a subject of amazingly many uses and surprisingly few effective practitioners. The traditional road to statistical knowledge is blocked, for most, by a formidable wall of mathematics. Our approach avoids that wall. The bootstrap is a computer-based method of statistical inference that can answer many real statistical questions without formulas.*"

> *– Bradley Efron*

A motivating example with odds ratios

In the original book on the jackknife and bootstrap (Efron and Tibshirani 1993), the authors gave an interesting motivating example. Since this example shows the advantages of a particular resampling method (the bootstrap) in an excellent manner, we use it here as well with our own words, code and comments. This example just should give reliability on resampling methods, since the same results are obtained as with the classical (non-resampling) approach.

The New York Times had on January 27, 1987 on its front page an article entitled *Heart Attack Risk Found to be Cut by Taking Aspirin*. This double-blind trial ultimately led to the following table; see also Efron and Tibshirani (1993):

	Heart attacks	#Persons
Aspirin	104	11037
Placebo	189	11034

The odds ratio of the two components is the following:

(104/11,037) / (189/11,034) = 0.55

A header in the newspaper could possibly be: *Those who take aspirin regularly have only 55% as many heart attacks as people who take no aspirin.*

As statisticians, we want to estimate the real population parameter θ. Of course we are not really interested in θ only, since θ is still only a point estimate of θ. If we conducted the study again and collected new data, we would get another result (different from 0.55).

We are interested in the accuracy/variability/uncertainty of $\theta = 0.55$ (statistical inference).

But how do we calculate the confidence interval (CI) for θ?

	Heart attacks	#Persons
Aspirin	a	b
Placebo	c	d

The odds ratio $\theta_{or} = (a/b)/(c/d) = (a * d)/(b * c)$. If we look at Wikipedia or literature, we see that the 95 percent confidence interval for $\log(\theta_{or})$ can be calculated by:

$$\log\theta_{or} \pm 1.96 * \sqrt{1/a + 1/b + 1/c + 1/d}$$

θ_{or} and the confidence interval has to be back-transformed by using their exponentials. With 95 percent probability, we cover the actual parameter with this interval:

```
dat <- matrix(c(104,11037,189,11034),2,2, byrow=TRUE)
dat
##        [,1]   [,2]
## [1,]   104 11037
## [2,]   189 11034
library("vcd")
## confidence intervals
confint(oddsratio(dat, log=FALSE))
##        2.5 %     97.5 %
## / 0.4324132 0.6998549
```

The following questions remain unanswered:

- How do we know that the formula for estimating the KI performs well? Where we can find the proof that this formula is valid?
- Are there better analytical estimates of the confidence interval available?
- Do we have simpler methods for the determination of the confidence interval?

The first question can be answered by some literature search. It turns out that the analytical expression to estimate the confidence interval of the odds ratios is an approximation. When looking at the literature, one can see that there are another 20 different formulas for estimating the confidence intervals of the odds ratios; in some cases, other formulas provide better results. If one looks carefully at the literature, it will take a lot of time to get enlightened and still it would be difficult to decide which formula to take. But do not worry, since we can answer the question "Do we have simpler methods for the determination of the confidence interval?". This question can be answered unequivocally with "YES!", namely by using a resampling method, consecutively with a bootstrap method.

The bootstrap for the aspirin example could be constructed as follows:

The first group consists of 104 ones and 11,037 - 104 zeros, the second one of 189 ones and 11,034 - 189 zeros.

Bootstrap sample: We draw from the first group a sample of size 11,037 with replacement, and from the second a sample of size 11,034 with replacement.

Bootstrap replication: The bootstrap replication of θ_{or} is now:

$$\theta_{or}^* = \frac{\text{Ratio of ones in first group}}{\text{Ratio of ones in the second group}}$$

We repeat this process (drawing bootstrap samples and calculating the corresponding bootstrap replicates), for example, 10,000 times and get 10,000 bootstrap replicates. The 95 percent confidence interval is determined by the 0.025 and 0.975 quantiles of the distribution of the bootstrap replicates (the motivation for this confidence interval follows later).

We can do this practically in R using the following code. Note that this example could be implemented more efficiently by using the `prob` parameter in the sample function; for didactical reasons, we initialize the whole vector of TRUE (heart attack) and FALSE (no heart attack):

```
## original surveyed data
s1 <- rep(c(TRUE, FALSE), times = c(104, 11037))
```

```
s2 <- rep(c(TRUE, FALSE), times = c(189, 11034))
## function for drawing a bootstrap sample
## and estimating the boostrap replicate
boot_aspirin <- function(s1, s2){
  ## odds ratio
  sum(sample(s1, replace = TRUE)) / sum(sample(s2, replace = TRUE))
}
## 10000 draws and replicates
boot_repl <- replicate(10000, boot_aspirin(s1, s2))
## confidence interval
quantile(boot_repl, c(0.025, 0.975))
##      2.5%      97.5%
## 0.4312796 0.6964336
```

For this example, the confidence intervals by bootstrap are very close to the one estimated previously from the analytical method. The estimation of confidence intervals using bootstrap was data-based, without preconditions (except the assumption that a good random number is chosen) and assumptions, and done in a (almost) very intuitive manner without mathematics.

Why the bootstrap works

Before we describe the bootstrap in detail, we want to point out the philosophical concept of the bootstrap. It is important to understand why the bootstrap is a valid approach for doing statistical inference. Readers who trust the bootstrap without questioning the philosophical principles of the bootstrap can skip this section.

This is a typical question (from http://stats.stackexchange.com/):

> *"I recently used bootstrapping to estimate confidence intervals for a project. Someone who doesn't know much about statistics recently asked me to explain why bootstrapping works, i.e., why is it that resampling the same sample over and over gives good results. I realized that although I'd spent a lot of time understanding how to use it, I don't really understand why bootstrapping works."*

Note that θ is a function of the random variables $X_1, X_2, \ldots, X_n$ and hence has a probability distribution, its sampling distribution, which is determined by n, and the distribution function F. In the following, we immediately go to the empirical case, we consider the empirical sample **x**. Its values are formed by the observation vector X_i, for $i = 1, \ldots, n$. **x** should serve as a sample from a population.

You want to ask a question of a population but you can't since you don't know the whole population. Therefore, you take a sample and ask the question of it instead. The idea is thus that we have just one vector **x**. Note that, for simplicity, we just work with a vector of values, but everything holds true for a -dimensional dataset **X** as well. When we estimate a population parameter (a statistic) $\theta = f(\mathbf{x})$ from this empirical dataset, we usually don't have a clue about the uncertainty (variability) of this estimate. But we know that there must be an uncertainty since – in theory – if we were to conduct another second sample data set empirically, say $\mathbf{X}_2$ from the same population, the resulting estimate, $\theta_2 = f(\mathbf{x}_2)$, would differ from θ. In other words, how confident are you that the sample answer is close to the population?

There are basically **four kinds** of approaches to answer this question, but not all are feasible in practice. For didactical reasons, we point out all four approaches according to a situation that may regularly happen in an enterprise. Imagine a meeting with the big boss, the vice big boss, the expert from accounting, the mathematical methods department boss and a data scientist:

- Get information about all (**Big Boss** approach):

  The big boss, unfortunately, has no idea about statistics; with a red face, he hits his fist on the table, since he is angry that the variability of θ cannot be easily expressed. He shouts: *Then let's get the whole population!* In cases where the population is finite (such as socio-economic populations), the accounting guy, of course, cannot provide him with an estimate of the variability, but he provides the big boss with an estimate of the millions of dollars it would cost to collect the necessary information about the whole population. (For infinite populations, the costs would be infinite.) The big boss respects that his own idea was not the best one, and he looks around the table for solutions from his *slaves*.

- Get information repeatedly (**Big Boss 2** approach):

  The big boss failed with his suggestion, but the second big boss feels that he is next in line to express his own brilliant idea. Self-assured, he expresses it with a superior smile on his face: *Then let's conduct more than one data set, repeat the survey, and conduct several data sets! Then we can evaluate our estimate and report if we can trust it!*

Let us give further comments on these suggestions. If you don't know the population, one way you might learn about the uncertainty of your population estimates is to take samples from the population again and again. For each of the samples taken, we would apply the same estimators to obtain the statistic of interest for each of these samples. We then would see how variable the sample answers tend to be.

The second big boss's smile freezes on his face when again the accounting guy claims that if k data sets are surveyed, the costs are (almost) k times higher. This approach is also not visible and thus everybody then looks at the mathematician – they think the mathematician is their last hope. So, even they know that they will again not understand the surely genius mathematician, everybody holds the eyes on the mathematician with full of expectation to receive any solution:

$$\left((1 - 2\hat{p})\, z_{\alpha/2}^2/2n \pm z_{\alpha/2}\sqrt{\hat{p}(1 - \hat{p})/n = z_{\alpha/2}^2/4n^2}\right)/(1 + z_{\alpha/2}^2/n)$$

- (Mathematician approach):

The mathematician says: *Imagine you decide to make assumptions, for example, that the statistic you want to estimate is approximately normal, or, for example, t-distributed. With some mathematics, you might then be able to calculate a confidence interval for the parameter of interest.* The bosses feel uncomfortable with the assumptions, but they think that a mathematician surely knows how to proceed in order to get a solution. They are just happy to get a solution, since the mathematician says that he might be able to express the variability of this complex estimator. However, then the mathematician replies: *The investigation and development needs five person months and I currently do not have the resources for it. We have to immediately hire an additional mathematician.* Of course, the accountant guy is already shaking his head to reject the idea of employing additional employees, because this has not been considered in the budget for this year. The bosses sink down in their chairs and with scattered depressive voice, the big boss says that they should apply a task force that will have weekly meetings on this issue. Thus, he is without hope that he will get a solution. By feeling truly helpless and without a vision, he just wants to close this meeting, but ...

- A job for the computer (**Data Scientist** approach):

  ... but the data scientist clears his throat, raises his hand and interrupts the closing of the meeting. He says: *I can give you a solution for any estimate you like in seconds.* The big boss raises his eyebrow, and the second big boss looks boringly to the data scientist since this young data scientist is in his eyes a rookie and does not know any realities. The accountant guy never trusts IT guys, and the mathematician looks with a pitiful face to the data scientist since he – the mathematician – thinks that he is the only serious person. The data scientist says: *Imagine you are not satisfied to assume a distribution of the parameter of interest as the mathematician wanted to assume. The option left is to use the information in the sample, from that only sample that you have. An alternative to conducting new samples from a population, as the second big boss suggested beforehand, is to take the only sample that you have and sample from it repeatedly. Sampling "with replacement" is now just a convenient way to treat the sample like it's a population and to sample from it in a way that reflects its shape. Do you agree with me that this is reasonable? The underlying sample that you have collected is the best information you can have about what the population actually looks like. And you surely agree with me that most samples will, if randomly chosen, look quite like the population they came from. Consequently, it is likely that your sample does too. Let us sample a large number of data sets from our underlying sample and compute the statistic of interest on each of these datasets. Thus we receive a distribution of our statistic. This distribution expresses the variability of our estimate. Just let the computer do the work for us.*

  Speechless, the bosses still haven't closed their open mouths. They are happy to get a quick and cheap solution of high quality.

  From now on, the bosses consult the data scientist on a regular basis to find solutions for data analysis problems. The data scientist becomes a hero and is so needed in his organization so that the bosses depend on his work (who is now the *slave*?).

A closer look at the bootstrap

The basis is to draw a random sample of size n from a probability distribution F; each drawn element is included in the sample with probability $1/n$. In other words, a random sample is given by: $x_i \sim F$ (i.i.d.) with $i = 1, \dots, n$ values drawn from the population.

Be $X_1, X_2, \dots$ random variables (in) with probability distribution $F(X)$, then the empirical probability function is for the realizations $\mathbf{x} = (x_1, \dots, x_n)$ defined by

$\hat{F}(x) = \frac{1}{n} \sum_{i=1}^{n} I_{(-\infty, x]}(x_i)$, where I is the indicator function.

It is true that (theorem of Glivenko-Cantelli, 1933)

$\parallel \hat{F} - F \parallel_{\infty} = \sup_{x \in \mathbb{R}} |\hat{F}(x) - F(x)| \to 0$. In other words, the distribution of the bootstrap samples converges almost surely to the actual probability distribution. This works because:

- The fact that for bootstrap samples the selection probability of an observation is still $1/N$

- The (strong) law of large numbers $P\left(\lim_{n \to \infty} \hat{X}_n^* = \mu\right) = 1$

- The central limit theorem – the bootstrap samples mimic the population

A bootstrap sample is usually of size n, the same size as the sample. A question could be: *Why not take bootstrap samples of size* $m \neq n$? The answer is easy. Most statistic/estimates are dependent on the sample size. The bootstrap distribution would just have potentially more spread when m < n and less spread if m > n, which would lead to an over- or underfitted estimated variance.

The full proof of the convergence of bootstrap samples almost surely to the actual probability distribution put a lot of knowledge of the measure theory and go over several pages; see, for example, Shao and Tu (1995). We will not repeat such a proof but use the evidence of the proofs in this book: we already trust proven theorems and concentrate on more applied stuff.

The plug-in principle

The bootstrap is based on the plug-in principle, that is, if something is unknown, then substitute an estimate for it. This principle is a familiar approach in statistics. For example, in *Chapter 4, Simulation of Random Numbers* we already plugged in the empirical standard deviation for the estimation of confidence intervals, since we didn't know the true variance, but the variance is noted in the formula for the confidence interval. With the bootstrap, we go a step further. Instead of plugging in an estimate for a single parameter, we plug in an estimate for the whole distribution (Hesterberg 2015).

Under the plug-in principle is meant nothing more than we replace $\theta = t(F)$ with the distribution function of the empirical distribution $\hat{F}$, $\hat{\theta} = t(\hat{F})$. Note: Often one writes the parameter θ directly as a function of the distribution of $\theta = t(F)$ instead of $\theta = t(\mathbf{X})$). It is assumed that θ can be calculated by the function $t(F)$. In the following section, the bootstrap is used to estimate standard errors and bias, where exactly this plug-in principle is exploited.

Estimation of standard errors with bootstrapping

In the following, we discuss the bootstrap in detail also by taking hands-on R. Before the estimation of the standard error is in focus, some definitions are repeated in more detail.

Let's consider the following toy example with the following seven numbers. We use such a small sample and toy example just to explain the bootstrap in R. The estimator of interest should be the arithmetic mean in our example:

```
x <- c(5, 7, 8, 2, 15, 12, 3)
```

We next define the bootstrap sample. A **bootstrap sample** is **random** sample

$x^* = (x_1^*, ..., x_n^*)$ **with replacement** from the sample $x = (x_1, ..., x_n)$. One **bootstrap sample** is given by:

```
## for reproducibility we use a seed
set.seed (123)
## bootstrap sample (with replacement)
s1 <- sample(x, replace = TRUE)
s1
## [1]   8 12   8   3   3   5   2
```

We see that this bootstrap sample does not include a 7 and a 15, but two times the 3 and 8. This can happen since we sample with replacement, meaning that if we draw a number, it will be replaced so that the next draw is again from *c(5, 7, 8, 2, 15, 12, 3)*.

Of course, we can repeat this to get another bootstrap sample, which of course differs with a high probability from the previous bootstrap sample:

```
s2 <- sample(x, replace = TRUE)
s2
## [1]   3   2   2   3   2  15  15
```

The arithmetic mean of our toy sample is:

```
mean(x)
## [1] 7.428571
```

The **bootstrap replicate** of $\theta = t(x)$ is denoted by $\theta^* = t(x^*)$. Exemplarily, be $t(x)$ the arithmetic mean $\overline{x}$ then the bootstrap replicate $t(x^*)$ is the arithmetic mean of the bootstrap samples $\overline{x}^* = \frac{1}{n}\sum_{i=1}^{n} x_i^*$.

For our bootstrap samples drawn, the arithmetic means (= **bootstrap replicates**) are as follows:

```
mean(s1)
## [1] 5.857143
mean(s2)
## [1] 6
```

Let's take a larger sample, for example, the `Prestige` data from the R package `car`. One variable is related to income. Again, let's take a bootstrap sample and estimate the bootstrap replicate.

But first, look at the statistic of interest from the sample. Let's assume that the statistic of interest is the arithmetic mean:

```
library("car")
data("Prestige")
mean(Prestige$income)
## [1] 6797.902
```

A bootstrap replicate for the arithmetic mean is:

```
set.seed(123)
mean(sample(Prestige$income, replace = TRUE))
## [1] 6393.882
```

Another can be achieved by repeating the previous line of code (without the `seed`):

```
mean(sample(Prestige$income, replace = TRUE))
## [1] 6662.529
```

The crucial thing is now how to express the variability of our statistic of interest. Before we discuss confidence intervals, we discuss how to estimate the standard error of an estimator. The bootstrap algorithm to estimate the standard error of an estimated parameter is as follows:

1. Select independent bootstrap samples $\mathbf{x}^{*1}, \mathbf{x}^{*2}, ..., \mathbf{x}^{*R}$ of x.
2. Calculate the bootstrap replications for each bootstrap sample:

$$\theta^*(r) = f(\mathbf{x}^{*r}), r = 1, 2, ..., R$$

3. Estimate the standard error se_F on the standard deviation of replications.

4. $se_R = \left\{ \sum_{r=1}^{R} [\theta^*(r) - \theta^*(\cdot)]^2 / (R-1) \right\}^{1/2}$ with $\theta^*(\cdot) = \sum_{r=1}^{R} \theta^*(r) / R$.

5. The following applies: $\lim_{R \to \infty} se_R = se_F$.

An illustration of the non-parametric bootstrap in the original definition of the bootstrap is given in Efron and Tibshirani (1993). We want to go a step further and show the bootstrap to estimate the standard error, as shown in *Figure 7.2*:

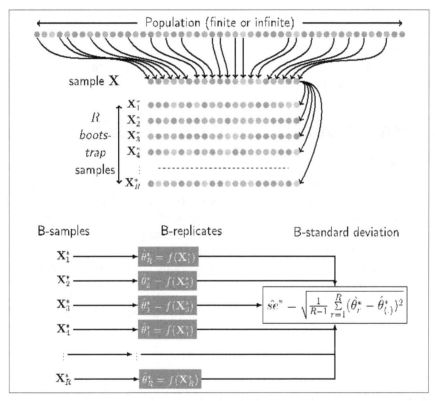

Figure 7.2: Bootstrap algorithm to estimate the standard error of a statistic $\theta = f(x)$ according to the original definition of Efron. The parameter R denotes the number of bootstrap replications

At the top of *Figure 7.2*, we see a whole population. This population is unknown but we have drawn one sample from it, say **x** of size n. From this sample, we draw bootstrap samples with replacement. All in all, we draw bootstrap samples of size n each. From these bootstrap samples, $\mathbf{x}_1^*, \ldots, \mathbf{x}_R^*$, the bootstrap replicates $\theta_1^*, \ldots, \theta_R^*$ are estimated. We obtained a distribution of bootstrap replicates. From the bootstrap replicates, the standard error se^* can be estimated.

To obtain stable and good results, one needs a certain number of bootstrap replications. In general, this course always depends on the problem and the distribution of the data. Basically, we often obtain stable results (when re-running the bootstrap, the same results obtained) with just 25 bootstrap replications, and 50 replications give very stable results for the standard error. Often 100 replications are chosen; more than 200 replications bring mostly no more profit. How can we check if, for example, R = 50 replications are enough to estimate the standard error? Just run the bootstrap a few times with R = 50 and evaluate how much the result varies. If the variation is relatively large, increase the number of replications.

In general, when other estimates are of interest, for example, the confidence intervals or model-based results, many more replications are needed. For estimating confidence intervals, more than 5,000 replications are useful. We see this in the section "Confidence intervals by bootstrap".

An example of a complex estimation using the bootstrap

It is often very hard to express standard errors in an analytical manner, even for simple estimators. We will show an example for the standard error for the (robust) correlation coefficient. The robust correlation measure can be achieved with the **Minimum Covariance Determinant** (**MCD**) algorithm (Rousseeuw and Driessen 1998). This is a rather complex estimator, where it is a huge challenge to estimate standard errors using a formula. We will see by using the bootstrap this is as easy as estimating the standard error for the arithmetic mean.

In R the MCD-based correlation can be calculated as follows. For simplicity, we only estimate the robust correlation between `income` and `prestige`:

```
library("robustbase")
## data
df <- Prestige[, c("income", "prestige")]
## robust MCD-based covariance
covMcd(df, cor=TRUE)$cor
##              income  prestige
## income    1.0000000 0.8240127
## prestige  0.8240127 1.0000000
```

The following legitimate question can be asked: How can one estimate the standard error for the correlation coefficient? Some further questions arise:

- Do you know how to estimate the standard error for the classical correlation coefficient (Pearson) analytically? If so, do you know the formula for the standard error of the correlation coefficient if...
- The data does not follow a multivariate normal distribution?
- Can you provide an appropriate analytical approximation?
- Can you calculate it for this example?
- Do you know it for the MCD-based correlation coefficient?

The answers are probably the following:

- Yes, when searching in Google or in a good book.
- No, I suppose there are only estimates for normally distributed data.
- No, but presumably this has been dealt with by someone else.
- Yes! Quite easily with the bootstrap!

Then let's do it. We sample (with replacement) the `Prestige` data using `sample()` and estimate the MCD-based correlation with function `covMcd`. We replicate this 200 times and estimate the standard error:

```
set.seed(1234) ## for reproducibility (seed)
## standard error with bootstrap
sd(replicate(200,
        covMcd(df[sample(rownames(df),  replace=TRUE), ],
               cor=TRUE)$cor[1,2]))
## [1] 0.09270074
```

In R, we can also make use of the function `boot`. We see that we get very similar results for the standard error. The fundamental concept of the `boot` function is to express how bootstrap samples should be drawn. This is done by writing an own function with a function argument regarding the data and another one about the index that should be sampled with replacement:

```
library("boot")
## function for bootstrapping in boot
cr <- function(d, w) covMcd(d[w, ], cor=TRUE)$cor[1,2]
## application of the boot function
boot(data=df, statistic=cr, R=200)
##
```

```
## ORDINARY NONPARAMETRIC BOOTSTRAP
##
##
## Call:
## boot(data = df, statistic = cr, R = 200)
##
##
## Bootstrap Statistics :
##      original        bias      std. error
## t1* 0.8240127  -0.001434576     0.088415
```

The parametric bootstrap

Generally speaking, when we have a properly specified model, simulating from the model often provides reliable estimates even with smaller number of replicates than the non-parametric bootstrap. However, if the parametric model is mis-specified, the solution converges to the wrong distribution. Thus, when using the parametric bootstrap, the assumptions must hold.

We would like to show an application of the parametric bootstrap to show the properties of this method. Suppose that we have information that allow us to conclude that the two variables income and prestige in the dataset Prestige (package car) are drawn from a bivariate normal distribution – this is the model here to be assumed. We now estimate the mean and covariance from the empirical data and draw from the theoretical normal distribution with the corresponding parameter values of the empirical data:

```
## MASS needed for drawing random numbers from multivariate normal
library("MASS")
## parameters from empirical data (income and prestige)
m1 <- colMeans(df)
m2 <- cov(df)
## number of observations
n <- dim(df)[1]
## parametric bootstrap
parboot <- replicate(200,  covMcd(mvrnorm(n, mu=m1, Sigma=m2),
cor=TRUE)$cor[1,2])
## standard error
sd(parboot)
## [1] 0.08318432
```

If we want to look at the computational speed also in comparison to the computation time of the non-parametric bootstrap, we increase the number of replicates and use the classical estimate of correlation:

```
## parametric bootstrap
system.time(sd(replicate(5000,
        cor(mvrnorm(n, mu=m1, Sigma=m2))[1,2])))
##    user  system elapsed
##   0.663   0.017   0.681
## non-parametric bootstrap
system.time(sd(replicate(5000,
        cor(df[sample(rownames(df),  replace=TRUE), ])[1,2])))
##    user  system elapsed
##   0.925   0.020   0.945
```

We see that there is not as much difference in computation time for the parametric and non-parametric bootstraps in this example. However, in the literature, often it is said that the difference is about the stability of results; in other words, it is often mentioned that if well specified, the parametric bootstrap provides stable results for the standard error for smaller sample sizes. However, this must not be true in the general case, and basically this is not even true for our example. We replicate the estimation of the standard error 20 times with R = 50 each and look at the range of results:

```
## parametric bootstrap
range(replicate(20, sd(replicate(50,
                    cor(mvrnorm(n, mu=m1, Sigma=m2))[1,2]))))
## [1] 0.04194079 0.06062707
## non-parametric bootstrap
range(replicate(20, sd(replicate(50,
        cor(df[sample(rownames(df),  replace=TRUE), ])[1,2]))))
## [1] 0.03479239 0.05161005
```

We see that the standard errors differ slightly.

Let's finally compare the results from the non-parametric and the parametric bootstrap. We draw 1,000 bootstrap samples:

```
## parametric bootstrap
pboot <-replicate(1000,
    cor(mvrnorm(n, mu=m1, Sigma=m2))[1,2])
## non-parametric bootstrap
```

```
npboot <- replicate(1000,
    cor(df[sample(rownames(df),
    replace=TRUE), ])[1,2])
mi <- min(pboot, npboot)
ma <- max(pboot, npboot)
```

Visually, these differences can be shown, for example, with histograms of the distribution of bootstrap replicates. Now we plot *Figure 7.3*:

```
par(mfrow=c(1,2), pty="s")
hist(npboot,
    main="non-parametric",
    xlab="1000 bootstrap replicates",
    xlim=c(mi,ma), breaks = 25)
hist(pboot,
    main="parametric",
    xlab="1000 bootstap replicates",
    xlim=c(mi,ma), breaks = 25)
```

The comparison is visible in *Figure 7.3*, generated from the preceding code. The results are very similar in this case:

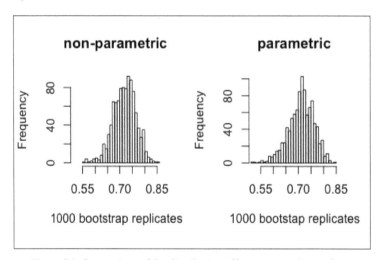

Figure 7.3: Comparison of the distribution of bootstrap replicates from a non-parametric and a parametric bootstrap

From *Figure 7.3*, we see that the distribution of bootstrap replicates is not very different for the parametric and non-parametric bootstraps in our example.

Estimating bias with bootstrap

Previously, the standard error was used as a measure of the accuracy of an estimator θ. We now want to look at the bias, the difference of the estimator θ and the parameters to be estimated the population θ – we want to look at systematic distortions of the estimator θ.

The reasons for bias in the data can be very different: systematic errors in registers, poor sampling design, heavy earners not reported, outliers, robust estimates of sampling means or totals in complex sampling designs, and so on.

The bias of $\theta = f(\mathbf{x})$ is the deviation from the actual parameter of the population, that is, $\theta = \text{bias}_\theta = E(\hat\theta) - \theta$. Since θ is generally unknown, the bias can usually only be expressed using resampling. In the following, we only concentrate on this mathematical bias and do not consider any other kind of bias (such as systematic bias from data collection).

For the estimation of the bias, independent bootstrap samples, $\mathbf{x}^{*1}, \mathbf{x}^{*2}, ..., \mathbf{x}^{*R}$, are drawn, see Efron and Tibshirani (1993), and the bootstrap replications estimated,

$\mathbf{x}^{*1}, \mathbf{x}^{*2}, ..., \mathbf{x}^{*R}$. $\theta_r^* = f(\mathbf{x}_r^*)$ is approximated with the help of the bootstrap replicates, $E_{\hat{F}}[f(\mathbf{x})]$ via $\theta_{(.)}^* = \sum_{r=1}^{R} \theta_r^*/R = \sum_{r=1}^{R} f(\mathbf{x}_r^*)/R$ and $t(F)$ via $t(\hat{F})$.

The bootstrap estimate of the bias is based on bootstrap replications:

$$\hat{\text{bias}}_R = \theta_{(.)}^* - t(\hat{F})$$

We again use the `Prestige` data and select the variable `income`. The parameters to be estimated of the population is the coefficient of variation, $\nu = \frac{\hat{s}}{\bar{x}}$ with $\hat{s}$ the estimated standard deviation and $\overline{\mathbf{x}}$ the arithmetic mean. This can be done in R like this:

```
x <- Prestige[, "income"]
v <- function(x) sd(x) / mean(x)
v(x)
## [1] 0.624593
```

1,000 bootstrap samples can be drawn easily, and the bootstrap replicates are easy to calculate:

```
vboot <- replicate(1000, v(sample(x, replace = TRUE)))
```

The bias is then given by the mean of bootstrap replicates estimate and the sample estimate:

```
vbias <- mean(vboot) - v(x)
vbias
## [1] -0.01215573
```

A bias-corrected estimator is then given by:

```
v(x) - vbias
## [1] 0.6367488
```

 Just being aware that a statistic is biased may help you to proceed more appropriately.

Confidence intervals by bootstrap

Confidence intervals are a very useful way to express uncertainty intervals, already broadly discussed in *Chapter 6, Probability Theory Shown by Simulation*. It's not always visible and easy to estimate the confidence interval for a complex estimator in a classical manner, but as before it's much easier when using the bootstrap.

The easiest method to estimate confidence intervals is just by plugging in the estimate of the standard error by bootstrap in the analytical formula for the confidence interval. But we will see that this is not the best idea.

As already described in *Chapter 6, Probability Theory Shown by Simulation* the classic estimate of the confidence interval of the arithmetic mean or total estimator is

$$\hat{\theta} \pm t_{n-1;\frac{\alpha}{2}} \cdot \hat{se}.$$

Now for, $\hat{se}$ then $\hat{se}^*$, the bootstrap standard error, is used.

For the previous example, one can determine this confidence interval as follows:

```
cat("CI(e): [", v(x) - vbias - qt(0.975, length(x)-1) * sd(vboot), ", ",
v(x) - vbias + qt(0.975, length(x)-1) * sd(vboot), " ]\n")
## CI(e): [ 0.5059086 ,  0.7675889  ]
```

However, expect from the bias correction these confidence intervals are always symmetric. However, one big advantage of the bootstrap is that the intervals might not be symmetric. For example, think of a ratio estimator, for example, the ratio of votes for a small party according to all votes in elections, and say this party has 1.5 percent of the votes. With classical methods and also with this approach for estimating the confidence interval with bootstrapping, it is likely that the left side of the symmetric confidence interval is negative. Negative votes! Impossible in practice. Thus we go to a much more reliable approach.

Especially if the bootstrap distribution of an estimator is symmetric, then percentile confidence intervals are often used. Efron's percentile method for bootstrap confidence intervals is the most popular method and it has good properties when the number of bootstrap replicates is large.

Instead the classic estimate of the standard error is replaced with the estimate obtained by bootstrapping, the lower and upper percentile of bootstrap distribution is used.

Efron's method of **percentile confidence intervals** using bootstrap is given by:

$$(\theta_{lo}, \theta_{up}) = (\theta^*_{(\frac{\alpha}{2})}, \theta^*_{(1-\frac{\alpha}{2})})$$

If we choose, for example, R = 1000 and for the significance level $\alpha = 0.05$, the percentile confidence interval is determined by the 25th and 975th values of the 1,000 sorted bootstrap replicates $\theta^*_{(r)}$, namely $(\theta^*_{(0.025)}, \theta^*_{(0.975)})$.

For our example, this confidence interval is determined as follows:

```
cat("CI(p): [", quantile(vboot, 0.025), ", ", quantile(vboot, 0.975), "
]\n")
## CI(p): [ 0.4816879 ,   0.7349403  ]
```

There are variants of this approach, like the confidence interval method by Hall:

```
cat("CI(h): [", 2*v(x) - quantile(vboot, 0.975), ", ", 2*v(x) -
quantile(vboot, 0.025), " ]\n")
## CI(h): [ 0.5142458 ,   0.7674982  ]
```

The bootstrap **Bias Corrected alpha (BCa)** confidence interval method (Efron 1987) makes use of another kind of bias estimate, the fraction of the bootstrap distribution that is $< \theta$.

The confidence interval of the BC_α method is also based on the percentiles. These percentiles depend on two numbers, the *acceleration* $\hat{a}$ and the *bias correction* $\hat{z}_0$. The BC_α confidence interval is given by:

$$BC_\alpha: (\hat{\theta}_{lo}, \hat{\theta}_{up}) = (\hat{\theta}^*_{(\alpha_1)}, \hat{\theta}^*_{(\alpha_2)})$$

With:

$$\alpha_1 = \Phi\left(\hat{z}_0 + \frac{\hat{z}_0 + z_{(\alpha/2)}}{1 - \hat{a}(\hat{z}_0 + z_{(\alpha/2)})}\right)$$

$$\alpha_2 = \Phi\left(\hat{z}_0 + \frac{\hat{z}_0 + z_{(1-\alpha/2)}}{1 - \hat{a}(\hat{z}_0 + z_{(1-\alpha/2)})}\right)$$

$\Phi(.)$ denotes the cumulative distribution function of the standard normal distribution, and $z_{(\alpha/2)}$ is the $\frac{\alpha}{2}$-quantile of the standard normal distribution. If $\hat{a} = \hat{z}_0 = 0$ then the BC_α method is equal to the percentile method.

Determination of $\hat{z}_0$:

The value of the bias correction $\hat{z}_0$ is the number of bootstrap replications, which are smaller than the (classical) estimate of θ, namely $\hat{\theta}$, that is:

$$\bar{z}_0 = \phi^{-1}\left(\frac{\#\{\hat{\theta}^*_{(r)} < \hat{\theta}\}}{R}\right)$$

Determination of $\hat{a}$:

The simplest method to determine $\hat{a}$ is by consulting the jackknife estimates *jackknife values* (details of this method can be found in the following *The jackknife* section). Let $x_{(i)}$ be the original sample without the th value x_i, and let $\hat{\theta}_{(i)} = f(x_{(i)})$ and $\hat{\theta}_{(.)} = \frac{1}{n}\sum_{i=1}^{n}\hat{\theta}_{(i)}$. Then the *acceleration* can be determined as follows:

$$\hat{a} = \frac{\sum_{i=1}^{n}(\hat{\theta}_{(.)} - \hat{\theta}_{(i)})^3}{6\{\sum_{i=1}^{n}(\hat{\theta}_{(.)} - \hat{\theta}_{(i)})^2\}^{3/2}}$$

The disadvantage of this method is that usually a large number of replications is required (min. 1,000).

Next, let's compare the confidence intervals of the percentile method with those of the BC_α method, and then compare it to all mentioned methods based on some simulated toy data:

```
## some crazy data (10 outliers)
x <- c(rnorm(100), rnorm(10,10))
## non-parametric bootstrap replicates
mb <- replicate(10000, mean(sample(x, replace=TRUE)))
## percentile method
cat("\nCI(perc): [", quantile(mb, 0.025), ", ", quantile(mb, 0.975), "
]\n")
##
## CI(perc): [ 0.4515313 ,  1.568372  ]
## BCa method
library("bootstrap")
b <- bcanon(x, 10000, mean, alpha=c(0.025,0.975))
cat("\nCI(BCa): [", b$confpoints[1,2], ", ", b$confpoints[2,2], " ]\n")
##
## CI(BCa): [ 0.5125295 ,  1.659545  ]
```

We compare all the mentioned methods by drawing the confidence intervals in a graphic; see *Figure 7.4*:

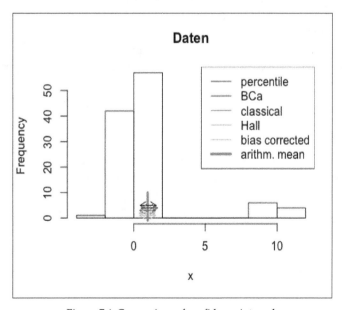

Figure 7.4: Comparison of confidence intervals

It is good to see the whole distribution of data in *Figure 7.4* but we need to have a closer look at the area of arrows of the confidence intervals. In *Figure 7.5*, we show this zoomed area:

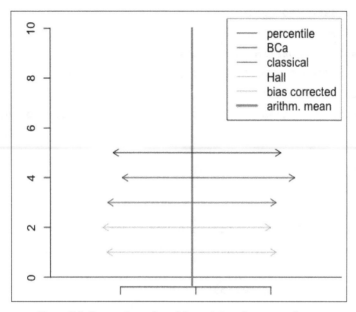

Figure 7.5: Comparison of confidence intervals – zoomed area

We note that even in the case of our extreme example with huge outliers, the differences are not dramatic. This is also true for other distributions, but it may depend on the parameter of interest and sample size as well as the number of bootstrap replicates. A non-smooth estimator is usually more problematic as the arithmetic mean in the previous example, especially for a resampling method that we present in the following section – *The jackknife*.

The jackknife

The jackknife is – like the bootstrap – a resampling method. The jackknife can be used to determine bias and standard error of estimators. It is simpler and faster than the bootstrap, since we do not draw new (bootstrap) samples, but we leave out one value from the original sample (for each jackknife sample). We just make estimations with one observation excluded.

The jackknife method was originally proposed by Quenouille (1949). Almost a century later, John Tukey (1958) extended the use of the method by showing how to use it for reducing the bias and estimating the variance. He invented the name "jackknife". Like a pocket knife, this technique can be used as an easy to use and fast to calculate "quick and dirty" tool that can solve a variety of problems. While the jackknife was very popular in the past because of its simplicity and fast computation, it generally has lower quality than the bootstrap, and it should be used only in rare, specific cases.

Let $\theta = f(\mathbf{x})$ be an estimator for a parameter of the population based on the given sample. The standard procedure of the classical jackknife is to estimate parameters of interest with n – 1observations instead of n.

$\mathbf{x}_{(i)} = (x_1, x_2, \dots, x_{i-1}, x_{i+1}, \dots, x_n)$ denotes the i-th **jackknife sample**. It is without the observation from $i \in \{1, \dots, n\}$, that is, the i-th jackknife sample is exactly the given data without the i-th observation.

The i-th **jackknife replication** of θ is given by $\theta_{(i)} = f(\mathbf{x}_{(i)})$.

The estimated bias calculated by jackknifing is given by $\widehat{Bias}_{jack} = (n-1)(\theta_{(.)} - \theta)$ with $\theta_{(.)} = \frac{1}{n}\sum_{i=1}^{n} \theta_{(i)}$.

The estimated jackknife standard error is given by $\widehat{se}_{jack} = \sqrt{\frac{n-1}{n}\sum_{i=1}^{n}(\theta_{(i)} - \theta_{(.)})^2}$.

The factor $\frac{n-1}{n}$ is a so-called *inflation factor*, which is needed because the Euclidean distances resulting from the jackknife $\theta_{(.)} = \frac{1}{n}\sum_{i=1}^{n} \theta_{(i)}$ are smaller than in case of the bootstrap $((\theta^*(r) - \theta^*(.))^2)$ that is, a typical jackknife sample is more similar to the original sample as a typical bootstrap sample. The exact form of the inflation factor, $\frac{n-1}{n}$, is fixed from the special case $\theta = \bar{x}$ - a consistent estimator for this special case.

A so-called *pseudo-value* is computed as the difference between the whole sample estimate and the partial estimate. Such pseudo-values reduce the bias of a partial estimate. The pseudo-values are then used instead of the original values to estimate the parameter of interest and their standard deviation is used to estimate the parameter standard error. It is assumed that pseudo-values allow us to write the estimate as a mean of n "independent" data values. However, this is often not the case in real applications. Expect that, in general, pseudo-values are not independent.

The jackknife pseudo-values are given by $\tilde{\theta}_i = n\theta - (n-1)\theta_{(i)}$.

The standard error estimated using jackknife pseudo-values is given by:

$$se_{jackPseudo} = \left\{ \frac{1}{(n-1)n} \sum_{i=1}^{n} (\tilde{\theta}_i - \tilde{\theta})^2 \right\}^{1/2} \quad \text{with } \tilde{\theta} = \frac{1}{n} \sum \tilde{\theta}_i$$

This corresponds to the usual formula for the variance of the arithmetic mean, thus we have an additional n in the denominator.

A possibility for specifying a confidence interval is: $\tilde{\theta} \pm t_{n-1;1-\frac{\alpha}{2}} se_{jack}$, with $t_{n-1;1-\frac{\alpha}{2}}$ also $(1 - \frac{\alpha}{2})$ quantile of a distribution with (n – 1) degrees of freedom. However, note again that the pseudo-values are rarely used in practice. In the following, we show results from both classical jackknife and jackknife using jackknife pseudo-values.

For the last example from the section about bootstrap, we now apply estimates with the jackknife in R. We use a toy data set with only few numbers. With this data set, we show the problems of the jackknife, especially later when we estimate non-smooth statistics such as the median. Before we come back to the variation coefficient:

```
## toy data
x <- c(1,2,2,2,2,2,7,8,9,10)
## remember, this is the variation coefficient
v <- function(x) sd(x)/mean(x)
## initialisation
n <- length(x)
vjack <- rep(0, n-1)
vpseudo <- rep(0, n)
## leave-one-out jackknife
for(i in 1:n){
  vjack[i] <- v(x[-i])
}
## jackknife pseudo values
pseudo <- n * v(x) - (n-1)*vjack
## confidence interval with pseudo values
cat("\nKI(pseudo): [", mean(pseudo) - qt(0.975, n-1) * sd(pseudo)/n, ",
", mean(pseudo) + qt(0.975, n-1) * sd(pseudo)/n, " ]\n")
##
## KI(pseudo): [ 0.6639477 ,   0.8618599  ]
## confidence interval with classical jackknife
```

```
se2 <- sqrt(((n-1)/n) * sum((vjack - mean(vjack))^2))
jbias <- (n-1) * (mean(vjack) - v(x))
cat("\nKI(jse): [", v(x) - jbias - qt(0.975, n-1) * se2 , ", ", v(x) -
jbias + qt(0.975, n-1) * se2, " ]\n")
##
## KI(jse): [ 0.4499772 , 1.07583  ]
```

From this example, we see that we may underestimate the confidence intervals, especially by using jackknife pseudo values, because we have a very small sample and, naturally, the confidence interval should thus be larger. In comparison, we show the results of a bootstrap that leads to broader confidence intervals:

```
quantile(replicate(10000, v(sample(x, replace = TRUE))), c(0.025, 0.975))
##      2.5%      97.5%
## 0.4977611 0.9860133
```

Disadvantages of the jackknife

This jackknife (later we see another kind of jackknife) is a very simple procedure to often receive good approximations, for example, for the bias and the standard error. However, the jackknife often does not converge to the true standard error, especially for non-smooth estimators. We give an extreme example in the following to see how the jackknife may underestimate the variation of the parameter. We use the same toy data set as before, but instead of the variation coefficient, we estimate a non-smooth estimator such as the median:

```
## sample estimate
median(x)
## [1] 2
## non-parametric bootstrap
qu <- quantile(replicate(10000,
        median(sample(x, replace = TRUE))),
      c(0.025, 0.975))
cat("\nCI(boot): [", qu[1], ", ", qu[2], " ]\n")
##
## CI(boot): [ 2 ,  8  ]
## jackknife, initialisation
n <- length(x)
jack <- rep(0, n-1)
pseudo <- rep(0, n)
```

```
for(i in 1:n){
  jack[i] <- median(x[-i])
}
## jackknife pseudo values approach
pseudo <- n * median(x) - (n-1)*jack
cat("\nCI(pseudo): [", mean(pseudo) - qt(0.975, n-1) * sd(pseudo)/n, ",
", mean(pseudo) + qt(0.975, n-1) * sd(pseudo)/n, " ]\n")
##
## CI(pseudo): [ 2 ,   2  ]
## classical jackknife
se2 <- sqrt(((n-1)/n) * sum((jack - mean(jack))^2))
jbias <- (n-1) * (mean(jack) - median(x))
cat("\nCI(jse): [", median(x) - jbias - qt(0.975, n-1) * se2 , ", ",
median(x) - jbias - qt(0.975, n-1) * se2, " ]\n")
##
## CI(jse): [ 2 ,   2  ]
```

We see that the jackknife completely underestimates the confidence interval: it was of zero length! The toy data set used had too many 2s, so when leaving out one value, the median is still 2. Thus the confidence interval estimated by the jackknife must be of zero length since all jackknife replicates have a value of 2. Of course, this was an extreme case, but the example should show that you should be aware when using the jackknife in practice. Especially for non-smooth estimators, the jackknife may underestimate the variability of an estimator.

The delete-d jackknife

The classic jackknife, as presented before, can be improved, especially when estimating non-smooth statistics. The principle *leave one out at a time* is replaced by leaving out d observations, where $n = d \cdot r$ (with r integer). The formula for the standard error with delete-d jackknife is $\sqrt{\frac{r}{\binom{n}{d}} \sum (\theta_{(s)} - \theta_{(.)})^2}$, with $\theta_{(.)} = \frac{1}{\binom{n}{d}} \sum \theta_{(s)}$ and the sum over all subsets s of size n – d , drawn from $X_1, X_2, \ldots, X_n$ without replacement. Often d is chosen as an integer value in $\sqrt{n} < d < n$.

However, the delete-d jackknife has the drawback that instead of calculating n leave-one-out estimates, we now have to calculate $\binom{n}{d}$ leave-d-out estimates – a much larger number, often bordering on the computationally infeasible.

Let's show this with the delete-2 jackknife. The aim is to create a matrix of $\binom{n}{d}$ combinations, in our case $\binom{n}{2}$, and apply a delete-d jackknife to that. Again, we want to estimate the median from the previous example:

```
## all combinations
co <- combn(10, 2)
## first 6 out of 45
co[, 1:6]
##        [,1] [,2] [,3] [,4] [,5] [,6]
## [1,]    1    1    1    1    1    1
## [2,]    2    3    4    5    6    7
## delete-2 jackknife replicates
jack_d <- apply(co, 2, function(i) median(x[-i]))
## standard error
n <- length(x)
r <- 2 / n
## n over 2
nd <- choose(n, 2)
## inflation factor
fac <- r / nd
m <- mean(jack_d)
## standard error
se_d <- sqrt(fac * sum((jack_d - m)^2))
## confidence interval:
cat("\nKI(jse): [", median(x)  - qt(0.975, n-1) * se_d , ", ", median(x)
+ qt(0.975, n-1) * se_d, " ]\n")
##
## KI(jse): [ 0.8077385 ,   3.192262  ]
```

The confidence intervals by the delete-2 jackknife seems reasonable. However, in general, the delete-d jackknife is not an efficient method. We investigated in a very small data set. For example, the number of possible combinations is for a sample of a slightly larger data set with 45 observations and *d* equals 10, we will get the following number of jackknife samples:

```
choose(45, 10)
## [1] 3190187286
```

You may imagine how this number would increase with even larger samples. It is thus better to apply a bootstrap instead of the delete-d jackknife.

Jackknife after bootstrap

This section explains how to estimate the variability of the standard error obtained by a bootstrap. In other words, we already estimated the variability (for example, standard error) using the bootstrap, but now we are interested in the uncertainty of our estimated variability. Let $\hat{se}_R = \left\{ \sum_{r=1}^{R} [\theta^*_{(r)} - \theta^*_{(\cdot)}]^2 / (R-1) \right\}^{1/2}$, with $\theta^*_{(\cdot)} = \sum_{r=1}^{R} \theta^*_{(r)} / R$ again be our standard error estimated by bootstrapping.

We are now interested in the uncertainty as to the estimation of $\hat{se}_R$ express them.

The **jackknife after bootstrap** method is a method to estimate the variance of the standard error $se(\hat{se}_R)$ or, in general, the uncertainty of a confidence interval estimate. To do this, one can make another bootstrap, but this means that for R= 1,000 to estimate the variance of the point estimator of interest and for another 1,000 replications to estimate the variance of the variance estimator leads to bootstrap replicates. Quite a large number.

But there is a trick to reduce this number considerably by using a jackknife after bootstrap in a special manner. Basically, we will see that only the information of the bootstrap samples is used.

The jackknife estimators of the standard error based on the following two steps:

- For $i = 1, \ldots, n$ exclude the i-th value and estimate $\hat{S}_R$. The result is $\hat{se}_{R(i)}$.
- $\hat{se}_{jack}(\hat{se}_R)$ is determined by:

$$\hat{se}_{wjack}(\hat{se}_R) = \left\{ \frac{n-1}{n} \sum_{i=1}^{n} (\tilde{se}_{R(i)} - \tilde{se}_{R(\cdot)})^2 \right\}^{1/2} , \text{ with}$$

$$\tilde{se}_{R(\cdot)} = \frac{1}{n} \sum_{i=1}^{n} \tilde{se}_{R(i)}$$

The thing left to estimate is $\hat{se}_{R(i)}$. As mentioned before, this estimation would need new bootstrap samples for each i. Since this is computationally expensive, the following trick is used. The probability is high that you find for the i-th value some bootstrap samples that do not include the i-th value. We estimate $\hat{se}_{R(i)}$ with the help of the standard deviation of $s(\mathbf{x}^{*r})$ of those bootstrap samples $\mathbf{x}^{*r}$ that do not include the i-th value. Let us denote C_i as the index of the bootstrap samples which do not include the data point i. If you have a total of such samples, then

$$\hat{se}_{R(i)} = \left[\sum_{r \in C_i} \frac{(s(x^{*r}) - \bar{s}_i)^2}{R_i} \right]^{1/2} \text{ with } \bar{S}_i = \sum_{r \in C_i} \frac{s(x^{*r})}{R_i} .$$

As a rule, for the estimate of $se_{jack}(se_R)$, more than 1,000 replications are needed to overhaul useful results. For R < 1000, one should weight . Be $\tilde{se}_{R(i)} = w_i se_{R(i)}$, then the weighted jackknife after bootstrap estimators is defined as follows:

$$se_{wjack}(se_R) = \left\{ \frac{n-1}{n} \sum_{i=1}^{n} (\tilde{se}_{R(i)} - \tilde{se}_{R(.)})^2 \right\}^{1/2} \text{, with}$$

$$\tilde{se}_{R(.)} = \frac{1}{n}\sum_{i=1}^{n} \tilde{se}_{R(i)}$$

A candidate for is given by $w_i = \frac{R_i}{\sum_{i=1}^{n} R_i/n}$ $, i = 1, ..., n$.

The jackknife after bootstrap plot, see Efron (1992) and Davison and Hinkley (1997), calculates the jackknife influence values from a bootstrap output object, and plots the corresponding jackknife after bootstrap plot. It is used to determine which observations have a high influence on the bootstrap replicates distribution and thus on se_R.

Let again be our vector with the income of the Prestige data. We again denote the function v as the estimation of the coefficient of variation. In order to be able to use the function boot(), we write down the function with two parameters:

```
data(Prestige, package = "car")
x <- Prestige$income
v <- function(x, indices){
  x <- x[indices]
  est <- sd(x)/mean(x)
  return(est)
}
```

The jackknife-after-bootstrap plot (*Figure 7.6*) is produced as follows:

```
library("boot")
bx <- boot(x, v, 2000)
## Figure 7.6.
jack.after.boot(bx)
```

From *Figure 7.6*, we see that observations 2 and 24 have great influence on the estimation of the coefficient of variation:

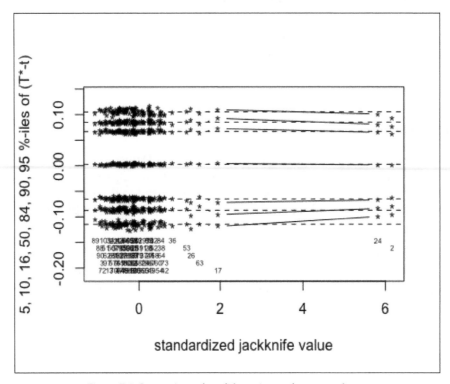

Figure 7.6: Comparison of confidence intervals - zoomed area

These two observations – you can see at the data values itself – have by far the largest jackknife values. The horizontal lines indicate the $(0.05, 0.10, 0.16, 0.50, 0.84, 0.90, 0.95)$-quantile of the bootstrap distribution, centered with respect to the value of the original data. The points that are connected to these lines denote the estimated (using bootstrapping) quantiles without the respective observation. One can see that especially for observations 2 and 24, the quantiles of the bootstrap replicates get smaller compared to the estimates when 2 and 24 are not excluded.

Generally, to mention is that the diagnosis by the jackknife-after-bootstrap plot cannot replace the usual diagnostics, for example, outlier diagnostics. However, the influence of particular values on the bootstrap replicates distribution is visible. Also, this approach is not affiliated designed to detect worse models. The jackknife-after-bootstrap plot merely gives an indication of which observations have great influence on the variance estimate.

Cross-validation

Cross-validation is a resampling method as well, similar to the jackknife. However, the aim is now not to make inference statistics but to estimate prediction errors.

Cross-validation is mainly used for the comparison of methods or to find the optimal values of parameters in an estimation model.

In the following section, we will explain cross-validation based on regression analysis. For readers who have never heard of regression analysis, we recommend to read a basic textbook about regression analysis. We only point out some very basic issues.

The classical linear regression model

The classical linear regression model in its simplest case with one response and one predictor is given by $y_i = \beta_0 + \beta_1 x_i + \epsilon_i$ with $i = 1, \ldots, n$. In matrix notation, this is

$y = X\beta + \epsilon$, with the response y a vector of values, design matrix X with observations and $p + 1$ variables (including a vector of ones in the first column for the intercept term), β a vector of size $p + 1$ and error term ϵ of length n. To keep it simple, we consider only one predictor, but stress that the assumptions and everything that follows can be formulated and translated to the multiple regression case.

The following model assumptions of the classical linear regression model are used:

- **A1**: The values of the independent variables X are fixed (not random) variables.

- **A2**: The values of the dependent variable y arising from the following components β_0, β_1 are parameters of the population.

- **A3**: The ϵ_i are random variables with the following properties:

    - **A3a**: $E(\epsilon_i) = 0$, for $i = 1, \ldots, n$

    - **A3b**: $\mathrm{var}(\epsilon_i) = \sigma_\epsilon^2$, for $i = 1, \ldots, n$ *(homoscedasticity!)*

    - **A3c**: $\mathrm{cov}(\epsilon_i, \epsilon_j) = 0$, for $i = 1, \ldots, n; j = 1, \ldots, n, \ i \neq j$

For valid inference, the error terms ϵ_i are assumed to be (approximately) normal.

The unknown parameters $\beta_0, \ldots, \beta_k$ of the population must be estimated based on the n observations of a concrete sample. Each solution **b** the normal equation is therefore a function **b** = g(y) of random observations. The empirically obtained regression coefficients **b** consequently vary from sample to sample. As linear combination of n random variable y, **b** = g(y) is also a random variable and g(y). β is the estimation for the parameters β of the population. This estimation is done based on an actual sample regression coefficients. **b** is thus the realization of the estimator $\hat{\beta}$.

It can be shown that the solution of the ordinary least squares problem,

$\hat{\beta} = (\mathbf{X}^T\mathbf{X})^{-1}\mathbf{X}^{-1}\mathbf{y}$, is the best linear unbiased estimator. Confidence and prediction intervals of $\hat{\beta}$ can be estimated in an analytical manner, or by using a bootstrap.

To *proof* if model assumptions hold, typically a residual analysis is carried out. With diagnostic plots showing the distribution of residual $\hat{e}_i$, the linearity assumption, the assumption of normal distribution of the error terms, constant variance of the error terms, and the assumption of the independence of the error terms are evaluated. We do not go into further details on this, but rather show cross validation.

The basic concept of cross validation

The idea of cross-validation is related to estimating the prediction error. In principle, a data set is divided into training and testing data. Based on the training data, parameters are estimated and evaluated on the basis of the test dataset.

Ideally, the training dataset contains the current data and the test dataset is determined by new measurements. Often, no new measurements are made for logistical or cost reasons. Then, dividing the current data into test and training data is usually made.

Cross validation was formulated long before the bootstrap; however, this procedure was able to prevail only with the help of powerful computers in recent years.

On the basis of a simple two-dimensional data set and according to the problem of ordinary least squares regression, cross validation and its variants are explained in the following.

The starting point should be a regression model $y_i = \beta_0 + \beta_1 \cdot x_i + \epsilon_i$, $(i = 1, \ldots, n)$. *Figure 7.7* shows three estimates for the regression line:

```
set.seed(12345)

## generate some data

x1 <- runif(100, 0, pi)

s <- data.frame(x1 = x1, x2 = rnorm(100, 0, 0.1) + sin(x1))
```

```
## plot data points for Figure 7.6
plot(s, xlab = "x", ylab = "y")
## simple model
reg1 <- lm(s[, 2] ~ s[, 1], data = s)
abline(reg1, lwd = 2)
## sinus model
reg2 <- lm(s[, 2] ~ sin(s[, 1]), data = s)
f <- function(x, coef) coef[1] + coef[2] * sin(x)
ss <- seq (-0.02, 3.2, 0.01)
lines(ss, f (ss, coef(reg2)), lty = 2, col = "blue", lwd = 2)
## locally reweighted regression
reg3 <- lowess(x = s[, 1], y = s[, 2], f = 0.1)
lines (reg3, col = "red", lty = 3, lwd = 2)
## legend for Figure 7.6
legend("bottom", col = c("black", "blue", "red"),
       lty = c(1, 2, 3), lwd = c(2, 2, 2),
       legend = c(expression(y = beta[0] + beta[1]*x),
                  expression(y = beta[0] + sin(x)),
                  "loess, 0.1"))
```

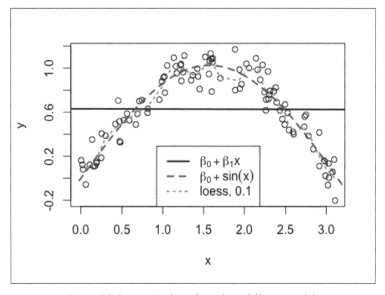

Figure 7.7: Regression lines from three different models

But which of these three lines in *Figure 7.7* represents the best fit? Of course, using a two-dimensional data set, this can best be chosen simply by looking at *Figure 7.7*. However, if more variables are used to predict **y** then this cannot be evaluated by viewing the data. Here, the models have to be evaluated using, for example, cross validation. In general, we are interested in how well we can predict data.

Classical cross validation – 70/30 method

As training data, we use as 70 percent of the data previously simulated. This 70 percent is selected randomly. The rest of the data serves then as the test dataset. Based on the training data, the three proposed methods are now applied and the performance of the methods is evaluated by the test dataset.

Let's have a look at our toy dataset:

```
str(s)
## 'data.frame':    100 obs. of  2 variables:
##   $ x1: num   2.26 2.75 2.39 2.78 1.43 ...
##   $ x2: num   0.715 0.575 0.688 0.385 0.924 ...
```

We want to select 70 percent of the observations randomly to serve as training dataset:

```
## index of training data
training_ind <- sample(1:nrow(s), 70)
## index of test data
test_ind <- which(!(1:100 %in% training_ind))
```

The model is now estimated on the training data; we can do that using the function lm. Basically, $\hat{\beta} = (X^T X)^{-1} X^{-1} y$ is estimated, but doing it in a numerical stable manner using a so-called QR decomposition:

```
lm1 <- lm(s[training_ind, 2] ~ s[training_ind, 1], data = s)
```

For a simple OLS model, $y_i = \beta_0 + \beta_1 x_i + \epsilon_i$ (here i represents 70 percent of the data, say $n_{training}$), the evaluation is easy; we just have to estimate the expected values by $\hat{y}_k = \beta_0 + \beta_1 \cdot x_k$ with: $k \in n_{test}$:

```
## expected values
f <- function(x) reg1$coef[1] + reg1$coef[2] * x
## prediction error, squared sum of expected and observed test data
error <- sum((f(s[test_ind, 1]) - s[test_ind, 2])^2)
error
## [1] 4.514495
```

The principles of Classical cross validation are explained visually in *Figure 7.8*:

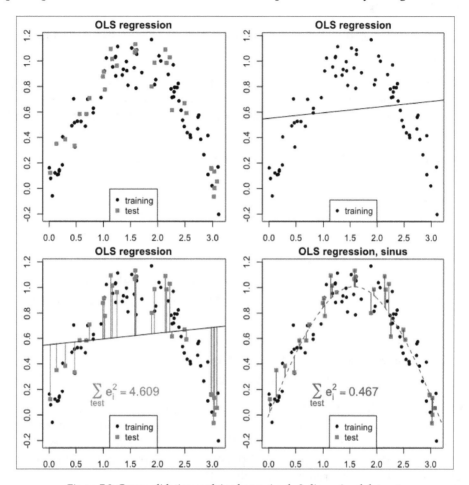

Figure 7.8: Cross validation explained on a simple 2-dimensional data set.
Black points represent the training data, red ones the test data

In the top left of *Figure 7.8*, we see the selection of training (black points) and test data (red points). This selection is done randomly. In the top-right graphics, the OLS regression result based on the training data is shown. We see that the fit (black solid line) is not well done. Note that we can see this only since we are in the special case of 2-dimensional data. The regression fit is evaluated by considering the squared distance between the expected (**y**) values from the test data and the observed (**y**) values of the test data. The prediction error is Classical cross validation **4.609**. For another model shown in the lower right of *Figure 7.7*, we see that the distance from predicted and observed test data is much less. The prediction error is **0.467**. Thus this second model is much better evaluated than the first one.

Of course, the selection of test and training data and the evaluation may repeated, for example, 1,000 times.

The sum of squared errors with respect to the test data is then distributed for model 2 as follows.

This basic principle – the selection of test and training data and evaluation – is now repeated 1,000 times with random division into training and test data. The sum of squared errors with respect to the test data is then distributed for model 2 (sinus) as follows:

```
f <- function (x) reg2$coef[1] + reg2$coef[2] * sin(x)
error1 <- numeric(1000)
n <- nrow(s)
training_ind <- numeric(1000)
for (i in 1:1000){
  training_ind <- sample(1:n, 70)
  reg2 <- lm(s[training, 2] ~ sin(s[training, 1]), data = s)
  error1[i] <- sum((f(s[-training_ind, 1]) - s[-training_ind, 2])^2)
}
summary (error1)
##    Min. 1st Qu.  Median    Mean 3rd Qu.    Max.
##  0.1927  0.3393  0.3869  0.3883  0.4308  0.5886
```

The advantages of this cross validation method by splitting into 70 percent training and 30 percent test data are mainly in the ease of use and relatively simple method of selection. However, the disadvantage is that a lot of the data has not been selected to estimate the model (here 30 percent). Specifically, the application of this method to very small data sets can therefore be problematic.

Leave-one-out cross validation

Similar to the jackknife, one observation is omitted from the fitting phase, and the model is evaluated based on the omitted observation. This single observation represents the whole test data set, shown in *Figure 7.9*:

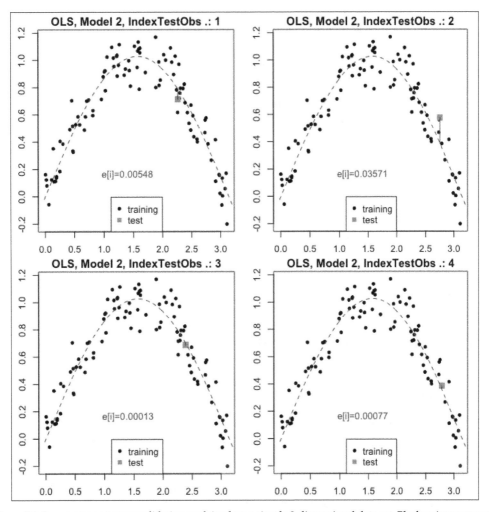

Figure 7.9: Leave-one-out cross validation explained on a simple 2-dimensional data set. Black points represent the training data, red ones the test data. The value of the prediction error is indicated in the plot

Figure 7.9 is constructed in a similar manner to *Figure 7.8*. Instead of a test data set of size 30 percent of observations, the test data set consists of one observation each. We show it for the first 4 (out of 100) test cases. First, the observation 1 is left out and the model (the sinus model now) is estimated on the remaining n – 1 observations. The model is evaluated by the squared distance between predicted value of the test data and observed test data. We see that leaving out observation 2 leads to larger prediction errors than 1, 3, and 4.

The full algorithm of leave-one-out cross validation is as follows:

1. Choose those n – 1 observations from the original data without the -th observation.

2. Make the estimation based on the n – 1 observations.

3. Calculate the prediction error regarding the i-th observation.

4. Do this for each i ∈ {1, ... , n} and report the mean prediction error.

In our example, this would be for our simple model:

```
n <- nrow(s)
error1 <- numeric(n)
for(i in 1:n){
  reg2 <- lm(x2 ~ x1, data = s[-i, ])
  error1[i] <- sum((f(s[i, 1]) - s[i, 2])^2)
}
mean(error1)
## [1] 0.1247593
```

k-fold cross validation

Here the data is divided in **k** groups randomly.

The algorithm for k-fold cross validation can be summarized as follows:

1. Partition the data randomly into k groups.

2. Choose those observations from the original data without the jth group, with $j \in \{1,...,k\}$ (training data).

3. Estimate the parameters based on these selected observations and evaluate the prediction error using the th group, the test data.

4. Perform points 2-3 for $j = 1,...,k$ and calculate a mean prediction error.

As a measure for the quality of the prediction (the prediction error), we can take the sum of squared residuals in the case of regression analysis. The arithmetic mean of estimates often serves as the prediction error of the model.

-fold cross validation is best made in the case of regression analysis using the R package cvTools (Alfons 2012). In the example below, we basically do the same as above, but using 5-fold cross validation, and in addition we repeat 5-fold cross validation 10 times and report the mean squared error:

```
library("cvTools")
fit <- lm(x2 ~ x1, data = s)
# perform cross-validation
cvFit(fit, data = s, y = s$x2, cost = mspe,
    K = 5, R = 10, seed = 1234)
## 5-fold CV results:
##         CV
## 0.1269221
```

The cvTools package makes it handy to select the best method. Let's come back to the dataset Prestige and let us apply some models and different regression methods to it:

```
library("robustbase")
# set up folds for cross-validation
folds <- cvFolds(nrow(coleman), K = 5, R = 10)
## compare LS, MM and LTS regression
## perform cross-validation for an LS regression model
fitLm <- lm(prestige ~ ., data = Prestige)
cvFitLm <- cvLm(fitLm, cost = mspe,
    folds = folds)
fitLm2 <- lm(prestige ~ income:type + education + women, data = Prestige)
cvFitLm2 <- cvLm(fitLm, cost = mspe,
    folds = folds)
## perform cross-validation for an MM regression model
fitLmrob <- lmrob(prestige ~ ., data = Prestige)
cvFitLmrob <- cvLmrob(fitLmrob, cost = mspe,
    folds = folds)
fitLmrob2 <- lmrob(prestige ~ income:type + education + women, data =
Prestige)
cvFitLmrob2 <- cvLmrob(fitLmrob, cost = mspe,
    folds = folds)
## Warning in lmrob.S(x, y, control = control, mf = mf): S refinements
did not
## converge (to refine.tol=1e-07) in 200 (= k.max) steps
## compare cross-validation results
cvSelect(LS = cvFitLm, LS2 = cvFitLm2,
```

```
            MM = cvFitLmrob, MM2 = cvFitLmrob2)
##
## 5-fold CV results:
##    Fit        CV
## 1   LS 48.70221
## 2 LS2 48.70221
## 3   MM 46.74886
## 4 MM2 47.06232
##
## Best model:
##     CV
## "MM"
```

> The function has further useful parameters and also other measures to estimate the prediction error.
>
> Changing the scale of the response variable makes it impossible to compare models, for example, comparing the model $y \sim x1 + x2$ against $log(y) \sim x1 + x2$ makes no sense since the different scale of the response leads automatically to different prediction errors. However, the comparison of, for example, $log(y) \sim x1 + x2$ against $log(y) \sim x1{:}x2 + log(x3)$ is a valid approach.

Summary

Statistical inference to evaluate the uncertainty/variability of estimations is usually challenging in classical statistics. But this is not true when resampling methods are used, data-oriented methods to make valid inference, perfectly suited for data scientists.

The bootstrap is a general tool to estimate the variance of an estimator. The estimation of the variance of a very complex statistic is as easy as estimating the variance of a simple estimator such as the arithmetic mean.

We saw that another popular resampling method – the jackknife – is by far not as trustable as the bootstrap, especially for non-smooth estimators. However, the jackknife is a useful tool to estimate the variance of the bootstrap variance estimate, for example.

Cross validation is very similar to the jackknife, but its aim is different. With cross validation, models can be compared and the prediction error is in the foreground.

Especially the bootstrap is now - in the next chapter - applied to practical more complex problems.

References

- Alfons, A. 2012. *CvTools: Cross-Validation Tools for Regression Models.* `https://CRAN.R-project.org/package=cvTools`.

- Chernick, M. R. 1999. *Bootstrap Methods: A Practitioner's Guide.* New York, NY: John Wiley.

- Davison, A. C., and D. V. Hinkley. 1997. *Bootstrap Methods and Their Application.* Cambridge: Cambridge University Press.

- Efron, B. 1987. "Better Bootstrap Confidence Intervals." *Journal of the American Statistical Association* 82: 171–85.

- Efron, B. 1992. "Jackknife-After-Bootstrap Standard Errors and Influence Functions (with Discussion)." *Journal of the Royal Statistical Society B* 54: 83–127.

- Efron, B., and R. J. Tibshirani. 1993. *An Introduction to the Bootstrap.* New York, NY: Chapman & Hall.

- Freeman, J. 2009. "Bootstraps and Baron Munchhausen." `Boston.com`.

- Good, P. 1993. *Permutation Tests.* New York: Springer Verlag.

- Hesterberg, T.C. 2015. „What Teachers Should Know About the Bootstrap: Resampling in the Undergraduate Statistics Curriculum." *The American Statistician* 69 (4): 371–86.

- Hjorth, J.S.U. 1994. *Computer Intensive Statistical Methods.* London: Chapman; Hall.

- Mammen, E. 1992. *When Does Bootstrap Work?* New York: Springer.

- Politis, D.N., J.P. Romano, and M. Wolf. 1999. *Subsampling.* New York: Springer.

- Quenouille, M.H. 1949. „Problems in Plane Sampling." *Ann. Math. Statist.* 20 (3). The Institute of Mathematical Statistics: 355–75.

- Rousseeuw, P.J., and K.van Driessen. 1998. „A Fast Algorithm for the Minimum Covariance Determinant Estimator." *Technometrics* 41: 212–23.

- Shao, J., and D. Tu. 1995. *The Jackknife and Bootstrap.* New York: Springer.

- Tukey, J. 1958. „Bias and Confidence in Not Quite Large Samples." *Ann. Math. Statist.* 29 (2). The Institute of Mathematical Statistics: 614–23.

- Westfall, P.H., and S.S. Young. 1993. *Resampling-Based Multiple Testing.* New York: John Wiley & Sons.

8

Applications of Resampling Methods and Monte Carlo Tests

The general idea of resampling methods is explained in the previous chapter where also a variety of simple examples has been shown. In this chapter we look at more complex applications of the most successful resampling method - the bootstrap. The examples will show that the bootstrap can be used for different kinds of complex problems, but will also show that conceptual adaptations of the bootstrap are needed. In other words, we will see that the bootstrap has to be modified.

First, we see the bootstrap applied to regression analysis, then we see the bootstrap in the context of imputation of missing values, followed by an application in times series analysis and to applications in complex survey designs.

Afterwards, we focus on resampling tests. We will see that each statistical test can be formulated as a Monte Carlo resampling test, with the (great) advantage that distribution of the test statistics must not be fixed as is the case with classical tests.

The bootstrap in regression analysis

We saw already in *Chapter 7, Resampling Methods* for estimation of the variance of MCD-based standard errors of correlation coefficients, resampling methods might be the only choice for estimating the variance for complex estimators. This is also true for regression analysis as soon as the classical, **ordinary least-squares (OLS)** regression is - for good reasons - skipped, and more robust methods are chosen.

Motivation to use the bootstrap

One might ask; "Why do we need a bootstrap to estimate the variance of regression coefficients when analytical expressions are known for it?". The answer is simple: because only for the ordinary least-squares regression, in addition to many model assumptions, are the analytical expressions valid.

Let's first look at the choice of more complex regression methods on a simple example using artificial data that best shows the problem that frequently occurs in practice:

```
library("robustbase")
data("hbk")
## structure of the data
str(hbk)
## 'data.frame':    75 obs. of  4 variables:
##   $ X1: num   10.1 9.5 10.7 9.9 10.3 10.8 10.5 9.9 9.7 9.3 ...
##   $ X2: num   19.6 20.5 20.2 21.5 21.1 20.4 20.9 19.6 20.7 19.7 ...
##   $ X3: num   28.3 28.9 31 31.7 31.1 29.2 29.1 28.8 31 30.3 ...
##   $ Y : num   9.7 10.1 10.3 9.5 10 10 10.8 10.3 9.6 9.9 ...
```

We next fit an OLS regression using Y as a response and all other variables as predictors:

```
lm_ols <- lm(Y ~ ., data = hbk)
## print summary
summary(lm_ols)
##
## Call:
## lm(formula = Y ~ ., data = hbk)
##
## Residuals:
##     Min      1Q  Median      3Q     Max
## -9.3717 -0.7162 -0.0230  0.7083  4.5130
##
## Coefficients:
##              Estimate Std. Error t value Pr(>|t|)
## (Intercept)   -0.3875     0.4165  -0.930  0.35527
## X1             0.2392     0.2625   0.911  0.36521
## X2            -0.3345     0.1551  -2.158  0.03434 *
```

```
## X3              0.3833     0.1288   2.976  0.00399 **
## ---
## Signif. codes:  0 '***' 0.001 '**' 0.01 '*' 0.05 '.' 0.1 ' ' 1
##
## Residual standard error: 2.25 on 71 degrees of freedom
## Multiple R-squared:  0.6018, Adjusted R-squared:  0.585
## F-statistic: 35.77 on 3 and 71 DF,  p-value: 3.382e-14
```

From this output everything looks fine. For X2 and X3 we cannot reject the null hypothesis that the regression coefficient is 0, the R2 is relatively high and the whole model is significant.

We may also look at one residual diagnostic plot, see *Figure 8.1*.

```
plot(lm_ols, which = 3)
```

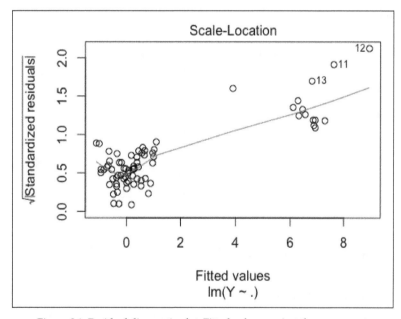

Figure 8.1: Residual diagnostic plot. Fitted values against the square root of absolute standardized residuals

All standardized residuals are small and thus no outliers are detected in *Figure 8.1.* For large fitted values, the absolute residuals are slightly larger than for the rest. All in all, the model looks well. But is this really true? Might the model already be influenced from outliers so that the model outcomes are already so disturbed that we cannot detect abnormalities?

Let's fit a robust MM-based regression (Maronna, Martin, and Yohai 2006) and compare it to the previous OLS-based result:

```
lm_rob <- lmrob(Y ~ ., data = hbk)
## print summary
summary(lm_rob)
##
## Call:
## lmrob(formula = Y ~ ., data = hbk)
##   \--> method = "MM"
## Residuals:
##      Min       1Q   Median       3Q      Max
## -0.92734 -0.38644  0.05322  0.71808 10.80013
##
## Coefficients:
##              Estimate Std. Error t value Pr(>|t|)
## (Intercept) -0.18962    0.11674  -1.624   0.1088
## X1           0.08527    0.07329   1.164   0.2485
## X2           0.04101    0.02956   1.387   0.1697
## X3          -0.05371    0.03195  -1.681   0.0971 .
## ---
## Signif. codes:  0 '***' 0.001 '**' 0.01 '*' 0.05 '.' 0.1 ' ' 1
##
## Robust residual standard error: 0.7892
## Multiple R-squared:  0.03976,   Adjusted R-squared:  -0.0008186
## Convergence in 9 IRWLS iterations
##
## Robustness weights:
##  10 observations c(1,2,3,4,5,6,7,8,9,10)
##   are outliers with |weight| = 0 ( < 0.0013);
```

```
##   7 weights are ~= 1. The remaining 58 ones are summarized as
##    Min. 1st Qu.  Median   Mean 3rd Qu.   Max.
##   0.8522  0.9268  0.9624  0.9532  0.9865  0.9986
## further output suppressed
```

We see that the R2 is almost zero and that we must reject each variable in the model. In addition, the residuals in the diagnostic plot look different, see *Figure 8.2*.

```
plot(lm_rob, which = 5)
```

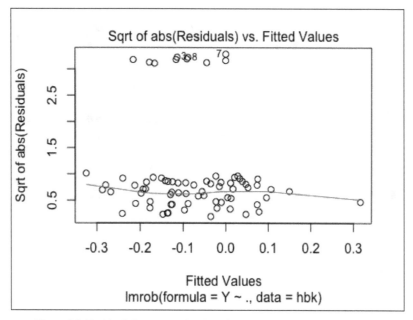

Figure 8.2: Residual diagnostic plot. Fitted values against the square root of absolute standardized residuals from a robust method

We can clearly see from *Figure 8.2* that there are a few outliers present, and from the preceding summary of lm_rob we see that there is no dependency between X and Y.

If we look at the pairwise scatterplot, we see that the robust regression method is correct and the OLS method completely fails, see *Figure 8.3*.

```
pairs(hbk, pch = 20, cex = 0.6)
```

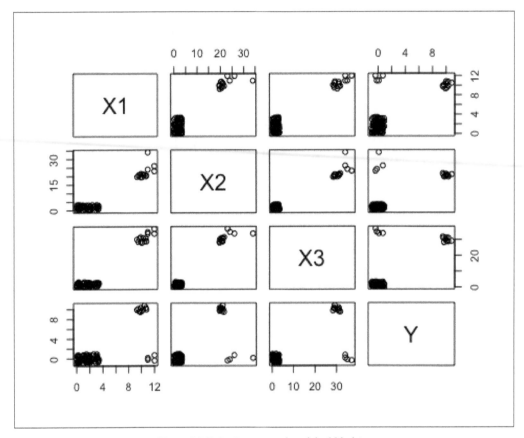

Figure 8.3: Pairwise scatterplot of the hbk data

From *Figure 8.3* we can observe that there is zero correlation between the variables and we also see the existence of few outliers. These outliers influence the OLS model in such a dramatic manner that it becomes completely corrupted, and the R2 will become high and two regression coefficients become highly significant.

With the classical OLS regression method, standard errors of the regression coefficients can be easily estimated using well-known analytical expressions. However, for the much more reliable robust regression method, such an analytical expression is hardly known. Bootstrap is again, the method of choice for estimating the corresponding standard errors. Its application is as simple as for the OLS method, that is to say; the complexity of the application of the bootstrap is independent of the complexity of an estimator.

The most popular but often worst method

We see in the following that there are two different kinds of methods for estimating the standard error of regression coefficients with the bootstrap.

First we show a method that is used in probably 95 percent of cases, but which in general overestimates confidence intervals. Afterwards we show a better method in case the model have good predictive power. This first method draws bootstrap samples from the whole dataset.

The estimation of a regression model $\mathbf{y} = \mathbf{X\beta} + \boldsymbol{\epsilon}$ plays the central role in this section. The data basis is therefore n observations, and $\mathbf{X}$ containing p + 1 predictors including a vector of 1's for the intercept. The whole data set (say $\mathbf{Z}$) can be represented as pairs of $\mathbf{y}$ and $\mathbf{X}$. In other notation this is $\mathbf{z_i} = (y_i, x_{i1}, x_{i2}, \ldots, x_{ip+1}), \; i = 1, \ldots, n$.

For $\mathbf{Z}$, R bootstrap samples are drawn and for each bootstrap sample the model is estimated, resulting in R estimations (bootstrap replicates) of the regression coefficients. From these bootstrap distributions, the confidence intervals can then be calculated with, for example, the percentile method from Efron (see *Chapter 7, Resampling Methods*).

Let us work again with the `Prestige` data from the `car` package and let us estimate the regression model:

prestige ~ log(income) + women + type

This means that we want to predict the variable `prestige` with the log values of income, percentage of incumbents who are women and type of occupation (blue collar, white collar, and professionals). Note that there are better models, but for simplicity in explaining the problems of this approach we use a simple example.

The model can be fitted using robust methods. Since for MM-regression, the bootstrap is already implemented in a very good way, we choose another robust regression method: least trimmed squares regression (Rousseeuw and Leroy 1987). In the output of the summary shown as follows, we see that the standard error estimated by the implementation of the function `ltsReg` is approx. `2.36`. We remember this value for later use:

```
data(Prestige, package = "car")
rob <- ltsReg(prestige ~ log(income) + women + type, data = Prestige)
summary(rob)
##
## Call:
## ltsReg.formula(formula = prestige ~ log(income) + women + type,
```

```
##      data = Prestige)
##
## Residuals (from reweighted LS):
##      Min      1Q  Median      3Q     Max
## -11.257  -3.562   0.000   4.252  12.927
##
## Coefficients:
##                Estimate Std. Error t value Pr(>|t|)
## Intercept    -186.19502   20.57510  -9.050 2.71e-14 ***
## log(income)    25.62408    2.36002  10.858  < 2e-16 ***
## women           0.17433    0.03364   5.182 1.34e-06 ***
## typeprof       13.48480    2.30026   5.862 7.42e-08 ***
## typewc          1.69518    1.96566   0.862    0.391
## ---
## Signif. codes:  0 '***' 0.001 '**' 0.01 '*' 0.05 '.' 0.1 ' ' 1
##
## Residual standard error: 6.467 on 90 degrees of freedom
## Multiple R-Squared: 0.8604,  Adjusted R-squared: 0.8542
## F-statistic: 138.7 on 4 and 90 DF,  p-value: < 2.2e-16
```

If we want to use the function `boot` from the R package `boot`, we should carefully prepare a `boot` function that the `boot` package can handle:

```
boot.lts <- function(x, indices){
  x <- x [indices,]
  model <- ltsReg(prestige ~ log(income) +
                  women + type, data = x)
  coefficients(model)
}
```

Having this function defined, we can put everything to the `boot` function:

```
library("boot")
set.seed(123)
rob_boot <- boot(Prestige, boot.lts, 1000)
## estimated standard errors
rob_boot
##
## ORDINARY NONPARAMETRIC BOOTSTRAP
##
```

```
##
## Call:
## boot(data = Prestige, statistic = boot.lts, R = 1000)
##
##
## Bootstrap Statistics :
##            original          bias     std. error
## t1* -188.9846989  -7.631124780   64.32621578
## t2*   25.9405809   0.882198382    7.37310316
## t3*    0.1789914  -0.001773418    0.07992569
## t4*   11.2511897   2.018062069    6.34813577
## t5*    1.5686363   0.919839439    3.94373349
```

Let's look at the coefficients for `log(income)` in more detail. We see that the standard error is approx. `3.84` while estimated from function `ltsReg` it was `2.36`.

It is also easy to see that the distribution of the bootstrap replicates is bimodal and deviations show up, especially in the upper tail of the distribution, see *Figure 8.4*.

```
hist(rob_boot$t[,2], 50, xlab = "bootstrap repl., log(income)", main =
"")
```

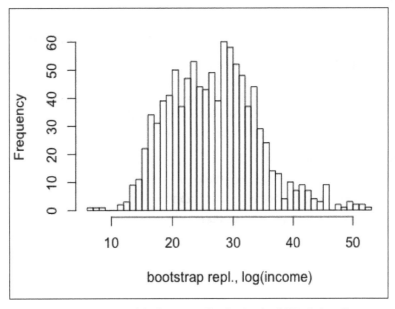

Figure 8.4: Histogram of the bootstrap distribution (and QQ-plot) replicates
of the regression coefficient log(income)

Also the distribution of bootstrap replicates of the coefficient regarding women does not look to be approx. normal, as seen in *Figure 8.5*:

```
hist(rob_boot$t[,3], 50, xlab = "bootstrap repl., women", main = "")
```

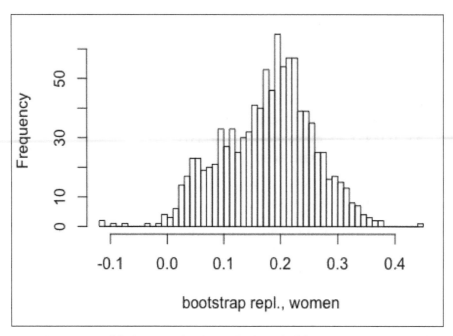

Figure 8.5: Histogram of the bootstrap distribution (replicates) of the women regression coefficient

We can do some further computations, like to estimate the confidence intervals of the estimated regression coefficients. With function `boot.ci` one can estimate different types of confidence intervals, such as the bias-corrected confidence intervals, confidence intervals with Efron's percentile method and confidence intervals by means of the BC_α method. For the coefficient `log(income)` the results are the following:

```
boot.ci(rob_boot, index = 2,
        type = c("norm", "perc", "bca"))
## BOOTSTRAP CONFIDENCE INTERVAL CALCULATIONS
## Based on 1000 bootstrap replicates
##
## CALL :
## boot.ci(boot.out = rob_boot, type = c("norm", "perc", "bca"),
##      index = 2)
##
## Intervals :
```

```
## Level        Normal           Percentile            BCa
## 95%     (10.61, 39.51 )    (14.58, 43.66 )     (13.96, 41.85 )
## Calculations and Intervals on Original Scale
```

In *Chapter 7, Resampling Methods* we learned about the *jackknife-after-bootstrap* plot to see the effect of single observations on the quantiles of the bootstrap distribution. This plot is shown for the coefficient `log(income)` and women in following *Figure 8.6*:

```
par(mfrow = c(2,1), mar = c(4,4,2,0.5))
jack.after.boot(rob_boot, index = 2, main = 'log (income) coefficient')
jack.after.boot(rob_boot, index = 3, main = 'woman coefficient')
```

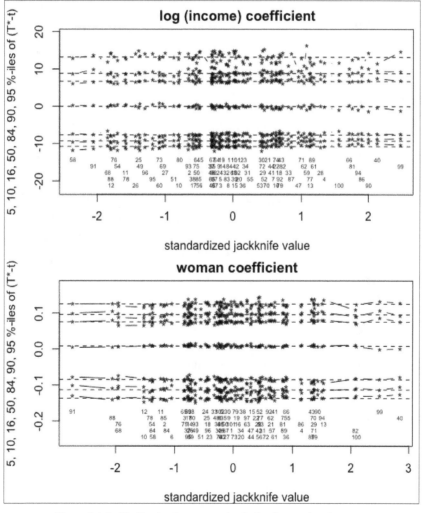

Figure 8.6: Jackknife after bootstrap plot for log(income) and women

From these graphics (*Figure 8.6*) we can observe that observation 58 and 54 have a strong influence on the bootstrap distribution; the bootstrap distribution gets larger by excluding these observations. Observation 40, for example, also has high impact on the bootstrap distribution but decreases the distribution when kept out. Thus observation 2 can be seen as an outlier.

We come back to these figures after we present a better method for bootstrapping in the regression context.

Bootstrapping by draws from residuals

In classical regression, one thinks of the **X** part as fixed (and independent). This can be considered by drawing from residuals instead of drawing bootstrap samples from **Z**. This approach is called the residual bootstrap.

To obtain a bootstrap sample, a random error based on the (bootstrapped) residuals $\hat{\mathbf{e}}$ are added to the predicted value $\hat{\mathbf{y}}$.

The rationale is that **y** can be reproduced by $\hat{y} + \hat{\in}$.

Let us motivate this concept on a simple 2-dimensional toy dataset:

```
set.seed(12)
df <- data.frame(x = 1:7, y = 1:7 + rnorm(7))
```

In the following code, we estimate the regression line and plot it to the data points. Afterwards we draw one bootstrap sample of residuals and add these residuals to the fitted values, that is; we get new values $\mathbf{y}_1^* = \hat{\mathbf{y}} + \hat{\mathbf{e}}^*$ that we use as input to the regression problem to obtain a new regression line:

```
par(mfrow = c(2,1), mar = c(4,4,1,0.3))
## fit to original data
lm_orig <- lm(y ~ x, data = df)
## plot original data
plot(y ~ x, data = df)
## add regression line from original data
abline(lm_orig)
## show the connection lines
## between original and fitted y
segments(x0 = df$x, x1=df$x,
         y0=df$y, y1=lm_orig$fit)
## fitted y
points(df$x, lm_orig$fit, pch=20, col="red")
legend("topleft", legend = c("y", expression(hat(y))),
       pch = c(1,20), col = c(1,2))
```

```
## second plot ---------------------
## plot of fitted values
plot(lm_orig$fit ~ df$x, col="red", pch = 20,
     ylab="y", xlab = "x")
## bootstrap sample by adding sampled residuals
y1 <- lm_orig$fit + sample(lm_orig$res, replace = TRUE)
## new bootstrap sample
points(df$x, y1, col="blue", pch = 3)
## connection lines new bootstrap sample to
## fitted values from original data
segments(x0 = df$x, x1 = df$x,
         y0 = lm_orig$fit, y1 = y1, col ="blue")
## regression line from original data
abline(lm_orig)
## regression line from bootstrap sample
abline(lm(y1 ~ df$x), col = "blue", lty = 2)
legend("topleft", legend = c("original", "bootstrap repl. 1"), lty =
c(1,2), col = c(1,4))
```

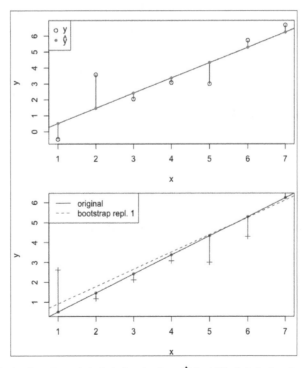

Figure 8.7: Top: Original values (round circles), fitted values $\hat{y}$ (red filled circles) and regression line from the fit of the original data. Bottom: Fitted values (red filled circles), one bootstrap sample represented by $\hat{y} + \hat{\epsilon}$, and regression line from original (black solid line) and the bootstrap sample (dotted blue line)

This approach cannot be repeated, that is to say; new bootstrap samples would lead to new regression lines in *Figure 8.7*.

Let's go back to a real case. We take again the *Prestige* data from the R `car` package and estimate the standard error of coefficients from a robust regression model via least trimmed squares regression. Let's first fit the model on original data:

```
Prestige <- na.omit(Prestige)
## fit model on original data
rob2 <- ltsReg(prestige ~ log(income) + women + type,
               data = Prestige)
```

We extract residuals and fitted values for later use, and also we need the model matrix later on. Note that this model matrix is fixed and thus only estimated from the original sample:

```
residuals <- residuals(rob2)
fit <- fitted(rob2)
## fix X, model matrix
X <- model.matrix(rob2, Prestige)[, -1]
```

Again we need a function for *boot* that creates the bootstrap sample, this time by adding random draws from residuals to the expected/fitted values from the original sample:

```
ltsBoot2 <- function(x, indices){
  y <- fit + residuals[indices]
  model <- ltsReg(y ~ X)
  coefficients(model)
}
```

Finally, we can do the residual-based bootstrap:

```
rob2_boot <- boot(Prestige, ltsBoot2, R = 2000)
## show results
rob2_boot
##
## ORDINARY NONPARAMETRIC BOOTSTRAP
##
##
## Call:
## boot(data = Prestige, statistic = ltsBoot2, R = 2000)
```

```
##
##
## Bootstrap Statistics :
##          original         bias    std. error
## t1* -188.9846989   3.847338290  23.93016057
## t2*   25.9405809  -0.422141347   2.73913510
## t3*    0.1789914   0.001174141   0.04058027
## t4*   11.2511897   2.652930311   2.67849883
## t5*    1.5686363  -0.055049721   2.42259399
```

We can see that the standard error is smaller compared to the previous approach (sampling from **Z**). Also the distribution of the bootstrap replicates related log(income) and women is now approximately normal (see *Figure 8.8*) and looks better shaped than with the previous approach:

```
par(mfrow = c(1,2), mar = c(4,4,1,0.2))
hist(rob2_boot$t[,2], 50, xlab = "bootstrap repl., log(income)", main =
"")
hist(rob2_boot$t[,3], 50, xlab = "bootstrap repl., women", main = "")
```

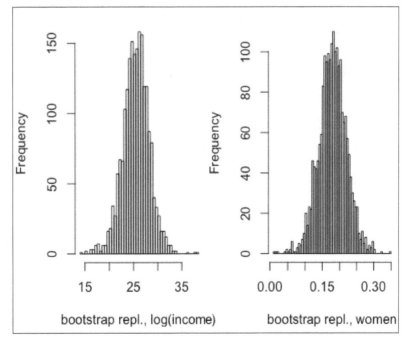

Figure 8.8: Histogram of the bootstrap distribution (replicates) of the regression coefficient log(income) (left) and women (right)

The *jackknife-after-bootstrap* plot confirms the comparatively better properties of the residual-based bootstrap than with the bootstrapping from **Z** before:

```
par(mfrow = c(2,1), mar = c(4,4,2,0.5))
jack.after.boot(rob2_boot, index = 2, main = 'log (income) coefficient')
jack.after.boot(rob2_boot, index = 3, main = 'woman coefficient')
```

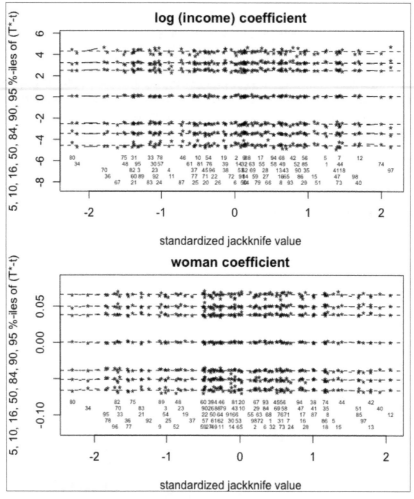

Figure 8.9: Jackknife after bootstrap plot for log(income) and women obtained from the bootstrap from residual approach

 In case of using the residual bootstrap in combination with robust methods, the bootstrap can be improved by sampling n residuals out of n - m outlier-free residuals (m... amount of outliers detected).

Proper variance estimation with missing values

Very often in practice, missing values are a major problem. Standard routines for estimation are typically not designed to deal with missing values. In the following we discuss a method to adequately deal with missing values when estimating the variance/uncertainty of an estimator.

Because of non-answered questions or measurement errors, data often has the following data structure:

$$
\mathbf{X} = \begin{pmatrix} x_{11} & \cdots & \cdots & x_{1p} \\ \vdots & \text{NA} & & \vdots \\ & & & \text{NA} \\ \vdots & & \text{NA} & \vdots \\ x_{n1} & \cdots & \cdots & x_{np} \end{pmatrix}
$$

Here we see **n** observations and **p** variables and some missing values (NA).

Often one will omit those observations that include missing values from the data set. However, this decreases the sample size and thus increases the variance of estimators, and in addition this may cause biased estimates if missing values are missing at random, that is; if the probability of missingness depends on covariates.

To work around this problem, another, better solution is to impute missing values. For some applications the imputations are done in a way to minimize a prediction error. For other applications it is important that the variance of an estimator is estimated in a proper manner (Rubin 1987). If one imputes values to minimize a prediction error, the variance of an estimator would be underestimated. But also if missing values are imputed by a single imputation method, the variance is underestimated since fixed values are used as imputations, rejecting the variability of the imputation. Thus for proper imputation, multiple imputation methods are usually applied. This means that not just one imputation is made using a probabilistic imputation method, but several. This results in multiple data sets, each data set containing one round of imputations. From these multiple files, proper variances of estimators can be obtained by using so called combining rules of each of the estimated variances (Rubin 1987).

However, imagine that you are working in an institution or company where one department is responsible for data collection, another one for data preprocessing, another one for analysis and another one for publications. Imagine that you work in the data preprocessing department. Do you believe that the other departments are happy if you send them, say 10 imputed data sets from one data set with missing values? Do you think the other departments can work with 10 data sets? In theory, multiple imputation is a very good concept, but in practice single imputation is often the only possible way to go. But will you feel well when you provide an imputed data set where you know that variances will be underestimated?

A way out of this dilemma is to use a resampling method such as the bootstrap or the jackknife. This method was already shown by Little and Rubin in 2002 but then somehow forgotten. However, we will see that it is very useful in practice.

Let **X** be a sample of **p** variables and **n** independent observations including missing values. The estimation of confidence intervals regarding a point estimate $\hat{\theta}$ from a population parameter θ is as follows. Note that the trick is to impute the bootstrap samples, not the original data. The philosophy again, is that the original sample is the best information you have, and that bootstrap samples of this original sample mimic the population, also regarding the missing values.

For $r = 1, \ldots, R$, repeat:

1. Draw a bootstrap sample $\mathbf{X}_i^*$ of the original (non-imputed) sample **X**.
2. Impute the missing values in $\mathbf{X}_i^*$.
3. Estimate the parameter $\theta_i^* = f(\mathbf{X}_i^*)$.

This results in R bootstrap replicates for θ_i^*, $i = 1, \ldots, R$. This bootstrap replicate distribution is then used for determining the confidence intervals or standard errors with respect to $\hat{\theta}$, for example, by using the percentile method from Efron, see *Chapter 7, Resampling Methods*.

Let's do this in practice. In the following example, confidence intervals are estimated for data with missing values using the mentioned bootstrap. To keep it simple, θ should be the arithmetic mean of one variable. Repeatably, bootstrap samples are drawn from the sample, the missing values in the bootstrap samples are imputed, and finally the arithmetic mean is estimated from the bootstrap samples. We use the sleep data set that includes missing values:

```
library("VIM")
data("sleep")
```

Let's first analyze the missing values structure a bit. The left plot from *Figure 8.9* shows the number of missing values in each variable of the sleep dataset, the right plot of *Figure 8.10* shows the missing pattern structure:

```
aggr(sleep, numbers = TRUE, prop = FALSE, cex.axis = 0.75)
```

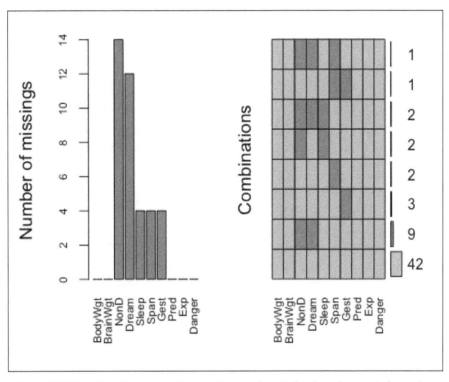

Figure 8.10: Simple statistics according to missing values in the sleep data set. Left: number missing per variable. Right: Frequencies of missing patterns

For example, 42 observations are fully observed, 9 observations have missing values in both the third and fourth variable, and so on.

The so-called matrixplot (Templ, Alfons, and Filzmoser 2011) in *Figure 8.11* shows the whole data matrix, sorted by variable `BrainWgt`. The darker the lines the higher the corresponding values of the data matrix. Red lines correspond to missing values in the data matrix. From *Figure 8.11* we see that the probability of missings in **NonD**, **Dream**, and **Sleep** might increase with higher values on `BrainWgt`:

```
par(mar = c(6,4,0.2,0.2))
matrixplot(sleep, sortby = "BrainWgt", interactive = FALSE)
```

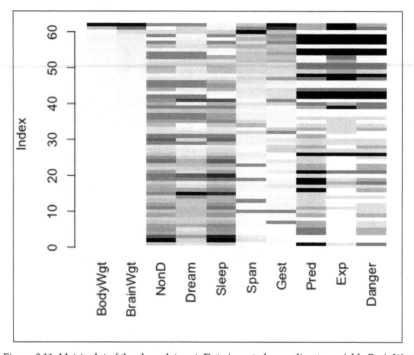

Figure 8.11: Matrixplot of the sleep data set. Data is sorted according to variable BrainWgt

A bootstrap sample (must) show similar behavior since we resample with replacement from the sample. From *Figure 8.12* we can observe that the number of missing values changed slightly. The frequencies according to the missing patterns (right graphics, *Figure 8.12*) differ. Instead of 42 observations without missing values, only 38 observations do not include any missings in the bootstrap sample. Also the frequencies of, for example, missing in **NonD** and **Dream** is now **11** instead of **9** before, compare for further details, *Figure 8.11* and *Figure 8.12*:

```
set.seed(123)
sleep_boot1 <- sleep[sample(1:nrow(sleep), replace = TRUE), ]
aggr(sleep_boot1, numbers = TRUE, prop = FALSE,
     cex.axis = 0.75)
```

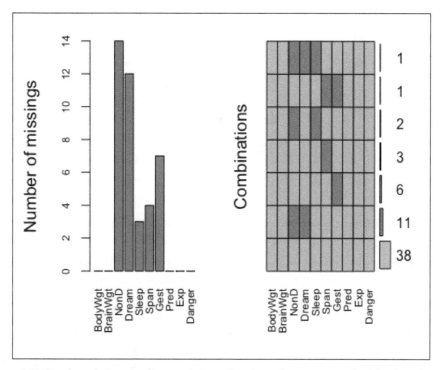

Figure 8.12: Simple statistics according to missing values in one bootstrap sample of the sleep data set. Left: number of missings per variable. Right: Frequencies of missing patterns

In the matrixplot, it is visible that slightly more patterns are selected for **NonD** and **Dream** combinations of missings, see *Figure 8.13*. Also in variable `Gest`, the probability of missingness is higher for small values of `BrainWgt` as before. See *Figure 8.13* for more detail:

```
par(mar = c(6,4,0.2,0.2))
matrixplot(sleep_boot1, sortby = "BrainWgt")
```

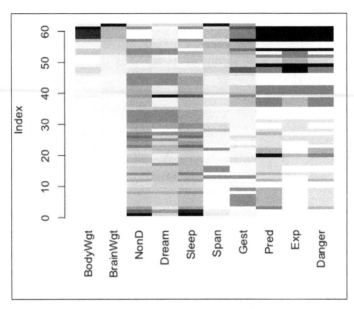

Figure 8.13: Matrixplot of one bootstrap sample of the sleep data set. Data is sorted according to variable BrainWgt

Many other figures would show the difference between the missing structure of a bootstrap sample to the original data. What is important is to also see the missing structure changes, that is; we mimic all situations that may occur in the population distribution using the bootstrap. Thus, this bootstrap seems to be a valid concept for estimating the variance with data including missing values. We show a practical example next, and we use some fully observed data (again the sleep dataset) and set some values to be missing. This simulation lacks a bit since we assume fixed values for missings. However, in practice a missing value has its own distribution. A way out would be to look at coverage rates for confidence intervals. However, we want to keep it simple and want to show how this bootstrap approach can be applied.

We give results for single imputation:

```
n <- nrow(sleep)
imputed <- kNN(sleep, imp_var = FALSE)
## Time difference of 0.0347321 secs
```

```
ci_single <- quantile(replicate(10000, mean(imputed[sample(1:n, replace =
TRUE), "Sleep"])), c(0.025, 0.975))
ci_single
##      2.5%     97.5%
##   9.280565 11.579073
```

Finally, we estimate the confidence interval with our proposed bootstrap approach. Here, the bootstrap samples are taken from non-imputed data. The following line of code needs longer computational time:

```
ci_boot <- quantile(replicate(10000, mean(kNN(sleep[sample(1:n, replace =
TRUE), ], imp_var = FALSE)$Sleep)), c(0.025, 0.975))
ci_boot
##      2.5%     97.5%
##   9.201613 11.658105
```

We see that this leads to a slightly larger confidence interval since we considered the uncertainty of imputation.

Of course we can also use the jackknife method for the estimation of confidence intervals when the data includes missing values. The approach is very similar to the bootstrap approach.

For $j = 1, ..., n$:

1. Impute the jackknife sample $\mathbf{X}_{(i)}$.
2. Estimate the parameter θ of the imputed dataset.
3. From the resulting jackknife replicates distribution, estimate the confidence intervals using the jackknife method from *Chapter 7, Resampling Methods*.

Bootstrapping in time series

Two methods are often used in bootstrapping of time series:

*   To estimate a model and draw from the residuals (see second last section on bootstrapping regression models by bootstrapping residuals)
*   Moving blocks bootstrap methods

We concentrate in the following, on the moving blocks bootstrap. It is a method that is often applied and mentioned in literature, but with limited success. To show the limitations of this approach is one goal of this section.

The idea is to divide the data in blocks and to sample with replacement within blocks. This allows us to not completely ignore the relationship between the observations. Relationships between observations are typically present in time series. For example, the next value will depend on the previous value. Think also on the trend, seasonality, and periodicity.

In principle, the time series can be divided in non-overlapping or overlapping blocks.

We will show an overlapping moving blocks bootstrap for estimating the autocorrelation. First we generate some toy data:

```
set.seed(123)
tseries <- rnorm(50)
## introduce auto-correlation
tseries[-1] <- tseries[-1] + tseries[-50]
```

The time series looks as shown in the following screenshot:

```
plot(ts(tseries), ylab = "values")
```

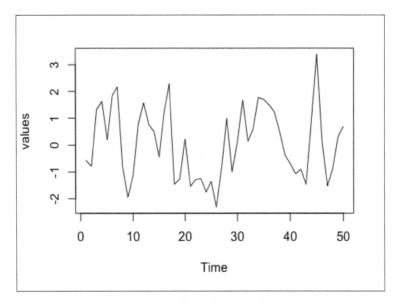

Figure 8.14: Example time series

Our moving blocks bootstrap needs the data, the blocksize, and the number of replications as input:

```
mbb <- function(x, R=1000, blocksize=6){
  ## initialization
  nc <- length(x)
  lagCorMBB <- ct <- numeric(R)
  seriesBl <- numeric(nc)
  ## function for moving blocks bootstrap
  corT <- function(x=tseries, N=nc, bl=blocksize){
    ## for N/bl blocks
    for(i in 1:ceiling(N/bl)) {
      ## endpoint of block
        endpoint <- sample(bl:N, size=1)
        ## put blocks together, bootstrap sample
        seriesBl[(i-1)*bl+1:bl] <- x[endpoint-(bl:1)+1]
    }
    seriesBl <- seriesBl[1:N]
    ## autocorrelation
    a <- cor(seriesBl[-1],seriesBl[-N])
    return(a)
  }
  ct <- replicate(R, corT(x))
  return(ct)
}
```

Now let's apply this function on our time series:

```
mb <- mbb(x=tseries, R=10000)
## first 10 bootstrap replicates
mb[1:10]
##  [1] 0.2899296 0.1966638 0.0771300 0.4065762 0.2561444 0.4276909
0.4419033
##  [8] 0.2332383 0.3501899 0.2468474
## auto-correlation coefficient from mean of bootstrap replicates
mean(mb)
## [1] 0.3410245
```

It is natural that if the time series is not white noise then the arithmetic mean of moving block bootstrap replicates is smaller than the point estimate from the data itself, since we lose some autocorrelation by partitioning the time series into new blocks. We see the autocorrelation (of lag 1) of the data in comparison:

```
acf(tseries)$acf[2]
```

```
## [1] 0.4302483
```

However, we are in any case only interested in estimating the 95% confidence interval (percentile method) of the autocorrelation coefficient:

```
qu_mbb <- quantile(mb, c(0.025,0.975))
cat("CI(mbb) : [", round(qu_mbb[1], 2), ",", round(qu_mbb[2], 2), "]")
```

```
## CI(mbb) : [ 0.12 , 0.57 ]
```

In comparison, the default method in the `forecast` package (Hyndman and Khandakar 2008) for the confidence interval of the autocorrelation coefficient is report the following:

```
library("forecast")
ac <- taperedacf(tseries)
cat("CI(classical) : [", round(ac$lower[1], 2), ",", round(ac$upper[1],
2), "]")
```

```
## CI(classical) : [ -0.02 , 0.43 ]
```

We saw how to implement a moving blocks bootstrap but we didn't mention in what situation a moving blocks bootstrap might not work properly. Cutting blocks and rejoining them will automatically destroy the trend and would lead to non-reliable results whenever the time series is not stationary. Thus before the application of a moving blocks bootstrap, the time series must be de-trended. In addition, the moving blocks bootstrap may only work for simple time series models, such as for the autoregressive of lag 1 (AR 1) process. Here it is assumed that the next value depends only on the previous one. For more complicated approaches such as general ARIMA processes, the moving blocks bootstrap may not give valid inference statistics.

Bootstrapping in the case of complex sampling designs

We already saw many applications where all these samples were drawn completely at random. However, this is often not the case when one has little information on a finite population, or when the data collection is based on a complex survey design. Of course such information is used to draw a sample in such a manner that costs are minimal. In other words, as an example from business statistics: a lot of small- and medium-sized companies exist in Austria but not many large ones. For precise estimates we need all the largest companies (selection probability 1), but the probability of selection of small companies can be much lower. A complex survey design allows us to draw a good sample with minimal costs.

In complex survey sampling, individuals are therefore sampled with known inclusion probabilities π_i ($i = 1, \dots, N$) from a population of size N to end up with a sample of size n. The inclusion probabilities can differ between strata (partitions of the population) or can even be different for each individual in the sampling frame.

For a population total we have an unbiased estimator of $T_y = \sum_{i=1}^{N} y_i$ is
$\hat{T}_y = \sum_{i:S_i=1} = 1\frac{1}{\pi_i}y_i$ with $S_i = 1$ if individual i is sampled and $S_i = 0$ if not.

Usually the population is divided into K strata with n_k ($k = 1, \dots, K$) observations drawn from stratum k. Then, bootstrap samples can be constructed by resampling n_k observations with replacement from the k-th stratum. Likewise, if observations are drawn into the sample in clusters rather than individually, for example; when drawing household and collect information on each household member, then the bootstrap should resample clusters rather than individuals. This is often mentioned as the naive bootstrap. Several authors discussed the limitations of this naive approach (Rao and Wu 1988), (Deville and Särndal 1992), (Deville, Särndal, and Sautory 1993).

When we estimate $\hat{Y}_d = \sum_{i:S_i=1} d_i y_i$, with design weight $d_i = 1/\pi_i$, we know some characteristics from the population. For example, we know from one variable x of the sample, the true total from the population, $X = \sum_{i=1}^{N} x_i$, and $\sum = 1 d_i x_i \neq x$. Then we search for new weights w_i with $\hat{y}_w = \sum_{i:S_i} = 1 w_i y_i$ with $\sum_{i:S_i} = 1 w_i x_i = X$ and $\sum_{i:S_i} = 1 w_i = N$. This becomes even more complex if we have more constraints/known population characteristics, and if the data have a cluster structure.

Of course, the bootstrap can be applied to complex sampling designs (involving, for example, stratification, clustering, and case-weighting) by resampling from the sample data in the same manner as the original sample was selected from the population. However, as mentioned before, the calibration should be taken into account.

Let's show the problem on a very simple (and simplified) toy data example. Consider the following simple sample data set and let's ignore that, typically, such data has a household structure:

```
x <- data.frame("location" = rep("Asten", 8),
         "income" = c(2000,2500,2000,2500,1000,1500,2000,2500),
         "weight" = c(1000,500,1000,500,1500,1000,1000,2000))
```

```
x
##     location income weight
## 1      Asten   2000   1000
## 2      Asten   2500    500
## 3      Asten   2000   1000
## 4      Asten   2500    500
## 5      Asten   1000   1500
## 6      Asten   1500   1000
## 7      Asten   2000   1000
## 8      Asten   2500   2000
```

We see a sample of eight people in Asten reporting the income and the sampling weights. We assume that the sampling weights are already calibrated and that, for example, the first observation stands for 1000 observations in the population, the second observation stands for 500 observations in the population, and so on. Thus, all in all, we can assume that the population size of Asten is 8500 people.

```
sum(x$weight)
## [1] 8500
```

The weighted total (Horwitz Thompson estimation), or the estimated total income of all people in Asten is:

```
sum(x$income * x$weight)
## [1] 16500000
```

Let's draw one bootstrap sample:

```
set.seed(123)
y <- x[sample(1:8, replace = TRUE), ] # Bootstrap Sample
y
```

```
##      location income weight
## 3      Asten    2000   1000
## 7      Asten    2000   1000
## 4      Asten    2500    500
## 8      Asten    2500   2000
## 8.1    Asten    2500   2000
## 1      Asten    2000   1000
## 5      Asten    1000   1500
## 8.2    Asten    2500   2000
```

The estimated total income of the people living in the village of Asten is then:

```
# non-calibrated estimation
sum(y$income * y$weight)
## [1] 23750000
```

Quite high isn't it? The condition $N = 8500$ is violated and thus the estimation of total income is distorted. For this bootstrap sample, the population size of Asten is:

```
sum(y$weight)
## [1] 11000
```

This is surely not equal to 8.500. This explains why the estimated income is completely overestimated from the first bootstrap sample.

Since we know that 8.500 people live in Asten and surely not 11.000, we will use this information about the population and we will calibrate the bootstrap sample according to this population information. In this case this is easy, we just have to multiply each weight by a constant 8.500/11.000:

```
constant <- sum(x$weight) / sum(y$weight)
## calibrated estimation
sum(y$x * y$w * constant)
## [1] 0
```

This example demonstrated the simplest case. Usually the sample must be calibrated according to various known population characteristics. However, this example clearly shows the need of a calibrated bootstrap, formally shown in the following.

Remember, the naive bootstrap algorithm for the estimation of the standard error was given by:

1. Choose R independent bootstrap samples $\mathbf{x}_1^*, \mathbf{x}_2^*, \ldots, \mathbf{x}_R^*$ from $\mathbf{x}$.

2. Estimate the bootstrap replications for each bootstrap sample.

3. $\hat{\theta}^*(r) = s(\mathbf{x}_r^*), \quad r = 1, 2, \ldots, R$.

4. Estimate the standard error $\widehat{se}_F$ using the standard deviation of the R bootstrap replications, $\widehat{se}_R = \left\{ [\sum_{r=1}^{R} [\hat{\theta}_r^* - \hat{\theta}_{(\cdot)}^*]^2 / (R-1) \right\}^{1/2}$ with $\hat{\theta}_{(\cdot)}^* = \sum_{r=1}^{R} \hat{\theta}_r^* / R$

The calibrated bootstrap needs an additional step between point 1 and 2 of the naive bootstrap:

First, calibrate the sampling weights so that the bootstrap sample exactly fits to known population characteristics, where the sampling weights should be changed as less as possible, that is; the sampling weights are multiplied by so-called g-weights that should be as close to 1 (optimization problem). These g-weights are typically estimated by raking methods such as iterative proportional fitting or least-squares regression methods.

We apply this calibrated bootstrap on a more complex data set in the following. The following example is about how to estimate the at-risk-of-poverty rate from the **European Union Statistics on Income and Living Conditions Survey (EU-SILC)**.

The at-risk-of-poverty rate is defined as the ratio of people with equalized household income below the poverty threshold. The poverty threshold corresponds to 60 percent of the median income of the population.

The poverty rate is thus defined as:

$ARPR = P(x_U < 0.6 \cdot med(x_U)) = F(0.6)$ with X_U being the equalized household income of the population. F_U is the distribution function of income.

For estimating the poverty rate, the sampling weights have to be considered. First we have to estimate the poverty threshold by:

$ARPT = 0.6 \cdot wmed(\mathbf{x})$ with $\mathbf{x}$ being the equalized household income from the sample and $wmed$ the weighted median, defined with:

$i = argmin_i \{ \frac{w_i}{\sum_{j=1}^{n} w_i} < p \}$ as $wmed(x) = x_i$ where i is odd and $wmed(x) = \frac{x_i + x_{i+1}}{2}$ if i is an even number.

The poverty rate can be estimated with the help of the index $\mathbf{y} = (y_1, ..., y_n)$

$$y_i = \begin{cases} 1 & \text{if } x_i < \text{ARPT} \quad i = 1, ..., n \\ 0 \end{cases}$$

Else as:

$$\text{ARPR} = \sum_{i=1}^{n} \frac{w_i y_i}{w_i}$$

These estimations can be practically done with the R package, `laeken` (Alfons and Templ 2013). The calibrated bootstrap is available with the function variance. Note that the totals are usually determined by a population. Here we estimate it from the sample:

```
library("laeken")
data("eusilc")
## point estimate of poverty rate
a <- arpr("eqIncome", weights = "rb050", data = eusilc)
## bootstrap with calibration
## define auxiliary 0-1 variables for regions
aux <- sapply(levels(eusilc$db040),
    function(l, x) as.numeric(x == 1),
    x = eusilc$db040)
## retrieve population totals from underlying sample
totals <- sapply(levels(eusilc$db040),
    function(l, x, w) sum(w[x == 1]),
    x = eusilc$db040, w = eusilc$rb050)
# bootstrap variance
variance("eqIncome", weights = "rb050", design = "db040",
    data = eusilc, indicator = a, X = aux, totals = totals,
    seed = 123)
## Value:
## [1] 14.44422
##
## Variance:
## [1] 0.09192744
##
## Confidence interval:
##    lower    upper
```

```
## 13.87865 15.19303
##
## Threshold:
## [1] 10859.24
```

We see that the point estimate of the at-risk-at-poverty rate is 14,444 and the confidence interval estimated by the calibrated bootstrap is [13,937; 15,012]. Note that in R there is no formula available for estimating the variance of the at-risk-at-poverty rate with an analytical expression. This is also true for many other poverty estimates. Existing formulas in the literature are complex and depend on assumptions and vary between sampling designs. The calibrated bootstrap is the only chance to estimate the variance in a user-friendly manner.

Monte Carlo tests

Do you know the test statistics of the multivariate Anderson-Darling test for multivariate normality? Don't worry, these test statistics have only been approximated for a few significance levels in terms of simulation experiments, and it is generally unknown. But then how we can estimate the value of the test statistics for a given number of observations, number of variables and a certain significance level? The answer is easy, and the procedure is as easy as for much simpler tests. We can do it with resampling methods for testing - the Monte Carlo tests.

A motivating example

Before we go to more formal descriptions of such tests, we introduce the Monte Carlo resampling test with a long introductory example. This should show why a Monte Carlo test works. The following example using body temperature data is motivated by a lecture given by Friedrich Leisch at the Vienna University of Technology and adapted for further follow-up lectures by the author of the book.

We first took some data, body temperature and heart rate data from 65 men and 65 women:

```
temp <- read.table("http://venus.unive.it/romanaz/statistics/data/
bodytemp.txt", header = TRUE)

temp$gen <- factor(temp$gen, labels = c("male", "female"))

str(temp)

## 'data.frame':    130 obs. of  3 variables:
##  $ tf : num  96.3 96.7 96.9 97 97.1 97.1 97.1 97.2 97.3 97.4 ...
##  $ gen: Factor w/ 2 levels "male","female": 1 1 1 1 1 1 1 1 1 1 ...
##  $ hr : int  70 71 74 80 73 75 82 64 69 70 ...
```

People who use degrees of Celsius instead of Fahrenheit can do the following transformation:

```
temp$celsius <- (temp$tf - 32) * 5 / 9
```

Let's visualize first, the densities related to male and female temperatures in *Figure 8.15*:

```
library("ggplot2")
ggplot(temp, aes(x = celsius, colour = gen, linetype = gen)) + geom_
density(size = 1.2) + theme(text = element_text(size=16)) + theme_bw()
```

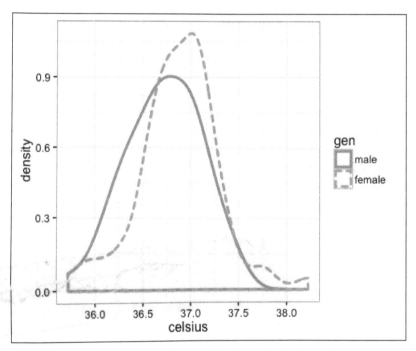

Figure 8.15: Density estimates of female and male temperatures

From *Figure 8.15* we see the different distributions according to male and female. Females have on average, higher temperatures in this dataset. We are coming back to the question on whether the Null hypothesis of equal population means can be rejected.

First issue is to test if the dataset is approximately normal, also an important assumption in many other tests. More precisely we want to know if the Null hypothesis sample that is drawn from a normal distribution can be rejected. We save the temperatures in its own vector, just for better visibility of code afterwards:

```
temperature <- temp$celsius
```

First let us visualize the empirical distribution function that gives mass $1/n$ at each sorted observation:

```
n <- length(temperature)
temperature <- sort(temperature)
y <- (0:(n-1)) / n
```

We can now plot the empirical distribution function, the sorted temperature values against a vector of length n of equidistant values between 0 and 1. The result is visible in *Figure 8.16*:

```
plot(temperature, y, pch=20, cex = 0.3)
lines(temperature, y, type="S")
```

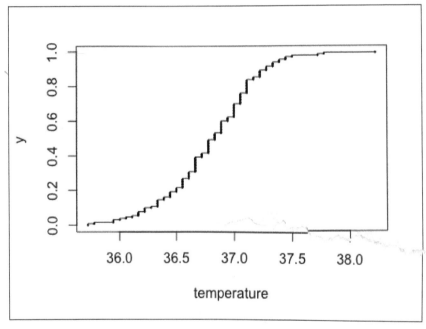

Figure 8.16: Empirical cumulative distribution function plot of the temperature data

We now can ask if these empirical values are drawn from a normal distribution. One possibility is to use diagnostic tools such as QQ plot, but this time we want to make a decision with numerical tools. Let's calculate the theoretical normal distribution with mean and standard deviation from our empirical data, plot and add it to the figure:

```
plot(temperature, y, type="S")
m <- mean(temperature)
s <- sd(temperature)
yn <- pnorm(temperature, mean = m, sd = s)
lines(temperature, yn, col=2)
```

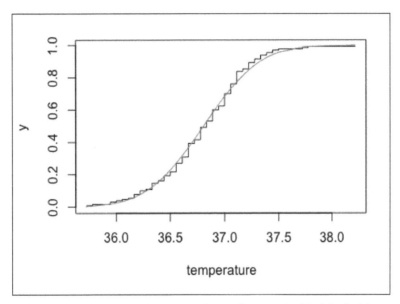

Figure 8.17: Empirical cumulative distribution function plot (black line) of the temperature data and the theoretical one (red line)

This is not too bad, but how do we get confidence bands for this red line?

We can either do some math or, alternatively, we can simulate confidence bands. Since we are lazy, we prefer to simulate it. But how this can be done? The trick is always the same. We draw random samples according to the null hypothesis using parameters estimated from the empirical sample data. In this case we draw from a normal distribution with mean and standard deviation from our temperature data, and see how much the resulting empirical cumulative distribution functions fluctuate. One draw is done as follows (note that we round the simulated data to one digit, as our original temperature data is represented):

```
z <- round(sort(rnorm(n, mean = m, sd = s)), 1)
```

We can repeat this and draw these lines in the plot:

```
set.seed(123)
plot(temperature, y, type="S")
for(k in 1:100){
    z <- rnorm(n, mean=m, sd=s)
    lines(sort(z), y, type="S", col="green")
}
```

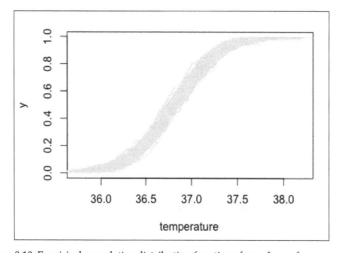

Figure 8.18: Empirical cumulative distribution functions from draws from a normal distribution with mean and standard deviation from the temperature data

The empirical cumulative distribution function of our original data should now have disappeared, that is; the black stepwise line representing the empirical cumulative distribution function of our temperature data should not be visible anymore in *Figure 8.18*. Thus the hypothesis of normality isn't complete nonsense.

Let's save the results from 1000 simulations from a normal distribution in a dataset:

```
Z <- NULL
for(k in 1:1000){
    z = rnorm(n, mean = m, sd = s)
    Z = cbind(Z, sort(z))
}
dim(Z)
## [1]   130 1000
```

z contains in each column, a sorted sample of size 130 from a normal distribution with mean m and standard deviation s. Another view is that z contains in each row, 1000 estimates for the *n / 130-quantile* of a normal distribution with mean m and standard deviation s.

Let's check this:

```
## mean of original temperature data
m
## [1] 36.80513
## simulated mean
(mean(Z[65, ]) + mean(Z[66, ])) / 2
## [1] 36.80581
## simulated median
(median(Z[65, ]) + median(Z[66, ])) / 2
## [1] 36.80621
```

The next plot shows an estimate of the normal distribution based on our random draws from a normal distribution. We also add lower and upper bounds - the confidence interval with significance level 0.05. See *Figure 8.19* for the result:

```
plot(temperature, y, type="S")
middle <- apply(Z, 1, median)
lines(middle, y, col = "blue", lwd = 2, type = "S")
## lower and upper bounds
lower <- apply(Z, 1, quantile, prob = 0.025)
upper <- apply(Z, 1, quantile, prob = 0.975)
lines(lower, y, col = 2, lwd = 2, type = "S")
lines(upper, y, col = 2, lwd = 2, type = "S")
```

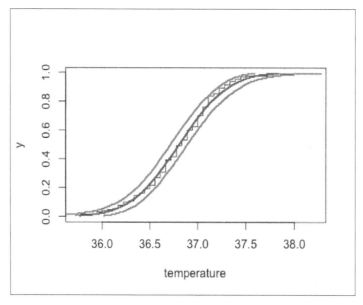

Figure 8.19: Confidence intervals obtained by simulation from the theoretical normal distribution

Our empirical data represented by its cumulative distribution function (the black stepwise line) is almost always inside the confidence bands. Again this is an indication that the normality assumption might not be rejected.

Probably the most popular test for distributions is the Kolmogorov-Smirnov test. Its test statistics is given by the maximum deviation of the observed empirical cumulative distribution function from a theoretical one.

Let's look at these deviations for each given temperature, reported in the bottom graphics of *Figure 8.20*. We also mark the maximum deviation with a big circle:

```
par(mfrow = c(2,1), mar = rep(1,4))
plot(temperature, y, type="S")
lines(temperature, yn, col=2)
lines(lower, y, col=2, lwd=2, type="S")
lines(upper, y, col=2, lwd=2, type="S")
plot(temperature, y - yn, type="h")
abline(h = 0)
## maximum deviation
D <- max(abs(y - yn))
w <- which.max(abs(y - yn))
points(temperature[w], y[w] - yn[w], col=2, pch=16, cex=3)
```

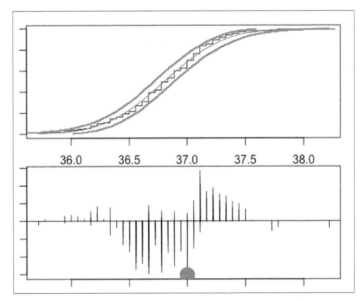

Figure 8.20: Top: ECDF of empirical data (stepwise black line), theoretical ECDF (middle line) and simulated confidence intervals. Bottom: Related differences between the ECDF of original data and the theoretical ECDF

How likely is it that the empirical cumulative distribution function of a normal distribution has at least the observed deviation?

We already simulated 1000 samples. We take a look at their maximum deviation by again doing the same that we did with the temperatures before:

```
## theoretical distribution
Z1 <- pnorm(Z, mean = m, sd = s)
## y will be recycled column-wise,
## extract the maximum for each column
D1 <- apply(abs(y - Z1), 2, max)
```

If we look at the distribution of D1 and compare it to the maximum deviation from our original data (D), we see that the value of D is not that unusual:

```
summary(D1)
##    Min. 1st Qu.  Median    Mean 3rd Qu.    Max.
## 0.02514 0.05457 0.06777 0.07163 0.08401 0.19120
D
## [1] 0.0607473
```

We can ask how many times our simulated maximum deviations are larger than the maximum deviation from our original data set. And even better, we may ask the ratio of it. It's already the *p-value*!

```
mean(D1>D)
## [1] 0.638
```

Let's have a look at the Kolmogorov-Smirnov test here:

```
ks.test(temperature, "pnorm", mean = m, sd = s)
##
##  One-sample Kolmogorov-Smirnov test
##
## data:  temperature
## D = 0.064727, p-value = 0.6474
## alternative hypothesis: two-sided
```

If we increase the number of columns of Z, that is; the number of draws from a normal, then the *mean(D1 > D)* should be equal the p-value of the Kolmogorov-Smirnov test. (beside problems of the Kolmogorov-Smirnov test with rounded values).

The permutation test as a special kind of MC test

Often, we compare two groups of observations with their respective arithmetic means and analyze them with respect to the significant differences of (arithmetic) means. In this case, the null hypothesis is $H_0: \mu_x = \mu_y$ with x and y vectors of size n_1 and n_2. The assumptions of the classical (t-) test consist of both populations, are normally distributed, and have equal variances. If the two samples $x_1, ..., x_{n_1}$ and $y_1, ..., y_{n_2}$ with arithmetic means μ_x and μ_y are independent and their means and variances given by $\bar{x}$, $\bar{y}$, s_x^2 and s_y^2, then the following test statistic follows a t-distribution with $n_1 + n_2 - 2$ degrees of freedom:

$$T = \sqrt{\frac{n_1 n_2 (n_1 + n_2 - 2)}{n_1 + n_2}} \cdot \frac{\bar{x} - \bar{y}}{\sqrt{(n_1 - 1)s_x^2 + (n_2 - 1)s_y^2}}$$

For the test $\mu_x = \mu_y$ the critical area for a one-sided test (the alternative $\mu_x > \mu_y$ is determined by $T > t_{n_1+n_2-2;1-\alpha}$). For a two-sided test α must be replaced by $\frac{\alpha}{2}$.

In the following example, the arithmetic mean of 45 US Americans (workers and employees) from 1950 are compared:

```
data(Duncan, package = "car")
x <- subset(Duncan, type %in% c("bc", "wc"), select = c("income",
"type"))
x$type <- factor(x$type)
## first four observations on income and type
head(x, 4)
##            income type
## reporter       67   wc
## conductor      76   wc
## bookkeeper     29   wc
## mail.carrier   48   wc
```

The classical t-test to test the previously mentioned null hypothesis is:

```
t.test(income ~ type, data=x)
##
##  Welch Two Sample t-test
##
## data:  income by type
## t = -3.045, df = 7.6945, p-value = 0.01669
## alternative hypothesis: true difference in means is not equal to 0
## 95 percent confidence interval:
##  -47.42134  -6.38818
## sample estimates:
## mean in group bc mean in group wc
##          23.76190          50.66667
```

The p-value is 0.01669. Thus the null hypothesis can be rejected for a significance level of 0.01, but not for a significance level of 0.05.

A strict assumption of the classical t-tests for two independent samples is that the population is normally distributed and that the variances should be equal. In addition, we basically do not know the test statistics when we replace the arithmetic mean with a, for example, robust estimator.

All these assumptions and weaknesses in translating the test for arithmetic means to other location estimates are not present in Monte Carlo tests.

The general idea is to mimic the null hypothesis, that is; to simulate values from the null hypothesis, apply the same test statistics to the original data and to the simulated one and compare these test statistics.

The p-value from the t-test shown before can also now be calculated by a permutation test (other Monte Carlo tests follow later).

1. Estimate the absolute difference of means of the two groups in the original sample (with original classes). Denote this as $\hat{\theta}$.

2. Simulate from the null hypothesis by permuting the grouping/classes. Random groups mimic the null hypothesis of equal means. Calculate the absolute difference between the means with the randomized grouping structure. Denote the results as θ_1^*. Repeat this at least:

$$R = 1.000 \text{ times} \rightarrow \theta_r^*, (r = 1, ..., R)$$

3. The p-value is then given by $\#\{\theta_r^* \geq \hat{\theta}\}/R$.

To permute the grouping structure, we simply use the function sample (without replacement):

```
## first 6 observations with permuted grouping structure
head(cbind(x, "p1" = sample(x$type),
              "p2" = sample(x$type),
              "p3" = sample(x$type)))
##                income type p1 p2 p3
## reporter           67   wc wc bc bc
## conductor          76   wc bc bc wc
## bookkeeper         29   wc bc wc wc
## mail.carrier       48   wc bc bc bc
## insurance.agent    55   wc bc wc bc
## store.clerk        29   wc bc bc wc
```

The groups still have n_1 and n_2 observations but their observations are randomized according to the group belongings. This mimics the null hypothesis of equal means.

Now let's write a permutation test in R. We use the class `htest` of R to receive standardized print output:

```
## define test statistics (workhorse)
teststat <- function(vals, group, lev){
  g <- sample(group)
  abs(mean(vals[g == lev[1]]) - mean(vals[g == lev[2]]))
}
## permutation test
permtest <- function(x, g, R = 1000, conf.level = 0.95){
    ## levels of the group vector
    lg <- levels(g)
    ## test statistics for original groups
    mdiff <- abs(mean(x[g==lg[1]]) - mean(x[g==lg[2]]))
    ## test statistics for permuted group data
    z <- replicate(R, teststat(x, g, lg))
    ## make nice print output
    DATA <- paste(deparse(substitute(x)),
                  "by",
                  deparse(substitute(g)))
    alpha <- 1 - conf.level
```

```
    conf.int <- quantile(z, prob = c(alpha/2, (1 - alpha)/2))
    attr(conf.int, "conf.level") <- conf.level
    res <- list(statistic=c(mdiff = mdiff),
                p.value = mean(abs(z) > abs(mdiff)),
                parameter = c(nrep = R),
                conf.int = conf.int,
                data.name = DATA,
                method = "Permutation test for difference in means")
    class(res) <- "htest"
    res
}
```

Now we can apply the permutation test to the Duncan data on income and type:

```
permtest(x$income, x$type, R = 10000)
##
##   Permutation test for difference in means
##
## data:  x$income by x$type
## mdiff = 26.905, nrep = 10000, p-value = 0.0039
## 95 percent confidence interval:
##   0.3095238 6.5238095
```

Also the permutation test would reject for a significance level of 0.05, but also for 0.01. The permutation test can be applied to any test problem where the groups/classes of a variable play a central role.

A Monte Carlo test for multiple groups

If more than one group should be compared, typically ANOVA is the choice. However, this could also be done by pairwise t-tests.

```
data(Duncan, package = "car")
pairwise.t.test(Duncan$income, Duncan$type)
##
##   Pairwise comparisons using t tests with pooled SD
##
## data:  Duncan$income and Duncan$type
##
```

```
##       bc      prof
## prof 2.9e-07 -
## wc    0.0039  0.2634
##
## P value adjustment method: holm
```

What is meant by p-value adjustment? The probability to reject (to reject the null hypothesis when the null hypothesis is true) all k tests is the product over all significance levels, that is; $(1 - \alpha)^k$. If $\alpha = 0.05$ and k = 100 then the probability of rejection is $(1 - 0.05)^{100} = 0.994$. This is also true if, for example, the data drawn from a normal distribution, randomly chooses 100 groups and a normality test is made since every single test will reject with probability 0.05 when the data is drawn from normal distribution and a normality test is made. Thus, one of the common problems in significance testing is the tendency for multiple comparisons to yield spurious significant differences even where the null hypothesis is true. Therefore, p-values must be adjusted for multiple comparisons.

The Bonferroni correction multiplies all p-values by the number of tests, the Holm correction multiplies the smallest p-value with n, the second with n – 1, and so on.

With the `pairwise.t.test` we looked for differences between any pairwise combination of groups. Another possible question is whether the mean value of all groups is the same:

```
mean(Duncan$income)
## [1] 41.86667
library("dplyr")
Duncan %>% group_by(type) %>% summarize(mean = mean(income))
## Source: local data frame [3 x 2]
##
##      type      mean
##    (fctr)     (dbl)
## 1      bc  23.76190
## 2    prof  60.05556
## 3      wc  50.66667
```

Our test statistic is the maximum absolute value of all test statistics, calculated by the following:

```r
tstat <- function(x, mu=0){
    (mean(x)-mu) / (sd(x) / sqrt(length(x)))
}
stats <- tapply(Duncan$income, Duncan$type, tstat,
mu=mean(Duncan$income))
stat <- max(abs(stats))
stat
## [1] 4.725815
```

Instead of thinking of a way to find test statistics in an analytic manner, we are lazy and remember the Monte Carlo way of easy living. Note that for a Monte Carlo test it is only important to obtain values of test statistics by respecting the null hypothesis. We can thus simulate random numbers from the null hypothesis, or if we know something about the distribution of the test statistics we can simulate random numbers directly from this distribution. In our case we know that the distribution of the test statistics of a z-test is a t-distribution:

```r
maxt.test <- function(x, g, R = 10000, conf.level = 0.05){
    m <- mean(x)
    stat <- tapply(x, g, tstat, mu = m)
    stat <- max(abs(stat))
    gsize = table(g)
    z <- NULL
    for(k in 1:length(gsize)){
        ## from a t-distribution:
        z <- cbind(z, rt(n=n, df=gsize[k]-1))
    }
    ## z now is a list with length(gsize) elements
    ## we need the maximum absolute value for each element
    z <- abs(z)
    z <- z[cbind(1:n,max.col(z))]
    ## make nice print output
    DATA <- paste(deparse(substitute(x)),
                "by",
                deparse(substitute(g)))
    alpha <- 1 - conf.level
    conf.int <- quantile(z, prob = c(alpha/2, (1 - alpha)/2))
```

```
    attr(conf.int, "conf.level") <- conf.level
    res <- list(statistic=c(stat = stat),
                p.value =  mean(z > stat),
                parameter = c(nrep = R),
                conf.int = conf.int,
                data.name = DATA,
                method = "Maximum t-test")
    class(res) <- "htest"
    res
}
```

Now let us apply this test on the Duncan data set with three groups of types:

```
maxt.test(Duncan$income, Duncan$type)
##
##   Maximum t-test
##
## data:  Duncan$income by Duncan$type
## stat = 4.7258, nrep = 10000, p-value = 0.007692
## 5 percent confidence interval:
##   1.271122 0.436830
```

We see that we can reject the null hypothesis.

Another possibility is to make a permutation test:

```
maxp.test <- function(x, g, R = 10000, conf.level = 0.05){
    m <- mean(x)
    stat <- tapply(x, g, tstat, mu=m)
    stat <- max(abs(stat))
    z <- numeric(n)
    for(k in 1:n){
        g1 <- sample(g)
        z[k] <- max(abs(tapply(x, g1, tstat, mu = m)))
    }

    retval <- list(tstat=stat, pval=mean(z>stat),
                   name="Permutation maximum t-test")
    class(retval) <- "ttest"
    retval
```

```
## make nice print output
DATA <- paste(deparse(substitute(x)),
              "by",
              deparse(substitute(g)))
alpha <- 1 - conf.level
conf.int <- quantile(z, prob = c(alpha/2, (1 - alpha)/2))
attr(conf.int, "conf.level") <- conf.level
res <- list(statistic=c(stat = stat),
            p.value =  mean(z > stat),
            parameter = c(nrep = R),
            conf.int = conf.int,
            data.name = DATA,
            method = "Permutation maximum test")
class(res) <- "htest"
res
}
```

Again we apply the test on the Duncan data:

```
maxp.test(Duncan$income, Duncan$type)
##
##   Permutation maximum test
##
## data:  Duncan$income by Duncan$type
## stat = 4.7258, nrep = 10000, p-value < 2.2e-16
## 5 percent confidence interval:
##   0.9895857 0.2037640
```

The p-value is even slightly smaller for the permutation test.

Hypothesis testing using a bootstrap

Generally, a bootstrap can also be used as a variant of a Monte Carlo test.

We continue the hypothesis test for a 2-sample test on equal population means. A bootstrap 2-sample test works quite similar to the permutation test. The basic difference is that we draw samples with replacement.

1. Draw R bootstrap samples of size $n_1 + n_2 = n$ with replacement. The first n1 observations now belong to sample 1 denoted by $\mathbf{X}^*$ and the rest of n_2 observations belong to the second sample $\mathbf{y}^*$.

2. For each bootstrap sample estimate $\theta_r^* = f(\mathbf{x}_r^*) - f(\mathbf{y}_r^*)$, $r = 1, ..., B$.

3. The p-value is then given by $\#\{\theta_r^* \geq \theta\}/R$, with θ estimated from the original samples.

Now let's look in R, this time we keep it simple and do not provide the print output as class `htest`:

```
boottest <- function(x, g, n=10000){
    lg <- levels(g)
    n1 <- length(x[g == lg[1]])
    N <- length(x)
    mdiff <- abs(mean(x[g == lg[1]]) - mean(x[g == lg[2]]))
    z <- double(n)
    for(k in 1:n){
        x1 <- sample(x, replace=TRUE)
        z[k] <- abs(mean(x1[1:n1]) - mean(x1[(n1+1):N]))
    }
    mean( z > mdiff )
}
```

The bootstrap test gives a p-value of 0, meaning that no test statistics of the sampled group structure provide a larger value of the test statistics as the test statistics obtained from the original data:

```
Duncan$type <- factor(Duncan$type)
boottest(Duncan$income, Duncan$type)
## [1] 0
```

A test for multivariate normality

As a last test we show a more advanced one where the test statistics are not known. We want to show a test for multivariate normal distribution, the **Anderson-Darling (AD)** test. Multivariate normality tests are important since the most multivariate statistical methods assume multivariate normality of the data. A test may check if this assumption is valid.

Generally important for tests are the *size of a test* and the *power* of a test. In case of the AD test the size of the test should be 0.05 whenever a significance level of 0.05 is chosen and random samples are drawn from a multivariate normal distribution, that is; for repeated draws, the mean of rejection should equal the significance level. The power of a test is used to compare tests. The one with highest power is the best test in case the size of test is correct.

Many multivariate normality tests are based on Mahalanobis distances.

If $\mathbf{X}$ is a sample with p variables, n observations and sample variance Σ, the aim is that the Mahalanobis distances, estimated by $d_i^2 = (\mathbf{X} - \bar{\mathbf{X}})'\Sigma^{-1}(\mathbf{X} - \bar{\mathbf{X}})$, are approx. χ^2 distributed with p degrees of freedom.

The test statistics for the univariate Anderson-Darling test (Anderson and Darling 1952) is defined as:

$A = -N - \bar{S}$, where $S = \sum_{i=1}^{n} \frac{2i-1}{n} (\ln F(x_{i(1:n)}) + \ln(1 - F(x_{i(n:1)})))$, with F as the cumulative distribution function of a normal distribution. $x_{i(1:n)}$ is the data vector's values in ascending order and $x_{i(n:1)}$ in descending order.

It is a one-sided test and the null hypothesis; *The sample was drawn from a normally distributed population*, is rejected if the test statistic A is larger than the critical value. For some cases of p, n and significance levels, the critical values are tabulated values, see Stephens, 1974.

In the multivariate case, replacing F from the previous formula with the cumulated distribution function of the χ^2 distribution and $x_{i(1:n)}$, $(i = 1, ..., n)$ are the quantiles of the χ^2 distribution of Mahalanobis distances.

The Anderson-Darling test statistic is usually multiplied by a constant depending on the sample size n.

In order to obtain a p-value a Monte Carlo method can be implemented. Repeated random sampling of data of size n x p with means and covariance of the original data is done to mimic the null hypothesis (multivariate normality). The ratio of the resulting test statistics (from the R artificially simulated data), and the test statistic of the original data then acts in turn as a p-value. The larger the number of simulations, the more stable are the results.

As a Monte Carlo test we can write the AD test as follows in R:

```
mvad.test <- function(x, R=1000){
    n <- nrow(x)
    ## test statistics
  stat <- function(x, N = n){
    cmean <- colMeans(x)
      cvar  <- var(x)
    u <- mahalanobis(x, center = cmean, cov = cvar)
    z <- pchisq(u, ncol(x))
    p <- sort(z)
```

```
    h <- (2 * seq(1:N) - 1) * (log(p) + log(1 - rev(p)))
    A <- -N - mean(h)
        return(A)
}
## value of test statistics for original sample
A <- stat(x)
    cmean <- colMeans(x)
cvar <- var(x)
p <- numeric(R)
## values of test statistics for draws of mvn
p <- replicate(R, stat(mvrnorm(n, cmean, cvar)))
pvalue <- mean(p > A)
    RVAL <- list(statistic = c(A = A),
                method = "A-D radius test",
                    p.value = pvalue)
    class(RVAL) <- "htest"
    RVAL
}
```

Size of the test

If a well performing random number generator has been selected and if data is drawn from a multivariate normal distribution, then the percentage of rejection should be equal to the chosen significance level.

This can easily be checked.

We simulate multivariate normal data with zero co-variances, and we repeat this 1000 times, that is; the Monte Carlo test is applied 1000 times. The significance level is set to be $\alpha = 0.05$. We then check how many times the p-value was smaller than 0.05. The result should be approx. 0.05 if the size of the test is correct:

```
library("MASS")
set.seed(123)
r <- replicate(1000, mvad.test(mvrnorm(100, mu=rep(0,3),
            Sigma=diag(3)))$p.value)
size <- mean(r < 0.05)
size
## [1] 0.05
```

Power comparisons

Once a test is constructed such that the size fits for different values, significance levels, and dimensions of data sets, it may be compared with other tests. The aim of checking the size of the test was to sample data repeatably from the null hypothesis (multivariate normality). Now the aim for power comparisons is to simulate data repeatably from the alternative hypothesis. If the data originating from the alternative hypothesis, of course the rejection rate (= the power of the test) should be as high as possible.

We compare our Monte Carlo AD test with the skewness test (Kankainen, Taskinen, and Oja 2007).

For this purpose, data is to be drawn from a multivariate t-distribution:

```
library("mvtnorm")
library("ICS")
## Monte Carlo AD test 100 times replicated
r <- replicate(100, mvad.test(rmvt(30, diag(3), df = 5), R=100)$p.value)
mean(r  < 0.05)
## [1] 0.51
## Skewness test 1000 times replicated
r2 <- replicate(1000, mvnorm.skew.test(rmvt(30, diag(3), df = 5))$p.
value)
mean(r2  < 0.05)
## [1] 0.368
```

We see that our Monte Carlo AD test has as high power as the well-known skewness test. However, we have to mention that in this case a so-called kurtosis test that evaluates the shape might be more successful than the skewness test where the main goal is to evaluate the symmetry of the distribution.

Summary

From this chapter we learned that the bootstrap can be applied to almost any complex problem, but we also learned that the bootstrap must be adapted for each complex problem. For regression analysis this was done by sampling from residuals instead of the whole data matrix. For times series analysis, the modification of the bootstrap was done by splitting the time series in blocks and resampling within blocks.

We also saw that uncertainty and proper variances can be estimated for data including missing values. This has huge advantages whenever multiple imputation cannot be applied for logistic reasons in a company or organization.

The bootstrap was also applied to complex survey samples drawn with complex survey designs. Here we defined the calibrated bootstrap to adequately estimate the variance of a statistic.

Monte Carlo tests served as a very general tool for hypothesis testing. Data scientists can make use of them for any statistical test. We did not use any theoretical knowledge about the distribution of our statistic under the null hypothesis, as is normally the case with classical tests. Instead, we simulated the distribution of the Null hypothesis. The Monte Carlo test works for all distributions of test statistics without making assumptions about them. That means that Monte Carlo tests, in the case of a violation of the central limit theorem (a small sample size and non-normal population), deliver more reliable results than classical tests. Of course there is also a disadvantage: the computation time. However, this should no longer be a problem with the current computational power of a desktop personal computer or notebook.

References

- Alfons, A., and M. Templ. 2013. "Estimation of Social Exclusion Indicators from Complex Surveys: The R Package laeken." *Journal of Statistical Software* 54 (15): 1–25. http://www.jstatsoft.org/v54/i15/.

- Anderson, T.W., and D.A. Darling. 1952. "Asymptotic Theory of Certain Goodness-of-Fit Criteria Based on Stochastic Processes." *Annals of Mathematical Statistics* 23: 193–212.

- Deville, J.-C., and C.-E. Särndal. 1992. "Calibration Estimators in Survey Sampling." *Journal of the American Statistical Association* 87 (418): 376–82.

- Deville, J.-C., C.-E. Särndal, and O. Sautory. 1993. "Generalized Raking Procedures in Survey Sampling." *Journal of the American Statistical Association* 88 (423): 1013–20.

- Hyndman, R., and Y. Khandakar. 2008. "Automatic Time Series Forecasting: The Forecast Package for R." *Journal of Statistical Software* 27 (1).

- Kankainen, A., S. Taskinen, and H. Oja. 2007. "Tests of Multinormality Based on Location Vectors and Scatter Matrices." *Statistical Methods and Applications* 16 (3): 357–79.

- Little, R.J.A., and D.B. Rubin. 2002. *Statistical Analysis with Missing Data*. 2nd ed. New York: John Wiley & Sons.

- Maronna, R., D. Martin, and V. Yohai. 2006. *Robust Statistics*. Chichester: John Wiley & Sons.

- Rao, J.N.K., and C.F.J. Wu. 1988. "Resampling Inference with Complex Survey Data." *Journal of the American Statistical Association* 83: 231–41.

- Rousseeuw, P.J., and A.M. Leroy. 1987. *Robust Regression and Outlier Detection*. Wiley; Sons, New York.

- Rubin, D.B. 1987. *Multiple Imputation for Nonresponse in Surveys*. J. Wiley & Sons, New York.

- Stephens, M.A. 1974. "EDF Statistics for Goodness-of-Fit and Some Comparisons." *Journal of the American Statistical Association* 69: 730–37.

- Templ, M., A. Alfons, and P. Filzmoser. 2011. "Exploring Incomplete Data Using Visualization Techniques." *Advances in Data Analysis and Classification* 6 (1): 29–47.

The EM Algorithm

9

The **Expectation Maximization (EM)** algorithm (Dempster, Laird, and Rubin 1977) is actually not really an algorithm, but a procedure for algorithms for the computation of the maximum likelihood estimators in data with missing values. The EM algorithm is typically used for problems where no closed-form solution is known; that is to say for the special kind of optimization problems where iteration is the only chance to get close to the optimal solution.

The EM algorithm is successfully used, especially in applications from data clustering in machine learning and computer vision, in natural language processing, in psychometrics, in price and managed risk of a portfolio and in medical image reconstruction, and it is the general procedure used to impute missing values in a data set.

All data scientists would benefit from knowing the functionality of the EM algorithm since it gives them a tool to solve many problems in practice where no exact solution exists.

The basic EM algorithm

Before we give a formal definition of the EM algorithm, let's discuss some basics about likelihood and maximum likelihood. This is necessary in order to understand the definitions. After satisfying these prerequisites, we will give a formal definition of the EM algorithm according to the problems of missing values imputation. This is where the EM algorithm originates (Dempster, Laird, and Rubin 1977). We will see that the complex formal definition is easy to catch with an introductory example.

Some prerequisites

Before we start with the EM algorithm we need to remind ourselves of some of the basics about likelihood and maximum likelihood.

For this we start by flipping a coin. If we have two possible outcomes, event A (*'head'*) and A' (*'tail'*), our parameter of interest is $\theta = P(A = \text{'head'})$, the probability of tossing the heads side of the coin. The probability of tossing the tails side of the coin is then $1 - \theta$.

Let's assume that we tossed the coin 10 times and the results were *head, tail, head, tail, head, head, head, head, head,* and *tail*. A natural approach is now to look just at the frequencies and calculate the number of successes divided by the number of trials,

$$\theta = \frac{7}{3+7} = 0.7$$

The likelihood of our observations depends on θ. The likelihood is given as the product of our parameter of interest:

$$L(\theta) = \theta(1 - \theta)\theta(1 - \theta)\theta\theta\theta\theta\theta\theta(1 - \theta)$$

The maximum likelihood can be written as:

$$\text{argmax}_\theta L(\theta) = \text{argmax}_\theta \theta^7 (1 - \theta)^3$$

But how do we find the maximum? This is always done by taking the derivation according to the parameter of interest and setting this derivation to zero:

$$\frac{\delta}{\delta\theta} = 7\theta^6(1 - \theta)^3 - 3\theta^7(1 - \theta)^2 = \ldots$$

Hmmm, we took the . . . since of laziness: way too many calculations for a lazy guy. We know that we receive the same results either by maximizing the likelihood or the logarithm of the likelihood. The solution is often much easier when we use logarithms. Thus, in our case, we want to maximize the log-likelihood denoted by $l(\theta)$:

$$\text{argmax}_\theta l(\theta) = \text{argmax}_\theta \log(\theta^7 (1 - theta)^3)$$

Again we take the derivative and set the derivative to zero to obtain the maximum:

$$\frac{\delta}{\delta\theta} = 7\log\theta + 3\log(1-\theta)$$

Set to zero:

$$7\log\theta + 3\log(1-\theta) = 0$$
$$\frac{7}{\theta} - \frac{3}{1-\theta} = 0$$
$$\rightarrow \theta = \frac{7}{10} = 0.7$$

In this case θ from the direct estimation equals to this solution θ_{ML}.

Formal definition of the EM algorithm

Let's first motivate the EM algorithm, according to its initial formulation as an algorithm, to estimate missing values in a data set.

Let $\mathbf{X}_{obs}$ and $\mathbf{X}_{miss}$ be the observed and the missing part of a data set $\mathbf{X}$ and let θ be a vector of unknown parameters to estimate. The likelihood function is given by $L(\theta; \mathbf{X}_{obs}, \mathbf{X}_{miss}) = p(\mathbf{X}_{obs}, \mathbf{X}_{miss}|\theta)$, and the unknown parameters are determined by the marginal likelihood of the observed data:

$$L(\theta; \mathbf{X}_{obs}) = p(\mathbf{X}_{obs}|\theta) = \Sigma^{\square}_{\mathbf{X}_{miss}} p(\mathbf{X}_{obs}\mathbf{X}_{miss}|\theta)$$

The closed-form solution of this equation is often too complex, and thus an iterative method is needed to solve this equation.

The EM algorithm is an iterative method that alternately performs two steps: the **E-step** (=Expectation step) and the **M-step** (=Maximization step). In this method, the likelihood function $L(\theta, \mathbf{X}_{obs}, \mathbf{X}_{miss})$ is maximized related to θ, which is equivalent to maximizing the log-likelihood function $l(\theta, \mathbf{X}_{o}bs, \mathbf{X}_{miss})$:

1. Choose a starting value for the parameter θ, say $\theta^{(0)}$, set $n = 0$.

2. Iterate until convergence 2a) **E-step**: Calculate the conditional expected value $\dot{Q}(\theta|\theta^{(h)}) = E(l(\theta; \mathbf{X}_{obs}, \mathbf{X}_{miss}))$. We took the log-likelihood function, $l(\theta, \mathbf{X})$ of the completed data set given by the current estimate $\theta^{(n)}$ to estimate this. 2b) **M-step**: Maximize:

$$\dot{Q}(\theta|\theta^{(n)}) \rightarrow \text{new estimate } \theta^{(n+1)}$$

Introductory example for the EM algorithm

As you may have noted, this is quite a complex general notation. However, in practice, this gets easier. In the following example, we want to explain the EM algorithm based on a simple 2 X 3 table with one missing cell:

```
y <- matrix(c(11, 22, 16, 24, 17, NA), nrow=2)
y
##      [,1] [,2] [,3]
## [1,]   11   16   17
## [2,]   22   24   NA
```

We took a linear model $x_{ij} = u + \alpha_i + \beta_j + e_{ij}$ with $\sum \alpha_i = 0$, $\sum \beta_j = 0$ and $e_{ij} \sim N(0, \sigma^2)$.

If we knew the cell value of x_{23} it would be simple to estimate the coefficients of the linear model, such as, $\hat{u} = \overline{x}$, $\hat{\alpha}_i = \overline{x}_{i.} - \overline{x}$ and $\hat{\beta}_i = \overline{x}_{.j} - \overline{x}$. Here $\overline{x}_i$ denotes the row-wise arithmetic means and $\overline{x}_{.j}$ the column-wise arithmetic means. Rather than giving more explanations as to why these are reasonable estimates of the parameters, we need to concentrate on the EM algorithm and how the EM can be formulated for this example.

What we always have to do in the EM algorithm is choose starting values. Thus we initialize the missing value, for example, we may choose the arithmetic mean of the observed values of y for initialization:

```
m <- mean(y, na.rm = TRUE)
m
## [1] 18
y[2,3] <- m
y
##      [,1] [,2] [,3]
## [1,]   11   16   17
## [2,]   22   24   18
```

Next we start the iteration. We iteratively impute the missing value x_{23} with plausible values using the following E and M steps:

```
## stop criterion
eps <- 0.001
## intitialisations
yalt <- y
n <- 0
```

```
converged <- FALSE
## iteration
while(!converged){
    n <- n + 1
    yalt <- y
    m1 <- mean(y)
    ## E-step (estimate parameters)
    a <- rowMeans(y) - m1
    b1 <- colMeans(y) - m1
    ## M-step (update y23)
    y[2, 3] <- m1 + a[2] + b1[3]
    ## stop criterion
    converged <- (abs(y[2, 3] - yalt[2, 3]) < eps)
}
list(yImp = y, iterations = n)
## $yImp
##      [,1] [,2]    [,3]
## [1,]   11   16 17.0000
## [2,]   22   24 26.4983
##
## $iterations
## [1] 21
```

We see that we needed 21 iterations to achieve the final result of the imputed value of X_{23}. We'll come back to the issue of imputation soon, but first we'll discuss another application of the EM algorithm.

The EM algorithm by example of k-means clustering

Probably the most famous algorithm for clustering observations to groups is the k-means algorithm. We will see that this algorithm is just a variant of the EM algorithm.

Given n objects, characterized by p variables, we like to partition them into n_c clusters $\{C_1, C_2, \ldots, C_{nc}\}$ such that cluster C_k has $n_{(k)}$ members and each observation is in one cluster. The mean vector (center, prototype), V_k, of a cluster C_k is defined as the centroid of the cluster and the components of the mean vector can be calculated

by $v_k(\in \mathbb{R}^p) = \left(\frac{1}{n_{(k)}} \sum_{i=1}^{n_{(k)}} x_{i1}^{(k)}, \ldots, \frac{1}{n_{(k)}} \sum_{i=1}^{n_{(k)}} x_{ip}^{(k)} \right)$ where $n_{(k)}$ is the number of observations in cluster C_k and $x_i^{(k)}$ is the i-th observation belonging to cluster C_k. For each cluster $C_1, \ldots, C_{n_c}$ the corresponding cluster means $V = \{v_1, \ldots, v_{n_c}\}$ are calculated.

We also need to determine the number of clusters in the output partition. Starting from the given initial locations of the n_c cluster centroids, the algorithm uses the data points to iteratively relocate the centroids and reallocate points to the closest centroid. The process is composed of these steps:

1. Select an initial partition with n_c clusters.
2. *E-step*: (Re)compute the cluster centers using the current cluster memberships.
3. *M-step*: Assign each object to the closest cluster center, new memberships.
4. Go to step 2 until the cluster memberships and thus cluster centroids do not change beyond a specified bound.

-means clustering optimizes the objective function:

$J(X, V, U) = \sum_{k=1}^{n_c} \sum_{i=1}^{n} u_{ik} d^2(x_i, v_k)$ where $X = \{x_1, \ldots, x_n\}$ is the data set with observation and variables, $v_1, \ldots, v_{n_c}$ is the matrix of cluster centers (prototypes) of dimension $n_c \times p$. $U = [(u_{ik})]$ is a matrix with the membership coefficients u_{ik} for observation x_i to a cluster n_c. U is therefore of dimension $n \times n_c$. d is the Euclidean distance between the observation and the cluster center. n_c determines the number of clusters.

The k-means algorithm can be implemented as follows. Fix $n_c, 2 \leq n_c < n$, and choose the termination tolerance $\delta > 0$, for example, *0.001*. Initialize $U^{(0)}$ (for example, randomly).

REPEAT for $r = 1, 2, \ldots$

1. **E-step**: Calculate the centers of the clusters:

$$v_k = \frac{1}{\sum_{i=1}^{n} u_{ik}} \left(\sum_{i=1}^{n} u_{ik} x_{i1}, \ldots, \sum_{i=1}^{n} u_{ik} x_{ip} \right) \quad , \text{for } k = 1, \ldots, n_c$$

2. **M-step**: Update $\mathbf{U}^{(r)}$: Reallocate the cluster memberships.

3. $u_{ij}^{(r)} = 1 \text{ if } d(\mathbf{X}_i, \mathbf{v}_j^{(r)}) = \min_{1 \le l \le n_c} d(\mathbf{X}_i, \mathbf{v}_l^{(r)})$

4. $u_{ij}^{(r)} = 0$ otherwise

$$\text{UNTIL } \| \mathbf{U}^{(r)} - \mathbf{U}^{(r-1)} \| < \delta.$$

We define the whole algorithm of k-means in the following. This is just to get in touch with the code and algorithm. For professional implementations of the k-means, see for example, (Leisch 2006).

For the cluster algorithm we need a distance function. We use the Manhattan distance:

```
distMan <- function(x, centers){
  if(class(x) == "data.frame") x <- as.matrix(x)
    d <- matrix(0, nrow=nrow(x), ncol=nrow(centers))
    ## dist center to observations for each cluster
    for(k in 1:nrow(centers)){
        d[,k] <- abs( colSums((t(x) - centers[k,])) )
    }
    return(d)
}
```

And we need a function that calculates means, for example, we may use the arithmetic mean, but we may also use the median as in the following:

```
means <- function(x, cluster){
    cen <- matrix(NA, nrow=max(cluster), ncol <- ncol(x))
    ## cluster means for each cluster
    for(n in 1:max(cluster)){
        cen[n,] <- apply(x[cluster==n,], 2, median)
    }
    return(cen)
}
```

We write a function for the k-means algorithm, which implements the formulas before. In order to make some plots show the EM-approach in detail, we do it in a `for` loop:

```
my_kmeans <- function(x, k, clmeans = means, distance = distMan, iter =
99999, seed = NULL){
  if(!is.null(seed)) set.seed(seed)
    cent <- newcent <- x[sample(1:nrow(x), size=k), ]
    oldclust <- 0
    j <- 0
    for(i in 1:iter){ # better: while()
      j <- j + 1
      cent <- newcent
      ## M-step
        dist <- distance(x, cent)
        clust <- max.col(-dist)
        ## E-step
        newcent <- clmeans(x, clust)
        if(all(clust == oldclust)) break()
        oldclust <- clust
    }
    res <- list(centers = cent,
                cluster = factor(clust),
                iterations = j)
    return(res)
}
```

As we can see, in k-means clustering the *E-step* is the fitting step and the *M-step* is the assignment step. Iterating the *E* and *M-step* iteratively improves the solution. This means that $J(\mathbf{X}, \mathbf{V}, \mathbf{U})$ gets smaller in each iteration. We break the algorithm if the cluster assignment is not changing anymore.

Let's crap some data. We want to keep it simple and we want to show the clusters visually. So we've taken a two-dimensional data set and shown it in *Figure 9.1*.

```
data(Nclus, package = "flexclust")
x <- data.frame(Nclus)
library("ggplot2")
qplot(X1, X2, data=data.frame(Nclus))
```

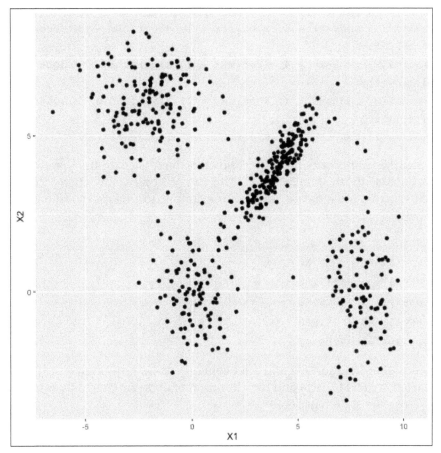

Figure 9.1: A simple two-dimensional data set used in the following example
for clustering (to find the four groups in this data set)

In the following we plot the results after iterations *1*, *2*, and after convergence. Instead of our simplified implementation of the k-means algorithm, we use the default k-means implementation of R. Some variants of the k-means exist, where we chose the algorithm of `"MacQueen"`, but only in order to explore the algorithm (the default method, `"Hartigan-Wong"` is converging too fast to show the steps of the algorithm). Note that the k-means algorithm starts with randomly chosen cluster centers. Thus we have to set the `seed` to ensure the same starts in each call of the k-means:

```
set.seed(123456)
cl1 <- kmeans(x, centers = 4, iter.max = 1, algorithm = "MacQueen")
set.seed(123456)
cl2 <- kmeans(x, centers = 4, iter.max = 2, algorithm = "MacQueen")
set.seed(123456)
cl3 <- kmeans(x, centers = 4, iter.max = 3, algorithm = "MacQueen")
set.seed(123456)
cl4 <- kmeans(x, centers = 4, algorithm = "MacQueen")
```

We then plot the results after the *E-step* and after the *M-step* for the first two iterations, but also for the final solution. This can be done easily when accessing the cluster centers from the k-means results, for example, for the first solution after one iteration with:

```
cl1$centers
##           X1          X2
## 1   4.787137   4.65547187
## 2   2.555571   2.20578465
## 3  -1.590451   4.32789868
## 4   7.997304  -0.08258293
```

The solutions after iteration *1*, *2* and after convergence is now shown in *Figure 9.2*. The calculated centers (*E-step*) and the allocation of observations to their nearest cluster (*M-step*) are shown in detail:

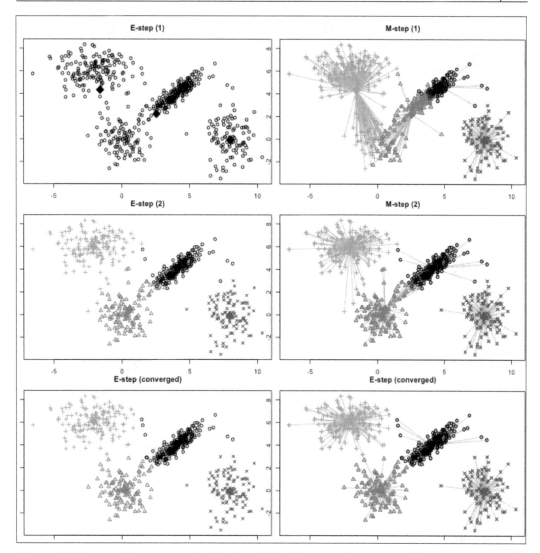

Figure 9.2: Solutions of the k-means algorithm. Top left: initial centers, the solution of the E-step in iteration 1). Top right: first assignment of points to estimated centers, the solution of the M-step in iteration 1. Middle left: new centers at iteration 2. Middle right: new assignment. Bottom left: final solution of the centers. Bottom right: final assignment of observations to cluster centers

Note that the k-means only takes the centers into account and works with a distance function to calculate the distance from the observations to the cluster centers. Another (more favorable) approach is to incorporate them within the shape of the clusters. This is implemented in the model-based clustering framework (Fraley and Raftery 2002). The model-based procedures mostly give better clustering results (Templ, Filzmoser, and Reimann 2008) but they are computationally more complex since in each *E-step* the covariance of each cluster must be additionally calculated.

The EM algorithm for the imputation of missing values

The EM algorithm is extensively used for the imputation of missing values. Implementations include (van Buuren and Groothuis-Oudshoorn 2011), (Schafer 1997), (Templ, Alfons, and Filzmoser 2011), (Raghunathan et al. 2001), and (Gelman and Hill 2011). In the following we want to show how an EM algorithm works generally for these kind of problems.

First we take a data set to impute. We select again the `sleep` data:

```
library("MASS")
library("robustbase")
library("VIM")
data("sleep")
str(sleep)
## 'data.frame':    62 obs. of  10 variables:
##  $ BodyWgt : num  6654 1 3.38 0.92 2547 ...
##  $ BrainWgt: num  5712 6.6 44.5 5.7 4603 ...
##  $ NonD    : num  NA 6.3 NA NA 2.1 9.1 15.8 5.2 10.9 8.3 ...
##  $ Dream   : num  NA 2 NA NA 1.8 0.7 3.9 1 3.6 1.4 ...
##  $ Sleep   : num  3.3 8.3 12.5 16.5 3.9 9.8 19.7 6.2 14.5 9.7 ...
##  $ Span    : num  38.6 4.5 14 NA 69 27 19 30.4 28 50 ...
##  $ Gest    : num  645 42 60 25 624 180 35 392 63 230 ...
##  $ Pred    : int  3 3 1 5 3 4 1 4 1 1 ...
##  $ Exp     : int  5 1 1 2 5 4 1 5 2 1 ...
##  $ Danger  : int  3 3 1 3 4 4 1 4 1 1 ...
```

Missing values are included in some of the all variables, like in variable `Sleep`:

```
apply(sleep, 2, function(x) any(is.na(x)))
## BodyWgt BrainWgt    NonD    Dream    Sleep    Span    Gest
Pred
##   FALSE    FALSE    TRUE    TRUE    TRUE    TRUE    TRUE
FALSE
##     Exp   Danger
##   FALSE    FALSE
```

How can we impute missing values in the variable Sleep? This might be done by performing regression fits. Ideally, we already initialize missing values from a well-performing algorithm for imputation, for example, a k-nearest neighbor imputation approach (Templ, Alfons, and Filzmoser 2011). However, to see the progress of the EM, we start very badly regarding the initialization of missing values in the variable Sleep, using a worst initialization just with a large number. Note that we also need the index of the missing values:

```
## index of missing values
ind <- data.frame(is.na(sleep))
## initialization
sleep <- kNN(sleep)
## Time difference of 0.04911399 secs
## overwrite missing initialization with bad choice
sleep$Sleep[ind$Sleep] <- 2240  # bad initialization
## initialized missing values in variable sleep
sleep$Sleep[ind$Sleep]
## [1] 2240 2240 2240 2240
```

We then fit a model for the first variable. The model results (regression coefficients) are then used to predict the missing values:

```
## E-step (1)
lm1 <- lm(Sleep ~ log(BodyWgt) + log(BrainWgt) + NonD + Danger, data =
sleep)
## M-step (1)
sleep$Sleep[ind$Sleep] <- predict(lm1)[ind$Sleep]
## print of updated missing values
sleep$Sleep[ind$Sleep]
## [1]  469.5127 559.9771 408.6845 229.0985
```

We may continue with the second iteration.

```
## E-step (2)
lm1 <- lm(Sleep ~ log(BodyWgt) + log(BrainWgt) + NonD + Danger, data =
sleep)
## M-step (2)
sleep$Sleep[ind$Sleep] <- predict(lm1)[ind$Sleep]
## print of updated missing values
sleep$Sleep[ind$Sleep]
## [1]  101.9265 121.6146   90.1618   48.7181
```

We see that the values still change a lot. Let's do this iteratively until the values will not change more than within a very small threshold. We can write a small function for the imputation of the variable `Sleep`:

```
EMregSleep <- function(method = lm, eps = 0.001, init = "bad"){
  ## index of missing values
  ind <- is.na(sleep)
  colnames(ind) <- colnames(sleep)
  indsleep <- ind[, "Sleep"]
  ## initialization
  if(init == "bad"){
    sleep <- kNN(sleep, imp_var = FALSE)
    sleep$Sleep[indsleep] <- 2240  # bad initialization
  }
  if(init == "worst"){
    sleep[ind] <- 2240  # worst initialization
  }
  iteration <- 0
  criteria <- 99999
  while(criteria > eps){
    iteration <- iteration + 1
    prev_sol <- sleep$Sleep[indsleep]
    ## E-step
    lm1 <- method(Sleep ~ log(BodyWgt) + log(BrainWgt) + NonD + Danger,
                  data = sleep)
    ## M-step
    sleep$Sleep[indsleep] <- predict(lm1)[indsleep]
    criteria <- sqrt(sum((prev_sol - sleep$Sleep[indsleep])^2))
  }
  res <- list("imputed" = sleep,
              "iteration" = iteration,
              lastmodel = lm1)
  return(res)
}
```

Again we load the data set `sleep`, impute it and look at the imputed values in the variable `Sleep`:

```
data("sleep")
sleepImp <- EMregSleep()
## Time difference of 0.179677 secs
missVals <- sleepImp$imputed$Sleep[ind$Sleep]
missVals
## [1]   3.845778 13.122764   3.658173 16.975766
sleepImp$iteration
## [1] 11
```

However, we imputed with expected values, which will lead to a decrease of variance since we didn't account for the uncertainty and distribution of missing values (compare the variance estimation with missing values in *Chapter 8, Applications of Resampling Methods and Monte Carlo Tests*). To consider the variance, we sampled residuals (compare the bootstrapping residuals regression approach in *Chapter 8, Applications of Resampling Methods and Monte Carlo Tests*):

```
missVals + sample(residuals(sleepImp$lastmodel), length(missVals))
##        13        33         6        59
##   3.763077 11.708266   4.191778 17.465241
```

> Note that for a proper estimation of variances we may impute not only once but several times, resulting in several imputed data sets from where proper variances can be calculated (the multiple imputation approach). Or alternatively, we use the Bootstrap approach to consider the uncertainty of missing values, see *Chapter 8, Applications of Resampling Methods and Monte Carlo Tests*.

Previously we saw that we needed 11 iterations. In addition, the OLS regression model might also be influenced from outliers, thus it is better to replace it with a robust method.

We already see good results after the first iteration (not shown here). We get slightly different results that are usually more trustable than using non-robust methods (Templ, Kowarik, and Filzmoser 2011).

The OLS results may become corrupted, especially with outliers also in the predictors. However, we see that even with the worst initialization (also huge outliers in the predictors) the results looks fine (although we prefer the robust method anyhow):

```
data("sleep")
## OLS regression
lm_ols <- EMregSleep(method = lm, init = "worst")
## M-estimation
lm_rlm <- EMregSleep(method = rlm, init = "worst", eps= 0.01)
lm_ols$imputed$Sleep[ind[, "Sleep"]]
## [1]   4.239191   8.169014   4.368256 13.775087
lm_rlm$imputed$Sleep[ind[, "Sleep"]]
## [1]   3.766792   7.788943   3.925772 13.700029
```

From these figures we can see that the OLS results are highly influenced by outliers. Compared to the previous estimates (using the bad initialization, not the worst one), the imputed values are too high. This is not as extreme when using an M-estimator, but compared to the implementation in the function irmi (see the following example) we underestimate the second and fourth value.

We have discussed how to impute one variable, but in general we want to impute all variables in a data set. The data set may also consist not only of continuous variables but also of a mix of continuous, semi-continuous, categorical, binary, and/or count variables. The robust EM-based imputation accounts for this (and more, such as specifying a model for each variable) and is implemented in the function irmi (Templ, Kowarik, and Filzmoser 2011) in the R package VIM (Templ, Alfons, and Filzmoser 2011):

```
data("sleep")
sleepImp <- irmi(sleep)
## Time difference of 0.03798294 secs
sleepImp[ind[, "Sleep"], "Sleep"]
## [1]   3.748899 10.089591   3.156300 17.085060
```

We see this is very close to the initial solution where we took a better initialization of the missing values. This is an indication of the successfulness of irmi. We may use another method, such as mice (as irmi is usually used for multiple imputation):

```
library("mice")
## Loading required package: Rcpp
## mice 2.25 2015-11-09
```

```
data("sleep")
em_mice <- mice(sleep, m = 1)
##
##  iter imp variable
##   1   1  NonD  Dream  Sleep  Span  Gest
##   2   1  NonD  Dream  Sleep  Span  Gest
##   3   1  NonD  Dream  Sleep  Span  Gest
##   4   1  NonD  Dream  Sleep  Span  Gest
##   5   1  NonD  Dream  Sleep  Span  Gest
em_mice$imp$Sleep
##        1
## 21 12.5
## 31 14.5
## 41  6.1
## 62 14.4
## now with bad intitialisation in predictors
sleep[is.na(sleep)] <- 2240
sleep$Sleep[ind[, "Sleep"]] <- NA
em_mice <- mice(sleep, m = 1)
##
##  iter imp variable
##   1   1  Sleep
##   2   1  Sleep
##   3   1  Sleep
##   4   1  Sleep
##   5   1  Sleep
em_mice$imp$Sleep
##        1
## 21  3.8
## 31  3.1
## 41  3.8
## 62 10.6
```

We see that we get a completely different result, as soon outliers are present in the data set. This is also true for other implementations of the EM algorithm, that are only suitable when the data set is approx. multivariate normal. As soon as this is violated (as typically is the case in practice), irmi might be a good choice.

Note that in `irmi` many other parameters can be specified (not discussed here):

```
args(irmi)
## function (x, eps = 5, maxit = 100, mixed = NULL, mixed.constant =
NULL,
##      count = NULL, step = FALSE, robust = FALSE, takeAll = TRUE,
##      noise = TRUE, noise.factor = 1, force = FALSE, robMethod = "MM",
##      force.mixed = TRUE, mi = 1, addMixedFactors = FALSE, trace =
FALSE,
##      init.method = "kNN", modelFormulas = NULL, multinom.method =
"multinom")
## NULL
```

Summary

The EM algorithm is a computation approach to find a solution for maximum likelihood estimators. Basically, the EM algorithm consists of two steps, the *E-step* for estimation of parameters and the *M-step* for maximization according to the actual parameters. The algorithm usually converges quickly and is applied in many areas.

In this chapter we saw the application in two areas, in clustering and in imputation of missing values. Clustering is an *NP-hard* problem; loosely speaking, we cannot find the exact closed-form solution in a reasonable time. The EM algorithm is therefore necessary to interactively find a good solution. In clustering, the EM algorithm is implemented for the k-means clustering algorithm, but also (not shown in this chapter) for model-based clustering and for mixture models in general.

Missing values occur frequently in data sets in practice. Data scientists are probably those people whose main job is in data pre-processing, thus they also have to impute missing values. We saw that the EM algorithm is a central tool for this task.

References

- Dempster, A.P., N.M. Laird, and D.B. Rubin. 1977. "Maximum Likelihood for Incomplete Data via the EM Algorithm (with Discussions)," *Journal of the Royal Statistical Society, Series B* 39 (1): 1–38.

- Fraley, C., and E. Raftery. 2002. "Model-Based Clustering, Discriminant Analysis and Density Estimation," *Journal of the American Statistical Association* 97: 611–31.

- Gelman, A., and J. Hill. 2011. "Opening Windows to the Black Box," *Journal of Statistical Software* 40.

- Leisch, F. 2006. "A Toolbox for K-Centroids Cluster Analysis," *Computational Statistics and Data Analysis* 51 (2): 526–44. doi: `10.1016/j.csda.2005.10.006`.

- Raghunathan, Trivellore E, James M Lepkowski, John Van Hoewyk, and Peter Solenberger. 2001. "A Multivariate Technique for Multiply Imputing Missing Values Using a Sequence of Regression Models," *Survey Methodology* 27 (1): 85–96.

- Schafer, J.L. 1997. *Analysis of Incomplete Multivariate Data.* Chapman & Hall/CRC Monographs on Statistics & Applied Probability. CRC Press. `https://books.google.at/books?id=3TFWRjn1f-oC`.

- Templ, M., A. Alfons, and P. Filzmoser. 2011. "Exploring Incomplete Data Using Visualization Techniques," *Advances in Data Analysis and Classification* 6 (1): 29–47.

- Templ, M., P. Filzmoser, and C. Reimann. 2008. "Cluster Analysis Applied to Regional Geochemical Data: Problems and Possibilities," *Applied Geochemistry* 23 (8): 2198–2213.

- Templ, M., A. Kowarik, and P. Filzmoser. 2011. "Iterative Stepwise Regression Imputation Using Standard and Robust Methods," *Comput. Stat. Data Anal.* 55 (10): 2793–2806.

- van Buuren, S., and K. Groothuis-Oudshoorn. 2011. "mice: Multivariate Imputation by Chained Equations in R," *Journal of Statistical Software* 45 (3): 1–67. `http://www.jstatsoft.org/v45/i03/`.

10

Simulation with Complex Data

Is an estimator biased in finite samples? Is an estimator consistent under departures from assumptions? Is the sampling variance under/overestimated under different assumptions? Does method A provide better properties than method B in terms of bias, precision, and so on? Is the size of a test correct (achieving nominal level of coverage under the null hypothesis)? Is the power of a test larger than for other tests?

All these questions can be answered by statistical simulation. Some of these questions have already been answered in *Chapter 6, Probability Theory Shown by Simulation* where the concept of bias, large numbers, and the central limit theorem was shown by simulation. We also saw Monte Carlo-based estimation of confidence intervals in *Chapter 7, Resampling Methods* (with the bootstrap, for example), and we have already discussed in detail the Monte-Carlo approach to testing in Chapter 8.

This chapter enhances previous chapters by introducing more complex simulations, but also complex data generation. So we will now give further answers to these questions in the absence of knowledge of analytical properties and analytical results. Generally, due to the complexity of modern statistical methods, obtaining analytical results about their properties is often virtually impossible. Therefore, simulation studies are widely used by statisticians as data-based, computer-intensive alternatives for gaining insight into the quality of developed methods, see also Alfons, Templ, and Filzmoser 2010a.

Simulations are now carried out to show if methods work well under certain conditions, whenever properties of an estimator cannot be shown in an analytic manner. This is nowadays often the case, especially for complex methods and complex estimators.

As already partially discussed in *Chapter 8, Applications of Resampling Methods and Monte Carlo Tests* in the *Monte Carlo tests* section, simulation studies typically include the following steps to answer questions on properties of an estimator:

1. Starting point is a given dataset or a set of assumptions about the nature and parameters of a dataset.

2. A synthetic data set $\mathbf{X}$ is simulated by a probabilistic model, where these assumptions should meet as best as possible. This is repeated to achieve R datasets $\mathbf{X}_1, \ldots, \mathbf{X}_R$, with R large (for example, R = 10,000).

3. The estimation $f(\mathbf{X})$ is carried out on each of the synthetic data sets (for example, estimating indicators, model coefficients, variance estimates, and so on), $T_i = f(\mathbf{X}_i)$, $i = 1, \ldots, R$. If we receive R numerical values, say $T_1, \ldots, T_R$ of the estimator/test statistic θ, we obtain an empirical distribution of parameter estimates.

4. The obtained distributions of parameter estimates from these simulated data sets are compared with the true parameter values. The summary statistics across $T_1, \ldots, T_R$ should be good approximations of the true sampling properties of the estimator/test statistic.

> Note that in a simulation setting the true parameter values are typically known beforehand. We simulate datasets with known properties. We repeat the simulation of synthetic datasets to *average-out* the randomness of the data simulation process. For power comparisons, (see *Chapter 8, Applications of Resampling Methods and Monte Carlo Tests* on the Anderson-Darling test) simulations should judge properties of hypothesis tests (the size and power of the test).

Different kinds of simulation and software

The structure of a simulation heavily depends on the particular task. Often statistical simulation experiments are carried out with simplified conditions. For example, to judge a method, a univariate or multivariate normal distribution is used to simulate random numbers. The method is then applied to the simulated data. Such simulations often don't show the features of an estimation method, since the data structures are often much more complex in practice and it is very difficult to derive a real world behavior. So methods to simulate random numbers, as presented in *Chapter 4, Simulation of Random Numbers* may not be sufficient for complex simulation studies. For teaching, micro-simulation studies, remote execution tasks, and complex simulation studies, complex data must be simulated.

Usually, we speak about and carry out **model-based** simulation studies. In the model-based simulation world, first, data is drawn randomly by a super-population model. The true parameters are known in this case. Secondly, the estimation methods are applied to this artificial data. The resulting estimates are compared with the *truth* - the known true parameter values of the population. One can then decide on bias and all other properties discussed in *Chapter 6, Simulation of Random Numbers* (consistency, asymptotic convergence...), for example, when all model assumptions hold, a method should yield the theoretically expected results.

If data is drawn with a complex sampling design, the best option is to consider this design when simulating data randomly. We can then talk about **design-based** simulation studies. In other words, in design-based simulations the random samples are drawn from a finite population according to a fixed sampling design. We do this to reproduce a survey process. One difficulty is to simulate a realistic population first that mimics important characteristics of the real population.

In this chapter, we will show how to simulate data for complex simulation tasks. We will also discuss the use of the R package *simFrame* (Alfons, Templ, and Filzmoser 2010a) for model and design-based simulation studies, starting with several examples for model-based simulation. The design-based simulation is particularly restricted to survey methodology. However, it is also of interest for data scientists who are not working in the area of official statistics, since with the complex simulation design we show a general framework for simulations. In general, projects commonly involve many people, often from different institutions, each focusing on different aspects of the project. If these people use different simulation designs, the results may be incomparable, which in turn makes it impossible to draw meaningful conclusions. So simulation studies in such research projects require a precise outline. In addition, to change a setting slightly may crash the whole simulation. A general framework of modular design helps to modify parts of the code and leads to less errors in the programming of the simulation. Consequently, a software framework for statistical simulation may contribute its share to avoid such problems. For this purpose, the R package `simFrame` (Alfons, Templ, and Filzmoser 2010a) has been developed. The object-oriented implementation with S4 classes and methods gives maximum control over input and output and provides clear interfaces for user-defined extensions. Moreover, the framework allows a wide range of simulation designs to be used with only a little programming.

The content for design-based simulation parts of this chapter depends on joint previous research work with Andreas Alfons, leading to the `simFrame` package.

Simulating data using complex models

"New opinions are always suspected, and usually opposed, without any other reason but because they are not already common". John Locke (1689).

When discussing the usefulness of synthetic data one is often confronted with the following opinions: "We have real data available so we don't need synthetic data!"; "Others also do not work with synthetic data!"; "Synthetic data is not real data!"; "With synthetic data we lose data credibility!"; "We have more important things to do!"; "Synthetic data is a hobbyhorse of science!"

But synthetic population data sets are not intended to replace traditional data sets for all research purposes, and will certainly not reduce the need to collect more and better data. But they are increasingly used for multiple practical applications. Synthetic data generation makes the dissemination and use of information contained in confidential data sets possible, by creating *replacement datasets* that can be shared as public use files for research, training purposes, or structural data files for remote execution tasks in statistical disclosure control when researchers are not allowed to work with real data. Synthetic data generation also allows the creation of new, richer, or *augmented* datasets that provide critical input for micro-simulation (including spatial micro-simulation) and agent-based modeling. Such data sets are particularly appealing for policymakers and development practitioners, who use them as input into simulation models for assessing the ex-ante distributional impact of policies and programs. Examples are found in multiple sectors, including health (Barrett et al. 2011), (Brown and Harding 2002), (Tomintz, Clarke, and Rigby 2008), [Smith, Pearce, and Harland (2011)}, transportation (Beckman, Baggerly, and McKay 1996), (Barthelemy and Toint 2013), environment (Williamson, Mitchell, and McDonald 2002), and others. Finally, synthetic data is needed for complex simulation studies to compare and validate methods.

We will start with easy examples and end this chapter by creating a whole population that can be used for the many previous tasks described.

A model-based simple example

To simulate a data set $\mathbf{X} \sim MVN(\mu, \Sigma)$ with 100 observations from a standard multivariate normal we can use the following code:

```
library("mvtnorm")
synth <- rmvnorm(100, mean = rep(0,5), sigma = diag(5))
## first three observations
head(synth, 3)
##                [,1]        [,2]        [,3]        [,4]        [,5]
```

```
## [1,]  0.644138924 -0.02072223 -0.746322 -0.9706192 -0.04744456
## [2,] -0.154906805 -1.45176977  1.791701  1.0259287 -0.07375616
## [3,] -0.004602993  0.54685023 -1.353268 -0.2535821  1.38033904
```

If we want to simulate data to be more "similar" to real data, we may use the mean and covariance matrix estimated from such real data. We once again took the `Prestige` data from package `car`, but only the first four columns since we didn't discuss how to simulate a mix of different kinds of distributions and the last two columns of `Prestige` are different (categorical) compared to the first four columns (continuous). We will select the dataset first:

```
data(Prestige, package = "car")
## first three observations of Prestige
head(Prestige, 3)
##                   education income women prestige census type
## gov.administrators    13.11  12351 11.16     68.8   1113 prof
## general.managers      12.26  25879  4.02     69.1   1130 prof
## accountants           12.77   9271 15.70     63.4   1171 prof
## subset of variables
real <- Prestige[, 1:4]
```

The following code is used to simulate a new data set from $MVN(\bar{x}, S)$ with $\bar{x}$ being the column mean and S being the estimated covariance of the original data set X:

```
## set seed for reproducibility
set.seed(12)
## simulate from multivariate normal
synth2 <- data.frame(rmvnorm(100, mean = colMeans(real), sigma =
cov(real)))
colnames(synth2) <- colnames(real)
## first three observations
head(synth2, 3)
##   education    income    women prestige
## 1  8.891485 13494.060 -23.687773 50.86117
## 2  6.095841  5635.296  20.595593 32.52649
## 3  8.822570  8609.970  -2.522208 34.78179
```

Is this result acceptable? Can we use this generation of synthetic data in a simulation study? The answer depends on the aim of the simulation, but most probably the simulation of random numbers was oversimplified. We can see that there are problems with the variable women where the values should be between 0 and 100.

```
summary(real$women)
##      Min. 1st Qu.  Median    Mean 3rd Qu.     Max.
##     0.000   3.592  13.600  28.980  52.200   97.510
summary(synth2$women)
##      Min. 1st Qu.  Median    Mean 3rd Qu.     Max.
##   -39.700   6.608  26.580  25.310  47.660  111.600
```

When we plot two variables from the original and the synthetic data, we can see that the multivariate structure differs. First, the increasing variance due to increasing prestige is not visible for the synthetic data, and in addition, the larger values from the synthetic observations are a bit shifted to the right, see *Figure 10.1*:

```
par(mar = c(4,4,0.2,0.2))
plot(prestige ~ income, data = real)
points(prestige ~ income, data = synth2, col = "red", pch = 20)
legend("bottomright", legend = c("original/real", "synthetic"), col =
1:2, pch = c(1,20))
```

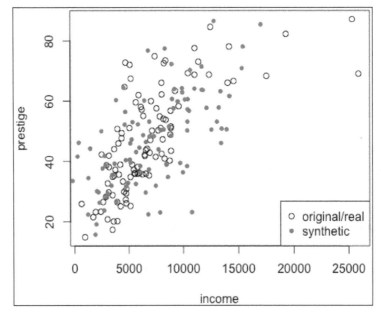

Figure 10.1: Two variables from the Prestige data (black circles) and the simulated synthetic ones (red full circles)

This is due to outliers, which may disturb the mean and covariance estimation. As a way out, we might simulate good data points and *bad* ones separately.

A model-based example with mixtures

Generally, a mixture model might be used if the data has a cluster structure. We only consider this now that there are two mixtures, one containing the good data points and the other one containing potential outliers. We simulate data from both distributions separately. An outlier-robust estimation of the covariance and location can be done with various estimators. We took a simple and fast one, the MCD estimator (Rousseeuw and Driessen 1998). In *Figure 10.2* (the left-hand graphics), we can see that the data fits better than before. If we separate the data generation of outliers and non-outliers we get an even better synthetic dataset, see *Figure 10.2*, (right-hand graphics).

```
library("robustbase")
cv <- covMcd(real)
synth3 <- rmvnorm(100, mean = cv$center, sigma = cv$cov)
par(mfrow = c(1,2), mar = c(4,4,0.2,0.2))
plot(prestige ~ income, data = real)
points(prestige ~ income, data = synth3, col = "red", pch = 20)
## add outliers
rmd <- mahalanobis(real, center = cv$center, cov = cv$cov)
## outliers defined by large Mahalanobis distances
out <- rmd > qchisq(0.975, ncol(real) - 1)
cv_good <- covMcd(real[!out, ])
## simulate good points
synth3_good <- rmvnorm(100, mean = cv_good$center,
                              sigma = cv_good$cov)
cv_out <- covMcd(real[out, ])
## simulate outliers
synth3_out <- rmvnorm(100, mean = cv_out$center,
                             sigma = cv_out$cov)
## Figure 10.2.
plot(prestige ~ income, data = real)
points(prestige ~ income, data = synth3_good,
       col = "red", pch = 20)
points(prestige ~ income, data = synth3_out,
       col = "red", pch = 20)
```

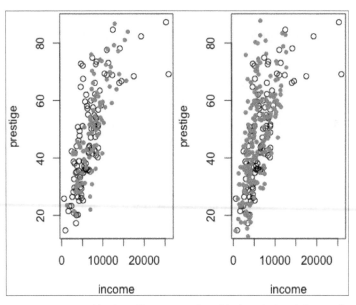

Figure 10.2: Two variables from the Prestige data (black circles) and the simulated synthetic ones (red full circles). For the graphics on the right, the simulation was done for outliers and non-outliers independently

Of course, we may also use other distributions than the multivariate normal, such as a multivariate Cauchy or multivariate t-distribution. An alternative to create data sets including outliers is the barrow wheel contamination setting (Stahel and Mächler 2009). Here, outliers are generated from a distribution that could create a large shape bias. We will not go into details with this approach but refer to the R package robustX (Stahel, Maechler, and others 2013) that contains functionality on it. Robust estimators from multivariate data sets might use this for benchmarking datasets.

Model-based approach to simulate data

We may also use a model-based approach. To simulate education, we can simply regress education against a set of well-chosen predictors. For simplicity in explaining this issue, we will take all other variables as predictors without interactions. We can take the fit on the real data and then use the model to replace education (in a new data set) and add some errors based on the residuals of the mode. Remember, errors were also added in *Chapter 9, The EM Algorithm*:

```
synth4 <- real

lm1 <- lm(education ~ ., data = real)

synth4$education <- predict(lm1, synth4[, 2:ncol(synth4)]) +
sample(residuals(lm1))
```

We can do this for all variables. For example, we can take the second variable of the Prestige data as response and use the rest as predictors. Again, we fit the model on the real sample and make the fit on the synthetic data:

```
p <- ncol(real)
for(i in 1:ncol(real)){
  df <- real[, i]
  df <- cbind(df, real[,-i])
  colnames(df)[1] <- "response"
  lm1 <- lm(response ~ ., data = df)
  synth4[, i] <- predict(lm1, synth4[, -i]) + sample(residuals(lm1))
}
```

It would be easy to further modify this imputation approach to gain an EM algorithm (see *Chapter 9, The EM Algorithm*).

An implementation of model-based data generation is given in the R package simPop (Templ, Kowarik, and Meindl 2016) whereby a bunch of models can be used to simulate variables (multi-nominal models, two-step approaches, linear models, regression trees, random forests, probabilistic methods, and so on).

An example of simulating high-dimensional data

In the last example, a specific model fitted on the data was used to simulate new data sets. But for various settings, relationships between variables are expressed by a latent model. This is especially useful for simulation of high-dimensional data, assuming that there is a latent model that may generate the high-dimensional data. For this purpose, we can simulate a data set $\mathbf{X}$ with observations and variables, for example, by the following latent model $\mathbf{X} = \mathbf{TB}^{\mathrm{T}} + \mathbf{E}$, where the columns of $\mathbf{E}$ are normally independently distributed with $\mathbb{N}(0, 0.01)$. The columns of the $n \times k$ matrix are drawn from a standard normal distribution, and the elements of $\mathbf{B}$ are drawn from a uniform distribution in $[-1, 1]$. In R, this could look like:

```
simLatent <- function(n = 200, p = 50, k = 3){
  T <- matrix(rnorm(n * k, 0, 1), ncol = k)
  B <- matrix(runif(p * k, -1, 1), ncol = k)
  X <- T %*% t(B)
  E <-  matrix(rnorm(n * p, 0, 0.1), ncol = p)
  XE <- X + E
  return(XE)
}
```

To simulate, for example, 1000 variables on 50 observations with a six component latent model, we can type the following:

```
x <- simLatent(n = 50, p = 1000, k = 6)
dim(x)
## [1]    50 1000
```

Simulating finite populations with cluster or hierarchical structures

Typically, in design-based simulation studies the influence of the sampling design on methods is evaluated. By simulating a population and drawing surveys by a complex sampling design from this synthetic population, we mimic reality. So the first aim is to simulate a population.

The synthetic data set must be realistic, that is, statistically equivalent to the actual population of interest, and present the following characteristics (Münnich et al. 2003), (Münnich and Schürle 2003), (Alfons et al. 2011), (Templ and Filzmoser 2014), (Templ, Kowarik, and Meindl 2016):

- The distribution of the synthetic population by region and stratum must be very similar to the distribution of the true population
- Marginal distributions and interactions between variables must be accurately represented
- Heterogeneities between subgroups, especially regional aspects, must be allowed
- Cluster and hierarchical structures should be preserved
- The records in the synthetic population should not be created by pure replication of units

Synthetic data generation allows us to distribute confidential data and also allows the creation of new, richer, or *augmented* datasets that provide input for micro-simulation and agent-based modeling.

The idea of generating synthetic population data is not new. (Rubin 1993), suggested generating synthetic microdata using multiple imputation. But the methods and algorithms are in constant evolution. The public availability of tools such as the R package simPop contributes to further assessments and improvements of the techniques.

simPop provides a highly optimized S4 class implementation of various methods in R, including calibration by iterative proportional fitting and simulated annealing, and modeling or data fusion by logistic regression.

Multiple approaches have been proposed for the generation of synthetic population data, which can be classified into three broad categories: synthetic reconstruction, combinatorial optimization, and model-based generation of data. The latter method is explained briefly in the following paragraph.

It consists of first deriving a model of the population from existing microdata, then *predicting* a synthetic population. So, the fitting is done on existing microdata and the prediction on population level. In an initial step, the household structure (for example, by age and sex, and potential other variables) is created by resampling of existing data with probabilities depending on the sampling weights. Additional categorical variables are then simulated using multi-nominal logistic regression models by random draws from observed conditional distributions. In the third step, continuous and semi-continuous variables are generated using regression modelling.

We will briefly show how a synthetic population can be simulated using the R package simPop. We will start from given microdata:

```
library("simPop")
data("eusilcS")
dim(eusilcS)
## [1] 11725    18
```

Please have a look at ?eusilcS for the description of these 18 variables.

The number of households is:

```
length(unique(eusilcS$db030))
## [1] 4641
```

Before simulating variables, we can create (using specifyInput()) an object of class dataObj that will hold all information needed to construct the synthetic population. We can identify the variables providing information on clustering here: households, household size, strata, and sampling weights (variable rb050):

```
inp <- specifyInput(eusilcS, hhid = "db030", hhsize = "hsize",
                    strata = "db040", weight = "rb050")
```

A summary of the content of this `dataObj` class object is displayed using the print method:

```
print(inp)
##
##    --------------
## survey sample of size 11725 x 19
##
##   Selected important variables:
##
##   household ID: db030
##   personal ID: pid
##   variable household size: hsize
##   sampling weight: rb050
##   strata: db040
##    --------------
```

The function `simStructure` generates the structure of the synthetic population using a replication approach:

```
synthP <- simStructure(data = inp,
                   method = "direct",
                   basicHHvars = c("age", "rb090", "db040"))
```

Categorical variables are simulated using the household structure of the synthetic population and the sample microdata as input, both included in the `synthP` object of the class `simPopObj`. In our example, we generate categorical variables on economic status (variable `p1030`) and citizenship (variable `pb220a`) by applying `simCategorical()`:

```
synthP <- simCategorical(synthP,
                   additional = c("p1030", "pb220a"),
                   method = "multinom")
```

The following variables: `age category`, `gender`, `household size`, `economic status`, and `citizenship` are used as predictors of `personal net income` by calling `simContinuous`:

```
synthP <- simContinuous(synthP, additional = "netIncome",
                        upper = 200000, equidist = FALSE,
                        imputeMissings = FALSE)
```

Basic information on the final population is shown as follows:

```
synthP
##
## --------------
## synthetic population   of size
##   81838 x 11
##
## build from a sample of size
## 11725 x 19
## --------------
##
## variables in the population:
## db030,hsize,age,rb090,db040,pid,weight,pl030,pb220a,netIncomeCat,netIn
come
```

This population can now be input in design-based simulation studies from where samples are drawn from this population.

Model-based simulation studies

As already mentioned, for some situations the formulation of and conduction of a precise mathematical treatment is often too difficult or too time-consuming. By using model-based simulation we may approximate real-world situations and results whenever the data is not sampled with a complex sampling design. Model-based simulation studies especially require much less time, effort, and/or money than a mathematical proof of properties of estimators or methods.

Latent model example continued

We will continue with the latent model from the previous example. Such datasets we may use for the comparison of methods. For example, one can mark values to be missing, impute them by suitable imputation methods and evaluate and compare the imputation methods. We can do this by example for a smaller dataset and compare mean imputation, nearest neighbor imputation, robust model-based imputation, and imputation by mice by using a simple precision-based error criterion based on distances:

```
library("mice")
library("VIM")
x <- orig <- simLatent(n = 50, p = 10, k = 6)
## evaluation criteria
eval <- function(real, imputed, nas){
  sqrt(sum((real - imputed)^2)) / nas
}
set.seed(123)
R <- 100
e1 <- e2 <- e3 <- e4 <- numeric(R)
for(i in 1:R){
  x <- orig
  x[sample(1:nrow(x), 10), 1] <- NA
  e1[i] <- eval(orig, e1071::impute(x), 10)
  e2[i] <-    eval(orig, kNN(data.frame(x), imp_var = FALSE), 10)
  e3[i] <-    eval(orig, irmi(x), 10)
  e4[i] <-    eval(orig, complete(mice(x, m = 1, printFlag = FALSE)), 10)
}
df <- data.frame("error" = c(e1,e2,e3,e4), method = rep(c("mean", "kNN",
"irmi", "mice"), each = R))
```

Boxplots are the most convenient method to compare the distributions of simulation results. See *Figure 10.3* for the comparison of methods according to our simple precision error measure:

```
library("ggplot2")
ggplot(df, aes(x = method, y=error)) + geom_boxplot() +
        theme(text = element_text(size = 20)) + theme_bw()
```

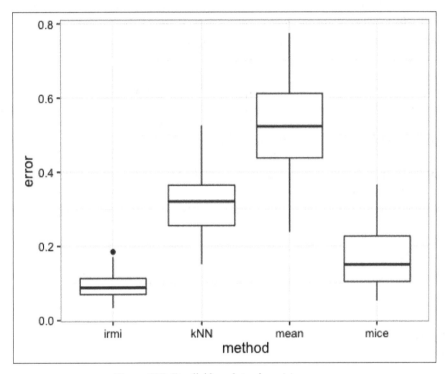

Figure 10.3: Parallel boxplots of precision errors

To compare these imputation methods, additional criteria (error measures) are needed and also coverage rates should be estimated. We will skip this and refer to Templ, Kowarik, and Filzmoser (2011) where results on this can be found. Our aim was to generally show a simulation that can be simply adapted for these new measures. We will later show how to use the package simFrame for such kinds of simulations.

A simple example of model-based simulation

We will start with a simple example. In *Chapter 6, Probability Theory Shown by Simulation* we drew 10 samples of size $n = 50$, each from an $\exp(1)$-distribution. So the super-population model was an exponential distribution (density is given by $f(x) = \lambda e^{-\lambda x}$) with the population parameter $\lambda = 1$. We want to compare four estimators for the population mean μ of an independent identical distributed sample: the arithmetic mean $\overline{x}$, the median $\tilde{x}$, the 10% trimmed mean $\overline{x}_{(20\%)}$, and the Huber mean (Huber 1981). In the following example, we want to know if the Huber mean (Huber 1981) is an unbiased estimator of the mean, and in addition, whether the confidence intervals estimated by bootstrap have good coverage of the true mean. Since the distribution is not symmetric, we expect that for data without outliers the arithmetic mean is 1 but for any other estimator the result will not equal 1. We will show this through simulation. The Huber mean is based on the Huber loss function that is less sensitive to outliers in data than the squared error loss. Outliers are down-weighted to have bounded influence, while in contrast the arithmetic mean outliers can have unbounded influence on an estimator. We want to see if the Huber mean is equal to the arithmetic mean. Note that this can be shown analytically as well, but remember that with simulation we can do it much easier. In addition, we want to compare all mean estimators, in terms of precision, in presence of measurement errors and efficiency:

```
library("robustbase")
set.seed(123)
x <- rexp(n = 50, rate = 1)
mean(x)
## [1] 1.130371
huberM(x)$mu
## [1] 0.9416643
```

On first view this seems to be correct. Both estimators are close to 1, though the Huber mean is closer to 1 than the arithmetic mean. But let's have a look at the result if we repeat the simulation of random numbers and mean calculation 10,000 times. We will report the arithmetic mean of the 10,000 results. We will see that the arithmetic mean is an unbiased estimator, that is, $bi\hat{}as = \hat{\theta}_{(\cdot)} - \mu$, with $\hat{\theta}_{(\cdot)}$ the arithmetic mean of $\hat{\theta}_1, \ldots, \hat{\theta}_2$:

```
m <- mean(replicate(10000, mean(rexp(n = 50, rate = 1))))
m
## [1] 0.9993768
m - 1
## [1] -0.0006231643
```

We can see that the Huber mean of exponential distributed variables is not 1 but around `0.854,` and the bias is about `-0.146`:

```
mh <- mean(replicate(10000, huberM(rexp(n =50, rate = 1))$mu))
mh
## [1] 0.8542077
mh - 1
## [1] -0.1457923
```

This is normal, since the exponential distribution is a non-symmetric distribution, so the comparison with the Huber mean was probably not the best choice. Next we want to have a look at the coverage of the arithmetic mean estimator. Each simulated random sample leads to a different estimation of μ. We may wonder how many intervals contain the true value of $\mu = 1$? The function below estimates the confidence intervals for random numbers of an exponential distribution:

```
set.seed(123)
alpha <- 0.05
ci <- function(x, z = qnorm(1 - alpha / 2)){
  s <- rexp(n = 50, rate = 1)
  m <- mean(s)
  se <- sd(s) / sqrt(50)
  ci_est <- c(m - z * se, m + z *se)
  ci_est
}
ci()
## [1]  0.7970204 1.4637213
```

We will replicate this 100,000 times and report how many intervals contain the value of 1:

```
set.seed(123)
ciR_n <- replicate(100000, ci())
isCovered <- function(x){
  apply(x, 2, function(x){
  if(x[1] > 1 & x[2] > 1) return(FALSE)
  if(x[1] < 1 & x[2] < 1) return(FALSE)
  return(TRUE)})
}
cn <- isCovered(ciR_n)
sum(cn) / length(cn)
## [1] 0.92872
```

We obtain good coverage of about 0.929. If we assume that our estimator (the arithmetic mean) is related to a t-distribution rather than the normal distribution, we can plug-in the quantiles of a t-distribution:

```
ciR_t <- replicate(100000, ci(z = qt(1 - alpha / 2, 49)))
ct <- isCovered(ciR_t)
sum(ct) / length(ct)
## [1] 0.93501
```

The coverage rate increased slightly. We also want to compare it to bootstrap estimates of the confidence intervals:

```
ci_boot <- function(x, R = 1000){
  s <- rexp(n = 50, rate = 1)
  ci_est <- quantile(replicate(R,
            mean(sample(s, replace = TRUE))),
            c(0.025, 0.975))
  return(ci_est)
}
ciR_boot <- replicate(1000, ci_boot())
cb <- isCovered(ciR_boot)
sum(cb) / length(cb)
## [1] 0.925
```

This also leads to the same conclusions, which we can now compare visually. *Figure 10.4* shows the lower and upper bounds of the confidence intervals from our simulation:

```
df <- data.frame(t(ciR_n))
df <- data.frame(rbind(t(ciR_n), t(ciR_t), t(ciR_boot)))
df$method <- rep(c("normal", "t", "boot"), times = c(100000,100000,1000))
colnames(df) <- c("lower", "upper", "method")
library("reshape2")
df <- melt(df)
library("ggplot2")
ggplot(df, aes(x = value, colour = method)) + geom_density() + facet_
wrap(~ variable) + theme(text = element_text(size=16))
```

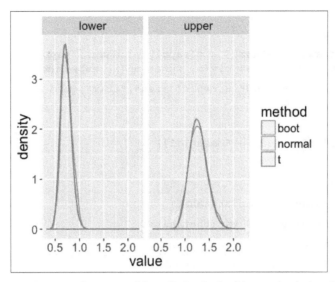

Figure 10.4: Lower and upper confidence limits obtained from a simulation of three
different methods to estimate the confidence bands

When speaking about bias and variance, the most important two properties of an
estimator, we always speak about the **mean squared error** (MSE), see also *Chapter
6, Probability Theory Shown by Simulation*. The mean squared error estimated by a
simulation experiment is $M\hat{S}E = \dfrac{1}{R-1}\sum_{i=1}^{R}\left(\hat{\theta}_i - \hat{\theta}_{(\cdot)}\right)^2 + \left(\hat{\theta}_{(\cdot)} - \theta\right)^2$ *variance + bias²*. The
relative efficiency of estimator 2 to estimator 1 is given by $RE = \dfrac{\text{var}\left(\theta_{(1)}\right)}{\text{var}\left(\theta_{(2)}\right)}$.

We sum up all things learned in this section to carry out the estimation of the
population mean of a normal distribution. The following function contains the
simulation of data and the estimation part:

```
simMean <- function(simFun = function(x) rnorm(100)){
  ## 1000 samples
  set.seed(123)
  R <- 1000
  m <- list()
  ## 1000 data sets
  for(i in 1:R){
    m[[i]] <- simFun()
```

```
}
## estimation
df <- data.frame("thetahat" = c(sapply(m, mean), sapply(m, mean, trim =
0.1), sapply(m, median), sapply(m, function(x) huberM(x)$mu)),
                "method" = rep(c("mean","trim","median","huber"), each
= R))
## summary
vm <- var(df[df$method == "mean", 1])
df %>%
  group_by(method) %>%
  summarize("bias" = mean(thetahat) - 0,
           "variance" = var(thetahat),
           "mse" = variance + bias^2,
           "re" = vm / var(thetahat))
}
```

We call the function to get all of the results for the different mean estimators. We can see that the arithmetic mean is the most efficient one with the smallest mean squared error:

```
library("robustbase"); library("dplyr")
simMean()
## Source: local data frame [4 x 5]
##
##    method        bias     variance          mse          re
##    (fctr)       (dbl)        (dbl)        (dbl)       (dbl)
## 1  huber 0.0015911419 0.009542405 0.009544936 0.9474960
## 2   mean 0.0009767488 0.009041390 0.009042344 1.0000000
## 3 median 0.0001103496 0.015578749 0.015578761 0.5803669
## 4   trim 0.0015793808 0.009742862 0.009745357 0.9280014
```

Let's modify this example a bit. We can assume the presence of measurement errors and also assume that the data is sampled from the distribution F of contaminated data. F is typically modeled as a mixture of distributions $F = (1-\in)G + \in H$, where $\in$ denotes the contamination level, G is the distribution of the non-contaminated part of the data and H is the distribution of the contamination.

We do basically the same as previously mentioned, but using another data generation process with 5 percent outliers included:

```
set.seed(123)
simMean(simFun = function(){c(rnorm(95), rnorm(5,15))})
## Source: local data frame [4 x 5]
##
##    method       bias      variance         mse        re
##    (fctr)      (dbl)        (dbl)        (dbl)      (dbl)
## 1   huber 0.09645247 0.009946125 0.01924920 0.9090364
## 2    mean 0.75097675 0.009041390 0.57300747 1.0000000
## 3  median 0.06853618 0.016427966 0.02112517 0.5503658
## 4    trim 0.09101656 0.010061782 0.01834580 0.8985874
```

We can see that the mean is highly influenced from these outliers, the MSE is much higher than for the Huber mean, the trimmed mean, or the median. So in case of the presence of outliers in a dataset, robust estimators are the preferable choice with the lowest mean squared error for this example.

A model-based simulation study

In previous chapters, the imputation of missing values was focused on. Also, in this chapter, we have already shown an example where we evaluated imputation methods in terms of precision error.

In this section, we will compare some imputation methods again. More precisely, model-based simulation, which will be demonstrated using an example of the imputation of missing values in compositional data. The examples enhance the previous examples and - their main aim - is to show the use of the simulation framework and R package `simFrame` (Alfons, Templ, and Filzmoser 2010a).

An observation $\mathbf{x} = (x_1, \ldots, x_D)$ is by definition a D-part composition if, and only if, $x_i > 0, i = 1, \ldots, D$, and all relevant information is contained in the ratios between the components (Aitchison 1986). The information is essentially the same if an observation is multiplied with a positive constant, since the ratios between components are of interest only. Examples of compositional data are: element concentrations in chemical analysis, household expenditures of a sample material, or monthly household expenditures on different spending categories such as housing, food, or leisure activities.

It is important to note that compositional data has no direct representation in the Euclidean space and that their geometry is entirely different, see Aitchison 1986. The sample space of D-part compositions is called the simplex and a suitable distance measure is called the Aitchison distance d_A (Aitchison 1992), (Aitchison et al. 2000). Fortunately, there exists an isometric transformation from the D-dimensional simplex to the real space $\mathbb{R}^{D-1}$, which is called the **isometric log-ratio** (**ilr**) transformation (Egozcue et al. 2003). With this transformation, the Aitchison distance can be expressed as $d_A(x,y) = d_E(ilr(x), ilr(y))$, where d_E denotes the Euclidean distance.

Hron, Templ, and Filzmoser 2010 introduced imputation methods for compositional data, which are implemented in the R package `robCompositions` (Templ, Hron, and Filzmoser 2011). While the package is focused on robust methods, only classical imputation methods are used in this example. The first method is a modification of **k-Nearest Neighbor** (**k-NN**) imputation (Troyanskaya et al. 2001), the second follows an iterative model-based approach (EM algorithm, see Chapter 9) using **least squares** (**LS**) regression, the third is equal to the second except a robust version is used. Also, the EM algorithm implemented in the `mice` package is compared. Before any computations are performed, the required packages are loaded and the seed of the random number generator is set for reproducibility:

```
library("simFrame"); library("robCompositions"); library("mvtnorm");
library("mice")
```

```
set.seed(123)
```

The data in this example is generated by a normal distribution on the simplex, denoted by $\mathbb{N}_S^D(\mu, \Sigma)$ (Mateu-Figueras, Pawlowsky-Glahn, and Egozcue 2008). A random composition $\mathbf{x} = (x_1, \ldots, x_D)$ follows this distribution if, and only if, the vector of ilr-transformed variables follows a multivariate normal distribution on $\mathbb{R}^{D-1}$ with mean vector and covariance matrix Σ. The following commands create a control object for generating 150 realizations of a random variable $X \sim \mathbb{N}_S^4(\mu, \Sigma)$ with $\mu = (0,2,3)^T$ and $\Sigma = ((1,-0.5,1.4)^T, (-0.5,1,-0.6)^T, (1.4,-0.6,2)^T)$. The function `isomLRinv` regards to the inverse isometric log-ratio transformation. The function `DataControl` allows us to take control of the data simulation process:

```
## data generation
crnorm <- function(n, mean, sigma) data.frame(isomLRinv(rmvnorm(n, mean,
sigma)))
sigma <- matrix(c(1, -0.5, 1.4, -0.5, 1, -0.6, 1.4, -0.6, 2), 3, 3)
## data control class
dc <- DataControl(size = 150, distribution = crnorm,
       dots = list(mean = c(0, 2, 3), sigma = sigma))
```

Furthermore, a control object for inserting missing values needs to be created. In every variable, 5 percent of the observations are set as missing completely at random:

```
nc <- NAControl(NArate = c(0.05, 0.1))
```

For the two selected imputation methods, the relative Aitchison distance between the original and the imputed data (cf. the simulation study in (Hron, Templ, and Filzmoser 2010)) is computed in every simulation run. Important to note is that the results are provided as a vector:

```
sim <- function(x, orig) {
    i <- apply(x, 1, function(x) any(is.na(x)))
    ni <- length(which(i))
    x <- x[, -ncol(x)]
    xMean <- e1071::impute(x)
    xMice <- mice(x, printFlag = FALSE, diagnostics = FALSE, m = 1)
    xMice <- complete(xMice)
    xKNNa <- impKNNa(x)$xImp
    xLS <- impCoda(x, method = "lm")$xImp
    xLTSrob <- impCoda(x, method = "ltsReg")$xImp
    c(xMean = aDist(xMean, orig)/ni,
      xMice = aDist(xMice, orig)/ni,
      knn = aDist(xKNNa, orig)/ni,
      LS = aDist(xLS, orig)/ni,
      LTSrob = aDist(xLTSrob, orig)/ni)
}
```

The simulation can then be run with the command runSimulation, where all parts are put together in the function arguments - the DataControl object, the NAControl object, and the simulation function that actually includes the call of the estimation methods. Here, 25 datasets are simulated and the estimators are applied to those datasets:

```
results <- runSimulation(dc,
                    nrep = 25,
                    NAControl = nc,
                    fun = sim)
```

The results can be inspected using `head()`, `aggregate()`, or `simBwplot()`:

```
aggregate(results)
##    NArate     xMean     xMice      knn        LS     LTSrob
## 1    0.05 17.219489 17.273910 17.26099 17.238508 17.239409
## 2    0.10  9.872175  9.932083  9.91985  9.892985  9.907121
```

A Box plot of the **simulation** results is presented in *Figure 10.5*:

```
simBwplot(results)
```

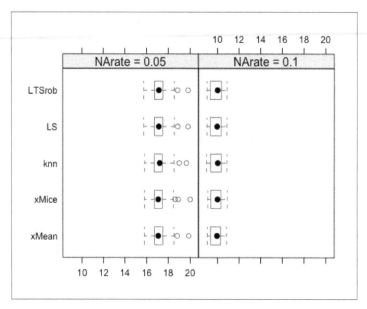

Figure 10.5: Simulation results and comparison of different imputation methods

Since the imputation methods in this example are evaluated in terms of a relative distance measure, values closer to 0 indicate better performance. The data simulation was too easy to show differences in the other methods.

For real life situations it is of interest to also include outliers, since they are present in virtually every dataset:

```
dcarc <- ContControl(target = c("X1"),
        epsilon = c(0.01,0.03,0.05,0.1),
        dots = list(mean = 150, sd = 1), type = "DCAR")
results <- runSimulation(dc,
                    nrep = 3,
                    NAControl = nc,
```

```
                          contControl = dcarc,
                          fun = sim)
aggregate(results)
##    Epsilon NArate    xMean      xMice        knn         LS      LTSrob
## 1    0.01   0.05  1.169989  0.9501772  0.8440359  0.8873185  0.7044925
## 2    0.03   0.05  1.867719  1.6452466  1.5593942  1.6538767  1.3555124
## 3    0.05   0.05  2.629600  2.5774409  2.4796152  2.6403572  2.1760300
## 4    0.10   0.05  4.180403  4.1640710  4.0308395  4.3412581  3.8326223
## 5    0.01   0.10  1.083472  0.9438792  0.7513994  0.8230325  0.5997533
## 6    0.03   0.10  1.542900  1.4860973  1.1938551  1.4082617  1.0123190
## 7    0.05   0.10  1.790335  1.8517452  1.5830545  1.6937968  1.3795612
## 8    0.10   0.10  2.867004  2.8748454  2.7553507  2.9715110  2.4287011
```

We plot the results in *Figure 10.6* to compare the distributions of simulation results:

```
simBwplot(results)
```

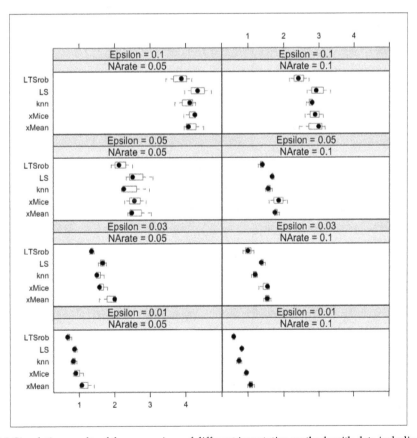

Figure 10.6: Simulation results of the comparison of different imputation methods with data including outliers

Clearly, the iterative model-based procedure leads to better results than the modified k-NN approach with respect to the relative Aitchison distance for both rates of missing values and all contamination levels. This is not a surprising result, as the latter is used as a starting point in the iterative procedure. Mean imputation performs the worst, `mice` is slightly worse than the EM algorithm from Hron, Templ, and Filzmoser 2010. For serious evaluation of the imputation methods, however, other criteria also need to be taken into account, for example, how well the variability of the multivariate data is reflected; see Hron, Templ, and Filzmoser 2010.

We will now leave almost everything unchanged for a new simulation. The new simulation function should now compare covariances instead of distances:

```
sim2 <- function(x, orig) {
    rdcm <- function(x, y){
        ocov <- cov(isomLR(x))
        rcov <- cov(isomLR(y))
        return(frobenius.norm(ocov-rcov)/frobenius.norm(ocov))
    }
    i <- apply(x, 1, function(x) any(is.na(x)))
    ni <- length(which(i))
    x <- x[, -ncol(x)]
    xMean <- e1071::impute(x)
    xMice <- mice(x, printFlag = FALSE, diagnostics = FALSE, m = 1)
    xMice <- complete(xMice)
    xKNNa <- impKNNa(x)$xImp
    xLS <- impCoda(x, method = "lm")$xImp
    xLTSrob <- impCoda(x, method = "ltsReg")$xImp
    c(xMean = rdcm(xMean, orig),
      xMice = rdcm(xMice, orig),
      knn = rdcm(xKNNa, orig),
      LS = rdcm(xLS, orig),
      LTSrob = rdcm(xLTSrob, orig))
}
```

Now, let's run the simulation again:

```
library("matrixcalc")
results <- runSimulation(dc,
                         nrep = 3,
                         NAControl = nc,
```

```
                    contControl = dcarc,
                    fun = sim2)
```

```
aggregate(results)
```

##	Epsilon	NArate	xMean	xMice	knn	LS	LTSrob
## 1	0.01	0.05	0.2052108	0.1888341	0.1677975	0.1746085	0.1581507
## 2	0.03	0.05	0.3707707	0.3556715	0.3447043	0.3607931	0.3407841
## 3	0.05	0.05	0.5094309	0.5009143	0.5082797	0.5075591	0.4938353
## 4	0.10	0.05	0.7008258	0.6825972	0.6809999	0.6860417	0.6658453
## 5	0.01	0.10	0.2284774	0.1783459	0.1741286	0.1849407	0.1621681
## 6	0.03	0.10	0.3847136	0.3726923	0.3477511	0.3749449	0.3424004
## 7	0.05	0.10	0.5484875	0.5096264	0.5148351	0.5428007	0.5106629
## 8	0.10	0.10	0.6914287	0.6790557	0.6846771	0.6876906	0.6677574

Again, we can see that the robust EM approach (*LTSrob*) from package
`robCompositions` performs the best for this error measure.

Design-based simulation

Design-based simulations are particularly important when the selection probabilities for statistical units of a finite sampling frame are not equal, that is, when samples are drawn with a complex sampling design. This primarily relates to any sampling from finite populations, for example, samples drawn from a population register.

The costs of a sample survey can be reduced if the sample is drawn with a certain complex sampling design. For example, for poverty measurement, a household with a single parent and children might be included with a higher probability than households with another composition of household members, because it's likely that the single parent household is poor (basically the target *variable*).

 Basically, in design-based simulations R samples from a finite population are drawn using a complex sampling design, wherein the population is simulated in a close-to-reality manner.

For each sample, a parameter θ of the population is estimated and the estimations $\hat{\theta}_1,\ldots,\hat{\theta}_R$, and $\hat{s}^2(\theta_1),\ldots,\hat{s}^2(\theta_R)$ are compared with the population parameter θ and $\sigma^2(\theta)$.

An example with complex survey data

Each design-based simulation may differ depending on the aim of what the simulation should show. However, some basic issues stay the same. We will show a very complex design-based simulation in which a lot of difficulties arise. These difficulties are related to outliers, missing values, different sampling designs, complex indicators to estimate, and their variance estimation.

The indicators on social exclusion and poverty are estimated from the **European Union Statistics on Income and Living Conditions (EU-SILC)** dataset.

In the simulation, studies will be conducted with the help of an artificially generated population (see the subsection on simulating finite populations). Samples will be drawn from that population. This means that we know the true values of the parameters that will be estimated from the drawn samples.

The design of the simulation study should correspond very closely to reality. This means that in addition to a good artificial population, outliers and missing values should be well-defined in the data. For example, missing values represent non-responses in questionnaires and outliers represent wrong answers.

The general concept of the simulation study should also be as close to reality as possible. Starting from population data, samples are drawn repeatedly using the real-life sampling methods. In each simulation run, the quantities of interest (in most cases, the indicators on social exclusion and poverty or their variances) are estimated from the corresponding sample. The results of all simulation runs are then combined to form a distribution. Finally, certain evaluation criteria are used to compare the estimates to the true values.

Concerning outliers and non-responses, the most realistic perception of the world is that they exist on the population level. Whether a person has an extremely high income or is not willing to respond to certain questions of a survey does not depend on whether that person is actually in the sample. So the most realistic simulation design is to insert contamination and non-responses into the population.

A disadvantage of this approach is that the number of outliers or missing values in the samples is unpredictable.

If robust properties of the considered estimators are the main focus of a simulation, or if outlier detection methods are investigated, maximum control over the amount of contaminated observations is necessary for a thorough evaluation. The same principle with respect to the amount of missing values applies if the treatment of incomplete data is the main interest. This problem can be solved by adding contamination and non-responses to the samples instead of the population. While this approach may not truly reflect the real processes, it may be more practical from a statistician's point of view in the aforementioned situations. Nevertheless, it should be noted that adding contamination and non-responses to samples comes with increasing computational costs for an increasing number of simulation runs. *Figure 10.7* visualizes the general outline of such a simulation design:

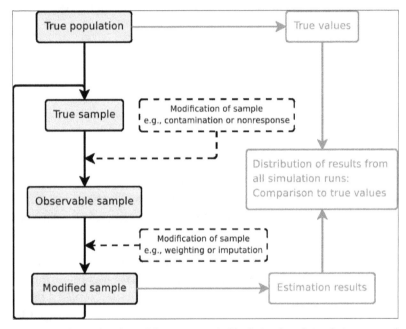

Figure 10.7: General outline of the most practicable design-based simulation approach

Simulation of the synthetic population

It is most convenient to use the R package simPop (Templ, Kowarik, and Meindl 2016) to simulate a population. We have already partially shown how to simulate a population using this software in the previous section (example of a finite population simulation).

We can assume that such a population already exists, and use the one which is available in the R package `simFrame`, simulated with the R package `simPop`:

```
data("eusilcP")
```

This population is smaller than the real population but for demonstration issues it is perfectly suited. The following variables are included:

```
colnames(eusilcP)
##  [1] "hid"         "region"      "hsize"       "eqsize"
"eqIncome"
##  [6] "pid"         "id"          "age"         "gender"      "ecoStat"
## [11] "citizenship" "py010n"      "py050n"      "py090n"      "py100n"
## [16] "py110n"      "py120n"      "py130n"      "py140n"      "hy040n"
## [21] "hy050n"      "hy070n"      "hy080n"      "hy090n"      "hy110n"
## [26] "hy130n"      "hy145n"      "main"
```

For detailed information on these variables, please call `?eusilcP`.

Estimators of interest

Next, we define the estimators of interest. In our case, this is the Gini coefficient (Gini 1912). We also want to compare the classical estimator of the Gini coefficient with the Hill estimator (Hill 1975) and the robust estimation of the Gini using a robust weighted partial density component estimator proposed by Alfons, Templ, and Filzmoser 2013.

Then the function to be run in every iteration is defined, we will call it `sim`. Its argument, k, determines the number of households whose income is modeled by a Pareto distribution. Since the `Gini` coefficient is calculated based on an equalized household income, all individuals of a household in the upper tail receive the same value:

```
sim <- function(x, k) {
  require("laeken")
  x <- x[!is.na(x$eqIncome), ]
  ## classical Gini
  g <- gini(x$eqIncome, x$.weight)$value
  ## Hill estimator
  eqIncHill <- fitPareto(x$eqIncome, k = k, method = "thetaHill",
    groups = x$hid)
  gHill <- gini(eqIncHill, x$.weight)$value
```

```
## partial density component estimator
eqIncPDC <- fitPareto(x$eqIncome, k = k, method = "thetaPDC",
  groups = x$hid)
gPDC <- gini(eqIncPDC, x$.weight)$value
## results as a vector
c(standard = g, Hill = gHill, PDC = gPDC)
}
```

Defining the sampling design

In order to achieve a realistic portrayal of the real-life processes in the simulation study, the true sampling methods should be used for drawing samples from the population. Others may be used additionally to get a more complete picture of the behavior of the methodology in different situations. However, there are a large number of sampling methods described in the literature regarding survey statistics, so it is necessary to select a few representative methods to be used in the simulations. The effects of simple methods on the outcome might provide some insight, so simple random sampling should be considered. Nevertheless, unequal probability sampling is frequently used in reality and should be covered in the simulations. Since each household is linked to a region in EU-SILC data, stratified sampling should certainly be investigated. Furthermore, more advanced methods such as multistage sampling or balanced sampling may be of interest. In any case, the designs to be tested should cover the most frequently used.

The previously defined function sim is used in the following examples, which are designed to exhibit the strengths of the framework. The sampling design is specified by the following function:

```
sc <- SampleControl(grouping = "hid", size = 1500, k = 100)
```

In this basic simulation design, 100 samples of 1500 households are drawn using simple random sampling. In order to change from one simulation design to another, all we need to do is define or modify the control objects and supply them to the function runSimulation():

```
library("laeken") # for function gini
set.seed(123)
## run the simulation
results <- runSimulation(eusilcP, sc, fun = sim, k = 175)
```

In order to inspect the simulation results, methods for several frequently used generic functions are implemented. Besides `head()`, `tail()`, and `summary()` methods, a method for computing summary statistics with `aggregate()` is available. By default, the mean is used as a summary statistic. Moreover, the `plot()` method selects a suitable graphical representation of the simulation results automatically. A reference line for the true value can thereby be added as well:

```
head(results)
##   Run Sample standard    Hill      PDC
## 1   1      1 27.15482 26.68633 26.23039
## 2   2      2 28.00388 28.45642 28.49079
## 3   3      3 26.40009 27.01484 25.72001
## 4   4      4 26.98088 26.80504 26.52683
## 5   5      5 27.08909 27.61471 25.07168
## 6   6      6 27.34760 27.16358 27.94456
aggregate(results)
## standard     Hill      PDC
## 26.72984 26.83082 26.91765
```

Figure 10.8 shows the resulting box plot of the simulation results for the basic simulation design:

```
tv <- laeken::gini(eusilcP$eqIncome)$value
plot(results, true = tv)
```

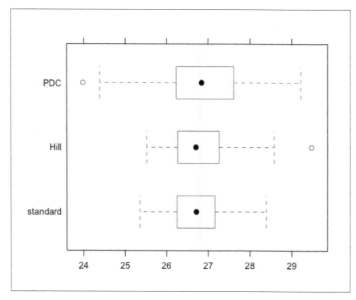

Figure 10.8: (Design-based) Simulation results for estimating the Gini coefficient. Comparison of methods

While the PDC estimator comes with larger variability, all three methods are on average quite close to the true population value. This is also an indication that the choice of the number of households for fitting the Pareto distribution is suitable.

Using stratified sampling

The most frequently used sampling designs in official statistics are implemented in simFrame. In order to switch to another sampling design, only the corresponding control object needs to be changed. In this example, stratified sampling by region is performed. The sample sizes for the different strata are specified by using a vector for the slot size of the control object:

```
set.seed(12345)
sc <- SampleControl(design = "region", grouping = "hid",
   size = c(75, 250, 250, 125, 200, 225, 125, 150, 100),
   k = 100)
## run new simulation
results <- runSimulation(eusilcP, sc, fun = sim, k = 175)
```

Like before, the simulation results are inspected by head() and aggregate().
A plot of the simulation results can be produced as well (it has been skipped for this example):

```
head(results)
##    Run Sample standard     Hill      PDC
## 1   1      1   27.08652 27.22293 27.66753
## 2   2      2   26.80670 27.35874 25.93378
## 3   3      3   26.68113 27.03964 26.60062
## 4   4      4   25.84734 26.52346 25.18298
## 5   5      5   26.05449 26.26848 26.60331
## 6   6      6   26.98439 27.01396 26.48090
aggregate(results)
## standard     Hill      PDC
## 26.71792 26.85375 26.86248
```

Adding contamination

Outliers are virtually present in any data set and it is of high interest to evaluate methods in presence of outliers, that is, to study the influence of outliers on the estimators. In simFrame, contamination is specified by defining a control object. Various contamination models are thereby implemented in the framework. Keep in mind that the term contamination is used in a technical sense here and that contamination is modeled as a two step process, see also Beguin and Hulliger 2008 and Hulliger and Schoch 2009. In this example, 0.5 percent of the households are selected to be contaminated using simple random sampling. The equalized income of the selected households is then drawn from a normal distribution with mean $\m = 500.000$ and standard deviation s = 10.000:

```
set.seed(12345)

## define contamination

cc <- DCARContControl(target = "eqIncome", epsilon = 0.005,
  grouping = "hid", dots = list(mean = 5e+05, sd = 10000))

## run new simulation

results <- runSimulation(eusilcP, sc, contControl = cc, fun = sim, k =
175)
```

The head(), aggregate(), and plot() methods are again used to take a look at the simulation results. Note that a column is added that indicates the contamination level used:

```
head(results)
##     Run Sample Epsilon standard       Hill       PDC
## 1   1      1    0.005 32.71453 29.12110 27.03731
## 2   2      2    0.005 34.22065 31.62709 26.24857
## 3   3      3    0.005 33.56878 28.49760 28.00937
## 4   4      4    0.005 35.26346 29.57160 26.25621
## 5   5      5    0.005 33.79720 29.15945 25.61514
## 6   6      6    0.005 34.72069 28.58610 27.22342
aggregate(results)
##     Epsilon standard     Hill      PDC
## 1    0.005 34.88922 30.26179 27.02093
```

In *Figure 10.9*, the resulting box plot is presented. We can see the high influence of outliers to the Hill and standard estimator - the Gini becomes arbitrary large for those estimators:

```
tv <- gini(eusilcP$eqIncome)$value
plot(results, true = tv)
```

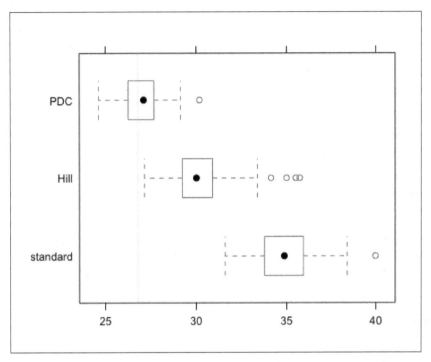

Figure 10.9: (Design-based) simulation results for different methods to estimate the Gini coefficients in presence of a few outliers. The gray vertical line represents the known true parameter value of the Gini coefficient

In other words, the figure shows that such a small amount of contamination is enough to completely corrupt the standard estimation (and also the Hill estimator) of the Gini coefficient. The PDC estimator leads to very accurate results.

Performing simulations separately on different domains

Data sets from official statistics typically contain strong heterogeneities, therefore indicators are usually computed for subsets of the data as well. So it is often of interest to investigate the behavior of indicators on different subsets in simulation studies. In simFrame, this can be done by simply specifying the design argument of the function runSimulation(). In the case of extending the example from the previous section, the framework then splits the samples, inserts contamination into each subset and calls the supplied function for these subsets automatically:

```
set.seed(12345)
sc <- SampleControl(design = "region", grouping = "hid",
  size = c(75, 250, 250, 125, 200, 225, 125, 150, 100), k = 100)
cc <- DCARContControl(target = "eqIncome", epsilon = 0.005,
  grouping = "hid", dots = list(mean = 5e+05, sd = 10000))
results <- runSimulation(eusilcP, sc, contControl = cc,
  design = "gender", fun = sim, k = 125)
```

The results can be inspected again using head() and aggregate(). The resulting plot is shown in *Figure 10.10* showing the distribution of estimated Gini coefficients from each method. The true parameter is represented by the gray vertical lines:

```
tv <- simSapply(eusilcP, "gender", function(x) gini(x$eqIncome)$value)
plot(results, true = tv)
```

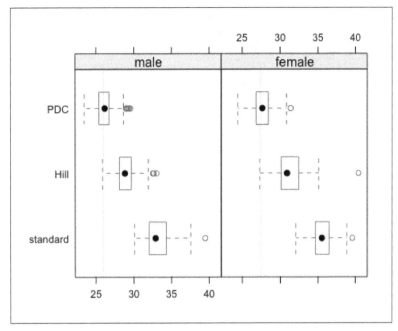

Figure 10.10: Simulation results for the simulation design with stratified sampling, contamination, and performing the simulations separately for each gender

Clearly, the PDC estimator leads to excellent results for both subsets, while the two classical approaches are in both cases highly influenced by the outliers.

To get a more complete picture of the behavior of robust methods, more than one level of contamination is typically investigated in simulation studies. The only necessary modification of the code is to use a vector of contamination levels as the slot epsilon of the contamination control object. We won't cover this but refer to Alfons, Templ, and Filzmoser 2010b for more information.

Inserting missing values

Survey data almost always contains a considerable amount of missing values. In close-to-reality simulation studies, the variability due to missing data therefore needs to be considered. Three types of missing data mechanisms are commonly distinguished in the literature. For example, (Little and Rubin 2002): **missing completely at random (MCAR)**, **missing at random (MAR)**, and **missing not at random (MNAR)**.

In the following example, missing values are inserted into the equalized household income of non-contaminated households with MCAR, that is, the households whose values are going to be set to NA are selected using simple random sampling. In order to compare the scenario without missing values of a scenario with missing values, the missing value rates 0 percent and 5 percent are used. The number of samples is reduced to 50 and only the contamination levels 0 percent, 0.5 percent, and 1 percent are investigated to keep the computation time of this motivational example low. With `simFrame`, only a control object for missing data (`NAControl`) needs to be defined and supplied to `runSimulation()`, the rest is done automatically by the framework:

```
set.seed(12345)

sc <- SampleControl(design = "region", grouping = "hid",
    size = c(75, 250, 250, 125, 200, 225, 125, 150, 100), k = 50)

cc <- DCARContControl(target = "eqIncome", epsilon = c(0, 0.005, 0.01),
dots = list(mean = 5e+05, sd = 10000))

nc <- NAControl(target = "eqIncome", NArate = c(0, 0.05))

results <- runSimulation(eusilcP, sc, contControl = cc,
    NAControl = nc, design = "gender", fun = sim, k = 125)
```

As always, the `head()`, `aggregate()`, and `plot()` methods are used to take a look at the simulation results. It should be noted that a column is added to the results that indicates the missing value rate used and that `aggregate()` in this example returns a value for each combination of contamination level, missing value, rate, and gender:

```
aggregate(results)
```

##	Epsilon	NArate	gender	standard	Hill	PDC
## 1	0.000	0.00	male	25.89948	25.99777	25.74944
## 2	0.005	0.00	male	33.52791	29.30477	26.14659
## 3	0.010	0.00	male	39.45422	32.74672	26.64929
## 4	0.000	0.05	male	25.88434	25.87824	25.80541
## 5	0.005	0.05	male	33.87975	29.60079	26.18759
## 6	0.010	0.05	male	39.99526	33.44462	26.31274
## 7	0.000	0.00	female	27.17769	27.30586	27.19275
## 8	0.005	0.00	female	35.46414	31.37099	27.98622
## 9	0.010	0.00	female	41.28625	35.22113	28.19677
## 10	0.000	0.05	female	27.16026	27.37710	27.20892
## 11	0.005	0.05	female	35.85305	31.56317	27.80455
## 12	0.010	0.05	female	41.86453	35.44025	27.98948

We can see once again the influence of the few outliers on the standard Gini estimator and the Hill estimator. If multiple contamination levels and multiple missing value rates are used in the simulation study, conditional plots are produced by the `plot()` method for the simulation results (not shown here).

Summary

The simulations shown in this chapter are of two different kinds: model-based simulation and design-based simulation. Model-based simulations simulate data from a certain (super-population) model. We saw that model-based simulations are easy to set-up. The aim is to always know true parameters – here, from the model that simulates random distributions of interest. The estimation is applied to each of the simulated data and compared with the true parameter values.

Design-based simulation studies differ in that sense that the sampling design must be incorporated. This is why we firstly showed how to simulate a finite population from where samples can be drawn. Whenever data sets are sampled with simple random sampling, there is no need for design-based simulations.

We also showed the efficient use of package `simFrame`. The examples showed that the framework allows researchers to make use of a wide range of simulation designs with only a few lines of code. In order to switch from one simulation design to another, only control objects need to be defined or modified. Even moving from basic to highly complex designs requires only minimal changes to the code. The use of this package leads to cleaner code, less error-prone coding, and efficient simulations.

References

- Aitchison, J. 1986. "The Statistical Analysis of Compositional Data." Chapman & Hall, London.

- Aitchison, J. 1992. "On Criteria for Measures of Compositional Difference." *Mathematical Geology* 34 (4): 365–79.

- Aitchison, J., C. Barceló-Vidal, J.A. Martín-Fernández, and V. Pawlowsky-Glahn. 2000. "Logratio Analysis and Compositional Distance." *Mathematical Geology* 32 (3): 271–75.

- Alfons, A., S. Kraft, M. Templ, and P. Filzmoser. 2011. "Simulation of Close-to-Reality Population Data for Household Surveys with Application to EU-SILC." *Statistical Methods & Applications* 20 (3): 383–407.

- Alfons, A., M. Templ, and P. Filzmoser. 2010a. "An Object-Oriented Framework for Statistical Simulation: The R Package simFrame." *Journal of Statistical Software* 37 (3): 1–36. http://www.jstatsoft.org/v37/i03/.

- — — —. 2010b. "An Object-Oriented Framework for Statistical Simulation: The R Package SimFrame." *Journal of Statistical Software* 37 (3): 1–36.

- — — —. 2013. "Robust Estimation of Economic Indicators from Survey Samples Based on Pareto Tail Modelling." *Journal of the Royal Statistical Society: Series C (Applied Statistics)* 62 (2). Blackwell Publishing Ltd: 271–86. doi:10.1111/j.1467-9876.2012.01063.x.

- Barrett, C.L., S. Eubank, A. Marathe, M.V. Marathe, Z. Pan, and S. Swarup. 2011. "Information Integration to Support Model-Based Policy Informatics." *The Innovation Journal: The Public Sector Innovation Journal* 16 (1).

- Barthelemy, J., and P.L. Toint. 2013. "Synthetic Population Generation Without a Sample." *Transportation Science* 47 (2): 266–79.

- Beckman, R.J., K.A. Baggerly, and M.D. McKay. 1996. "Creating Synthetic Baseline Populations." *Transportation Research Part A: Policy and Practice* 30 (6): 415–29.

- Beguin, C., and B. Hulliger. 2008. "The BACON-EEM Algorithm for Multivariate Outlier Detection in Incomplete Survey Data." *Survey Methodology* 34 (1): 91–103.

- Brown, L., and A. Harding. 2002. "Social Modelling and Public Policy: Application of Microsimulation Modelling in Australia." *Journal of Artificial Societies and Social Simulation* 5 (4): 6.

- Egozcue, J.J., V. Pawlowsky-Glahn, G. Mateu-Figueras, and C. Barceló-Vidal. 2003. "Isometric Logratio Transformations for Compositional Data Analysis." *Mathematical Geology* 35 (3): 279–300.

- Gini, C. 1912. "Variabilità E Mutabilità: Contributo Allo Studio Delle Distribuzioni E Delle Relazioni Statistiche." *Studi Economico-Giuridici Della R. Università Di Cagliari* 3: 3–159.

- Hill, B.M. 1975. "A Simple General Approach to Inference About the Tail of a Distribution." *The Annals of Statistics* 3 (5): 1163–74.

- Hron, K., M. Templ, and P. Filzmoser. 2010. "Imputation of Missing Values for Compositional Data Using Classical and Robust Methods." *Computational Statistics & Data Analysis* 54 (12): 3095–3107.

- Huber, P.J. 1981. Robust Statistics. Wiley.

- Hulliger, B., and T. Schoch. 2009. "Robustification of the Quintile Share Ratio." *New Techniques and Technologies for Statistics*, Brussels.

- Little, R.J.A., and D.B. Rubin. 2002. Statistical Analysis with Missing Data. 2nd ed. New York: John Wiley & Sons.

- Mateu-Figueras, G., V. Pawlowsky-Glahn, and J.J. Egozcue. 2008. „The Normal Distribution in Some Constrained Sample Spaces." http://arxiv.org/abs/0802.2643.

- Münnich, R., and J. Schürle. 2003. On the Simulation of Complex Universes in the Case of Applying the German Microcensus. DACSEIS research paper series No. 4. University of Tübingen.

- Münnich, R., J. Schürle, W. Bihler, H.-J. Boonstra, P. Knotterus, N. Nieuwenbroek, A. Haslinger, et al. 2003. Monte Carlo Simulation Study of European Surveys. DACSEIS Deliverables D3.1 and D3.2. University of Tübingen.

- Rousseeuw, P.J., and K.van Driessen. 1998. "A Fast Algorithm for the Minimum Covariance Determinant Estimator." *Technometrics* 41: 212–23.

- Rubin, D.B. 1993. "Discussion: Statistical Disclosure Limitation." *Journal of Official Statistics* 9 (2): 461–68.

- Smith, D.M., J.R. Pearce, and K. Harland. 2011. "Can a Deterministic Spatial Microsimulation Model Provide Reliable Small-Area Estimates of Health Behaviours? An Example of Smoking Prevalence in New Zealand." *Health Place* 17 (2): 618–24.

- Stahel, W. A., and M. Mächler. 2009. "Comment on Invariant Co-Ordinate Selection." *Journal of the Royal Statistical Society* B 71: 584–86.

- Stahel, W., M. Mächler, and potentially others. 2013. robustX: "EXperimental Functionality for Robust Statistics." https://CRAN.R-project.org/package=robustX.

- Templ, M., and P. Filzmoser. 2014. "Simulation and Quality of a Synthetic Close-to-Reality Employer–employee Population." *Journal of Applied Statistics* 41 (5): 1053–72.

- Templ, M., K. Hron, and P. Filzmoser. 2011. "RobCompositions: An R-Package for Robust Statistical Analysis of Compositional Data." *In Compositional Data Analysis*, 341–55. John Wiley & Sons, Ltd.

- Templ, M., A. Kowarik, and P. Filzmoser. 2011. "Iterative Stepwise Regression Imputation Using Standard and Robust Methods." *Comput. Stat. Data Anal.* 55 (10): 2793–2806.

- Templ, M., A. Kowarik, and B. Meindl. 2016. "Simulation of Synthetic Complex Data: The R-Package SimPop." *Journal of Statistical Software*, 1–39.

- Tomintz, Melanie N., Graham P. Clarke, and Janette E. Rigby. 2008. "The Geography of Smoking in Leeds: Estimating Individual Smoking Rates and the Implications for the Location of Stop Smoking Services." Area 40 (3): 341–53.

- Troyanskaya, O., M. Cantor, G. Sherlock, P. Brown, T. Hastie, R. Tibshirani, D. Botstein, and R. Altman. 2001. "Missing Value Estimation Methods for DNA Microarrays." *Bioinformatics* 17 (6): 520–25.

- Williamson, P., G. Mitchell, and A. T. McDonald. 2002. "Domestic Water Demand Forecasting: A Static Microsimulation Approach." *Water and Environment Journal* 16 (4). Blackwell Publishing Ltd: 243–48.

11

System Dynamics and Agent-Based Models

Judging by the title of this chapter, you may think that we are going to discuss a completely different topic compared to previous chapter topics. But this is not true. We already did some simple system dynamics in *Chapter 6, Probability Theory Shown by Simulation* when we flipped the coin (over time). The evolution over time was just the frequency counts of one side of the coin. In addition, we did Markov chain Monte Carlo experiments that also develop over time and possibly converge against a solution. However, this chapter differs in terms of only constants and probabilities playing a role. Statistical uncertainty is – unfortunately – not directly related to system dynamics.

In this chapter, we want to discuss some more advanced modeling over time. Generally, dynamic systems, in terms of the evolution of systems in time, have widespread applications, for example, the growth of organisms, stock markets in finance, traffic, chemical reactions, the spread of diseases, the movement of planets, demographic changes, and so on.

What makes using system dynamics different from other approaches to studying complex systems is the use of feedback loops and stocks and flows. Empirically, a dynamical model is described in a mechanistic manner as input-output, a certain kind of black box. We consider the change of single objects (agents, automata, individuals), populations, and interactions over time.

Relative to the overall scope of the book, in this chapter we will deal with basic topics. We will not cover the whole area of dynamic systems. We will cover practical examples, including agent-based modeling, the dynamic game of love and hate, and the abundance of animals in a predator-prey Lotka-Volterra type model.

Agent-based models

"Prediction is very difficult, especially if it's about the future."

– Niels Bohr

This quotation gives a warning about forecasting in the future. This quotation states problems about the traditional approach to forecasting - the prediction of estimators/summary statistics. However, agent-based models (microsimulation) provide prediction for each single individual in the future. In following sections, we will show some background into how individual predictions used to be done.

Microsimulation models are favored in the area of demographics for population forecasts, simulating the spread of diseases, and to forecast social or economic changes. In population statistics three continuous time scales are important, the individual's age, time, and the time that an individual has already spent in a specific state.

The input of such a stochastic model is a population of time T_0 transition rates, and possibly a population of migrants. We are interested in the state of times $T_1, T_2, \dots$.

Optimally, a microsimulation starts with a true complete population. Since this is rarely the case that a population is available, a true population must be "augmented" or even completely simulated. A synthetic population is already simulated in *Chapter 10, Simulation with Complex Data* and it should contain information on individuals that is demographically relevant, such as sex, marital status, fertility status, and information on education level.

We should first take some notes on fertility and mortality rates.

For any category that can change over time we basically need a transition matrix or probabilities from a regression model. Zinn, 2014 gives the example of the Hadwiger mixture model (T., Coleman, and Horns 1999) that can be used to describe the transition rates among women giving birth to a second child. The function inputs are age, calendar time, and lastbirth (time since the firstbirth in years):

```
fert2Rate <- function(age, time, lastbirth){
 a <- ifelse(time <= 2020, 32, 33)
 b <- ifelse(time <= 2020, 6.0, 5.7)
frate <- (b / a) * (a / age) ^ (3 / 2) *
             exp(-b ^ 2 * (a / age + age / a - 2))
 frate[age <= 15 | age >= 45 | lastbirth < 0.75] <- 0
 return(frate)
}
```

The fertility rate for a 30 year old women that has a three year old baby until the year 2030 is this, according to the (simplified) model of (T., Coleman, and Horns 1999):

```
fert2Rate(30, 2030, lastbirth = 3)
## [1] 0.1483116
```

The older the women, the lower the fertility:

```
fert2Rate(40, 2030, lastbirth = 3)
## [1] 0.03874834
```

This is just an example of modeling the fertility rate, in the real-world the fertility rate will depend on much more covariates such as education level, income, living area, ethnical background, and so on. However, there might be other ways to increase individual fertility rates as well as happiness in life with a partner.

Mortality rates will also depend on many covariates. We will give just a simplified version also used in (Zinn 2014):

```
mortRate <- function(age, time){
  a <- 0.0003
  b <- ifelse(time <= 2020, 0.1, 0.097)
  mrate <- a * exp(b * age)
  return(mrate)
}
```

The mortality rate of the 40-year-old author of this book in the year 2056 is:

```
mortRate(40, 2056)
## [1] 0.01452726
```

Not very realistic, considering the lifestyle of the author.

For the initial population of time T_0, we use the one simulated in *Chapter 10, Simulation with Complex Data*, which is already available in R. We basically only need a few demographic variables out of this data set:

```
library("simFrame")
data(eusilcP, package = "simFrame")
pop <- eusilcP[, c("age", "gender", "hsize", "hid")]
```

In our population, no information is given about fertility. So we will construct it, ignoring the case of single mothers. We will also add a variable that indicates whether one is being partnered or single.

```
pop$nchildWomen <- ifelse(pop$gender == "female" &
   as.integer(pop$hsize) > 2 &
   pop$age > 17, as.integer(pop$hsize) - 2, 0)
pop$partnered <- factor(ifelse(as.integer(pop$hsize) >= 2 &
   pop$age > 17,
"P", "A"))
```

The first six observations of our population at time T_0 look like this:

```
head(pop)
##          age gender hsize hid nchildWomen partnered
## 39993   25    male     2   1           0         P
## 39994   24  female     2   1           0         P
## 31004   57  female     2   2           0         P
## 31005   53    male     2   2           0         P
## 29071   30  female     1   3           0         A
## 41322   32    male     3   4           0         P
```

We now can easily define the state space:

```
stateSpace <- expand.grid(sex = levels(pop$gender),
                          partnered =  levels(pop$partnered))
```

Our simplified state space is as the following:

```
stateSpace
##        sex partnered
## 1    male         A
## 2  female         A
## 3    male         P
## 4  female         P
```

We are shown what a transition matrix might look like:

```
trMatrix_f <- cbind(c("female/A->female/P", "female/P->female/A"),
                    c("rates1", "rates2"))
trMatrix_m <- cbind(c("male/A-male/P", "male/P-male/A"),
```

```
                        c("rates3", "rates4"))
allTransitions <- rbind(trMatrix_f, trMatrix_m)
absTransitions <- rbind(c("female/dead", "mortRate"),
                        c("male/dead", "mortRate"))
```

We use a function from the `MicSim` package to build the transition matrix:

```
library("MicSim")
transitionMatrix <- buildTransitionMatrix(allTransitions =
allTransitions, absTransitions = absTransitions, stateSpace = stateSpace)
```

After manual correction of the transition matrix (`rates3` and `rates4` were not considered by build `transitionMatrix`), the transition matrix looks as follows:

```
transitionMatrix[1,3] <- "rates3"
transitionMatrix[3,1] <- "rates4"
transitionMatrix
##           male/A  female/A male/P   female/P dea
## male/A    "0"     "0"      "rates3" "0"      "mortRate"
## female/A  "0"     "0"      "0"      "rates1" "mortRate"
## male/P    "rates4" "0"     "0"      "0"      "mortRate"
## female/P  "0"     "rates2" "0"      "0"      "mortRate"
```

We need to determine the maximum age of a person, for example:

```
maxAge <- 100
```

To define further transitions is now straightforward, for example, regarding newborns, educational level, enrolment to school, and migration. We will skip this but refer to Zinn, 2014 for examples. Generally, a transition matrix of the size as large as the number of states must be made available. We skip the determination of all transition functions for any event of interest and refer to software packages `MicSim` (Zinn 2014), `simario` (`https://github.com/compassresearchcentre/simario`), Modgen (`http://www.statcan.gc.ca/eng/microsimulation/modgen/modgen`), and OpenM++ (`http://ompp.sourceforge.net/wiki/index.php/Main_Page`). The software tool Modgen and OpenM++ are probably the most reliable tools. The author's experience with R package `MicSim` at the time of writing the book is that it does produce errors when any other example data is used, other than the examples given in `?micSim`. So we will stop here, waiting for better tools to become available in R.

Dynamics in love and hate

In the original text of *A Midsummer Night's Dream* by Shakespeare, Hermia says: "The more I hate, the more he follows me" and "I curse him, but he loves me." Also, Helena says in this work from Shakespeare: "The more I love him, the more he hates me." A short search using an Internet search engine such as Google will produce a bunch of articles and research questions on the topic "The more he hates me the more I love him, the more he loves me the more he hates me."

We want to give another simple example of a dynamic system, the dynamics of a love affair, but for other examples than for example, reported in Strogatz, 1994.

You can consider the situation of Hermia and Lysander, Helena and Lysander, or Romeo and Juliet, but we want to transfer it to the modern age. Those of you in Britain, have possibly already read what Cosmopolitan wrote (22 February 2012) about celebs who love bad boys: "Prince Harry is known for being the more cheeky, troublesome Prince, but his on-off girlfriend Chelsy Davy appears to love his mischievous side." We want to help the Royal Family of Britain.

Let:

- $P(t)$ be Prince Harry's love/hate for Chelsy Davy while $P(t) < 0$ is hate otherwise love
- $C(t)$ can be Chelsy Davy's love/hate for Prince Harry

In addition, we will consider the following constraints/conditions:

- Prince Harry is in love with Chelsy Davy.
- The more Prince Harry loves Chelsy Davy, the more frightened she is and the more she wants to run away.
- But when Prince Harry starts to hate Chelsy Davy, Chelsy Davy finds Prince Harry attractive and her love grows.
- Prince Harry is simple in his love. He loves Chelsy Davy when she loves him, and he starts to hate her when she hates him.

A dynamic model may help to open the eyes of the Royal Family on Prince Harry's love affair given the conditions described.

We will use differential equations to solve this problem and when formulated, these equations we will carry on with system dynamics. The derivative:

$$\frac{dP}{dt} = aC$$

Regarding time *t* expresses that Prince Harry's love grows in proportion to Chelsy Davy's love. The derivative:

$$\frac{dC}{dt} = -bP$$

This derivative expresses that Chelsy Davy's love grows if Prince Harry shows his mischievous side and her love decreases the more Prince Harry acts nicely to her. The coefficients a and b are positive constants (response coefficients). We will formulate a function called `love` which we will pass through all parameters:

```
love <- function(t, x, parms){
  with(as.list(c(parms, x)), {
    dPrince_Harry <- a * Chelsy_Davy
    dChelsy_Davy <- -b * Prince_Harry
    res <- c(dPrince_Harry, dChelsy_Davy)
    list(res)
  })
}
```

We then fix the parameters and the length of the love affair. In addition, we assume that at time 0, Prince Harry loves Chelsy Davy but Chelsy Davy does not love him:

```
parms   <- c(a = 1, b = 2)
times   <- seq(0, 30, length = 31)
## Start values for steady state
y <- xstart <- c(Prince_Harry = 1, Chelsy_Davy = -1)
```

We solve the dynamic system using a general solver for ordinary differential equations:

```
library("deSolve")
out <-  ode(xstart, times, love, parms = parms)
```

Figure 11.1 shows the result of how Prince Harry's and Chelsy Davy's love develops over time:

```
matplot(out)
```

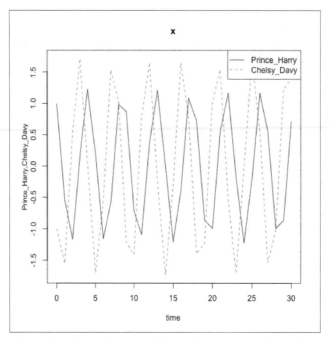

Figure 11.1: Prince Harry's and Chelsy Davy's love and hate affair

Chelsy Davy hates him in the beginning since Harry loves her too much. This influences Prince Harry's love that immediately cools down and is already frozen at time 1. Up to this time he start to act like as a bad boy and on time 2 his love is such frozen that he behaves terrible. However, this attracts Chelsy Davy since she like the bad boy in Harry, and he start to have strong feelings of love for him. This results in the Prince also starting to love her until the point that Chelsy gets cold. The periodicity in their love and hate is clearly seen.

Let's think about other maybe more realistic starting values and parameter values. Prince Harry is a bit interested in Chelsy Davy at time 0. Chelsy Davy is full with love at first sight. Prince Harry's loves grows when Chelsy Davy loves him, but his love develops not as fast as before. Chelsy Davy wants to escape with parameter b = 0,7 depending if Prince Harry is too nice to her. The result is shown in *Figure 11.2*:

```
y <- xstart <- c(Prince_Harry = 0.2, Chelsy_Davy = 1)
parms   <- c(a = 0.3, b = 0.7)
out <-   ode(xstart, times, love, parms = parms)
matplot(out)
```

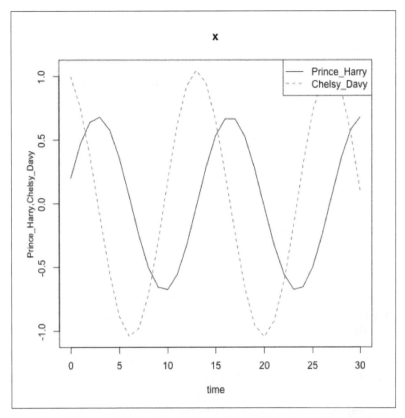

Figure 11.2: Prince Harry and Chelsy Davy's love and hate affair using another set of parameters

The interpretation of *Figure 11.2* is straightforward and so it is not described here. A continuous change in love and hate, whilst Chelsy goes more to the extreme end of love and hate than Prince Harry. We wish them all the best.

Dynamic systems in ecological modeling

Dynamic systems play a vital role in ecological modeling to model absence and presents and interaction of species or interactions between economic systems and ecological systems. An ecological system is generally dynamically complex. When thinking of the simplest case, the predator and prey, it is obvious that the predator population is dependent on the presence of prey and vice versa.

Most ecological models can be formulated as a state space representation with:

$\dot{x} = \mathbf{f}(t, \mathbf{x}(t), \mathbf{u}(t), \mathbf{p})$

$\mathbf{y} = \mathbf{g}(t, \mathbf{x}(t), \mathbf{u}(t), \mathbf{p})$

Here, **x** is the derivative of the state of the system **x**. t is the time, **u** is the input vector of boundary conditions, and **y** is the output vector. **p** is a vector of constants/parameters and function **f** is the state transition function while **g** is the observation function, see also (Petzoldt and Rinke 2007). **f** is written in bold for the reason that it can also be a system of ordinary differential equations. In our love and hate example, this was our function `love` in combination with the ordinary differential equation solver.

The Lotka-Volterra predator-prey model (Lotka 1910) is a pair of first-order, non-linear two differential equations used to describe the dynamics of simple biological systems in case of the interaction of two species, one as a predator *(y)* and the other as the prey *(x)*:

$$\frac{dx}{dt} = k_1 x - k_2 xy \qquad \text{(prey model)}$$

$$\frac{dy}{dt} = -k_3 y + k_4 xy \qquad \text{(predator model)}$$

The prey grows at a linear rate of *k1* and gets eaten by the predator at the rate of *k2*. The predator gains a certain amount of vitality by eating the prey at a rate of *k4* while dying off at another rate of *k3*.

So it describes natural oscillations between the populations of predators and their prey. Let's take this to the ground with an example of toads and snakes. In a region of Upper Austria in the Alps, more precisely in an area called Zeitschen nearby the village of Rosenau, the population of toads and snakes develops periodically. As soon as the snakes eat the population of toads, the snakes don't find enough food and escape. Then the population of toads steadily increase and the snake population as well with some shift. They have enough to eat now until they over-populate and eat almost all the toads. In reality, this can be observed. We can take the parameters *k1* = *1* (the toad population grows fast), *k2* = *0.5* (rate of snakes eating toads), *k3* = *0.2* (the dying rate of snakes), and *k4* = *0.6* (the vitality gained by snakes when eating toads).

We can write the Lotka-Volterra model in a function:

```
lv_mod <- function (time, state, parms) {
    with(as.list(c(state, parms)), {
        dx <- k1 * x - k2 * x * y
        dy <- -k3 * y + k4 * x * y
        return(list(c(dx, dy)))
    })
}
```

Specify the parameters (linear growth of the prey and prey gets eaten by the predator at the rate of *1.5, …*):

```
parms <- c(k1 = 1, k2 = 1.5, k3 = .2, k4 = .6)
state <- c(x = 10, y = 10)
time <- seq(0, 200, by = 1)
```

We can solve the ordinary differential equations using the ode function from the deSolve package:

```
res <- ode(func = lv_mod, y = state, parms = parms, times = time)
res <- as.data.frame(res)
```

We can now plot the results that can be seen in *Figure 11.3*:

```
par(mar = c(4,4,0.5,0.1))
matplot(res[,-1], type = "l", xlab = "time", ylab = "population")
legend("topright", c("Toads", "Snakes"), lty = c(1,2), col = c(1,2), box.
lwd = 0)
```

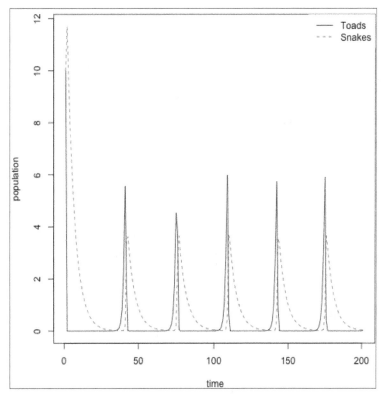

Figure 11.3: The natural oscillations between the populations of snakes and toads

The snakes died slowly after they ate all of the toads. When the snakes disappeared, the population of toads increased quickly. This caused the population of snakes to recover since they could find enough toads to eat. As soon as the snake population gets too large, they will eat all of the toads and again they will not find enough food anymore and die slowly.

Summary

The basic concept of system dynamics is to predict time based on given scenarios/assumptions.

We looked at simple applications for population demographics using microsimulation modeling. Microsimulation modeling became popular since managers and politicians wanted to have predictions of the future. While this was done in the past with aggregated information, with agent-based microsimulation models we do it on an individual level. A criticism of this is that statistical uncertainty is not taken into account and that selected scenarios are unlikely to be true in the future since political changes or unobservable events may happen that cannot be considered beforehand.

Dynamic systems are popular in business and finance but they also play a central role in ecological research. We looked at the Lotka-Volterra model in one example that the author of this book regularly observes in a place in the Upper Austrian mountains. But most importantly, and ironically speaking, we have shown the relationship in time - the love and hate affair of Prince Harry and Chelsy Davy, and have done the Royals a huge favor by doing so.

References

- Lotka, A.J. 1910. "Contribution to the Theory of Periodic Reaction," *Phys. Chem.* 14 (3): 271–74.

- Petzoldt, T., and K. Rinke. 2007. "Simecol: An Object-Oriented Framework for Ecological Modeling in R," *Journal of Statistical Software* 22 (1).

- Strogatz, S.H. 1994. *Nonlinear Dynamics and Chaos: With Applications to Physics, Biology, Chemistry, and Engineering.* MA: Addison-Wesley.

- T., Chandola., D.A. Coleman, and R.W. Horns. 1999. "Recent European Fertility Patterns: Fitting Curves to Distorted Distributions," *Population Studies* 53 (3): 317–29.

- Zinn, S. 2014. "The MicSim Package of R: An Entry-Level Toolkit for Continuous-Time Microsimulation," *International Journal of Microsimulation* 7 (3): 3–32.

Index

A

aes(). assignment 67
aesthetic mapping 67
agent-based modeling (ABM) 3, 9, 364-367
alias method 105, 106
arithmetic random number generators 92

B

Beta distribution 113-116
BFGS method 157
bias
  estimating, bootstrap used 221
Bias Corrected alpha (BCa) confidence
      interval method 223
Big Boss 2 approach 209
Big Boss approach 209
bootstrap
  about 6, 204-212
  bias, estimating 221
  by draws from residuals 258-262
  complex estimation, example 216, 217
  confidence intervals 222-226
  in case of complex sampling
      designs 273-278
  in regression analysis 247
  in time series 269-272
  method 253-258
  motivating example, with odds
      ratios 205-208
  to estimate standard error 213-216
  using 248-252
  working 208-211

C

central limit theorem 190-195
CG method 157
classes 27
classical linear regression model 235, 236
complex models
  used, for simulating data 324
Comprehensive R Archive
      Network (CRAN)
  about 14
  reference link 14
computational statistics 1
confidence intervals
  about 197-199
  by bootstrap 222-226
congruential generators 93
  linear 94
  multiplicative 94-97
contamination
  adding 354, 355
cross-validation
  about 235
  basic concept 236-238
  classical cross validation 238
  classical linear regression model 235, 236
  k-fold cross validation 242-244
  leave-one-out cross validation 240-242

D

data
  model-based simple example 324
  simulating, complex methods used 324
data manipulation
  apply, using 28-30

data.table package, using 42
dplyr package, using 31
in R 28
data science 1, 2
Data Scientist approach 211
data.table package
calculations, in groups 46
fast subsetting 45
indexing 43, 44
keys 44
subsetting 43, 44
used, for data manipulation 42
variable construction 42
data types, R
about 18
array 24, 25
data.frame 22, 23
factors 21
list 21
vectors 19, 20
design-based simulation (DBS)
about 9, 323, 347
complex survey data, example 348
contamination, adding 354, 355
interest, estimators 350
performing, separately on different
domains 356, 357
sampling design, defining 351, 352
stratified sampling, using 353
synthetic population, simulation 349, 350
dplyr package
aggregates 38-40
grouping 38-40
local data frame 32
order 34
selection of columns 35, 36
selection of lines 33, 34
uniqueness 37
used, for data manipulation 31
variables, creating 37
window functions 41
dynamics 368-371
dynamic systems
in ecological modeling 371-374

E

EM algorithm (Expectation Maximization)
about 301
explaining, by k-means clustering
example 305-311
formal definition 303
introductory example 304, 305
prerequisites 302, 303
used, for imputation of missing
values 312-318
estimators
confidence intervals 197-199
properties 195-197
robust estimators 200, 201

F

finite populations
simulating, with cluster or hierarchical
structures 330-333
Fortran 47-49
function optimization 149

G

generators 98
generic functions 26, 63
Gibbs sampler
about 129
linear regression, application 132, 133
multiphase Gibbs sampler 131
two-phase Gibbs sampler 129, 130
gradient ascent/descent method 154
graphics package
about 62
graphics parameters, controlling 64-66
high-level plot example 62-64
high-level graphics functions 62
interactive functions 62
low-level graphics functions 62

H

high-dimensional data
simulating, example 329, 330
highest spot
finding, strategies 150-153

high-level plot functions 64
high performance computing
  about 47
  benchmarking 49-55
  interfaces to C++ 58-60
  parallel computing 56, 57
  slow functions, detecting with
    profiling 47, 48
Hohe Wand 150

I

independent and identically distributed
  (i.i.d) random numbers 89
information visualization
  about 60
  graphics package 62
  graphics system, in R 61, 62
  package ggplot2 66-70
interactive graphics 61
inversion method 101-104

J

jackknife
  about 226-229
  after bootstrap 232-234
  delete-d jackknife 230, 231
  disadvantages 229, 230
  sample 227

K

k-fold cross validation 242, 243
k-means clustering
  used, for EM algorithm
    demonstration 305-311
k-Nearest Neighbor (k-NN) 342

L

L-BFGS-B method 157
leave-one-out cross validation 240-242
lottery
  winning 176-178
low-level functions 64

M

machine numbers
  64-bit representation, example 77
  and rounding, issues 74-76
  convergence 77
  convergence, example 78-86
Markov chain Monte Carlo (MCMC)
  about 9
  methods 4
Marsaglia
  URL 141
Mathematician approach 210
method dispatch 63
methods 27
Metropolis Hasting algorithm
  about 117
  Markov chains 118
Metropolis-Hastings 163, 164
Metropolis sampler 126-128
micro-simulation 3
Minimum Covariance Determinant (MCD)
  algorithm 216
missing completely at random (MCAR) 357
missing not at random (MNAR) 357
missing values
  imputating, with EM algorithm 312-317
  inserting 357, 359
mixtures
  model-based example 327, 328
model-based approach
  to simulate data 328
model-based example
  with mixtures 327, 328
model-based simple example 325-327
model-based simulation (MBS)
  about 9, 333-347
  example 336-341
  latent model example 334, 335
Modgen
  URL 367
Monte Carlo simulations 9
  about 4
  Bayesian statistics 4
  Markov chain Monte Carlo (MCMC)
    methods 4
  multi-dimensional integrals 5

numerical optimization 5
statistical uncertainty 5
Monte Carlo tests
about 278
for multiple groups 290-294
Hypothesis testing, bootstrap used 294, 295
motivating example 278-286
multivariate normality, test for 295, 296
permutation test, as special kind
of MC test 287-290
power comparisons 298
test, size 297

N

Nelder-Mead method 157
Newton-Raphson method 154-156
non-uniform distributed random variables,
simulation
about 101
alias method 105, 106
counts in tables, estimation with
log-linear models 106-108
Gibbs sampler 129
inversion method 101-104
Markov chains 118-125
MCMC samples, diagnosis 134-137
Metropolis Hasting algorithm 117
Metropolis sampler 126-128
random numbers, simulating from Beta
distribution 113-116
rejection sampling 108
truncated distributions 116, 117
values, simulating from normal
distribution 109-112
numerical optimization
about 153
BFGS method 157
CG method 157
general-purpose optimization
methods 157-159
gradient ascent/descent method 154
L-BFGS-B method 157
Nelder-Mead method 157
Newton-Raphson method 154-156
SANN method 157

O

OpenM++
URL 367
optimization (O) 9

P

parametric bootstrap 218-220
percentile confidence intervals 223
plug-in principle 212
probability distributions
about 174
continuous probability distributions 175
discrete probability distributions 174, 175
probability theory
basics 173, 174
problems
conditions 86
pseudo random number generators
about 92
arithmetic random number generators 92
recursive arithmetic random number
generators 92

R

R
about 13, 14
basics 15
data manipulation 28
data types 18
help option 17
installation 16
installation link 16
missing values 25, 26
overview 15
statistical environment 14
updates 16
updation link 16
working directory 18
workspace 18
random
URL 91
random numbers
about 90, 92
congruential generators 93

congruential generators, linear 94-97
congruential generators,
    multiplicative 94-97
example 142-144
generators 98, 99
lagged Fibonacci generators 98
pseudo random numbers, simulating 92, 93
testing 141, 142
recursive arithmetic random number
    generators 92
reference links 71, 72, 318
resampling method 6
robust estimators 200, 201
R Project
reference link 14
RStudio
reference link 15

S

sampling design
defining 351-353
SANN method 157
simario
URL 367
simulation
about 3, 5
agent-based modeling 3
and big data 7, 8
applying, in sampling 3
burning fire simulation, URL 10
micro-simulation 3
Monte Carlo simulations 4
technique, selecting 8-10
uses 6
simulations
performing, separately on different
    domains 356, 357
types 322, 323

software environment R 1
statistical simulation 2, 4
stochastic optimization
about 159
Gradient-based 165-168
Metropolis-Hastings 163, 164
Spaceballs 159, 163
Spaceballs princess 159-163
Star Trek 159-163
stratified sampling
defining 353
synthetic population
simulating 349, 350
system dynamics (SD) 3, 9

V

variables 67
vector selection
logical way 20
negative way 20
positive way 20

W

weak law of large numbers
about 178
displaying, by simulation 182-189
Emperor penguins, and boss 178-180
random variables, convergence 180, 181
random variables, limits 180, 181
sample mean, convergence 181
window functions
about 41
cumulative functions 41
offsets 41
ranking/ordering 41

9 781785 881169